Walter Map
and the
Matter of Britain

THE MIDDLE AGES SERIES

Ruth Mazo Karras, Series Editor
Edward Peters, Founding Editor

A complete list of books in the series
is available from the publisher.

Walter Map
and the
Matter of Britain

Joshua Byron Smith

PENN

UNIVERSITY OF PENNSYLVANIA PRESS

PHILADELPHIA

Published by
University of Pennsylvania Press
Philadelphia, Pennsylvania 19104-4112
www.upenn.edu/pennpress

Printed in the United States of America on acid-free paper
1 3 5 7 9 10 8 6 4 2

Library of Congress Cataloging-in-Publication Data
Name: Smith, Joshua Byron, author.
Title: Walter Map and the matter of Britain / Joshua Byron Smith.
Other titles: Middle Ages series.
Description: 1st edition. | Philadelphia : University of Pennsylvania
    Press, [2017] | Series: The Middle Ages series | Includes
    bibliographical references and index.
Identifiers: LCCN 2016056690 | ISBN 9780812249323 (hardcover : alk.
    paper)
Subjects: LCSH: Map, Walter, active 1200. | Map, Walter, active 1200.
    De nugis curialium. | Latin literature, Medieval and modern—
    England—History and criticism. | English literature—Middle
    English, 1100–1500—History and criticism. | English literature—
    Middle English, 1100–1500—Celtic influences.
Classification: LCC PA8380.Z5 S65 2017 | DDC 878/.0307—dc23
LC record available at https://lccn.loc.gov/2016056690

For Lora

Contents

Abbreviations

CPGC	*Contes pour les gens de cour*, trans. Alan Keith Bate (Turnhout: Brepols, 1993).
DMLBS	*Dictionary of Medieval Latin from British Sources*, ed. R. E. Latham et al. (London: Published for the British Academy by Oxford University Press, 1975–2013).
DNC	Walter Map, *De nugis curialium: Courtiers' Trifles*, ed. and trans. M. R. James, rev. C. N. L. Brooke and R. A. B. Mynors (Oxford: Clarendon Press, 1983).
GCO	*Giraldi Cambrensis opera*, ed. J. S. Brewer, James F. Dimock, and George F. Warner, 8 vols. (London: Longman, 1861–91).
GPC	*Geiriadur Prifysgol Cymru*, ed. R. J. Thomas (Cardiff: University of Wales Press, 1950–2002).
HRB	Geoffrey of Monmouth, *The History of the Kings of Britain: An Edition and Translation of "De gestis Britonum,"* ed. Michael D. Reeve, trans. Neil Wright (Woodbridge: Boydell Press, 2007).
LSM	Peter Stotz, *Handbuch zur lateinische Sprache des Mittelalters*, 5 vols. (Munich: Beck, 1996–2004). [References are to book, page, and section number.]
OLD	*Oxford Latin Dictionary*, ed. P. G. W. Glare (Oxford: Clarendon Press, 1996).

A Note on Translations

With the exception of the *History of the Kings of Britain*, the *Lancelot-Grail Cycle*, and the Vulgate, all translations, including those from the *De nugis curialium*, are mine unless otherwise noted. Translations from the Vulgate are the Douay-Rheims.

Introduction

In either 1209 or 1210, Walter Map, a British churchman, courtier, and writer, died. While the year of his death remains in doubt, the month and day are clearly recorded: April 1.[1] Of course, the association of this date with practical jokes had not yet arisen when Walter passed away, but enough of his mischievous personality comes through in his work to suggest that he would surely appreciate the serendipitous alignment of his obituary with a day devoted to hoaxes. He had a wry sense of humor, and, fittingly, much of his literary career can be summed up as a series of hoaxes—some intentional, some not. Walter has been mistaken for St. Jerome, an ancient Roman, a Welshman, a precocious Greek translator, a vicious satirical poet, and the son of a Welsh princess and Norman lord. Indeed, a significant portion of scholarship on Walter Map has been devoted to sifting the real Walter out of this preponderance of fake Walters. This book seeks to understand another of Walter's mistaken identities: his role as author of the *Lancelot-Grail Cycle*, a sprawling thirteenth-century French prose narrative and one of the highlights of medieval Arthurian literature. Why did Walter Map, who apparently did not write in French and who had seemingly no interest in Arthurian material, become attached to the *Lancelot-Grail Cycle*?

In unraveling this question, this book makes two larger arguments concerning the literary history of the twelfth and thirteenth centuries. The first is that Walter Map's *De nugis curialium* is not the disheveled and disorganized text that scholars have imagined—or, at least, its disorganization is of a completely different nature than has been realized. This better understanding of Walter's work in turn provides new evidence in support of a second, larger argument. I show that ecclesiastical networks of textual exchange played a major role in exporting Welsh literary material into England in the twelfth century. Overall, this book attempts to rewrite the history of how narratives about the pre-Saxon inhabitants of Britain, including King Arthur and his knights, first circulated in England. It contends that inventive clerics like

Walter Map, and not traveling minstrels or professional translators, were responsible for popularizing these stories about ancient Britain. In the early thirteenth century, someone envisioned Walter Map withdrawing ancient documents about the Holy Grail from a monastery and putting them in order for Henry II. This story cannot be true. But it is not the literary equivalent of an April Fools' joke, either. As this book will show, it was a succinct and clever way of summarizing how literary material about ancient Britain made its way to numerous gifted and innovative writers in the twelfth century.

Walter Map's posthumous lives have in the past overwhelmed the real, historical Walter Map. Thankfully, Walter's actual career is relatively well documented for a twelfth-century author, and several good biographies have rendered clear the major phases of his life.[2] The details of his early life, however, are rather more cloudy. Walter's exact birthplace is unknown, but he seems to have been born in southwestern Herefordshire, sometime in the late 1130s.[3] Walter tells us that his family was "faithful and useful" to Henry II, both before his coronation and after, and that his promotion to Henry's court was due to their loyalty.[4] (Frustratingly, he never names these members of his family.) As several scholars have suggested, and as I argue as well, Walter may have begun his education at St. Peter's Abbey in Gloucester, before moving on to Paris, where we find him studying theology with Gerard la Pucelle in 1154. Upon his return from the schools, Walter entered the service of the church when the bishop of Hereford, Gilbert Foliot (1148–63), employed him as a clerk. It is very likely that Gilbert already knew Walter, having met him as a youth when he was abbot of St. Peter's, Gloucester (1139–48). When Gilbert Foliot became bishop of London (1163–87), Walter followed him there, and by 1173 he was a canon of St. Paul's. By 1173 he had also entered royal service, traveling with King Henry II to Limoges. He served as a royal justice in England in 1173, and in 1179 he was one of the king's representatives at the Third Lateran Council. He was at Saumur in 1183 when the Young King Henry died at Martel. All in all, Walter seems to have been a trusted courtier. Gerald of Wales, Walter's colleague and friend, calls him a *clericus familiarius* of the king and gives two anecdotes that suggest Walter had King Henry's ear.[5] Walter proved useful at court, and he seems to have remained in Henry's service until his death in 1189. Like so many of Henry's courtiers, Walter may well have found himself out of favor with Richard. Nonetheless, we have no evidence that Richard or even John was particularly hostile to Walter.[6] Indeed, in 1202 John even gave Walter the revenues from the archdeaconry of Brecon.[7]

While Walter is mostly remembered today as a witty courtier, he probably considered himself to be a servant of the church more than the king. He seems to have accumulated some benefices early on, likely in the 1170s. He held the church of Westbury-on-Severn in Gloucestershire, and Ashwell in Hertfordshire. Probably sometime in the 1180s, he became a canon of Hereford, where he would be joined by a rather illustrious group of intellectuals under Bishop William de Vere.[8] From Gilbert Foliot he received a prebend in St. Paul's. Additionally, Walter became a prominent figure in the diocese of Lincoln. By 1183–85 he was a canon, and by 1186 he became chancellor. Upon the death of Henry II, he become precentor of the cathedral. Finally, in 1196 or 1197 he moved south and became the archdeacon of Oxford, which was to be his final ecclesiastical position. Although he was nominated for two bishoprics, Hereford in 1199 and St. Davids in 1203, neither was granted to him. Like his contemporaries Peter of Blois and Gerald of Wales, he ended his career as an archdeacon; literary prowess and a quick wit only got one so far in the twelfth century. In the *cursus honorum* of the English church, Walter could claim a respectable, though not outstanding, career. His death in 1209 or 1210, however, proved to be the best career move he could have made.

The thirteenth century witnessed the rise of two Walter Maps. The first is the subject of this book: early in the century, probably only a little more than a decade after his death, he became associated with the *Lancelot-Grail Cycle*, an attribution that, if true, would have made him one of the most influential authors of medieval Europe. Equally impressive is the fact that Walter Map's name quickly became attached to the corpus of satirical poetry widely known as Goliardic verse. This, too, first began in the thirteenth century. While it is clear that Walter did compose satiric verse—one of his poems, for example, provoked a feisty reply from an Oxford contemporary— the vast majority of these attributions are spurious.[9] Thomas Wright's 1841 volume *The Latin Poems Commonly Attributed to Walter Mapes* testifies to the wide variety of poetry that attracted Walter's name, as does Alfred Lord Tennyson's play *Becket*, in which an incorrigibly satirical Walter Map is criticized for "Goliazing and Goliathizing."[10] Interestingly, this reputation seems to have developed haphazardly throughout the thirteenth and fourteenth centuries, when the works of several satirical poets by the name of Walter circulated together in manuscripts, which ultimately gave way to the name Walter being associated with a certain type of irreverent, satirical poem.[11] Walter Map (or "Mapes" as he is often called in this tradition) became the foremost of these Walters, and many poems that were written by other Walters, as well as many that were anonymous or had the misfortune of being composed by someone not named Walter, came into his orbit. In Medieval Latin poetry, the name *Walter Map* became more a marker of genre than of authorship. It is hard to know what exactly Walter would have thought about this development, but it seems that the man who could craft exquisite monastic and curial satire would not have been entirely displeased with some of his more biting pseudepigrapha.

These first two alternative lives, Arthurian author and Goliardic poet, are well known to scholarship, but the least familiar development in Walter's posthumous reputation occurred in nineteenth-century Wales, when the most famous Welsh intellectual of his day, Edward Williams (1747–1826), better known by his bardic name *Iolo Morganwg*, endeavored to turn Walter into a leading figure of medieval Welsh literary culture.[12] Iolo took to Walter with customary inventiveness, making him responsible for Geoffrey of Monmouth's *History of the Kings of Britain* and a medieval Welsh agricultural treatise. So great was Walter's pull on his imagination that he created the *Llyfr Gwallter Demapys* (The Book of Walter Demapys), an agricultural treatise that contained spurious—but attractively romantic—biographical information about Walter. He also brazenly claimed that Walter had translated works from Greek. Additionally, Iolo made Walter the son of a Norman knight and a Welsh princess, and he used Walter as one example of the literary precocity of the peculiar Cambro-Norman culture of the southern Welsh Marches. It took Welsh scholarship at least a century to work out Iolo's forgeries, but once his machinations were laid bare, Walter Map ceased to be the greatest Welsh writer of his age.

Given the impressive scope of Walter's fictitious lives, it is easy to see how his pseudepigrapha overshadowed his genuine work until the twentieth century. While it is common to read that the *De nugis curialium* is Walter's only work to survive, this assertion is not quite true. The *Dissuasio Valerii*, an anti-matrimonial tract, circulated widely and was a medieval favorite. Indeed, it gathered anti-matrimonial exempla from antiquity with such range and verve that it struck a chord with misogynist readers everywhere. It is, in essence, Jankyn's "book of wikked wyves," made famous in Chaucer's *Wife of Bath's Prologue*. Recognizing its appeal, Walter revised the *Dissuasio*, and a copy of this revision appears in *distinctio* 3 of the *De nugis curialium* alongside Walter's mournful comments about having to use a pseudonym to gain literary fame. Nonetheless, in 1468 the *Dissuasio*'s popularity earned Walter the noteworthy distinction of being the first English author whose work appeared in print; however, he would have surely been disappointed to see that he had been confused with St. Jerome.[13] Apart from the *Dissuasio* and the rest of the *De nugis curialium*, scraps of verse survive here and there in addition to a few of Walter's witty anecdotes.[14] Finally, it is possible that a few of the satiric verses that bear his name are genuine, though not nearly to the extent that the attributions would have us believe.

Nonetheless, Walter's modern fame rests on this strange book known as the *De nugis curialium*, which survives in only one manuscript, Bodley 851. In spite of the existence of only one medieval copy of this work, Walter's name is ubiquitous in studies not only of twelfth-century British history and literature but of the European Middle Ages in general. His ability to craft engaging, peculiar vignettes of figures such as Henry II makes for memorable reading. For example, his use of Bernard of Clairvaux's failed miracles to mock a monkish predilection for pedophilia is unforgettable, and any discussion of the French language in England includes Walter's ridiculing of Geoffrey Plantagenet for speaking what he terms "Marlborough French."[15] Walter is often praised as one of the best satirical writers of his age. His anti-monastic satires, in particular, are deliciously compelling in their well-directed scorn and baroque farce, especially in their treatment of the Cistercians, who at one point are compared unfavorably to the barbarous Welsh. Walter's interest in the Welsh, for that matter, pervades several tales, and the presentation of the Welsh therein has become one of the major sources for Anglo-Norman views of their western neighbors. As mentioned above, Walter also has the dubious honor of writing one of the most vicious and popular anti-matrimonial tracts of the Middle Ages, the *Dissuasio Valerii*. The *Dissuasio*'s deft command of classical and patristic sources has impressed modern and medieval readers alike. Although Walter could wield the vast array of *auctoritates* expected of a secular cleric, he was to a surprising extent open to what we would now call the popular culture of his day. His stories of fairy lovers, zombies, and phantasms provide folklorists with some of the first medieval witnesses of certain folkloric motifs, and his knowledge of Welsh folklore has even been used to reconstruct the archetypes of a few Celtic myths. Finally, the *De nugis curialium* has garnered significant scholarly attention for its construction of authorship and its presentation of reading practices. In several provocative passages, Walter addresses his shortcomings as an author, voices his complaints for contemporary literary taste, and explicitly instructs readers how to approach his text.

The above has certainly not exhausted the reasons for Walter's continuing appeal, but it should help explain why scholars from all disciplines so often quote the *De nugis curialium*. Urbane, learned, and occasionally scurrilous, the *De nugis curialium* is a potpourri of twelfth-century literary culture. Yet Walter Map is typically treated as scholarly window dressing. He is often called in to deliver a witticism or anecdote before being shown the door, and when he is encouraged to stay for a little longer, the interest usually lies in only one or two of his tales. In many respects, this behavior is hard to fault: Walter, always prepared with a bon mot, seems to have been something of a twelfth-century Oscar Wilde. While this book does not aim to offer a complete synthesis of Walter's work, it does, I hope, provide a clearer path for those who may desire to do so in the future.

Unlike its modern-day popularity, the *De nugis curialium* does not appear to have been widely read in the Middle Ages, thus seemingly fulfilling Walter's prophetic complaint: "For when I have begun to rot, then my work will begin to gain flavor for the first time, and my decease will compensate for all its defects, and my antiquity will make me an authority in the most distant future, since then, as now, old copper is preferred to new gold."[16] Yet while the *De nugis curialium* has gained modern currency, the nature and extent of its "defects" are still misunderstood. Indeed, few modern readers have thought the text without defect. With a quip that has resonated widely in discussions of Walter, C. N. L. Brooke and R. A. B. Mynors, the most recent editors of the *De nugis*, have called the work "the untidy legacy of an untidy mind."[17] And while I will show that this characterization is unfair—its untidiness, in fact, results from the disorderly transmission of the only manuscript of the *De nugis curialium*—the presentation of Walter as inattentive and scatterbrained in the edition most consulted by Anglophone scholars has perhaps had an outsized impact. Framing the *De nugis curialium* as the disconnected jottings of a hectic courtier has in turn produced untidy readers of Walter's work, readers who are content to examine a few tales or sections at a time, without pausing to examine the place of individual tales in their overall context. After all, if there is no discernible structure to the work, or if its textual transmission has been hopelessly bungled by a scribe, or even by Walter himself, why should one try to understand the text as a whole?

Of course, the otherwise excellent edition of Brooke and Mynors is not entirely to blame for this phenomenon; the eclectic nature of the *De nugis curialium*, its confused textual state, and its anecdotal approach to history with only a passing regard for what we may call historical fact all invite readers to approach the work in snatches. Perhaps it is for these reasons that only one book-length study of Walter has been completed.[18] The *De nugis curialium* belongs to that curious category of a text that is widely known and carefully read, but consulted only in part and not as a whole: it is the *Lonely Planet Great Britain* of the late twelfth century.

The *De nugis curialium* deserves a better reputation than a series of hastily scribbled anecdotes, and in exploring Walter's involvement with the *Lancelot-Grail Cycle*, this book also offers a reappraisal of textual history of the *De nugis curialium*. I argue that the work was never meant to be a single, unified text, but likely represents at least five works in various stages of completion. Its presentation as one work called the *De nugis curialium* results from several layers of scribal interference, not from a haphazard process of composition on Walter's part, as many have believed. Moreover, the *De nugis curialium* preserves several instances of revision, passages that Walter has reworked from earlier versions.[19] Seen in this light, the *De nugis curialium* provides important evidence for the practice of revision in twelfth-century literature. In its exploration of the *De nugis curialium* as a text in the process of revision, this book offers a timely reappraisal of Walter and his work, one that shows Walter to be a careful, focused reviser in the vein of Gerald of Wales or even William Langland.

While this reevaluation has wide-ranging implications for all aspects of Walter's work, it is particularly helpful in understanding how he became associated with the *Lancelot-Grail Cycle*. In one instance, recognizing Walter's revisions allows us to see a tale about ancient Britain taking shape before our eyes. Walter, although he never mentions Arthur, was in fact interested enough in stories about ancient Britain that he wrote one himself, almost from scratch. Moreover, noticing the extent of the scribal interventions and corruptions that pepper the *De nugis curialium* provides a clearer picture for how Walter dealt with Welsh material. He, as will be seen, tended to know what he was talking about when it came to Wales, a fact often obscured by later scribal tinkering. Finally, viewing Walter as a careful reviser better accords with how the *Lancelot-Grail Cycle* portrays him. Giving Walter, a supposedly undisciplined author, a hand in the creation of the *Cycle* is not absurd as some critics have thought. His modern reputation no longer must remain at odds with this medieval one.

Using Walter Map as a case study, this book overturns long-established narratives of how Welsh literary material first circulated outside of Wales. Instead of identifying Breton minstrels as the agents of transmission, I show that Walter and others had access to Welsh-Latin documents that circulated throughout a monastic network in southern Wales and western England. Latin literature, and not folktales, brought Arthur out of Wales and into

England. I also argue that Walter Map participates in the widespread phenomenon of reworking existing tales in order to fit them into the newly
popular setting of ancient Britain, in effect creating faux-Celtic stories. Taken
together, these two discoveries suggest a new approach for understanding the
"Celtic" element in medieval French and English literature. Rather than the
sources-and-analogues approach that has dominated scholarship for decades,
I propose an approach that is historically sensitive, one that asks what kind of
literary work the concept of ancient Britain does in a culture in which the
inheritors of ancient Britain—the Welsh—are often at odds with the ruling
elite. Twelfth-century clerics were at the forefront of a vibrant literary culture, collecting Welsh-Latin documents and reshaping the Welsh material
they found for their own ends. In the thirteenth century, Walter Map, or at
least the figure of Walter Map, became an Arthurian author precisely because
he fit the profile: he was a clerical Latin writer with a strong interest in Wales
and its past.

Chapter 1 examines Walter's affiliations with Wales and with the genre of
romance, providing important context for how Walter could be seen as someone who worked with the Matter of Britain. Walter took a special interest in
Wales and the Welsh, and while these Welsh tales have generally been said to
reflect common anti-Welsh stereotypes, they are often more sophisticated
than has been assumed. They show that Walter viewed himself as somewhat of
an expert on the Welsh; his stories display a relatively nuanced view of Anglo-
Welsh politics. This chapter also argues that Walter was a skilled writer of romance. *Distinctio* 3 of the *De nugis curialium* contains four polished romances
that demonstrate that Walter could write a series of thematically linked stories. While these romances are not set in ancient Britain, they nonetheless
show that Walter had read widely in contemporary French literature and that
he incorporates many elements of popular romance into his own work.

Chapters 2 and 3 concern the only surviving copy of the *De nugis curialium* found in Bodley 851. I argue that the *De nugis curialium* was originally
five separate works in various stages of completion that were erroneously
taken by later scribes to be a single work. Chapter 2 examines all of the doublets in the *De nugis curialium*, arguing that Walter was reusing earlier material in later work. This chapter does the meticulous work of comparing all of
the doublets found in the *De nugis curialium* and finds that some of the tales
in *distinctiones* 1 and 2 are indeed polished revisions of their counterparts
found in *distinctiones* 4 and 5. Walter's work is therefore not a messy collage of
courtier notes. Rather, it is a collection of unfinished works, some of which

are frozen in the act of revision. Chapter 3 argues that many of the text's infelicities, which are often attributed to Walter himself, are the result of scribal interpolation. Overall, I suggest that Walter's work is not as sloppy or "untidy" as earlier critics have assumed.

Chapter 4 examines in detail the process of revision that lies behind the tale of King Herla, one of Walter's most celebrated tales. This tale is not in fact authentically Welsh, as is widely believed, but is rather a reworking of a continental tale, fitted into Welsh garb—a practice that I argue was widespread. Reworking tales to make them fit into the Matter of Britain could have very specific ideological effects. Walter, for example, has his own way of bringing Henry II into ancient Britain. This chapter also includes an overview of other medieval works that have been incorporated—some skillfully, some sloppily—into the Matter of Britain. Overall, I conclude by arguing that this phenomenon was commonplace in medieval literature and that many instances of Celtic narrative material may in fact be the invention of medieval authors.

Chapter 5 takes up the thorny question of the transmission of the Matter of Britain. How did so many Welsh, Cornish, and Breton characters, themes, and stories make their way into medieval French literature? Walter Map's *De nugis curialium* provides a good deal of indirect evidence, as well as some direct evidence, that transmission occurred through written Latin documents, instead of itinerant multilingual minstrels, who are thought to be the usual channel for transmission. It also explicitly details a network of exchange among minor Marcher aristocrats, which Walter took advantage of to find material for his own work. Arguing that Latin clerics like Walter played a larger role in the transmission of the Matter of Britain than has previously been acknowledged, this chapter concludes by examining other instances in which Latin clerics were instrumental in moving narrative material out of Wales. In particular, this chapter argues that Walter obtained the sources for two of his Welsh tales from the monastic archive of St. Peter's, Gloucester.

Chapter 6 reviews Walter Map's reception in the thirteenth century and beyond, asking why so many readers and writers ascribed to him parts of the *Lancelot-Grail Cycle*. I argue that the earliest attributions to Walter, written only a decade after his death, do not portray him as the author or translator of any of these Arthurian romances. Instead, Walter is merely imagined as a clerk of Henry II who rummaged through monastic archives to compile the Latin source for the French romances. This image corresponds well to what we know about Walter Map and to our revised understanding of how Welsh material passed into the larger European world. Although Walter almost certainly had no hand in the *Lancelot-Grail Cycle*, the author who first introduced him into the *Cycle*'s list of putative authors knew more about how legends of Arthur and his court circulated out of Wales than he has been given credit for.

Walter Map, Wales, and Romance

Medieval readers appreciated knowing the pedigree of a story, and medieval authors obliged them, even if their explanations were often well-crafted fiction. It is no wonder then that the *Lancelot-Grail Cycle* insists that Master Walter Map played an integral role in writing, translating, or discovering these wondrous adventures about ancient Britain.[1] But invoking a source, as the *Cycle* invokes Walter Map, could do more than satisfy the curiosity of readers; it could also perform important literary work. This chapter begins to ask what kind of literary work the name *Walter Map* might have accomplished for the *Cycle*'s author and its first readers. In doing so, it recovers Walter Map's literary reputation, with particular attention to Wales and to the genre of romance. Both of these topics would be of special concern to writers and readers of the *Cycle*. Texts dealing with the pre-English, Arthurian past of Britain often established a plausible tie with the British past, usually through Wales or Brittany.[2] Moreover, early romances tended to position themselves in a larger literary network, sometimes by claiming patronage and sometimes by claiming to be translations or adaptations of earlier romances. Part of the appeal of Walter's name was that it evoked expertise in both the Welsh and romance. As Chapter 6 shows, these two aspects are not the only reasons that the *Cycle* claims Walter's involvement, but they are a good place to begin the investigation.

Walter the Marcher

In November of 1203, Gerald of Wales faced the rather cruel task of nominating candidates to serve as the bishop of St. Davids, a position that he himself

had just been denied. Gerald, however, had to follow one important qualifica-
tion: the candidates must have been born in England, unlike Gerald himself.[3]
One of the two men he grudgingly suggested was Walter Map, the archdeacon
of Oxford. Although Gerald and Walter had known one another for some
years, perhaps even since their youth, Gerald was not merely doing a favor for
an old friend; Walter was a strategic choice. Part of Gerald's rhetoric for his
own promotion had been that recent bishops of St. Davids, appointed by
English kings and Canterbury, had been altogether ignorant of Welsh customs and could not speak Welsh. "We seek a doctor of souls," Gerald wrote,
"not a funeral attendant; we wish to have neither a mute dog, nor a speechless
shepherd."[4] If they could not have a Welsh bishop who could preach in the
language of their diocese, then Walter Map might be a suitable compromise.
Not only was Walter witty, learned, and generous, but he was familiar with
the Welsh and their customs, since he called the Anglo-Welsh border home.[5]
Conveniently for Gerald, Walter could also claim to have been born in England: while he could call the Welsh his compatriots, England was, in his own
words, his mother. Had Gerald's proposal been accepted instead of ignored,
one wonders how Walter's new diocese would have responded to his trenchant
observations that "the glory of the Welsh lies in plunder and theft" and that
the Welsh are "completely unfaithful to everyone," or any number of like remarks that Walter was in the habit of making.[6] In the end, St. Davids might
well have preferred a mute dog to Walter's sharp tongue.

This tension between Walter's familiarity with the Welsh and his disparaging remarks toward them, between his creative use of Welsh culture and his
status as an English courtier, pervades the *De nugis curialium*. However, Walter is not alone in having a seemingly vexed opinion of the Welsh. Medievalists commonly group Walter Map with Gerald of Wales and Geoffrey of
Monmouth—a trio of roughly contemporary Latin authors who called the
Welsh border home. Gerald, never shy in describing his mixed Norman and
Welsh heritage, provides the clearest evidence that those like him, of mixed
background and inhabiting contested lands, were in the twelfth century perhaps beginning to think of themselves as a hybrid people, as a gens apart from
the rest: "Marchers," or *marchiones* in Latin.[7] As for Geoffrey, it is difficult to
tell whether he considered himself a Marcher in these terms; he has left behind little biographical information. Nonetheless, his connection with Monmouth allows for a relatively unproblematic designation as a border dweller.
Our knowledge of Walter Map lies somewhere in between Gerald's garrulous
self-reporting and Geoffrey's nearly total silence on biographical matters.

Walter provides just enough information about himself to produce confusion in critics. One can read confidently that Walter was "born in Wales" and that "he was not even born in Wales."[8] In articles published within a year of one another, Walter the "clerc gallois" becomes Walter the "clerc anglais."[9] And although patriotic Welsh scholars in the nineteenth century celebrated Walter as a preeminent Welsh writer and the son of a Welsh princess, in 1940 R. T. Jenkins curtly announced that "the idea that he is a Welshman must be rejected."[10] Such contradictory statements could easily be multiplied. Yet many scholars, sensing that the evidence itself is contradictory, have remained content to call Walter Anglo-Welsh or simply a Marcher.

It is certainly safe to call Walter a Marcher; indeed, he explicitly declares himself to be one. More interesting, I believe, is that a closer look at some of Walter's Welsh tales illustrates how he used his identity as a Marcher to his own advantage. This section, in addition to exploring Walter's identity as a Marcher, also argues that Walter used his status as a border dweller to become, in a way, a foreign policy expert on the Welsh. Many of the Welsh stories in the *De nugis curialium* anticipate an elite audience of policy makers, including the royal court and the local elite of the Welsh March. Their political import suggests that for his colleagues and peers Walter may well have been seen as an expert on Welsh affairs. This reputation, in turn, helps illuminate Walter's pseudonymous authorship of the *Lancelot-Grail Cycle*.

Any discussion of Walter Map's ethnicity must first grapple with his quirky-sounding name—*Map*.[11] The name has commonly been explained as a version of the Middle Welsh word *map* (son), which made up the linking element in male patronymic surnames.[12] Dewi map Ceredic, for example, is David son of Ceredig. Given its ubiquity in Welsh names, *map*, so the theory goes, seems to have been viewed as a token of Welshness by the Normans and English. It was thus duly applied to people of Welsh descent or affiliation in a playful, mocking sort of way. (A good parallel seems to be *Maccus*, used to designate those with some Gaelic affiliations.)[13] In support of this view is the fact that when other instances of the cognomen *Map* occur, they do so in places where English and French speakers would have encountered Welsh and Cornish speakers (the word for "son" in both languages is written *map/mab*). In the tenth-century Bodmin Gospels, a Godric Map appears in Cornwall, and Domesday Book records an Ælfric Mapesone in Worcester and a Godric Mapeson in Herefordshire during the eleventh century.[14] If Map is indeed a nickname of sorts, it was not heard as too derogatory, since Walter claims it as his own, describing Map as his *agnomen*—a word that can, frustratingly, mean both "nickname" and "surname."[15] This agnomen also seems to have been jokingly incorporated into a group of prebends at St. Paul's that received their names from men of Walter's generation: Walter's prebend was called Mapesbury.[16]

Yet it is challenging to work out what this nickname may have meant to contemporaries: Was Walter Welsh? Or just Welsh-*ish*? Testimony from the Welsh side of the border may help in this respect. The Welsh could use the term *Sais* (lit. "Saxon/English") for a Welshman who was familiar with either English habits or the English language or even for Welshmen who enjoyed English patronage.[17] Importantly, Welsh evidence shows that the term *Sais* says little about ethnicity. The son of Rhys ap Gruffudd, a powerful Welsh prince and contemporary of Walter's, serves as a good reminder in this respect. Rhys's son Hywel spent thirteen years as a hostage at Henry II's court, and when he returned to Wales in 1171, he was granted a new addition to his name—*Sais*.[18] Certainly, Hywel Sais, as a son of a very influential and politically powerful Welsh ruler, had few doubts as to his own ethnicity. Rather, his new nickname, which, one may suspect, may not have been wholly welcome, suggests "how his exile had shaped his attitude and behavior."[19] Perhaps *Map* meant something similar: a nickname bestowed upon men of non-Welsh descent who nonetheless had spent time among them or who were familiar with Welsh traits and customs. This description would suit Walter nicely.

Although this understanding of Walter's name has received widespread approval, it is not without problems. First of all, some evidence points to *Map* having been a family name, rather than a personal nickname. Walter's nephew Philip carried the *Map* name, and in the early thirteenth century a "Walter Map son of Walter Map of Wormsley" appears in a series of charters concerning Wormsley church.[20] We have no way of knowing for sure that these last two are related to the author of the *De nugis curialium*, but it is not unlikely, especially because Walter held nearby interests.[21] If *Map* is a family name, then it may say more about Walter's ancestors than Walter himself. Second, a few have doubted that *Map* is in any way related to the Middle Welsh word *map* (son).[22] A. K. Bate, following studies of English surnames, hesitantly suggests that *Map* derives from Medieval Latin *mappa* (cloth; map), which may indicate that Walter's ancestors held some sort of administrative position.[23] Bate also claims that the distribution of the name in border countries suggests a regional family—not a nickname—and he implies that the desire to have a Welsh or a half-Welsh Walter results from some passé stereotypes of Celtic storytellers.[24] This last point undoubtedly has some truth to it, but deriving

Map from Latin *mappa* does not make much sense. Why *mappa* and not something like **mappator*?[25] Moreover, the name never unambiguously appears as "Mappa" or "Mappe," the latter of which would be the expected early Middle English outcome.[26] Deriving *Map* from an Old English borrowing of Latin *mappa* seems no less problematic than the Welsh explanation.

Another wrinkle does little to clarify matters. *Map* (son) seems to have been an epithet common in the Brittonic world, with attestations in Wales, Cornwall, and Brittany.[27] Out of the dozen or so Welsh occurrences, two instances help explain what *map* means when used in this way: "Gruffudd Ddu ap Ieuan Fab ap Ieuan Las" and "Gruffudd Fab ap Gruffudd Gŵyr ap Cydifor."[28] (The word *fab* is merely *mab* with an expected initial mutation.) Since both Ieuan and Gruffudd have the same name as their fathers, it seems here that the use of *map* as an epithet parallels the way some British authors use Latin *filius* (son) to mean "junior" or "the younger."[29] French *fitz* (son) and English *son* were also used in a similar manner.[30] It is not surprising that Welsh witnesses an analogous development. Nevertheless, this use of *map* does not seem to have been widespread, and it never overtook the much more common *bychan* (lit. "little") in this regard. Nonetheless, the few instances of *Map* along the border could be explained as borrowings of this Welsh practice, perhaps in mixed families, rather than a nickname that the English and French applied to those of Welsh affiliations. Welsh attestations, after all, outnumber those from east of the border, and the English instances of *Map* appear only in places where Welsh (or Cornish) speakers were nearby.

Reading *Map* as "junior" also has the advantage of making the two occurrences of the surname *Mappeson* more intelligible. The semantic path from the nickname *junior* to the first name *Junior* is quite clear, as witnessed by the rise of *Junior* as a first name in the United States. These Mappesons, therefore, might have had a father whose nickname *Map* (junior) overtook his baptismal name. Yet such an interpretation remains puzzling given "Walter Map son of Walter Map of Wormsley," since the entire point of *Map* was to distinguish father from son. Perhaps the meaning of *Map* was lost when it passed out of Welsh usage and into an Anglo-Norman context? In any case, even if it is not entirely certain that *Map* was a nickname bestowed upon those with Welsh affiliations, it does seem reasonable to understand the name as one of the many tokens of the cultural mélange of the Anglo-Welsh borderlands.

Indeed, although we have no sure evidence, Walter's familiarity with the border strongly suggests that he was a native of the March. He twice refers to the Black Mountain, which straddles southwest Herefordshire and Powys.[31]

He also displays some detailed local knowledge of Ross, Wollaston, Beachley, Aust Cliff, and the Forest of Dean.[32] Furthermore, some of the Welsh tales are set in the lordships immediately east of the Black Mountain.[33] And he sets a short exemplum illustrating the hotheadedness of the Welsh at Hay-on-Wye, a strategic border town in the area.[34] He also held land, at least later in his life, at Ullingswick in Herefordshire, about fifteen miles west of Offa's Dyke. Moreover, the patronage of Gilbert Foliot may not have been the only factor in Walter's election as a canon of Hereford, as the chapter had a strong preference for local sons.[35] In light of these facts, the general critical impression has been that Walter's homeland is "somewhere south of Hereford."[36]

One possibility that deserves special consideration is Archenfield, or Ergyng in Welsh, the southwestern portion of Herefordshire, where Walter held the church of Westbury-on-Severn. Although Archenfield lay on the English side of the river Wye and although today it is a thoroughly anglicized part of Herefordshire, during Walter's time Archenfield was starkly Welsh in character and overwhelmingly populated by Welshmen.[37] Even late into the fifteenth century, the area was still regarded as a place "where the king's writ could not be served."[38] Archenfield fits with all of the available facts of Walter's life. Here, the Welsh would have definitely been his countrymen, yet he could claim without any evasion that he was born in England. If he did not call Archenfield home, he was nonetheless intimately familiar with the general area—much more so than with any other place mentioned in the *De nugis curialium*.

Certainly, not all border dwellers were the same, and, as far as can be inferred, Walter's background differed from that of his colleague Gerald of Wales in a few important ways. In Walter's case, the scale of English-Welsh identity is tipped toward the English side. Gerald's birth in Wales and kinship with Welsh princes proved easy targets for his enemies, who managed to thwart his aspirations, in part by making his identity as a Marcher suspect.[39] Walter never mentions any persecution of this sort. His royal patronage, it must be said, rested on surer footing. His parents had served Henry II, both before and after he took the throne, and so even if Walter did have some ancestral relationship with Wales, it did not cause unease in either Gilbert Foliot or the king, his two major patrons.[40] But if Walter was part Welsh, at any remove, he never claimed it, as the *De nugis curialium* speaks with one voice in describing Walter as a Marcher, but not a Welshman. Walter never once uses the words *Cambria* and *Cambrensis* to refer to Wales and the Welsh, but rather the nonnative terms *Wallia* and *Wallenses*. (In this respect, however, Walter could merely be an early adopter, as the terms *Wallia* and *Wallenses* were being adopted by Welsh writers in the twelfth century.)[41] Moreover, Walter calls the Welsh his "compatriots" (*compatriote*)—a remark that has at times led readers astray.[42] But *compatriota* implies little about ethnicity or culture, meaning only someone from the same district, county, or country as oneself.[43] Though he may have lived among the Welsh, he still considered England his country. In a particularly revealing passage, Walter speaks of a promising young man and boasts they are related ("de cuius cognacione glorior").[44] When his young relative passes overseas to serve Philip I, Count of Flanders, Walter says that "he left England, his mother and mine" (matrem nostram et suam Angliam exiuit).[45] A clearer statement of national identity would be hard to find.

Yet for all that, Walter shows a deeper familiarity, and even understanding, of the Welsh than might be expected of someone who calls England his mother. He uses a few Welsh terms: *brycan* (cloth; blanket) and *brenhin* (king).[46] And he has some decent knowledge of southeastern Wales, gained through personal experience, oral culture, and literary sources.[47] While many of his Welsh stories are tailor-made for relating Welsh stereotypes, others show a more nuanced interest in Welsh history and culture. Walter even knows a bit about Welsh law.[48] Further testimony of Walter's knowledge of Welsh culture is found in Gerald's nomination of Walter for the bishop of St. Davids. When the archbishop of Canterbury asked him to put forward the names of suitable candidates who were born in England ("de Anglia oriundus"), Gerald begrudgingly suggested John of Brancaster and Walter Map in 1203.[49] John, according to Gerald, is learned and knows Welsh ("linguae nostrae non inscium").[50] Walter, whom Gerald celebrates for his eloquence and wit, has knowledge of the mores of both the Welsh and the English in Wales (*morumque gentis utriusque terrae*), because they are his neighbors (*vicinitate locorum*) and because he has had repeated dealings with them (*frequentia*).[51] Since Gerald showed an interest in language surprising for his age, his silence on Walter's ability to speak Welsh, especially after he has just praised John of Brancaster for knowing it, strongly implies that Walter would not have been able to converse with many residents of his diocese had he become bishop.[52] Still, Walter was familiar enough with the area's *mores*, a term that for Gerald meant the distinctive social practices of a people, though it also could encompass psychological traits.[53] Gerald's description of Walter agrees with the portrait that emerges from the *De nugis curialium*: familiar with the Welsh, yet born in England; unable to speak Welsh, yet able to catch a few words here and there; a purveyor of Welsh anecdotes; an amateur Welsh historian—all of which fit perfectly with Walter's own description as a Marcher.

A Welsh Specialist

On one occasion, Walter baldly states that he is "a Marcher to the Welsh" (*marchio sum Walensibus*).[54] We are lucky to have such a clear statement of self-identification, but we are even luckier that its immediate context has been preserved, allowing us a glimpse into how Walter deployed his status as a border dweller at court. The remark follows Walter's discussion of the exceptional welcome Edward the Confessor received from King Llywelyn, who displayed admirable courtesy and humility in greeting his enemy. Walter reports that peace did not last; it was broken soon thereafter, as the Welsh are wont to do (*more Walensium*).[55] Llywelyn's fickleness allows Walter the opportunity to reflect upon a conversation he once had with Thomas Becket during his tenure as royal chancellor (1155–62). The two may have met in Paris, and, if Walter is to be believed, Thomas may well have been contemplating the Welsh campaign of 1157 and approached Walter for advice about how to best deal with the Welsh.[56] At any rate, he sought out Walter presumably because he, as a Marcher, had some special insight. Walter implies as much: "he asked me, a Marcher to the Welsh, what is their faithfulness and how they can be trusted."[57] Walter does not disappoint him, either, as he gives Becket a lively parable (*parabolam*) in response: Franco, a German knight in exile in France, happens upon King Louis, whose attendants have left him alone to guard a felled stag, after they rush off in pursuit of another. Franco asks to speak to the king, but Louis keeps his identity concealed, saying that he will return shortly. King Louis then helps the knight dismount, and, as he holds the saddle, he spies Franco's large sword. Taken by the size and the beauty of the sword, the king asks to examine it, and Franco complies. While holding the sword, the king forgets he is in disguise, and in a royal manner orders Franco to bring him a stone to sit on. Fearing the sword, Franco complies, but when he receives the sword back, he tells the king: "Take that stone back to its place!"[58] The king, likewise fearing the sword, does as he is told. Walter explains this parable to Becket: "And from this incident, I can demonstrate to you the faithfulness of the Welsh: as long as you hold the sword, they will submit; when they hold it, they will command."[59] The very threat of violence can move rocks and men.

Walter's conversation with Becket, even if it contains retrospective embellishment, suggests that being a Marcher at court could be expedient, especially if one is quick with a memorable anecdote. In this regard, Walter's behavior with Becket has a performative aspect about it; being a Marcher at court means being able to discourse on the Welsh. Becket's request for insight surely was not the only time Walter was called on to explain the Welsh. Walter knew about the pretentions of the diocese of St. Davids, which he apparently denigrated on numerous occasions.[60] Moreover, other passages in the *De nugis curialium* have the polished feel of repeated recitation. The Welsh are scrupulous (*probi*) only in their unscrupulousness (*improbitate*).[61] They value hospitality to a fault, so much so that a Welshman once killed his wife for insulting a guest.[62] Plunder and theft are so important to the Welsh that few grow old willingly: "Die young, or beg old," as they say.[63] So rash and irrational are the Welsh when angry that they will even kill their friends out of spite.[64] True to form, Walter can furnish an exemplary story for each of these claims. These short stories are crafted to distill the essence of the Welsh into a few pithy words: they show that Walter is a man in the habit of explaining the Welsh.

Walter was not, however, the only Welsh specialist at Henry's court. Gerald of Wales was rewarded, though not as much as he hoped, for his local knowledge of Wales during his time as a royal clerk.[65] He often boasts of his usefulness in dealing with the Welsh. Indeed, according to Gerald, he was first summoned to Henry's aid when the king was "in the borders of the March, for the purpose of pacifying Wales."[66] Moreover, Gerald's Marcher family knew how to counter the military tactics of the Welsh, and their strategies proved successful in invading Ireland as well.[67] Gerald, ever eager to please, invoked his Marcher expertise to advise Henry and his court on cultural and military matters pertaining to the Welsh. Walter played the same role, and his royal invitation to possess the revenues of the archdeaconry of Brecon in 1202 might attest to the fact that he could parlay his Marcher know-how to his advantage.[68] There was profit to be had in knowledge of the Welsh, and Marchers seem to have cornered the market.

Gerald's comments on Walter also speak to the complexity of the March: Walter knows the mores not only of the Welsh but "of both people of the land" (*gentis utriusque terrae*).[69] The other people to whom Gerald is referring are, of course, the Anglo-Norman Marcher aristocracy. Walter knew what it was like to live in a frontier society, and he was certainly comfortable in a Marcher milieu. He traded tales with Marcher barons, knights, aristocrats, and bishops.[70] Several of his stories are rooted in the March, and they respond to the peculiar situation of living on the border, recording dangerous Welsh raids and buttressing contemporary property rights with the misty past of legend. And his church of Westbury-on-Severn lay in an area of southwestern Herefordshire where Welsh presence was strong. This benefice, in effect, made Walter a member of the Marcher gentility, though in a modest fashion.

It is tempting to overstate the importance of Walter's status as a Marcher. It was, after all, just one of the many identities available to him. He was also English, and a member of the French-speaking English elite at that. And he was at home in the international world of Latin Christendom. He was entertained by Marie de Champagne and her husband, Count Henry, at their chateau in Troyes, and he was one of Henry II's representatives at the Third Lateran Council.[71] Although Walter's vocation as a secular cleric caused him less angst than it did Peter of Blois, his day-to-day life as a churchman, both in and out of court, held clear importance to him; the strong moral and didactic overtones of his satire show that he thought both monastic and curial life needed reform.[72] Yet Walter's reputed role in producing the *Lancelot-Grail Cycle* suggests that one of the most salient of these identities was status as a learned intermediary between Wales and England. Walter's exemplum for Thomas Becket bears this out. It does not end by stating only that threat of violence at the tip of a sword is all that is needed to subjugate the Welsh. Rather, Walter tells us what happens to Franco, the wandering German knight who inadvertently threatened the king of France: "And to let you know what came of Franco when his men had reached him, the king at once held him back, by praising him greatly as he tried to flee in fear, and the king told his men how bravely and courteously he had made him carry the stone back, and he gave him Crépy-en-Valois as his inheritance."[73] Walter has already authorized us to read this parable in terms of Anglo-Welsh relations. Although he leaves this ending unglossed, the meaning is plain to see. The threat of violence, though of utmost importance, cannot on its own fashion a long-lasting political solution. The English must accommodate the Welsh in some manner, allow them some degree of respectability. By identifying Crépy-en-Valois ("Crespium in Valesio") as the specific site of the Franco's inheritance, Walter may well be punning off the French word for Wales (attested as *Gales*, *Galeys*, *Wales*, and so on), in effect suggesting that the English king grant the Welsh at least some land to control.[74] And Henry II did just that when he adopted a strategy of rapprochement in his later dealings with Wales, especially after 1171.[75] In this regard, Walter's anecdote mirrors royal policy. To be clear, what Walter is advocating is not a pro-Welsh policy but merely a reflection of the reality of the accommodation and coexistence that obtained throughout the March. Walter, when dealing with the Welsh and border culture in general, shows the savvy and flexibility that one would expect of a Marcher who gladly flaunted his specialist knowledge when requested.

The parable of the armed German knight is not the only story in the *De nugis curialium* that reads as political commentary on the Welsh. Walter's story of Cynan the Fearless plays on anxiety over Welsh military raids, anxiety that was very real for Walter and his fellow border dwellers. The story takes place "over the Severn in Glamorgan," in an area that had been under Anglo-Norman control for the better part of a century, and it describes a raid on a certain "valiant and rich" knight in typical Welsh fashion.[76] Welsh military resistance in the March most commonly took the form of swift, guerrilla-style attacks, as the Welsh were generally reluctant to be drawn into large-scale military campaigns.[77] They frequently attacked at night and utilized wooded areas to surprise their enemies, whereupon they would melt back into the forest to escape unharried.[78] The tactics that Cynan's band employs are the same: Cynan "left the forest that towers over the whole district by himself, with a large band hidden in it, and he devised a murderous ambush for the innocent man."[79] Moreover, Cynan and his band do not attack the knight's house openly, but try to sneak through a window in secret (*furtim*).[80] There can be no doubt that Walter portrays Cynan as a typical Welsh raider; it is a portrait that no Marcher would fail to recognize. And Walter Map himself was clearly familiar with the tactics of Welsh raiders in the March, whether from his acquaintances or firsthand experience, though likely both.[81]

In addition to depicting the reality of border skirmishes, the tale presents Cynan not as a powerful scourge but as a humbled and contrite raider.[82] It does so by emphasizing a Welsh stereotype—the importance of hospitality to the Welsh. Here, the knight whom Cynan and his band are set to attack receives a guest. Cynan, not wanting to breach his people's reverence for hospitality, beseeches his companions to hold back. Cynan's speech has strong religious overtones: "for he has received a knight with hospitality who, as is our custom, sought it out in the name of charity, and in him he has God for a guest, and with God any battle is unequal."[83] By echoing Abraham and Sarah's reception of the three guests who are in fact angels of the Lord, Cynan's willingness to hold hospitality sacred makes his subsequent violation of it all the more striking.[84] After his companions browbeat him into acquiescence by mocking his name—"how rightly he is called fearless!"—Cynan leads his crew toward the house, where, alerted by the guard dogs, the guest lies armed and ready.[85] Two of Cynan's nephews are caught unaware and killed. The story ends with more religious imagery; as Cynan carries the corpses away, he remarks, "I knew that God was in there, and I know that Judas Maccabaeus, the strongest champion of God, said: 'For the success of war is not in the multitude of the army, but strength cometh from heaven,' and therefore I was afraid to prolong this attack; and the Lord did not forget to take vengeance on my nephews for the pride of their abuse."[86] With these words the story ends. And Cynan, recognizing his errors, retreats back into the woods.

This tale is a wonderful piece of fantasy for a Marcher audience who is used to dealing with Welsh raids. It creates a mechanism that punishes the Welsh on their own terms. Within this tale Walter Map brings two Welsh "customs" into blunt opposition—their taste for plunder and their respect for hospitality. Not only does rapacity overcome hospitality, perhaps hinting at what really drives the Welsh, but it does so in a way that emphasizes Cynan's weakness. In short, Welsh raiders—a serious and constant threat to Marchers—are here reduced to somewhat comical characters, subject only to their greed, even to the point of ignoring one of their most cherished mores. Indeed, throughout *distinctio* 2 the defining characteristics of the Welsh are their reverence for hospitality and their inclination toward rash violence. The religious streak of this tale also has significance in this context. The Welsh were routinely said to have suffered at the hands of the Saxons because of their religious failings. For a Marcher audience, particularly those who had read their Geoffrey of Monmouth, this story would imaginatively defang the persistent threat of Welsh raids. It reduces the shortsighted nature of their raids into parody and elides the failure of Cynan to heed hospitality into the widely held belief that the Welsh people's military and political stumblings are divine retribution for their sinful behavior.

While the story of Cynan addresses the anxieties of the Marcher elite, those like the valiant knight Cynan attacks, other stories show that Walter was interested in "the problem of the Welsh" on a national level as well. The most detailed portrait of a Welshman in the *De nugis curialium* is that of Llywelyn ap Gruffudd, king of Wales.[87] Walter never intends to be a careful writer of history, and it has long been suspected that he has switched the name of the son and father around.[88] (Those who have worked with Welsh dynastic names will forgive this mistake.) Gruffudd ap Llywelyn (d. 1063), who became king of Gwynedd and Powys in 1039 and gained all of Wales in 1055, is most probably the historical figure who lies behind Walter's Welsh king.[89] In addition to being the leading political figure of his day, inspiring one Welsh chronicler to style him the "head and shield and defender of the Britons," Gruffudd swore fealty to Edward the Confessor in 1056, an event that Walter records, with no small help from his own imagination.[90] The historical Gruffudd was a dynamic figure who allied himself with Earl Ælfgar of Mercia—an alliance that some English observers cast in a positive light.[91] But Walter's Llywelyn is much more one-dimensional, termed at the outset a "faithless man, just as almost all his predecessors and successors were."[92] This characterization is unsurprising, since Walter's home country had been on the receiving end of Gruffudd's success a few generations before. Of all Gruffudd's campaigns into English territory, the most memorable was his harrying of Hereford in 1055, when he laid waste to the city and its cathedral; in the next year at Glasbury he even slew its bishop Leofgar, several of the cathedral's canons, and the sheriff Ælfnoth, all of whom had attacked Gruffudd in retaliation.[93] The minster lost almost everything. Very few documents survive from before 1055, and the relics of St. Æthelbert were likewise destroyed, thus depriving the chapter of significant spiritual cachet. Moreover, Westbury-on-Severn, whose church Walter held, had also suffered at the hands of Gruffudd in 1053.[94] It is unsurprising that Walter, himself a canon of Hereford, describes a cruel, jealous, and untrustworthy Llywelyn ap Gruffudd. Even if he did not get the name quite right, he knew that the southern borders had been ravaged by a fearsome Welsh king a century before.

Walter recounts four short anecdotes about Llywelyn; all but the last serve to defame him. Nonetheless, these Llywelyn passages are not merely personal invective—Walter has not bothered to get the name of this Welsh king exactly right, after all—but general illustrations of Welsh backwardness. For Walter's English contemporaries, these stories would exemplify several distasteful aspects of Welsh culture: their odd legal system, cultivation of prophecy, and extreme political violence.

Welsh law differed considerably from English practice, a fact that contemporary observers were well aware of and that could present practical problems in places where English and Welsh law were both in use.[95] Walter, who had himself been an itinerant justice, was familiar with this cultural difference. His first anecdote relates the mechanics of one aspect of Welsh law with surprising accuracy. Llywelyn, overcome with jealously, desires vengeance from a handsome and well-born man who had merely dreamt of having an affair with Llywelyn's wife the queen; the injured king "said that he had been duped and boiled with rage as if the deed had actually taken place."[96] The dreamer is captured, and all his relatives offer themselves as surety so that he can be brought to trial. An insult to the king's honor must be punished. Although Walter does not use the term, he understands one of the key elements of Welsh law: *sarhad*, or the compensation owed for harming someone's honor. This strange case of *sarhad* vexes lawmen—how does one punish a thought crime? In the end, one exceedingly clever man solves the problem, and in doing so he gives an overview of the legal elements at play:

> We should follow the laws of our land, and we cannot, for any reason, do away with the laws that our fathers established as precepts and that have been confirmed by extensive use. Let us follow them and, until they reach any verdict in public at odds with custom, let us suggest nothing new. Our most ancient laws declare that anyone who dishonors the queen of the king of Wales through adultery will depart free and uninjured once he has paid a thousand cows to the king. In the same manner, the penalty was set at a certain amount for the wives of princes and other noblemen according to the honor of each. This man is accused of having sex with the queen in a dream, and he does not deny the charge. Given that he has confessed to the truth of his crime, it is settled that a thousand cows should be handed over.[97]

The ingenious solution is to line up one thousand cows along the shores of the lake of Brycheiniog, and to have Llywelyn gaze upon their reflection. He may then collect his payment in the form of the reflection of the cows, since dreams are merely a reflection of reality. Thus the punishment matches the crime, all while upholding Welsh legal tradition. This passage, in addition to succinctly explaining the basic concept of *sarhad*, closely echoes a passage in a southern recension of Welsh law.[98] In the Welsh lawbook known as the *Llyfr Blegywryd*, one of the three ways a king can be dishonored is by "violating his wife" (*kamarueru o'e wreic*), the fine for which is set at one hundred cows for every cantref a king controls.[99] Although stories of escaping legal quandaries while obeying the letter of the law are commonplace in folk literature, Walter's story is grounded in actual Welsh legal theory. Importantly, Walter does not expect his audience to have a clear understanding of Welsh legal practice, and he therefore provides a brief explanation. The anecdote reads as both informative and entertaining and shows Walter at his best in crafting border tales from his knowledge of Welsh culture. The story also educates, even if derisively, its readers in Welsh legal difference—they do things differently over there.

The next two episodes also discredit Llywelyn, though they do so not by explaining peculiar Welsh institutions but by relying on contemporary Welsh stereotypes. Llywelyn was, according to Walter, an underachieving child, one who "sat beside his father's ashes."[100] His sister scolds him, begging him to follow the "custom of the country" (*mos huius terre*) to venture out on New Year's Eve to raid, steal, or even to eavesdrop.[101] Those who choose to eavesdrop have the chance to hear a prophetic saying about their future. Inspired, Llywelyn creeps up to a house and listens to a cook inside contemplating the beef chunks in his stew: "Here I have found one remarkable piece among the others, since I always send it to the bottom and place it under the others, and right away it reappears above all the other pieces."[102] Llywelyn takes himself to be this unsinkable chunk of beef, and gladdened by such a "clear omen" (*manifesto pronostico*), he begins his rise to becoming "the most cunning thief and the most violent raider of the property of others."[103] Political prophecy is certainly not unique to Wales, but Welsh political prophecy takes on particular significance when read in an English context.

The Welsh nursed their loss of the island of Britain by cultivating a rich body of prophetic lore that told of a national savior who would come to destroy the English and restore the sovereignty of the island to its rightful holders. Gerald of Wales was not the only one to observe that the Welsh "foretell and boast with the utmost confidence—and their entire populace wondrously holds to this hope—that soon their countrymen will return to the island, and, in accordance to the prophecies of their own Merlin, both the foreign nation and its name will perish, and the Britons will once more rejoice in their old name and privilege in the island."[104] Walter was familiar with the figure of Merlin as a prophetic figure, and his description of Llywelyn's omen humorously undercuts Welsh pretensions.[105] Not only is Llywelyn's prophecy amusingly mundane—a pot of beef stew in the place of dragons and other allegorical beasts—but it fails to produce a great national redeemer. While Llywelyn does become an outstanding Welsh leader, in Walter's eyes that simply means that he is the best thief and raider in a land full of thieves and raiders. This anecdote speaks to an English perception that plunder, and not noble claims to recovering the crown of the Island of Britain, is what truly motivates Welsh rulers, in spite of what their grand prophecies may say.

Walter's description of Llywelyn's reign bears this assumption out. He ruled peacefully, with the sole exception of "the suffering that he inflicted upon his own people."[106] Llywelyn proceeds to murder and maim any promising young man that he sees, adopting the proverb "I kill nobody, but I blunt the horns of Wales so that they do not harm their mother."[107] Sensing that his nephew Llywarch will grow to be his rival, Llywelyn finally corners him and, asking why he has fled his presence, he offers to provide guarantors in case he is afraid. Llywarch then proceeds to name as guarantors several promising young men whom his uncle has already slain. Violence and treachery were common aspects of medieval aristocratic life, but Anglo-Norman and Angevin dynastic politics were relatively tame compared to the constant bloodshed of Welsh petty kings.[108] Walter's Llywelyn therefore embodies two salient aspects of Welsh political life that would have been recognized by English readers: prophecy and violence.

Among Llywelyn's many acts of wickedness, Walter records one noble and honorable deed. When Edward the Confessor, troubled by Llywelyn's violent incursions into England, humbly approaches the Welsh king in a boat to discuss the situation, Llywelyn is so moved by his modesty in crossing over to him, rather than the other way around, that he does homage to his English rival. The event is at least partly based in truth, since Gruffudd ap Llywelyn did in fact pay homage to King Edward in 1056.[109] But in Walter's telling, this rapprochement becomes an opportunity to highlight two opposing myths about who is the rightful heir to the Island of Britain. At Aust Cliff and Beachley on the Severn River, the two kings meet at one of the clearest markers of division between England and Wales. Neither king wishes to cross to the other's side, and the debate quickly turns to political theory: "Llywelyn claimed greater precedence; Edward equal rank. Llywelyn claimed that his people had taken possession [*conquisissent*] of all England, along with Cornwall, Scotland, and Wales from the giants, and asserted that he was the heir with the most lawful descent. Edward claimed that his own ancestors had obtained England from those who had taken possession of it [*conquisitoribus*]."[110]

Condensed into this short exchange are both Welsh and English claims to the Island of Britain. In particular, Walter relies upon Geoffrey of Monmouth's *History of the Kings of Britain*, where a battle against giants lies at the very foundation of Britain.

Geoffrey's *History* describes how once the Trojan refugees have landed on the fruitful and promising island, inhabited by nobody "save for a few giants," they begin to explore the territories, "driving off to mountain caves any giants they [come] upon," and soon thereafter Brutus names the island Britain and its people Britons after himself.[111] Corineus, favoring the southwestern portion of the island, chooses Cornwall, since "there were more [giants] to be found there than in any of the districts divided amongst his companions."[112] Eventually, a frighteningly strong giant named Goemagog, leading twenty other giants, attacks Brutus and his men as they hold a feast in Totnes, the spot where they are said to have landed. After reinforcements arrive, the giants are all destroyed, except Goemagog, the last of his kind, who is spared only because Brutus desires to watch Corineus and Goemagog wrestle. It is only after Corineus kills Goemagog that the work of building and settling the island really begins, for immediately afterward Brutus surveys the whole island and decides to build Trinovantum, New Troy, which would later become London. Thus, with the Trojans now settled in their new home, the first book of Geoffrey's *History* comes to a close.

As the climax of the first book of *The History of the Kings of Britain*, Corineus's defeat of Goemagog cements the Trojan's control over Britain and marks the point at which Brutus and Corineus divide the island among themselves.[113] This episode is the first of several passages in the *History* in which divisions of Britain are explained, usually with reference to an eponymous founder.[114] These passages famously foreshadow and justify many of the political, legal, and ethnic boundaries of Geoffrey's day: the kingdoms of Wales, England, and Scotland, for example, reflect how Brutus parceled out Britain among his three sons.[115] The Trojans' skirmish with the giants over supremacy of the island thus becomes the exemplar of how British land is contested and appropriated in Geoffrey's *History*. Crucially, Walter's Llywelyn knows the history of this battle and its meaning.

While Llywelyn cites the beginning of Geoffrey's *History*, Edward cites the end. If the Welsh gained Britain by conquering the giants, the English gained their territory by conquering the Welsh. The last books of Geoffrey's *History* explain how the Britons lose their former territory on account of their sins. Their future looks bleak: "The Welsh, unworthy successors to the noble Britons, never again recovered mastery over the whole island, but, squabbling pettily amongst themselves and sometimes with the Saxons, kept constantly massacring the foreigners or each other."[116] As far as Edward is concerned, the English hold Britain with just as much right as the Welsh—both had it from previous peoples. This brief exchange nicely encapsulates the debate on the aim of Geoffrey of Monmouth's work, a debate that has continued into modern scholarship. Walter, typically, refuses to weigh in on behalf of either Edward or Llywelyn, since it is ultimately Edward's personal charisma, rather than any quasi-mythical claim, that moves Llywelyn. For Walter's courtly audience, the moral of Llywelyn and Edward's meeting is simple: argument over English and Welsh claims to the rightful possession of Britain will end in a stalemate. The solution seems to be personal action, rather than principled debate. In particular, Walter suggests that the personal action most effective in dealing with the Welsh is not humility, but rather intimidation. Llywelyn's peace "was, in the habit of the Welsh, kept only until they had the chance to harm."[117] Walter immediately moves on to his parable delivered to Thomas Becket, which explains how the Welsh can only be coerced into obedience by the threat of the sword. Citing Geoffrey of Monmouth, it would seem, is a poor strategy when dealing with perceived Welsh recalcitrance.

Walter anticipated readers who dealt with the Welsh on a political level and who appreciated his wry insight into the Welsh. Cynan the Fearless addresses the anxieties of the Marcher gentry, dissolving the horror of a Welsh raid into a comedic juxtaposition of Welsh stereotypes, reading their love of violence against their love of hospitality. Elsewhere, I have discussed how Walter supports Hereford Cathedral's claim to Lydbury North, an important estate that sat along the border, making the bishop, in effect, a Marcher lord.[118] Walter kept a close eye on border politics. His portrait of Llywelyn, moreover, demonstrates that his Welsh stories could address national, not merely regional, concerns. Welsh law, Welsh prophetic tradition, and even the Welsh claim to dominion over Britain all coalesce in Walter's discussion of this Welsh king. Walter's presentation of these weighty topics would have found eager ears in English courtiers, for whom the Welsh were a constant political headache. Finally, Walter's Welsh stories have a didactic value. If readers are unaware of Welsh stereotypes, Walter has provided an overview of them in *distinctio* 2, along with memorable anecdotes. The Welsh are untrustworthy, vengeful, murderous, and hospitable to a fault. Walter teaches you how to view the Welsh through a medieval English lens. These stories mark Walter as a man who was in the habit of leveraging his background as a Marcher to explain the Welsh to people who mattered, to the Marcher gentry, to the English court, and, of course, to Thomas Becket.

Walter and Romance

When Gottfried von Strassburg invokes Thomas of Britain as the best authority on *Tristan*, or when Layamon names Wace as one of his sources, seasoned readers of medieval romance give an excited, agreeable nod, even if the actual chain of transmission in both instances is more complicated than their authorial claims might appear. After all, there is nothing amiss, especially from a medieval perspective, about one romancer citing another for his source. But a general feeling of critical unease arises from the association of Walter Map with the *Lancelot-Grail Cycle*.[119] Somehow, this claim does not feel quite right. For many, Walter Map seems incongruous in terms of genre: what does a Latin satirist have to do with an Arthurian romance written in French? Nevertheless, Walter's relationship with the genre of romance is less vexed than his relationship with Wales. While Chapter 6 will address the question of whether or not Walter wrote French romances, this section examines Walter's engagement with romance as witnessed by the *De nugis curialium*. It is clear that Walter was a voracious reader of romance, and he even wrote some himself: four short, but skillfully written, romances of his survive in *distinctio* 3, and these show the influence of a broad range of contemporary romances. Nonetheless, Walter's modern reputation as a satirist and as a supposed collector of folktales has often overshadowed this aspect of his career. Yet if the contents of the *De nugis curialium* are even somewhat representative of Walter's literary output, he spent much of his artistic energy on reading, contemplating, and composing romance.

While glimpses of romance appear throughout the *De nugis curialium*, *distinctio* 3 provides the easiest demonstration that Walter had read widely in this popular genre. The entire *distinctio*—which, as I argue in Chapter 3, should be read as its own independent work—consists of four polished romances, all of which feature a love triangle. These romances seem addressed to a fellow secular cleric, someone who has to recover his breath after "consulting the philosophic or sacred page."[120] Naturally, the fact that these romances are in Latin also strongly suggests a clerical audience. Moreover, this anonymous addressee seems to have a specialty in the law, since Walter announces that he will not be touching upon the disputes of the law court (*fori lites*) or the sober matters of those pleading (*placitorum . . . seria*), matters that presumably occupy the time of his addressee.[121] In a nod to current literary debates, Walter opens this work by playing on the topos of *sens* and *matière*, of meaning and subject matter. Even though Walter's stories are, in his own words, "base and bloodless absurdities," it is nonetheless possible for good men to make good use of them.[122] Walter's task is simple; his readers, on the other hand, must do the work of making sense of the matter that has been gathered before them.[123]

The first romance of the four, *Sadius and Galo*, is the longest and has attracted the most interest from critics.[124] In order to appreciate its debt to contemporary romance, a brief overview will be helpful.

Sadius and Galo, two noble knights, are peers in almost every manner. Sadius is the beloved nephew of the king of the Asians, while Galo is intensely desired by the queen. Foreseeing trouble, Sadius attempts to cool the queen's illicit desire by implying that Galo does not have masculine genitals: "Although he could acquire everything from women, he has confessed—but only to me—that he is completely unable to perform that act."[125] This plan, true to fashion, goes awry when the queen decides to test Galo to make sure that he truly is unable to perform. She sends one of her servants to investigate matters. The queen instructs her "how to slide into Galo's embrace, how to unite her naked body to his naked body, and orders her to lay her hand on his privates and to report whether he can or whether he can't, all while remaining pure."[126] The servant goes out and stays gone much too long, stirring up worry and envy in the queen. When the servant returns, she tells the queen, "I almost pleased him, and I felt him to be all man and ready for the occasion, if he had only perceived you. But when he realized that I was smaller than you, that I was harder to handle, and that I was not as suited to him, I was cast out at once!"[127] The queen realizes this is a lie—she has, after all, never been with Galo—and she becomes furious and vengeful.

At the king's birthday feast, she seizes an opportunity for revenge. When the king grants the queen the opportunity to have whatever present she wants, she pounces upon Galo, who has been sitting at the banquet clearly nursing some internal anguish. The queen demands that Galo admit to the entire court what is causing him such harm. Reluctantly, he recounts a marvelous adventure, stopping at times, but always forced to continue by the merciless queen.

Galo tells how a year ago on Pentecost, while recovering from a fever, he had gone out in arms to test his strength. His horse led him through a dark forest until he entered a palace without any inhabitants, except for a maiden sitting under a tree. Despite his attempts to greet her, she remained silent. Galo admits that he tried to rape her, but Rivius, a giant, came to the maiden's aid and pinned Galo to a tree. Another maiden appeared and begged Rivius to relent, persuading the giant to grant Galo a year's truce before the two should enter into single combat.

Galo laments that today is the day on which he must fight Rivius. He leaves the banquet, but Sadius catches him and requests that he fight the giant in place of Galo. Galo counters that they should exchange armor, making it only appear that Sadius is the one fighting the giant. They switch armor and the battle begins. Galo, disguised as Sadius, fights valiantly, getting the best of the giant on several occasions, only to grant him mercy. All the while, the queen berates Galo, though it is actually Sadius in disguise. Finally, Galo triumphs over the giant, and the two friends slip away to exchange armor. They reveal their ruse to the court, and Galo is praised while the queen is vilified.

This brief summary makes it clear that Walter knew his romance motifs: intractable male friendship; banquet speeches; a rash boon; a knight errant wandering through a dark forest into a strange land; the importance of Pentecost; a desolate city; a maiden under a tree; a hostile giant; and an exchange of identities. Studies of analogues to *Sadius and Galo* show that Walter's romance has many close similarities to *Gawain and Bran de Liz*, *Guerehés*, *Amis and Amiloun*, *Eger and Grime*, *Tristan and Isolde*, the *Lai de Graelent*, *Petronius Rediuiuus*, and perhaps some of Chrétien's work.[128] Stylistically, Walter takes part in the new twelfth-century vogue of writing inner monologues for his characters, of describing "the subtleties of inner debate and the scenes of emotional see-sawing."[129] While the queen in *Sadius and Galo* is the clear villain, she is without a doubt the most compelling character, an effect largely created by her wonderfully impassioned inner monologue. "I am my own deception," she laments at one point, "my own betrayer; I've caught myself in my own net."[130] In these long inner monologues, Walter reveals that he has absorbed not only the motifs of romance, but its stylistic innovations as well.

The question of exactly what romances Walter had read is not particularly important for my purposes. Rather, I merely wish to draw attention to the fact that Walter had read broadly in contemporary romance, a fact that *Sadius and Galo* easily demonstrates. That said, the other three romances in *distinctio* 3 have received considerably less critical attention than *Sadius and Galo*. Yet all four romances are thematically linked and respond to one another, indicating that Walter thought about romance in a sophisticated manner, on par with the best romancers of his age. All four romances in Walter's collection concern problematic love triangles that eventually reach some resolution, destroying the original triangle in the process—a plot structure that has much in common with Marie de France's *Lais*. Marie's *Eliduc* suggests that religious sublimation is the only acceptable way to disentangle the love triangles of romance. Walter, on the other hand, prefers another strategy. Every romance reasserts what we might call traditional male values, usually at the expense of women.[131]

The second romance, which the chapter heading calls *On the Variance Between Parius and Lausus* (*De contrarietate Parii et Lausi*), contrasts the perfect friendship of Sadius and Galo with the poisonous one of Parius and Lausus.[132] The two men are chamberlains of King Ninus of Babylon, and their friendship is broken when Parius grows envious of Lausus. He murders Lausus and covers up any evidence of the murder, thus committing homicide, as well as what Walter playfully calls morticide.[133] However, King Ninus soon grows fond of Lausus's surviving son, which stirs up Parius's jealously once again. Parius devises a plan to remove the boy from the king's favor. He tells the boy that his breath stinks so badly that he should take care not to offend the king with his stench. In turn, Parius tells the king that the boy, now reluctant, has been avoiding him because he has compared the king's own breath to sewage water. Incensed, the king plans to murder the boy during a public celebration. Lausus, however, convinces the boy to yield his place of honor to him, and thus when the murderer attacks, he kills Lausus—not the boy. After some confusion, the truth comes out and King Ninus restores the boy to his high position in court.

The homosocial love triangle of Parius, Lausus, and Ninus is the only romance from *distinctio* 3 not to feature a woman in any prominent role. Nevertheless, the beginning of the romance dwells on the feminized allegorical figure of Invidia (Envy). We read that Invidia was born in the heart of Lucifer and crept into Paradise to cause the fall of man. A conqueress (*victrix*), but expelled from heaven, she now makes her home with us, attacking everyone, regardless of station.[134] Invidia is explicitly made the cause of the outbreak of jealousy at the Babylonian court: "She secretly entered the seat of proud Babylon."[135] Thus, this romance begins with a feminine allegorical figure attacking the Babylonian court. Moreover, Parius murders Lausus in a way that invokes female deceit. While trying to discover a way to murder Lausus, he finally calls to mind Hercules and Deianira and the poisonous sheet that she almost inadvertently kills him with.[136] For Walter, this classical example is a memorable act of female betrayal, one that he also recounts in his antimatrimonial treatise, the *Dissuasio Valerii*.[137] While no female characters exist in this romance, Walter still manages to give the story's betrayal a feminine veneer.

The next romance features Raso, Raso's wife, and an emir. Chaucer's Wife of Bath would have approved of Raso's approach to his marriage, since, moved by classical examples, he decides to grant his wife control over herself: "and so he released the horse from the bridle, so that she could seek fodder wherever her hunger directed her, and he praised her voluntary chastity to the stars."[138] Her appetite, however, leads her to the emir, whom Raso has captured and placed in confinement. Eventually, she helps the emir escape, and Raso is himself captured in the counterattack. Raso's son saves his father and kills the emir, but Raso's wife escapes with a knight whom she intends to take as yet another lover. Before the two can flee the city, Raso kills this knight, puts on his clothes, and travels in disguise with his estranged wife. The pair are attacked by hostile forces, but Raso's son again appears and saves his father, killing his stepmother in the process.

Those unfortunate enough to have read even a small selection of medieval misogynistic texts will be able to see from this bare summary that Raso's wife exhibits several stereotypical traits: she abuses her freedom, betrays her husband, and recklessly jumps from man to man. This story, however, is not a simple retelling of the unfaithful wife motif. Given the conventions of romance, one could imagine this story focusing on the bond of father and son, or even on a grudging, mutual respect between Raso and the emir. Walter, however, introduces an element that brings this romance close to parody. Raso's true love turns out to be his horse. The emir flees Raso's city "on Raso's favorite horse" (*equo Rasonis carissimo*).[139] The loss of this horse causes him the greatest grief when he learns his wife's deception: "He sobs without restraint, but not because of the loss of the emir, or his wife, or what they had taken from him—only from the loss of his horse. Neither his son's nor his household's consolation lifts his spirits."[140] When the lady evades Raso's counterattack, she escapes on "this excellent horse" (*optimum equuum*).[141] Later, when Raso is disguised as his wife's new lover, the two exchange horses, and so he finally gains what he has most desired. As they travel, Raso eventually falls asleep from exhaustion on his beloved horse. The horse proves to be a trustworthy companion, since it warns Raso of an impending attack: "Just as the men are drawing near, Raso's horse, who was not used to remaining idle in battle, lifts his head, neighs, and paws the sand with his feet to protect his lord from death."[142] Raso awakes, and in the ensuing battle he bursts through the enemies and "is carried wherever he wants thanks to his horse's speed."[143] Raso's horse becomes a better companion than his wife, and readers are implicitly invited to compare the two, since Raso's initial misguided laxity toward his wife has already been described in bestial terms: "he released the horse (*iumentum*) from the bridle that she could seek fodder (*pabula*) wherever her hunger directed her."[144] With the wife dead and Raso's son restored to his rightful place in the household, the romance suggests that keeping a bridle on female agency will help one avoid a cheating wife, hostile capture, and even horse theft.

The love triangle in the final romance in *distinctio* 3 consists of the nobleman Rollo, Rollo's wife, and a young knight named Rhys.[145] Rhys pines for Rollo's wife, but she scorns him, forcing Rhys to recognize that he has little renown, especially when compared to Rollo. Chastised, he sets out to make a name for himself in the world of chivalry. Guided by "Master Love" (*magister amor*), Rhys becomes famous and gains a name for himself.[146] Rollo takes note of his accomplishments and he praises the knight in conversation with his wife. Trusting Rollo's opinion, the wife decides she has been too proud and agrees to a tryst with Rhys. She then tells Rhys why she changed her mind: "Rollo was the cause," she baldly states.[147] Rhys is shocked. "Rhys will never repay Rollo's good will with wrong," he says, "since it is uncourtly of me to stain his bed, which all the world denied me and he himself granted me."[148] The romance ends by invoking Ovid, claiming that he was wrong when he stated that a lady cannot be made a virgin again.

It is tempting to read Rhys's love as ennobling, as the driving force making him into a superb knight, but that is not the case.[149] Walter describes Rhys's chivalric education in a thoroughly scornful manner. Outwardly, he appears a great knight, but inwardly he is, in Walter's opinion, one of the worse things a man can become—a woman.

> He conquers ranks of iron, walls, and towers, and the spirit [*animus*] that led him to all his victories makes itself womanly [*a seipso effeminatur*], but he becomes a woman [*sed infeminatur*], because his spirit changes into feminine weakness [*in femineam transit impotenciam*], so that he runs after his desires without a thought like women do—a lamb inwardly, but outwardly a lion—and the one who levels the castles of foreigners becomes castrated [*castratus*] by domestic concerns; he grows soft, weeps, begs, and cries. She, like neither a virgin nor a virago, but like a man, renounces, scorns, and shoves him into despair in every way she can.[150]

Like Chrétien's Erec, Rhys's devotion to love, to Magister Amor, has made him womanly. Moreover, Rollo's wife maintains control of her emotions and her restraint, making her more of a man than her suitor. When it comes to gender, Walter is an assuredly unsubversive writer, and this story's ending, which restores normative gender roles, is unsurprising given the three romances that have preceded it. Male order and control is reasserted, and female variability is scorned once again.

The four romances in *distinctio* 3 all explore love triangles, and they all praise homosocial male friendship, even if that friendship is, in one instance, with a horse. Each romance, moreover, introduces an element of inconstancy at a different point in the triangle, creating a series of romances that speak to one another. These romances are also notable for what they lack—courtly love. But this does not mean that Walter was not aware of the concept. Indeed, this sequence of romances seems to delight in being as opposed to courtly love as possible. Trysts are thwarted; Master Love leads knights astray; and by the end of the stories women are dismissed altogether. The fact that Walter consistently teases readers' expectations by setting up familiar courtly love situations, only to dash them, shows that he was very familiar with this popular literary concept. Tony Davenport, speaking specifically of the story of Rollo and Rhys, finds acknowledgment of courtly love in "its reference to Ovid and its obvious awareness of contemporary interest in debating degrees of honor and love."[151] Walter's romances are meant as a clerical satire of, or remedy to, courtly love in popular vernacular romances. Walter Map, like Marie de France and Geoffrey Chaucer, enjoys generating debate by asking readers to compare and contrast similar stories and by subverting generic expectations. The interconnected themes of Walter's romances demonstrate that he could approach the genre with a high deal of sophistication and expertise.

Walter Map knew contemporary romance, and he wrote romance himself; in spite of some misguided suggestions otherwise, nothing should be controversial about this.[152] Latin literature in the twelfth century, especially that associated with Henry II's court, found a fruitful partner in French-language literature. In terms of genre and style, influence sometimes flowed from French to Latin, in reverse of the normal medieval pattern.[153] And Latin literature could easily become a vehicle for romance or for other genres more closely associated with the vernacular.[154] Even though Walter wrote his romances in Latin, they display a consistent and unmistakable engagement with contemporary vernacular literature.

Reconstructing a Literary Reputation

Literary reputations are admittedly difficult to reconstruct, with opinions shifting depending on geography, chronology, and audience. Even so, the reputation that the *Lancelot-Grail Cycle* imagines for Walter—a writer with connections to Wales (thus ancient Britain) and to romance—agrees with several facets of Walter's own work. He presented himself as an expert on the Welsh, and he wrote romances. These two elements alone would have been enough to make Walter a plausible *auctoritas* for the *Cycle*, but another factor doubtlessly helped to cement his inclusion: his presence at the court of Henry II. It may be that Henry II's patronage of Arthurian literature was in reality less than has been commonly thought, but regardless of the king's actual involvement (or not) in the literary culture surrounding his court, the numerous references to

Henry and Eleanor as patrons of literature show that, in the popular imagination at the very least, they are strongly associated with romance.[155] The compilers of the *Lancelot-Grail Cycle* believed this association to be important: twice, the *Cycle* invokes Henry II alongside Walter Map.[156] Thus, for an early thirteenth-century reader, invoking Walter Map could call to mind at least three elements strongly linked to Arthurian literature: Henry II's court, romance, and Wales.

Walter Map may not have written a true Arthurian romance—at least one that survives—but that does not mean that he had no interest in ancient Britain. Chapters 4 and 5 demonstrate that Walter made use of Welsh literary material and that he could also write imaginative and clever literature set in ancient Britain. However, before exploring these aspects of Walter's work, this book must address a larger critical problem looming over Walter Map—his reputation for carelessness. Indeed, the incongruity of Walter's modern reputation as an unfocused author with the extended narrative of the *Cycle* has been one of the major reasons that critics believe Walter Map to be a poor or ironic choice for an *auctoritas*. He seems to have lacked the attention to detail necessary to complete such a long work. The next two chapters show that this view of Walter is mistaken.

Chapter 2

Works Frozen in Revision

Walter Map's *De nugis curialium* survives in a state of textual disarray. In the midst of sections that seem to have been written in the early 1180s, the work occasionally references events that occurred much later, making the internal chronology difficult to accept. Henry II is alive, then dead, then alive once again. Similarly, the *De nugis curialium* at one point references two "Bretons, about whom more is told above."[1] Yet, this passage refers to episodes that occur later in the work and not earlier. The rubricated chapter headings occasionally lapse into descriptions that are dull or vague even for the workaday conventions of medieval headings: in a book full of marvelous, otherworldly creatures and miracle-working saints, headings such as "a wonder" or "another wonder" offer little help to readers searching for specific passages. Moreover, the rubricated chapter headings almost disappear entirely toward the end of the work, with several folios having no chapter headings whatsoever. Curiously, the last chapter of the *De nugis curialium* ends with what the headings call "a recapitulation of the beginning of this book, differing in expression but not substance."[2] This recapitulation, however, does not echo the beginning of the book in an artistic fashion—as does the funereal ending of *Beowulf,* for example—but appears to be merely a different version of the book's first several chapters, maybe even their first draft. Several other doublets exist in the work as well, which gives the peculiar effect that Walter is at times plagiarizing himself. But perhaps the greatest oddity is that, set roughly in the middle of the work, *distinctio* 4 begins with a prologue that its editors think is meant for the entire book, and immediately following this invasive prologue lies an equally invasive epilogue. It, too, seems to have been meant for the whole of the work, according to the editors at least. Strange things are certainly afoot in the textual history of the *De nugis curialium.*

It is therefore hard to disagree with the characterization of the *De nugis curialium* as an "inchoate book," of its content as "miscellaneous and unedited," and of its structure as "jumbled and irregular."[3] It is frequently likened to a commonplace book, laden with personal recollections, topical folktales, fiery invective, and whatever else seems to have struck Walter's fancy at any given point over the span of a decade or two. Indeed, Walter himself seems to confirm the desultory nature of its composition when he writes, "I have written this little book by snatches on loose sheets at the court of King Henry."[4] This remark, coupled with the imperfect textual state of the *De nugis curialium*, has all but cemented the work's status as the product of a harried courtier who only took the time to craft a relatively unconnected series of short narratives and vignettes, without any consideration of a larger plan. In this account, the *De nugis curialium* is a piecemeal work for piecemeal reading.

The confused manuscript of the *De nugis curialium* has also been taken, unjustly as I hope to show, as evidence for a confused mind. James Hinton, who did much to explain the text, warned against the tendency to equate Walter's intellect and the sole manuscript of the *De nugis curialium*, which was written some two centuries after his death: "whether Walter Map had originally a plan, or not, the crudities manifest in the disposition of materials are not due to the author's slovenliness or mental incoherence so much as to the fact that he never completed his editing, but left his materials fragmentary and unpublished."[5] This plea, however, has largely passed unheeded.[6] Indeed, in reading scholarship on Walter, it takes little time to realize that "dismissive remarks on the nature of Walter's achievement are the rule."[7] Frederick Tupper and Marbury Ogle thought of Walter "as a gentleman, an amateur rather than as a professional author."[8] M. R. James believed Walter incapable of organization and driven by impulse: "As to the plan and date of the *de Nugis*, nothing can be clearer than that there is no plan, and that the work was jotted down at various times, as the fancy struck the author."[9] He also believed Walter guilty of a serious literary transgression—"he did not always know very clearly the meaning of the words he used."[10] Walter's wide-ranging interests have at times been seen as a fault, rather than the mark of a dynamic mind. He is "an author who struggled to exercise control over his highly varied material."[11] And some of his stories "reveal to us a Map both critical and credulous, divided between reason and irrationality."[12] Ian Short simply calls him "indescribable."[13] David Knowles, who may have felt the sting of Walter's anti-monastic satire too keenly, was no great fan, saying he "lacked both balance of mind and ethical sobriety."[14] Walter's most recent editors also imply that he lacked sobriety, but not of the ethical sort: "The *De nugis curialium* was the commonplace-book of a great after-dinner speaker; and if one is entirely sober when one reads it, it is easily misunderstood."[15] Most scholarship on Walter leaves the impression that if he were alive today, he might make a superb blogger: quick with a witty anecdote, an expert aggregator of popular culture, and given to passionate first impressions. The studied discipline of a novelist, however, would elude him.

This chapter and the next reevaluate both the textual state of the *De nugis curialium* and Walter's critical reputation. In this chapter, I show that Walter sometimes revised his earlier work and that he did so with meticulous care. And in the next, I argue that medieval readers, and not Walter Map, are responsible for the idea that the *De nugis curialium* should be considered a single, unified work. The title of the work and its chapter divisions are not Walter's. Moreover, several glosses, many of which are faulty, have found their way into the main text, adding another layer of textual difficulty to Walter's work. Overall, I suggest that the *De nugis curialium* as we have it is best understood as five separate works in various stages of completion that have been bound together, almost certainly after Walter's death. Seen in this light, it is clear that Walter does not deserve his reputation as a scatterbrained author. It is hardly his fault that the only surviving copy of his work has been taken as the definitive testament of his literary talents. Not only does this reevaluation render Walter's presence as an *auctoritas* for the *Lancelot-Grail Cycle* less incongruous—he had the patience and focus needed for such a work—it also bears directly on his reputation as a writer who worked in the Matter of Britain. As Chapter 4 shows, understanding Walter's practice of revision sheds new light on one method medieval authors used to write stories set in ancient Britain.

Evidence of Revision in the *De nugis curialium*

James Hinton was the first scholar to examine the structure and plan of the *De nugis curialium* in depth.[16] Although he recognized that Walter's text survives in an unedited state, he proceeded to reconstruct the text in the order in which he believed it had been composed. Identifying as many *termini a quo* and *termini ad quem* as possible, Hinton distinguished twenty separate "fragments," which he thought gave little evidence of a larger design: "From what has been noticed of the casual manner in which Map wanders from one topic to another even while he is writing straight ahead, it is clear that he was not restrained by a definite plan; he wrote willingly upon whatever occurred to his mind, careless of the drift of his discourse."[17] This is the Walter Map familiar to scholarship. Indeed, I will concede that dividing the *De nugis* up into small pieces and ordering them on the basis of chronology makes Walter's text even less coherent, but it must also be admitted that splitting up almost any literary work into the chronological order of its composition would result in disorganization, too. *The Canterbury Tales* would certainly look the poorer for it. And everyone, it seems, has followed Hinton in claiming that Walter all but announces his lackadaisical style of composition when he writes, "Hunc in curia regis Henrici libellum raptim annotaui scedulis" (I have swiftly [*raptim*] noted this little book down in pages of parchment in the court of King Henry).[18] Hinton takes *raptim* with its etymological force "by snatches," which lends credence to the belief that Walter's literary activity occurred at intermittent stages. However, this meaning is not attested in Medieval Latin (nor in Classical Latin for that matter).[19] Instead, it is best to take *raptim* here with its normal meaning of "swiftly" or "hurriedly"—a subtle, but important, distinction. Although Hinton's contributions remain valuable, especially his observations that the *De nugis curialium* is an unfinished work and that the chapter titles are the product of a later scribe or compiler, this chronological arrangement is unnecessarily complicated and relies on a rather constrained view of literary composition.[20]

Brooke and Mynors, Walter's most recent editors, accept many of Hinton's arguments regarding dating. However, they propose that the *De nugis curialium* has more structure than Hinton allows. Instead of a series of fragments thrown together by Walter or a later scribe with little attempt at order, they suggest that the work "was composed more or less as a single book, into which additions small and large were later inserted."[21] They show that apart from eight interpolations, the work belongs mostly to the early 1180s. In their view, the manuscript's current disarray results overwhelmingly from Walter's subsequent tinkering and erratic insertions.

> The bulk of it was drafted in 1181 and 1182, and it lay for a number of years in loose quires, roughly arranged in the order *dist.* iv, v, i, ii, iii. It was still a draft, not a finished work, and included two versions of the satire on the court; some chapters were never completed. From time to time the author added insertions small and large on slips of vellum; in 1183 he provided the whole work with a

prologue. At some date unknown, he decided to make the satire on the court the opening of the book, and so cut his loose quires like a pack of cards, arranging the material in approximately its present order.[22]

This explanation has the apparent benefit of originally placing the two versions of the satire on the court in succession, with the more polished version immediately following the earlier draft version (though exactly why this is preferable is left unexplained). Additionally, in the original order proposed by Brooke and Mynors the book begins with the *Dissuasio Valerii*, Walter's most popular work, which alone of the contents of the *De nugis curialium* circulated widely. Since it first circulated under a pseudonym, it would have been a good marketing ploy to open a work of some considerable size with the surprising revelation that Walter himself had composed the popular *Dissuasio Valerii*. But, as Brooke and Mynors admit, this account does not solve all the infelicities of the *De nugis curialium*. Here, Walter comes in for yet more criticism. Since they argue that the manuscript's current form results more or less from Walter's own meddling, the blame for all the faults of the *De nugis curialium* lies squarely on his shoulders. Brooke and Mynors, for example, are more inclined to believe the subpar rubricated chapter headings are Walter's own invention: they are "untidy in every possible way, and with an untidiness which clearly reflects in part the mind of Master Walter."[23] And what of the internal epilogue, which even in their reconstructed form still sits oddly in the middle of the work? They suggest that "since it was evidently written on a loose slip or bifolium, it is possible that Map, finding his prologue unhappily sandwiched in the middle of the book, with gay abandon attached the epilogue to it."[24] Just to be clear, what Brooke and Mynors propose is that Walter wrote a coherent book, cut it in half so that it began with the satire on the court, neglected to discard his first draft of said satire on the court, perhaps placed an epilogue in the now middle of the work because that is where his prologue lay, and afterward inserted a few stories here and there. This scenario, as they readily admit, is conjectural. Nonetheless, in my opinion it relies too heavily on the supposition that Walter Map is a flighty writer, unable or unwilling to write an orderly narrative—only thus could an author demonstrate such carelessness with his text. However, the only evidence for Walter's mental "untidiness" is itself the manuscript of the *De nugis curialium*. This is a significant problem.

There is, however, a way around the tautological explanation that the *De nugis curialium* is disorganized because Walter Map is disorganized, a fact that is in turn proven by the disorganization of the *De nugis curialium*. In an astute review, A. G. Rigg suggests that previous editors and scholars have confused "the order of *composition* with the final *intended* arrangement, as though only scribal incompetence could account for a nonchronological order."[25] In other words, writers do not work in a strict chronological fashion, starting a work with page one and completing it neatly with the final sentence; this scenario neglects the messy business of drafts, omissions and additions, and innumerable starts and restarts that are familiar to any writer. Walter is no exception. Indeed, Rigg seems to have been the first to grasp the importance that Walter was rearranging and revising previous material, and, as any good reviser will do, he moved sections about, cut some passages, and expanded others, while retaining some phrases verbatim.[26] Either Walter never finished this process of revision or the only surviving text reflects an earlier state of affairs. We should therefore view the doublets present in the *De nugis* not as two versions of the same tale, nor as the handiwork of a particularly inept scribe, but as Walter's earlier and later revisions of the same episode. Rigg claims that *distinctiones* 1–3 "are in nearly final state," while *distinctiones* 4 and 5 consist largely of outdated drafts and material that Walter either had not yet reworked or had not yet decided where to place.[27] While in the middle of reworking the *De nugis*, Rigg supposes that Walter "took the whole pile of material with him to Oxford in 1197, where it lay until a fourteenth-century editor copied it all out."[28] Walter's only surviving work lies frozen in the midst of revision.

While I do not agree with all of Rigg's brief suggestions—I remain unconvinced that Walter was writing a single, unified work and it is certain that the copyist of Bodley 851 was not working from an authorial copy—they do provide a valuable point of departure for a new investigation into the textual state of the *De nugis curialium*.[29] The following study of the doublets in the *De nugis curialium* confirms that material in *distinctiones* 1 and 2 has been revised from material in *distinctiones* 4 and 5. The resulting analysis also rules out the possibility that the doublets might represent Walter's recording of two separate versions of the same tale or that Rigg has suggested the wrong direction for revision (i.e., that 4 and 5 contain the revised tales, while 1 and 2 represent earlier material). Moreover, this chapter examines the mechanics of Walter's revision. What can these revisions tell us about Walter's overall plan or his habits as a writer? Walter, it will be seen, revised thoroughly, with few passages escaping his pen.

A careful comparison of the major and minor differences between the doublets of the *De nugis curialium* demonstrates that they are not merely two versions of the same story, recorded perhaps at separate times, but rather the same story at different stages of revision. Many passages share exact phrasing, which would be highly improbable had Walter impulsively recorded in his commonplace book the same story, metaphor, or idea ten years apart; he was clearly rewriting with a close eye to his earlier compositions. An analysis of Walter's diction, prose style, and larger literary aims bears this assumption out. The philologically faint of heart may be forgiven for skipping to the end of this section, but for those who stay, these comparisons offer a fascinating glimpse into the mind of a twelfth-century author at work. For ease of reference, I list the doublets along with their subject matter in Table 1.

I will deal separately with the major and minor differences between the doublets. Under major differences I include the addition and deletion of significant passages and changes in how a tale fits within the larger context of its neighboring tales. Because the minor differences show most clearly the process of revision, I will begin with them.

One of the most easily recognizable differences between the doublets is that small changes in diction are sometimes driven by the desire to insert as much alliterative effect as possible. In several cases the doublets occurring in *distinctiones* 1 and 2 contain more alliteration than their counterparts in IV and V. Since many Medieval Latin writers of the twelfth century took such a liking to alliteration—Walter is among those who could not resist its pull—it is much more plausible that Walter added alliteration during his process of revision, rather than purposefully omitting it. For example, "Cor autem illud saxo comparatur, quia Dominus ait" becomes "Cor illud bene comparatur saxo Sisiphi, quia scriptum est."[30] And toward the end of comparison of the court with hell, Walter works up a tour de force of alliterative imagery: "obuoluciones autem ignium, nebulas et fetorem, anguium <et> uiperarum sibila, gemitus et lacrimas, feditatem et horrorem" is amplified to "Obuolucionem

Table 1. Revised Passages in the *DNC*

Revised	Unrevised	Topic
1.1–10	5.7	Satire on the court
1.11	4.13	King Herla/Herlething
1.14	4.7	Militant monk of Cluny
2.12	4.10	Eadric the Wild
2.13	4.8	The sons of the dead woman (though see discussion)

autem ignium, densitatem tenebrarum, fluminum fetorem, stridorem a de-
monibus magnum dencium, gemitus exiles et miserabiles a spiritibus anxiis,
uermium et uiperarum et anguium et omnis reptilis tractus fedos, et rugitus
impios, fetorem, planctum et horrorem."[31] The increased alliteration of this
passage is hard to miss (i.e., *densitatem tenebrarum*; *fluminum fetorem*; *demoni-
bus . . . dencium*; *uermium . . . uiperarum*). Moreover, Walter has also added
the additional effect of rhyme with "exiles et miserabiles." In the tale of Eadric
the Wild, the same process is seen in the sentence "se iussit Herefordiam deferri" becoming "et se deferri fecit Herefordiam."[32] Here the meaning of the
two phrases is almost identical, but Walter has changed *iussit* to *fecit* in order
to answer the *f* in *deferri* and *Herefordiam*. He takes similar care in revising "et
relapsum cor in uallem auaricie secuntur" to "et relapsum in auaricie uallem
animum reuocare conantur," where *cor* is replaced by the closely related *animum*, thus nicely linking *auaricie* and *animum*. In another case, Walter's earlier material in *distinctio* 5 shows that he had already decided to include the
three judges of the dead, Rhadamanthus, Minos, and Aeacus, in his satire on
the court. In the process of revision, these judges take on ironic epithets,
which, of course, alliterate: "Minos est misericors, Radamantus racionem
amans, Eacus equanimis."[33] Furthermore, "Det Deus [sc. *cor*] et sic faciat curialibus" is improved to "Det Dominus cor curialibus carneum."[34] Likewise,
in the tale of the militant monk of Cluny, Walter improves the alliteration of
"lethali spiculo perforat inprouisum [sc. *monachum*]" to "monachum misso
letali telo perforat."[35] Walter may have made this change so that the alliteration falls on two stressed syllables (*pérforat inprouísum* versus *mónachum
mísso*).

But this last example also demonstrates that as Walter revises he sometimes abandons an alliterating pair of words in order to create alliteration
elsewhere. In many cases, however, it is difficult to say why exactly Walter
switches his alliterative targets, and it may in the end be fruitless to seek clear
explanations for each of these edits. Regardless, these changes confirm that
Walter did pay close attention to alliteration as he worked through his drafts.
Further examples of this type of alliterative vacillation are not hard to find:
"Sunt et hic qui diuiciarum altitudinem adepti nichil actum putant" is revised
to "Sunt et hic multi qui montem ascensi diuiciarum nil actum putant."[36]
Here, Walter seems to have preferred *montem* over *altitudinem* because it allows for the pair *multi . . . montem*, even though it cannibalizes the alliterative
triplet *altitudinem . . . adepti . . . actum*. Perhaps here Walter shows a preference for consonance over assonance. And in the story of the militant monk of

Cluny, Walter eliminates the varied alliteration of "Sentit monachus mortem in ianuis, confiteri cupit, nec adest preter puerum cui possit," preferring instead a relentless focus on the sound of *p*: "Ille se morti proximum sciens, puero qui solus aderat peccata fatetur, penitenciam sibi petens inuingi."[37] While these changes in alliteration may not be deeply significant on their own, taken together they show that as Walter revises, he remains in line with the general twelfth-century practice of minding one's alliteration.

In a few instances, we also see Walter changing his diction with a preference for a more striking or more appropriate term. "Porfirius dicit genus esse . . ." (Porphyry says a genus is . . .) becomes "ut Porphirius diffinit genus" (as Porhyry defines a genus).[38] The scholastic connotations of *diffinire* are more appropriate for Walter's mock intellectual exercise of comparing the court and hell than the commonplace verb *dicere*.[39] Moreover, in the revised version Walter uses *diffinire* once again: after a few paragraphs on the current state of the court and the degeneration of the modern age, he begins his famous comparison of the court with hell, though he hesitates, asking himself, "Hic tamen dubito an eam recte diffinierim" (Yet in doing so I wonder if I have defined it correctly).[40] Here, Walter alerts the attentive reader that what follows is in the mold of a scholastic exercise and that he will be as careful in his definitions as Porphyry. Another small change is found in the revision of "Non in omnes loquor iudices, sed in maiorem et in insaniorem partem" (I am not speaking against all judges, but against the larger and madder part) to "sed secundum maiorem et insaniorem loquor aciem" (but I am speaking with respect to the larger and madder fray).[41] That *acies* (blade; battle line, fray) is much more striking than *pars* (part; portion) is clear, but its use also picks up on the violence implicit in Walter's description of foresters, *uenatores hominum* (hunters of men), that precedes this remark. Moreover, puns, one of Walter's favorite literary devices, are clearly on his mind as he revises: "Sed parcendum est curie" (But the court must be spared) becomes "Sed curie parcere curiale uidetur" (But sparing the court seems a courtly thing to do).[42] And in revising the section on Ixion, Walter changes "hinc et illinc" (hither and thither) to "ultra, citra" (on this side, on that side), which, while not in the least rare terms, are however less clichéd than the original.[43] Finally, Walter makes a savvy change when describing the court's wheel of fortune: "nullius in ea sine spe locus est" (nobody's place on it is without hope) is tweaked to "nullius in ea sine spe casus est" (nobody's fall on it is without hope).[44] With its connotations of loss, chance, and the fall of man, *casus* fits this passage's context much better than *locus*.

Perhaps one of the clearest indications that Walter revised with a sharp eye is that many of the revised passages are stylistically superior to the earlier draft material. A good example of this tendency is found in the beginning of the work, just after Walter invokes Augustine's confusion over the definition of time. Compare the following draft passage with its revision below:

> Simili possum admiracione dicere, quod in curia sum et de curia loquor, et quid ipsa sit non inteligo. Scio tamen quod ipsa tempus non est.

> (With similar astonishment I am able to say that I am in the court and I speak of the court, and I do not understand what it is. Nevertheless, I know that it is not time.)

> Ego simili possum admiracione dicere quod in curia sum, et de curia loquor, et nescio, Deus scit, quid sit curia. Scio tamen quod curia non est tempus.

> (With similar astonishment I am able to say that I am in the court and I speak of the court, and I do not know—God knows—what the court is. Nevertheless, I know that the court is not time.)[45]

Walter has replaced the two instances of the pronoun *ipsa* with *curia*, resulting in *curia*—the ostensible topic of *distinctio* 1—being repeated four times at the work's opening. Moreover, Walter has emphatically added *ego* at the beginning of the sentence in order to heighten his witty paralleling of Augustine. Walter also echoes St. Paul's own struggle to define his mystical experience: "sive in corpore nescio, sive extra corpus nescio, Deus scit" (whether in the body, I know not, or out of the body, I know not; God knoweth).[46] Thus, both biblical and patristic authority coalesce in these revised opening lines to create satirical astonishment over the precise definition of Henry's court, neatly leading into the exploration of Walter's famous question—is the court hell?

Moreover, Walter adds two striking images: the court is "a hundred-handed giant which, though all its hands have been cut off, is still entirely the same hundred-handed giant," as well as a "hydra with many heads."[47] Walter also extends the court-as-time metaphor, adding the line "et hodie sumus una multitudo, cras erimus alia; curia uero non mutatur, eadem semper est" (And we are one multitude today; we will be another tomorrow. But the court is not changed—it is always the same).⁴⁸ This small addition, moving quickly through *hodie* (today), *cras* (tomorrow), and *semper* (always), transforms the initial invocation of Augustine from a mere quip into a prolonged, though still tongue-in-cheek, comparison. Finally, Walter concludes his introduction by offering one more playful comparison. Only now, instead of time, Walter measures the court against Boethius's definition of fortune—that it is only stable in its instability.⁴⁹ He of course finds this comparison fitting. The thorough revision of this introductory passage apparently found its mark, as it appears with dependable regularity in scholarship that touches upon Henry II's court.

Another stylistic improvement occurs when Walter rewrites his comparison of the denizens of hell with courtiers.⁵⁰ While many of the same images occur (e.g., Tantalus, Sisyphus, and Ixion), Walter simplifies and systematizes this section. The introduction to this section, which had contained a discussion taken from Macrobius on the human body as hell, as well as a brief passage on the allegorical significance of the four rivers of the underworld, is reduced to a few sentences. Thus Walter seems to have taken his own advice in omitting his discussion of Macrobius: "Quod quia longum est distinguere, leuiterque potest alias haberi, dimittimus" (But we put this aside, since working it out takes some time and it is easily found elsewhere).⁵¹ Instead of dwelling on the body as hell, a conceit that while somewhat pertinent does little to set up the comparison between court and hell, the revised passage concisely defines the court as a place of punishment and ends on the simple question: "Quis ibi cruciatus qui non sit hic multiplicatus?" (There [i.e., in hell] what torment exists which is not amplified here?).⁵² This *ibi-hic* (there-here) formula then repeats in each of the figures of hell that Walter introduces. The revised passage on Ixion, for example, begins "Sibi sepe dissimilis, super, subter, ultra, citra, Yxion ibi uoluitur in rota. Nec hic desunt Yxiones" (Never able to keep himself still, there Ixion spins about in his wheel—up and down, over here and over there. And here there is no lack of Ixions).⁵³ "Nec hic desunt Yxiones" (And here there is no lack of Ixions) replaces an earlier "Habemus et nos Yxiones" (We too have Ixions), thus bringing this passage into line with the those of Tantalus and Sisyphus and adhering to the newly introduced *ibi-hic* question now anchoring this section.⁵⁴

In this revising of the comparison of courtiers with those in hell, we see Walter tempering his ever-present desire to quote from the ancients in order to create a more focused piece of prose. Moreover, the newly systematized *ibi-hic* formula creates a strong sense of stylistic unity in this passage. It is a shame that a folio is lacking in this section, which originally continued on to make courtly comparisons with Tityus, the daughters of Belus, Cerberus, and Charon. (We know what passages are missing here because the table of contents for the *De nugis curialium* was written before the loss of this folio.) Had these survived, we would have even more evidence of Walter's revision of this section. But from what remains, it is clear that Walter could recognize and correct one of his supposed faults: his inability to refrain from learned digressions. Moreover, Walter's care in developing the *ibi-hic* formula demonstrates that he had a clear rhetorical plan for this section and that he could execute it.

Yet another stylistic improvement appears in the ending to the section on Ixion, whose transgressions caused Zeus to bind him to a fiery wheel. Walter here takes Ixion's spinning wheel as a courtly *rota fortunae*, capriciously lifting up and casting down courtiers, who despite this fickleness find the mere possibility of advancement difficult to resist. A comparison of the first draft with its revised version below shows that Walter stays close to the original.

Tota terribilis est, contra consciencias tota militat, nec inde minus appetitur.

(It is completely terrifying, completely at odds with good conscience. Nonetheless, for these reasons it is sought out.)

Tota terribiliter horret, tota contra consciencias militat, nec minus inde proficit alliciendo.

(It is completely and terrifyingly dreadful, completely at odds with good conscience. Nonetheless, it therefore succeeds in luring them away.)[55]

However, he makes a few small changes to improve the balance of the sentence. In his revised version, the first two clauses now both begin with *tota*, and the change of *terribilis est* to *terribiliter horret* results in both clauses having the same syntactic structure (i.e., predicate adjective + adverbial phrase + intransitive verb) and thus a pleasing balance. Finally, the change of logical subject from *appetitur* (it is sought out)—in which the courtiers seek the wheel—to *proficit alliciendo* (it succeeds in luring them away)—in which the wheel actively seduces them—not only makes the *rota* the logical subject of every verb in the sentence but also heightens the menace of the court. Rather than being sought out, the court now seeks its own victims.

Major Changes During Revision

While the above serves as representative of the nature of Walter's minor revisions, it is not an exhaustive treatment. His countless adjustments would require much more space to discuss in full. But equally revealing are Walter's major alterations: his addition or omission of entire passages, his repurposing of earlier tales for a different use, and his close attention to narrative continuity. In considering this type of revision, I first approach chapters 1 through 15 of *distinctio* 1. Here we have the best evidence for Walter's technique and aims, as we can watch as he composes a coherent narrative in both theme and structure. I will then address the revised sections of *distinctio* 2, which, while less extensive than those in *distinctio* 1, nonetheless show Walter working with the same consideration. I will, however, omit discussion of the tales of King Herla and Eadric the Wild, since I discuss them elsewhere.[56]

First of all, Walter has reworked his introduction in order to better reflect his subsequent critique of Henry's court. (Here I consider the first chapter the introduction, i.e., everything up to the beginning of the comparison of the court with hell.) Three new sections now follow the original introduction. The first new section addresses the court's distribution of *gratia* (favor) to the undeserving. The next describes *cupiditas* (cupidity) reigning as Lady of the Court. Cupidity reverses the natural correlation between a happy demeanor and inner righteousness; the good now appear sorrowful and the bad happy. To a reader even passingly familiar with the medieval court, the presence of both cupidity and ill-deserved favor needs no explanation—but Walter's next addition may. He begins his longest addition to the introduction by asking, "Quid autem est quod a pristina forma uiribus et uirtute facti sumus degeneres, cetera queque uiuencia nullatenus a prima deuiant donorum gracia?" (Why is it that we have degenerated from our original beauty, strength, and virtue, while no other living creature strays from the grace of its gifts?).[57] Walter, relying on common medieval conceptions of the prelapsarian state of man, explains that only mankind and the devils have fallen from original grace, and with that fall has come a reduction in the life span and physical vitality granted to man.[58] The ancients, because of their longevity, had the time to develop new technology and acquire great knowledge. In contrast,

Walter finds the modern age intellectually degenerate and wholly dependent on the wisdom of the past: "non est a nobis nostra pericia" (our expertise is not our own), he laments.[59]

A common twelfth-century topos, the pessimistic view of the present often, as it does here, constitutes "a form of social criticism," since highlighting the corruption of the current age has the potential to prompt reform.[60] Pessimism, then, is not out of place in satire, as both draw attention to moral decay. All three of these additions expand the critique of the court; its inconstancy was the sole concern of the earlier version. By widening the scope of the introduction to include jealousy, hypocrisy, and the promotion of the undeserving—all commonplaces in twelfth-century critiques of the court—Walter gives a more accurate representation of what follows. Moreover, this new section anticipates the juxtaposition of *moderni* and *antiqui*— another favorite topos of twelfth-century literature, and one that Walter often invokes.[61] In particular, this passage ironically sets up one of the better jokes in the *De nugis curialium*, in which the incessant wandering of Henry II's court is not a creation of the present, but rather an inheritance from an ancient king's entourage, who "have passed down their wanderings" (*suos tradiderint errores*) to the present court.[62] Walter took pains to get his introduction right: he added three sections that introduce common themes in *distinctio* 1. Moreover, he has altered the original introductory paragraph to extend the court-as-time metaphor, and he has incorporated an apt reference to Boethius.

Given this thorough revision, it is in some ways ironic that Walter decided to conclude the new introduction with a passage that reinforces his critical reputation as a flighty writer:

De curia nobis origo sermonis, et quo iam deuenit? Sic incidunt semper aliqua que licet non multum ad rem, tamen differri nolunt, nec refert, dum non atrum desinant in piscem, et rem poscit apte quod instat.

(The beginning of our discussion concerned the court, but it has already gone off course! Yes, some things always arise which are perhaps not very relevant but refuse to be put off. Yet as long as they do not end in a black fish and as long as the discussion at hand fittingly calls for the matter, it does not make a difference.)[63]

Certainly, these lines have served as one of the first indications of Walter's "waywardness"—he is incapable of finishing the introduction without embarking on a distracting tangent![64] However, the care with which Walter has revised the entire introduction shows that this waywardness is a carefully constructed conceit, and not a spontaneous, unaffected moment of self-awareness from our harried courtier. To ward off accusations that his digressions are inappropriate, Walter slyly invokes the beginning of Horace's *Ars poetica*, in which the narrator describes a painter setting the head of a lovely woman on top of a horse's neck, which itself is attached to a feathered body composed of various limbs. This ungainly image "shamefully ends in a black fish" (*turpiter atrum / desinat in piscem*).[65] For Horace, one of Walter's favorite authors, such a painting shows that a unified form is expected in art; deviations will be met with ridicule. Walter's own claim that diverse topics are acceptable "as long as they do not end in a black fish" (dum non atrum desinant in piscem) shows that his writing, in his own estimation at least, holds to a unified form.

Perhaps a better illustration of what a unified order meant for Walter is found in his contemporary Geoffrey of Vinsauf's *Poetria nova* (ca. 1208–13), a work that became extraordinarily popular. This treatise explains that order over one's material can be imposed naturally, with a straightforward order, or through "the by-paths of art": "This order, though reversed, is more pleasant and by far better than the straightforward order. The latter is sterile, but the former fertile, from its marvelous source sending out more branches from the parent trunk, changing one branch into many, a single into several, one into eight."[66] This principle helps explain Walter's system of arrangement not only in the introduction, but also the work as a whole. Rather than a general satire of twelfth-century life, systematically exhausting one topic before moving to another, *distinctio* 1 moves organically from topic to topic, following strands before doubling back to return to the point. This technique is visible throughout the *De nugis curialium*, as almost all episodes move to the next with clear transitions. Walter's defense of his digressions thus explicitly announces that his narrative will not proceed in what Geoffrey of Vinsauf calls a "natural order," strictly following chronological or logical arrangement. Another useful point of comparison is the *Disciplina clericalis* of Peter Alfonsi, a work that Walter probably knew.[67] Walter's interlinking of chapters is so similar to Peter's own technique of linking together groups of similar (and sometimes dissimilar) stories that he may well have modeled his own narrative style after it, especially in *distinctiones* 1, 2 and 4.[68] Indeed, most of the *De nugis curialium* progresses steadily in an artful, leisurely manner, with Walter linking stories together with quick transitions. The apparent digressions are exactly what give long sections of the *De nugis curialium* their self-sustained unity. Walter's seemingly candid admission of waywardness is in fact a planned and studied conclusion to a meticulously rewritten introduction.

Whoever invented the chapter headings for the only surviving copy of the *De nugis curialium* has done Walter no favors in this regard. (As discussed in detail in the next chapter, Walter did not write these headings.) The entire introduction up to Walter's defense of his digressions is served by one chapter title, "Assimulacio curie regis ad infernum" (A comparison of the king's court to hell).[69] But like many of the headings, this one poorly describes what follows. Consequently, Walter's own organizational strategy is often obscured in modern editions and translations of the text. A better heading for the first twelve chapters of *distinctio* 1 might be something along of the lines of "Diffinicio curie" (A definition of the court), since they all consist of Walter trying to make sense in one way or another of the court—its changeability, judgment, avarice, torment, and ungovernableness. And, as noted above, Walter twice makes explicit mention of his attempt to define (*diffinire*) the court. Moreover, in a lively example of arrangement through the "by-paths of art," these first twelve sections move seamlessly from defining the court, to arguing that the court, like hell, is a place of torment, to describing Walter's own ungovernable household (which explains in miniature why the court is ungovernable), to narrating the history of King Herla, which itself humorously provides an explanatory myth for the court's inconstancy, the very subject that opens the work. These chapters end with the tale of the king of Portugal, which illustrates the deceit and envy typical of courtiers. All of these episodes work to satirically explain and define the twelfth-century court. And, to adapt Walter's own phrase, all of these episodes are called for by the discussion at hand.

Another major addition to the beginning of the *De nugis curialium* is Walter's apology for Henry II. In the earlier version, the king takes some blame for his court's misconduct: "The king of this court, if he knows it well, is not free from blame, since he who is a ruler is obligated to be a reformer."[70] Most of the blame, however, lies with deceitful courtiers who purposefully misdirect the king, distracting him with hunting and flattery. The king, Walter explains in a memorable phrase, "is like a husband who is the last to learn that his wife has strayed."[71] In this earlier version, the king is guilty of ignorance. In rewriting this section, however, Walter adopts a more conciliatory tone toward Henry, saying, "Nor can we cast blame upon our lord and ruler, since in this world nothing is free from disturbance, and no one is able to enjoy any kind of tranquillity for long."[72] In lieu of blaming deceitful and ambitious courtiers for the king's ignorance—matters that have already been discussed—Walter rewrites this section to include a long but very humorous analogy that excuses the king's inability to manage his own court. Walter admits that through fraud and trickery his own household servants have thoroughly defeated him, with the result that his household no longer belongs to him but to his servants. After describing a few of these entertaining deceptions in detail, Walter announces that he has cataloged his own humiliation "for the benefit of our king."[73] "How," he asks, "will he keep thousands and thousands in check and guide them toward peace, even though typical householders like us are unable to control a few servants?"[74] Why Walter changes his tone toward the king in this passage is hard to tell. Certainly, while Walter's exasperation at his own household is more charming and original than stock complaints against scheming courtiers, there remains the possibility that he thought better of airing a grievance against the king in public.[75]

The tale of the militant monk of Cluny also undergoes major revision. In the earlier version in *distinctio* 4, Walter tells of a well-heeled man who, after leaving his land and wealth to his sons, decides to become a monk of Cluny.[76] After a few years in the monastery, he is asked to return to his native country to serve as an adviser. His abbot grudgingly permits him to leave the monastery but asks the monk to swear not to take up arms. The monk accedes to his abbot's wish. Eventually, however, war engulfs the monk's country, and, in the heat of the battle, the monk finds himself unarmed in the middle of his force, which is outnumbered and in retreat. Against his oath, he dons his armor, seizes his weapons, rouses his men, and leads his army to victory. Unused to such exertion—monastic life has apparently dulled his martial skills—he takes off part of his armor to rest and is promptly struck by an enemy's well-aimed arrow. Dying and finding no one fit for receiving his confession, he enjoins a small boy to do so, after which the repentant monk dies.

In this early version in *distinctio* 4, the tale of the Cluniac monk falls in the middle of a series of tales "about deaths in which God's judgment is uncertain."[77] In the tale that follows that of the Cluniac monk, God's judgment remains uncertain in a very literal fashion.[78] A knight of Brittany finds his deceased wife among a great band of women at night in a deserted area, in what seems to be a gathering of otherworldly fairies. Working up his courage, the knight snatches his wife away. Seemingly against the laws of nature, they live together for many years, and she even bears him children. Was she really dead? Moreover, the tale preceding the Cluniac monk's concerns Eudo, an impoverished nobleman who makes a deal with the devil to regain wealth and influence. With eternal damnation imminent, Eudo seeks penance from an angry bishop who hastily replies that for his extraordinary sins Eudo should leap into a fire. Without hesitation Eudo jumps into the flames and burns to ashes. The readers and hearers of this tale are then asked to debate "if this knight had the correct zeal"—that is, will he be saved?[79] Indeed, the ending of the Cluniac monk's tale echoes this question in its last words: "The monk passed away in the faith of Christ and with good hope and inflamed zeal of penance."[80] Readers here are also asked if the monk's confession to the young boy outweighs the breaking of his oath of pacifism to his abbot: the tale begins, "One can also question the salvation of a monk of Cluny."[81] All three of these deaths involve some type of uncertainty, whether spiritual or literal.

Dubious deaths, the context of the early version of the tale of the militant monk of Cluny, are one of Walter's favorite topics, but in his revision of this tale Walter leaves them aside in an effort to focus on the elements of sin and penance. Here in *distinctio* I, it fits comfortably into the series of stories concerning "recent events" that Walter places immediately after the tale of King Herla.[82] Its new context contains an exemplary story of the king of Portugal, a small encomium of the bishop of London, Walter's distress at the fall of Jerusalem in 1187, and, most important, an account of Guichard III of Beaujeu (d. 1137). Guichard retires to the monastery of Cluny in his old age and becomes an excellent poet. However, much to the dismay of his abbot, Guichard interrupts his leisure to retake his land from his rebellious son. After a successful military campaign, Guichard returns to Cluny, remains faithful to his vows, and dies a good death. Walter follows Guichard's tale with the militant monk of Cluny, which, though removed from its earlier context of dubious deaths in *distinctio* 4, sits happily in its new surroundings in *distinctio* I. Walter has, however, made several adjustments to the tale. First of all, he has added an appropriate transition between the two tales of extra-claustral activity: "But for others it can turn out otherwise. Far more pitiful was what happened to a noble and robust man who was likewise a monk at the same place and who was similarly called back to arms by the very same necessity."[83] Aside from the increased attention to continuity, Walter has excised material deemed unnecessary. Gone is any discussion of the monk's broken vow, a crucial element in the earlier story that concerns the efficacy of the monk's repentance. Similarly, in the unrevised tale the monk attempts to make a truce with the enemy, but they double-cross him and secretly gather a large force to ambush him and his men. This betrayal sets the scene for the monk's fateful battle and provides some extenuating circumstances for breaking his vow: it is only when the monk's own men are in dire need that he decides to take up arms. However, in the revised tale Walter has apparently decided that all these details are superfluous, and he removes any trace of the attempted truce and the monk's desperate situation. Instead, he quickly describes how the monk "suffered repeated reverses in battle with magnificent and unbroken spirit" and how he "rose again from defeat as if newborn to the fight; kindled as it were with quickened rage."[84] This compression curtails the nuances of the monk's dilemma by excising any discussion about betrayal and any explanations for the monk's breaking of his vow, with the result that the monk's moral dilemma has disappeared completely. Instead, in its revised form in *distinctio* 1 this tale illustrates another dilemma, one closer to Walter's everyday experiences in court: obtaining and keeping a peaceful, unharried life.

The first fifteen chapters of *distinctio* 1 do not concern moral quandaries or the afterlife. Indeed, although the court is the ostensible subject of these chapters, the theme that binds them all together is Walter's frustrated quest for *quies*, "quiet." The court, with its instability and torment, is the greatest manifestation of disquiet in Walter's own life. But, as he admits while excusing his lord Henry, disquiet is a symptom not merely of the court but of the fallen world in general: "in this world nothing is free from disturbance [*quietum*], and no one is able to enjoy any kind of tranquillity [*tranquillitate*] for long."[85] Henry's court, so Walter glibly claims, has inherited the ghostly wanderings of the ancient King Herla: "But from that time, that phantom circuit has been at peace [*quieuit*], as if they have passed down their wanderings to us for their own peace [*quietem*]."[86] Ironically, the only place in the world that seems to have peace in Walter's day is Jerusalem, where, after the defeat of the crusaders, Saladin and his forces "established peace [*pacem*] with the firmest of occupations, so that their will is now done on earth as it is in hell."[87]

For Walter, the chaos of the court and the world at large is antithetical to literary pursuits; he admits no romantic notions about inspirational chaos. Walter replies to Geoffrey, the unknown and possibly fictional person urging him to write:

> Writing poetry is for someone with a peaceful [*quiete*] as well as a collected [*collecte*] mind. Poets desire a completely safe abode [*residenciam*] where they can maintain a constant presence, and when the body and material wealth are at their peak, it will not do any

good unless the mind is set at ease [*tranquillus*] by internal peace [*interna pace*]. Therefore, what you are asking of me, that an ignorant and inexperienced man write from this place, is no less a miracle than if you were to command new boys to sing from the furnace of another Nebuchadnezzar.[88]

Walter again accuses Geoffrey of handing him an impossible task in another passage: "And although the mother of our afflictions and nurse of our wrath surpasses others in its storminess, you command me to be a poet in the midst of these discords [*discordias*]?"[89] Understandably, Walter is jealous of those men of letters who have the leisure and means to compose undisturbed. After singling out Gilbert Foliot, Bartholomew of Exeter, and Baldwin of Worcester, he writes, "These men are the philosophers of our time who lack nothing, who have abodes [*residenciam*] stuffed with every abundance and peace [*pacem*] outside: they have begun properly and will attain a good end. But where is a haven for me, who scarcely has the leisure to live?"[90] These first fifteen chapters form a lament for the courtier-cleric with literary pretensions, and they end with the clearest symbols of the *vita actiua* and *vita contempliua* known to the medieval mind—Jesus's visit to the house of Martha and Mary.[91] Walter, it is clear, prefers the constancy and calmness of the *vita contempliua*. Yet the court, to which he is both "bound and banished," refuses him peace and stability.[92] Walter's complaints about the difficulty of literary pursuits while in the court manifests what John Cotts has termed "the clerical dilemma": "the balancing of the professional, educational, and spiritual concerns in an uneasy synthesis," which is found in the writing of many twelfth-century secular clerics.[93] Walter's duties as a member of the court stymie (so he claims) his literary pretensions.

The two stories of the monks who leave Cluny to fight for their land exemplify the pressures of the secular world on those who would lead a life devoted to more elevated pursuits. Guichard's new life at Cluny is a matter of envy for Walter: "when [Guichard] had obtained an easy living and taken up newfound quiet [*quietem*], he brought his strength together into an undivided mind, which had previously been distracted when he lived as a soldier [*milicie secularis*]; he suddenly felt himself to be a poet, and shining forth brilliantly in his own way, that is, in the French tongue, he became the Homer of the laity. Ah, if only there were such a truce for me, to keep the wandering through the many beams of a scattered mind from creating barbarisms!"[94] Like Gilbert, Bartholomew, and Baldwin, Guichard's literary productivity directly—almost miraculously—results from his withdrawal from the commotion of the world. After necessity forces him to revisit his life as a soldier, he returns to his vow and to the monastery without any complications. The nameless monk of Cluny, however, has no such luck. In the moment of his triumph, he is struck down by a covert enemy's arrow, never again to enter the peaceful confines of Cluny. Revised and in a new context, the tale of the militant monk of Cluny offers a counterpoint to Guichard's experience: leaving the cloister, or any peaceful refuge from the world, can be fatal.

Understandably, in rewriting this story Walter focuses not on the monk's attempt at penance but on the dangers of the outside world. Moreover, the revised tale also acts as a transition in the larger narrative structure of *distinctio* 1. Up until this tale, the subject matter of the *distinctio* 1 almost exclusively concerns the court and the uneasy place of a writer in it. With the tale of the militant monk of Cluny, Walter begins to address the instability and tumult of the world outside the court. As in its original form, the tale ends with the militant monk asking for penance from a boy. However, in the revised version, Walter adds a few "words of mercy," quoting a well-known phrase, "In whatever hour the sinner laments, he shall be saved."[95] Given such mercy, Walter wonders how the Lord could not grant the militant monk salvation. This concluding discussion of penance, mercy, and salvation allows Walter to transition to these same topics in the world at large. He begins with jubilee years, which are years of "forgiveness and grace, of safety and peace, of exultation and pardon, of praise and joy."[96] For Walter's contemporaries, jubilee years—and the remission they offer—were closely associated with crusading. A few decades earlier, Bernard of Clairvaux had explicitly connected the two, and Walter has skillfully made use of this connection to move to the starkest reminder of instability in the late twelfth century—the fall of Jerusalem in 1187.[97] Thus, with the newly revised tale of the militant monk of Cluny Walter moves from private penance to public penance, and from the instability of court to the instability of the world. It is worth noting that this section, too, ends with a smooth transition to the next section on monastic satire. After cataloging Saladin's victory and the apparent absence of the Lord's mercy, Walter wonders why the prayers of so many thousands of monks are unable to alter the current discord of the world. These monks say that they serve the Lord as Mary does, devoutly sitting at Christ's feet in pursuit of the *vita contempliua*, but perhaps, Walter suggests, they are too involved with worldly pursuits. With these words the first half of *distinctio* 1, with its focus on *quies* and the court, ends, and Walter's famous satire on the monastic orders begins.

The survival of earlier versions of most of the material in chapters 1 through 15 shows that there is nothing haphazard in the organization of *distinctio* 1 of the *De nugis curialium*. In the foregoing discussion, I have, however, omitted Walter's revision of chapter 11, the tale of King Herla, because it is the subject of Chapter 4. As will be seen, this tale also shows all the hallmarks of careful revision found in the rest of *distinctio* 1.

On the surface, *distinctio* 2 seems to contain two stories that have been revised from earlier material: the tale of Eadric the Wild and the story Walter calls "The Sons of a Dead Woman." As I have explained elsewhere, in revising the tale of Eadric the Wild, Walter adds a famous Anglo-Saxon thane to an earlier story in order to shore up the rights of the bishop of Hereford.[98] One more doublet, then, remains to be explained. Both *distinctio* 2 and *distinctio* 4 contain broadly similar stories concerning the offspring of humans and fairy lovers, classifying them as "sons of a dead woman" (*filii mortue*).[99] Rigg considers these stories to represent the same episode in revised and unrevised forms. Thus, I have included them in Table 1. However, although these two chapters do touch upon the same subject matter, their identification as the same story is unwarranted. The only direct verbal similarity between the two tales is the tag "sons of a dead woman" (*filii mortue*). Moreover, *distinctio* 2 does not actually recount the story of one of these sons of a dead woman. Instead it directly follows the tale of Gastin Gastiniog's son Trunio Vagelauc and Eadric the Wild's son Alnoth, both of whose mothers are fairies.[100] (Fairy-bride stories have a certain pull on Walter.)[101] Walter explains that fairies and their ilk, or "phantasms" (*fantasma*) as he terms them, are merely demons whom God has permitted to change their appearance. This explanation would not surprise contemporary readers, as succubi and incubi, with which he equates these phantasms, have long been treated as demons in Christian thought. But what, Walter wonders, is one to make of cases in which the offspring of these unions "which remain and propagate themselves in good succession, as in this case of Alnoth or that of the aforementioned Britons, in which a certain knight is said to have buried his wife who was truly dead, and to have gotten her back after he snatched her from a ring of dancers, and afterward to have received children and grandchildren from her, and their offspring endures to this very day, and those who trace their origin from this source have become widespread—all of them are therefore called 'the sons of a dead woman' "?[102] Walter does not have a satisfactory explanation for these cases, gesturing merely to the incomprehensible ways of the Lord. Nonetheless, I think it is clear that Walter has not rewritten or retold the story of the sons of the dead woman here; he simply provides another version of the same type of story to increase his examples. This little vignette is made to stand on its own and requires no reference to the story in *distinctio* 4. No revision has taken place.

However, modern readers of the *De nugis curialium* have also found something puzzling about this passage, though not its demonology. The reference to "the aforementioned Britons" (*Britonum de quo superius*) here certainly seems to describe the story found in *distinctio* 4, in which a "knight from Brittany" (*miles quidam Britannie minoris*) rescues his dead wife from a great band of women and begets several children with her, the offspring of which are still numerous in Walter's day.[103] Problematically, no preceding story matches the description here. One suggestion is that *Britonum* here means "Welsh" and refers to the story of Gastin Gastiniog and his son Trunio Vagelauc, which does in fact precede this passage. But although Trunio does have a fairy mother, the particulars do not align: Gastin catches his fairy bride in a lake, and Trunio dies without any mention of his offspring. The erroneous *de quo superius* may be one more clue that *distinctio* 2 is still under revision. However, as I show in the next chapter, the *De nugis curialium* does include several interpolated glosses. I would suggest this *de quo superius* originally began its life as an interlinear gloss—it is certainly unnecessary and does feel rather awkwardly inserted.[104] Indeed, since Walter immediately and fully explains what he means by *ille Britonum*, there is no need for him to direct readers to another part of his work to gain the full story. Walter, in fact, never directs readers to another *distinctio*, except for this suspicious passage. Given this, I think it likely that *de quo superius* first existed as an interlinear gloss, not for *ille Britonum*, but for Alnoth, whose story we have just heard. When a scribe moved this gloss into the main text of the *De nugis curialium*, he was a few words off, and *de quo superius* became confusingly attached to *ille Britonum*. At any rate, I see no convincing evidence to consider this brief discussion of the sons of a dead woman as a revision of the thematically similar tale in *distinctio* 4.

Walter the Reviser

The above certainly does not document every change that Walter makes as he revises. It provides enough of an overview to address one major issue concerning the textual state of the *De nugis curialium*. The minor revisions all point to the same direction of change: if we grant Walter even the least bit of authorial competence, in each of the alterations discussed above the stories found in *distinctiones* 4 and 5 seems to be the earlier version of their counterparts in *distinctiones* 1 and 2. The major revisions, which focus mainly on narrative structure, also point to this direction of revision. However, to my mind the minor changes most convincingly demonstrate that the doublets do indeed result from the process of revision. Otherwise, one would have to suppose that as Walter rewrites, he is reducing his alliteration, choosing less striking or appropriate words, and generally impairing the rhetorical success of his work. A few may prefer this view of Walter; I find it unlikely. The man who could gleefully write "si me ruditus ruditas ridiculum reddiderit" almost certainly did not restrain his alliteration and wordplay as he revised.[105] Alternatively, one could suppose that the doublets are merely different versions of the same story, recorded decades apart. However, the direct verbal similarities, often exact, in the doublets prove that Walter had an earlier version in front of him as he reworked his prose. The unfinished textual state of the *De nugis curial-ium* has even tidily provided us with another group of doublets with which we can compare Walter's revisions. In *distinctio* 1, Walter twice recounts tales of the Carthusians and the Order of Grandmont. And while these doublets re-visit the same material, they do not represent the same story at different stages of revision; Walter has composed them at different times with different aims. Aside from the broadest of generalizations, they share no direct verbal or the-matic likenesses. After comparing these tales, the revised nature of the other doublets stands out in stark contrast.

Comparing Walter's revision of his own tales with his use of other sources also demonstrates that Walter was a careful reviser of his own work as well as that of others. Like most medieval writers, Walter saw no harm in reworking stories from other authors and sources, but in this respect, Walter is no verba-tim transcriber. When he uses another source, he tends to shape it to his needs, editing and rewriting it with a strong focus, unafraid to make radical, and felicitous, changes. Nowhere in his work do we see the wholesale borrow-ing that is not altogether uncommon in medieval composition, as in the *Gemma ecclesiastica* of Gerald of Wales, which lifts several passages from Peter the Chanter.[106] For example, Walter has carefully reworked a passage ulti-mately from Cicero's *De officiis* to good effect in his story of Earl Godwine of Wessex.[107] The tale of Sadius and Galo, one of Walter's most celebrated pieces, has been skillfully stitched together from several narrative sources.[108] And Walter's refashioning of a story from the collection known as the *Analecta*

Dublinensia is, according to one critic, "more coherent and more satisfying" than the original.[109] While an examination of Walter's use of sources is outside the scope of this book, initial studies all agree that Walter was an adroit adapter who carefully modified earlier material. Clearly, Walter took the same approach when it came time to revise his own work.

That Walter revised the material in the *De nugis curialium* sheds light on another textual mystery. The *Dissuasio Valerii*, Walter's anti-matrimonial tract found in *distinctio* 4, circulated separately from the *De nugis curialium*. Its popularity—it remains most famous as one of the major sources for Jankyn's "book of wikked wyves" in *The Canterbury Tales*—has ensured a complex and rich manuscript tradition. The work's most recent editors have argued that the transmission of the text was bifid, meaning that all witnesses of the *Dissuasio* stem from two families representing separate, irreconcilable archetypes.[110] These archetypes, which they term "alpha" and "beta," may well represent two different authorial versions of the *Dissuasio Valerii*.[111] Alpha appears to be the earliest, and seems to have been in circulation by 1184.[112] The copy of the *Dissuasio* found in the *De nugis curialium*, on the other hand, belongs to the beta family of manuscripts (though it is interestingly not the best representative of this family). This state of affairs would to be expected if the beta family represents a revised version of the *Dissuasio*, since by Walter's own testimony the *Dissuasio* was already popular by the time Walter revisited it in the *De nugis curialium*. It seems then, that these two families of manuscript are best thought of as earlier (alpha) and revised (beta) versions of the *Dissuasio Valerii*. This works well with what we know about the circulation of the alpha and beta groups. The alpha group appears to have spread rapidly throughout the continent and is by far the larger of the two families. Only eight manuscripts belong to the beta group. It is very revealing that in addition to the copy of the *Dissuasio* in the *De nugis curialium*, only one other manuscript, British Library Additional 34749, names Walter Map as the text's author—and both of these belong to the beta (revised) group.[113] In other words, the only manuscripts that name Walter Map as the author of the *Dissuasio Valerii* belong to the small family of manuscripts that I believe represents the revised version of the text, a situation that accords with what Walter himself tells us: that he only added his name after the *Dissuasio* became incredibly popular. Tellingly, lines 284–317, which contain an overtly Christian exhortation and thus destroy the illusion that the text is indeed ancient, seem to have their origin in the beta version.[114] Walter seems to have added this passage only after he revealed his own authorship of the *Dissuasio*. Only a thorough comparison of the alpha and beta traditions can confirm that he did in fact produce two separate versions—a task that the lack of a good alpha edition renders impossible for the moment. Nonetheless, internal evidence from the *De nugis curialium* has already shown Walter to be a thorough reviser. It is not surprising in the least that he revised his most successful work.

As a reviser, Walter is no anomaly in the twelfth century. Gerald of Wales wrote five versions of *Topographia Hibernica*.[115] Peter of Blois seemingly could not resist the urge to fiddle with his letters, and later in his life he gave his letter collection a fairly radical overhaul.[116] Likewise, the textual tradition of Nigel Wireker's *Speculum stultorum* suggests that this popular satire also underwent one revision.[117] Walter, like these and other authors, worked through his text with care, tinkering with words, rearranging phrases, and repurposing stories. Importantly, this care does not suggest a careless anecdotist who has hastily jotted down witty sayings. Walter Map may in fact have more in common with William Langland, the most well-known reviser in medieval England; it is a pleasant coincidence that an important copy of *Piers Plowman* resides in Bodley 851, a happy companion to the only copy of the *De nugis curialium*.

Chapter 3

Glosses and a Contrived Book

The *De nugis curialium*, like many favorite medieval texts, did not achieve a wide audience. Only one copy survives, and, outside the wildly popular *Dissuasio Valerii*, there exists no definitive proof that the *De nugis curialium* circulated in a form similar to what is found in Bodley 851. That our fourteenth-century manuscript is not an authorial copy is obvious enough; our text has passed through at least one round of transmission. This much is clear and uncontroversial. However, internal evidence suggests that at least one reader of Walter's work was interested enough to add chapter headings and gloss the manuscript rather extensively. Hinton dealt thoroughly with the rubricated chapter headings and concluded that they were not Walter's but the result of a scribe.[1] While his arguments remain convincing to me, Walter's recent editors have their doubts: "It can be said at once that the incompetence of the rubrics is not sufficient (as Hinton seems to have thought) to indicate that Map was not their author, nor that they were made after his death. It is clear that the numbering of chapters is the work of a copyist, and not a very intelligent one. But the state of the rubrics conforms to the general condition of the book, which is untidy in every possible way, and with an untidiness which clearly reflects in part the mind of Master Walter."[2] Because Walter's editors remain doubtful, this chapter revisits the evidence for Walter's authorship of the rubricated chapter headings, expanding and solidifying Hinton's arguments. Furthermore, I will show that over two dozen glosses have been interpolated into the text of the *De nugis curialium*. The *De nugis curialium* had a few readers interested enough to gloss the text, and, at some point during transmission, these interlinear glosses were interpolated into the main text, causing significant confusion to future readers.

It is in many ways unfortunate that the manuscript's chapter headings have been kept in the main text of every edition of the *De nugis curialium*. Although they are valuable as medieval reactions to Walter's text, their unquestioned inclusion has only misled readers. Hinton correctly warned that they give "a specious impression of finished and ordered composition."[3] But most important, Hinton demonstrated that the chapter headings ultimately result from a scribe promoting marginal navigation notes to the status of headings and titles. While the identity of the original annotator remains a mystery, his handiwork is seen throughout the *De nugis curialium*. Hinton identified several instances that betray his presence, and he demonstrated that Walter did not compose the headings himself. First of all, the headings consistently refer to "Mahap," while the text itself agrees with contemporary evidence in spelling the author's cognomen *Map*. Gerald of Wales, Hue de Rotelande, and all the documentary material agree on *Map*.[4] Moreover, MS British Library Additional 34749, a thirteenth-century manuscript that, outside of the *De nugis curialium*, alone preserves Walter's name as the author of the *Dissuasio Valerii*, has "Map."[5] Further evidence confirms Hinton's suspicions that the odd spelling *Mahap* is a later invention: Metrical evidence in a poem from Gerald of Wales shows that *Map* is the correct form. A disyllabic *Mahap* would break the pentameter line in the elegiac couplet.[6] The attributions to Walter in the *Lancelot-Grail Cycle*, which began in the early thirteenth century, prefer the spelling *Map* or *Mape*; they never have *Mahap*.[7] Of the few poems that Walter probably wrote, none preserve his name as *Mahap*.[8] Even in the Goliardic tradition, the curious spelling *Mahap* only rarely appears.[9] Nonetheless, the only other environment in which the spelling *Mahap* appears is Walter's pseudonymous work—a fact that does not inspire great confidence in the rubricated headings of Bodley 851. *Mahap*, as Hinton suspected, is a later development, and it would seem that the rubricated headings in the *De nugis curialium* have been influenced by pseudonymous traditions about Walter.[10] Indeed, Bodley 851 contains four other works that have been attributed to Walter, including the *Apocalipsis Goliae*, one of Walter's most famous pseudonymous works.[11] While the *Apocalipsis Goliae* is the only one of these four poems to claim Walter's authorship in Bodley 851, the spelling of Walter's name is the same as in the rubricated headings of the *De nugis curialium*: "Apocalipsis mag(ist)ri Galteri Mahap."[12] These headings were, in fact, written by the same scribe, so it is possible that the change of *Map* to *Mahap* in the headings to the *De nugis curialium* occurred during the composition of Bodley 851.[13]

Had Hinton continued looking for orthographic clues, he might have found a few others that suggest the chapter headings belong to a different textual layer than the rest of the text. For example, the chapter title for chapter 4 in *distinctio* 5 reads "De Cnutone rege Dacorum," but the body of the text consistently spells his name *Chnutus*.[14] Elsewhere, the headings read "Giscardeo," "Tarentaisie," and "Lodouuico," while the body has "Gischardeus," "Tharenthasie," and "Lodouicus."[15] Obviously, one cannot make too much of the variation of vernacular names in Medieval Latin manuscripts, especially since the rubricated chapter headings of the *De nugis curialium* where written by a different scribe than the main body.[16] Indeed, this variation in names is almost certainly due to individual scribal practice. Scribe A, who wrote the main body of the text, also wrote the table of contents at the end of the *De nugis curialium*. In the table of contents, we find "Gischardeo," "Tharenthasie," and "Lodouico," which is consistent with scribe A's practices elsewhere. Thus, either scribe A, or scribe X (who wrote the rubricated headings) altered the orthography of their exemplar.[17] These orthographic variations are thus somewhat misleading.

Much more convincing is the unsystematic and occasionally incorrect nature of the chapter headings. So untrustworthy are they that Hinton need only cite the first six rubricated chapter headings in the work to find illustrative mistakes. The first chapter, for instance, is titled "Assimulacio curie regis ad infernum" (A comparison of the king's court with hell), even though the actual comparison does not begin until chapter 2; the entirety of chapter 1 concerns defining the court and does not even mention hell. Chapter 2, on the other hand, is indeed labeled "De inferno" (Concerning hell), but this short chapter is merely the introduction to the following chapters on hell: Tantalus, Sisyphus, Ixion, and others all receive their own chapter headings when in fact they are subheadings and should not be promoted to chapters. Finally, the heading "De Yxione" (Concerning Ixion) is incorrectly placed in the manuscript, which can be confirmed by comparing it to the same passage in its earlier draft form.[18] Tellingly, the headings flag in the latter sections of the work: *Distinctio* 1 (roughly sixty pages of Latin text in the most recent edition) contains thirty-two chapters. *Distinctio* 5 (roughly forty-seven pages) has only seven. The attentiveness of the original annotator, it seems, waned as he worked through Walter's text. For instance, the title "De primo Henrico rege Anglorum et Lodouuico rege Francorum" (Concerning Henry I, king of the English, and Louis, king of the French) serves as the sole heading for several pages that encompass a diverse array of historical anecdotes.[19] One reads them with the impression that if the annotator had begun his reading with this *distinctio*, with the zeal of his pen not yet exhausted, our modern editions would here have several chapters instead of one.

The annotator also seems to have been confused about what he was reading at times. The first five chapters of *distinctio* 4, for example, are titled: "Prologus ," "Epilogus .ii.," "Dissuasio Valerii ad Ruffinum philosophum ne uxorem ducat .iii.," "Conclusio epistole premisse," "Finis epistole premisse v." Yet, the latter half of the section titled "Epilogue" is explicitly an introduction to the *Dissuasio Valerii*. (I will examine below the reasons that the glossator incorrectly marked the beginning of this section as "Epilogus.") Especially convincing that these headings do not belong to Walter is the very last chapter in *distinctio* 5, which contains the earlier draft of the introduction. This chapter is titled "Recapitulacio principii huius libri ob diuersitatem litere et non sentencie" (A recapitulation of the beginning of this book, differing in expression not substance).[20] As demonstrated in the previous chapter, this section of the *De nugis curialium*, however, is not a repetition, but an earlier draft of the beginning of *distinctio* 1. While Hinton suspected this was the case, the foregoing analysis has confirmed its status as an earlier version.

Moreover, the *sentencia* (substance) of the two versions actually does differ. Take, for example, Walter's decision not to cast too much blame on Henry II in his revised version—this is a significant change that the chapter heading does not register.[21] Finally, the general shoddiness of the chapter titles throughout the entire work, with their unrepresentative, bland, or incorrect descriptions, is everywhere consistent with Hinton's suggestion that these rubrics were originally the uninspired notes of an annotator, written out with little thought as he navigated through the text. Overall, I can find nothing to contradict Hinton's conclusion about the rubrication: "It is apparent, then, that the titles are in general devoid of authority, and further that the text must originally have been rubricated so insufficiently that we can hardly believe the author edited and published it."[22] In light of our new understanding of Walter's revisionary practices, I would add to Hinton's conclusion that it is inconceivable that a writer so careful in his revisions would compose inaccurate and dull chapter headings for his own unfinished work.

Independent evidence also suggests that the rubricated chapter headings are not Walter's. In the textual tradition of the *Dissuasio Valerii*, which circulated independently of Bodley 851, the headings "Conclusio epistole premisse" and "Finis epistole premise" occur only in Bodley 851.[23] Thus, the version of the *Dissuasio Valerii* that we find in the *De nugis curialium* stands alone in having these headings. Certainly, Walter could have added these headings during the process of revision, but given all the other evidence in favor of their being scribal relicts, that scenario seems on the whole unlikely.

Finally, in one instance we have what looks to have once been an annotation, but one that did not get promoted to the status of a chapter heading. The bald phrase "The Lord freed a hermit" (Liberauit Dominus heremitam) sits out of place in *distinctio* 2.[24] It seems to be an annotation of the same sort of those that became called into service as rubricated chapter headings. But unlike a similar annotation, it has not been turned into a chapter title because the annotation "De quodam hermita" (Of a certain hermit) immediately preceded it. If a scribe had also turned *Liberauit Dominus hermitam* into a chapter title, he would have created a chapter that consisted of a single sentence, which even for a rather dull scribe would seem unacceptable.

The only defense that may be given for Walter's authorship of the headings is to make him an extraordinarily slipshod writer, which is what Brooke and Mynors prefer. The carelessness of the chapter headings, they say, "conforms to the general condition of the book, which is untidy in every possible way, and with an untidiness which clearly reflects in part the mind of Master Walter."[25] It is perhaps unfair to the editors to linger on this point, since in their view the authorship of the headings is "not of much moment." [26] Nonetheless, the only evidence for Walter's carelessness is the single copy of a work that is clearly unfinished and caught in the middle of revision. On the contrary, it *is* important to recognize that the chapter headings are not Walter's. While they are surely valuable as a medieval response to Walter's work, their post-authorial composition should not be allowed to overdetermine our response to the text.

It is worth stopping to consider whether or not the scribes of Bodley 851 were responsible for creating the chapter headings as we currently have them. On the whole, codicological evidence suggests that they were already present in the exemplar. While scribe A wrote the body of the text of the *De nugis curialium*, scribe X contributed the rubricated chapter headings.[27] Importantly, scribe A anticipated the rubrication: depending on the length, he left one, two, or sometimes three lines blank. Usually he left enough space, but on occasion he did not, and scribe X had to spill out of the column to complete the rubrics.[28] And sometimes scribe A began a new chapter, wrote a few words, and then realized he had forgotten to leave space for the chapter heading, so he immediately stopped and skipped to the next line. For example, we see this process on folio 14ra, where scribe A begins chapter 18 of *distinctio* 1 by writing "Miles quida(m)" before moving to the next line to leave space for scribe X to squeeze in the rubric. This all suggests that scribe A knew when to expect a chapter heading and generally how long the chapter heading was. Thus, the chapter headings were present before scribe A started copying, and he had access to them. Moreover, two interesting mistakes in the chapter headings suggest that scribe X was himself working from an exemplar. On folio 33vb, the entire chapter heading for chapter 30 of *distinctio* 2 is missing. Scribe A left no room for it at all. (He might well have been confused by three chapters in a row beginning with the same heading: "Item aliud prodigium.") Yet scribe X remained undeterred and correctly numbered the next chapter 31. Similarly, on folio 47ra, scribe X forgot to give a number to chapter 4 of *distinctio* 4, although he includes the heading. Nonetheless, the numbering correctly continues at 5 for the next chapter. Had scribe X himself been responsible for the initial numbering of the chapter titles, we might have expected him to continue counting in sequence in these two instances, but he does not, which strongly suggests he was working from an exemplar that provided him with the numbering.[29] It is, however, conceivable that the scribes of Bodley 851 decided themselves to promote marginal notes to chapter titles and that this was done before either scribe started writing, and thus from earlier marginal notes they created a table of contents, like the one present at the end of *De nugis curialium*, on folios 72v–73v. That is certainly plausible. I do, however, doubt that the scribes of Bodley 851 did much more than follow their exemplar. After all, scribe A often uses *litterae notabiliores*, or enlarged letters, to mark out different sections of text, even within the same chapter, especially if the chapter is long; he usually does so quite sensibly. If he had been in charge of dividing up the text into chapters, based on his use of *litterae notabiliores*, I suspect he would have done a better job than what he inherited.

Interpolated Glosses

The chapter headings are not the only places in *De nugis curialium* that can be identified as scribal interpolations. Scattered throughout the text are more than two dozen phrases beginning with *id est* (that is)—the telltale sign of a lexical gloss. These phrases tend to bluntly explain metaphors, gloss difficult words or names, and clarify Walter's Latin. (Walter's penchant for a condensed prose style renders the last of these particularly understandable.) When examined as a whole, they give a strong impression that a glossator's handiwork has become interpolated into the main text of the *De nugis curialium*. Although editions of the *De nugis curialium* have identified a few of these interpolated glosses before, as a whole they have not been studied in detail.[30] Not every interpolation will receive a thorough treatment, but an examination of the glossing of names and hard words, metaphors, and general clarification of Walter's prose will show that these passages, like the chapter headings, are almost certainly the work of a later reader.

Fairly clear confirmation that a glossator has been at work is seen in the many explanations of proper names or recondite Latin words, sometimes correctly. Unsurprisingly, Welsh terms are often in need of commentary. At one point in a story concerning Welshmen, Walter uses the Welsh word *brycan* ("super brachanum") for a blanket or coverlet.[31] The nonchalance with which Walter uses this word implies that Walter, a border dweller, was quite familiar with this mundane item. The gloss, on the other hand, reads "id est tapetum optimum" (that is a very fine carpet), a somewhat overblown definition for what Gerald of Wales dismisses as "a durable and rough cloth."[32] Either the glossator is guessing here, or a patriotic Welsh-speaker has fed him a bit of an exaggeration. Less lucky, though, is his guess on the meaning of the Welsh word *Deheubarth* (though the manuscript has *Deheulard*).[33] *Deheubarth* denotes the general region of South Wales, but the glossator has written "id est Noruualie" (that is North Wales).[34] He could not have been more wrong. Context helps him with another Welsh regional name. The unexplained, corrupt—indeed the entire passage is certainly corrupt—word *Reynos* is glossed with "id est Brecheniauc" (that is Brycheiniog).[35] But this gloss requires no special knowledge of Wales: a few lines above, the text explains that the king who controls Reynos is named Brychan (*Brehein*) and his kingdom is named Brycheiniog (*Brekeniauc*). Whatever the word *Reynos* originally designated is of little import here; *Brycheiniog* is easily deducible from this context. Moreover, *Brycheiniog* could have been a familiar toponym to the glossator, since the name of this Welsh kingdom survived as the Norman lordship of Brecon. None of these glosses on Welsh terms seem to come from someone as familiar with the Welsh and the southern Marches as Walter. They have the hallmarks of someone completely unfamiliar with Wales, but who uses contextual clues to explain foreign terms.

Lexical glosses explaining proper names and difficult terms do not appear only for Welsh words. In two of these the glossator clarifies what would have been understood for Walter's immediate audience: "Noster dominus" (Our lord) is explained as "id est Henricus secundus" (that is Henry II), and "insulam nostram" (our island) attracts an explanation of "id est Anglia" (that is

England).[36] Both of these are rather banal, intrusive, and unlikely to have been deemed necessary by Walter. On the other hand, the rare word *nefrens*, "suckling piglet," deserving of a gloss, is somewhat incorrectly described as a "young and virgin sow" (id est adolescentem et uirginem suem).[37] But the glossator has correctly identified a less common meaning of *fides*, which usually means "faith," but which Walter uses to mean "faithfulness."[38] Similarly helpful is the definition of *Parthis* (inhabitants of Parthia): the glossator has written "id est Turchis" (that is Turks)—a common medieval conflation of the two.[39]

The glossator also liked to explain metaphors, and their inclusion in the edited text occasionally gives an unnecessarily pedantic feel. Clear examples of this are found in the draft of the comparison of the court with hell. In a moment of self-criticism, Walter identifies with the unlawful desires of the mythical Tityus, a would-be rapist, whose crime brought him eternal punishment in the form of two vultures who feed on his ever-regenerating liver. Walter asks, "Nunquid non ego sum in curia Ticius, et forsan alius aliquis, cuius cupido cordi vultures apponuntur, id est affectus nigri, diuellentes ipsum . . . ?" (In the court am I not also a Tityus—perhaps others are too—upon whose covetous heart vultures—that is, black passions—are set plucking it apart . . .?)[40] In the very next passage—apparently an interpretive mood struck the glossator as he read this section—two similar passages are found. For his next hellish comparison, Walter has chosen the daughters of Belus, who continually and ineffectually strive to fill perforated bowls with sieves. The impossibility of this task strikes Walter as an apt metaphor for the never satisfied ambition of those at court: "cribro quod a paleis grana secernit, id est, discrecione, vasa complere pertusa laboramus, id est, animos insaciabiles" (we labor to fill the pierced bowls, that is, our insatiable spirits, with a sieve that parts the grain from the chaff, that is, discretion).[41] Generally speaking, Walter is not in the habit of explaining his obvious metaphors, jokes, or puns. These small phrases, all headed by the revealing *id est*, seem suspiciously out of place, especially when compared to surrounding passages, which all use the same metaphorical technique but which do not have heavy-handed explanations. It seems this section, for whatever reason, spurred the glossator into action.

Another metaphorical passage that caught his eye is found in the anecdote about Theudus, a Welshman who while on a raid overhears a man saying, "This morning I saw a little cloud rise from the sea, and it became a great cloud, so that it covered the entire sea."[42] From this scrap of conversation, Theudus understands that he will one day become king: "arbitratus se nubeculam, id est paruulum, a mari, id est Wallia, que semper in motu est, natum, regem futurum" (he judged that he, the little cloud—that is, the young boy—born from the sea—that is, Wales—which is always in motion, would become king).[43] The glosses *id est paruulum* and *id est Wallia* are again unnecessary and their inclusion in the edited text clutters what would otherwise be a perfectly happy Latin sentence. One last example shows the glossator reading metaphorically where no metaphor is intended. When Walter excuses Henry II from blame for the unruliness of his court, he claims that it is altogether impossible for Henry to know every member of his vast court. "No one," he explains, "entirely succeeds in ruling a family whose thoughts and speech—that is, whatever their hearts speak—remain unknown to him."[44] While glossing "speech" (*linguam*) as "whatever their hearts speak" (*quicquid eorum corda loquuntur*) is not particularly farfetched, the context of this passage, however, makes it clear that with *linguam* Walter references Henry II's multilingual court and not the unknowable intentions of his courtiers. Not only would this aspect of court be familiar to Walter's peers, but the next sentence shows that Babel was on his mind. Combining a phrase from the creation of the world in Genesis with passages referencing God's division of man after the destruction of the tower of Babel, Walter writes, "The Lord divides waters from waters, people from people" (Dominus diuidit aquas ab aquis, populos a populis).[45] This scriptural resonance shows the glossator to have missed the mark here.

As might be expected, our glossator also works in a rather mundane fashion, clarifying what Walter's prose means. For example, toward the end of Walter's great anti-monastic satire, in which he has sarcastically adopted the term "Hebrews" for monks, parodying their holier-than-thou attitude, Walter summarizes, "I speak about them, that is, the Hebrews, what I know and what the church laments."[46] After so many pages of identifying the monks as Hebrews, this gloss is wholly unnecessary. Another clear gloss is found when Walter announces that he is returning to Henry II after a brief a digression: "But to return to the subject matter from which I have digressed—that is, Henry II—this same king Henry was . . ." (Sed ut ad materiam unde digressus sum, id est ad regem Henricum secundum, reuertar; erat idem rex Henricus . . .).[47] This interpolated gloss has made for an awkward repetition of Henry. Finally, the presence of a glossator helps explain one of the odder editorial decisions in the *De nugis curialium*. At the beginning of his monastic satire, Walter explains how monks, in a manner eerily reminiscent of a time-share pitch, lure men away to their monasteries. The manuscript reads "Hos alliciunt, et ad camineas suas a strepitu seorsum, ab hospitibus caritatis, id est publicibus longe . . ." (They entice these men, and by their fireside, away from clamor, away from charitable hosts, that is, far from *publicibus*).[48] With the phrase "a strepitu seorsum, ab hospitibus caritatis" Walter means that those staying at the monastery will be far from any other place to stay. The glossator clearly understood this, though he mistakenly writes *publicibus* for *publicis* (public), perhaps under the influence of the nearby *hospitibus*. Mistaken declension or not, the glossator is clarifying Walter's phrase "away from clamor, away from charitable hosts" in more prosaic terms: these men are far from the public. Oddly, Brooke and Mynors follow James in emending *publicibus* to the nonsensical *pulicibus* (fleas).[49] The best recourse, however, is to omit this probable interpolation from the edited text.

This survey has not included every *id est* phrase, but I am confident that in almost every occurrence they denote a gloss that has been interpolated into the main text in the course of transmission. In every case they are superfluous. The roughness of these phrases is often smoothed over in translation, and a reader straying from the Latin may miss them. Of course, not all scribal relicts are so neatly indicated, and there are doubtless others lurking in the text. Furthermore, several instances of *scilicet* seem suspicious, although many of them, it must be said, do seem to be integral to the text, much more consistently than those phrases with *id est*. Nonetheless, given the above, it is all the more tempting to identify passages such as "uiri predicti, Barnardi scilicet" (this man, that is to say, Bernard), "domini mei regi Henrici scilicet secundi" (to my lord King Henry, that is to say, the second), and "ad dominum nostrum regem scilicet Anglie" (to our lord king, that is to say, of England) as interpolated suppletive glosses.[50] Ultimately, however, it is impossible to accurately identify all of the interpolated glosses in the *De nugis curialium* without any sort of corroboration from another manuscript.

It is not my intention to systematically identify and purge anything that has the look of an interpolated gloss from the text of the *De nugis curialium*. (However, had Walter's modern reputation been that of a clear thinker, like John of Salisbury, the more obvious glosses would have likely already been edited out of the text.) Rather, by recognizing that the surviving copy of the *De nugis curialium* has passed through a layer of glossing and that its chapter headings result from a scribe promoting glosses to chapter titles, Walter's reputation improves and the work as a whole becomes more comprehensible. The current edition, for instance, explains the incorrect gloss of *nefrendem* (suckling piglet) as perhaps an example of Walter's "improvised explanations."[51]

Although medieval writers did occasionally gloss their own work, the errors and contradictions found in the glosses I have discussed strongly suggest that it was not Walter who created them.[52] Moreover, critics often call the *De nugis curialium* a text that had almost no medieval readership, but there were at least four readers, which as far as we know makes for more than *Beowulf* or *Sir Gawain*: the initial glossator/annotator; the scribe who internalized these glosses and promoted some to numbered chapter headings; the scribes who copied Bodley 851; and a reader of Bodley 851 who himself left glosses.[53] Four is what can be proven; there certainly could have been more. We need not postulate only one glossator, for example. Furthermore, comparisons with other extant versions of the *Dissuasio Valerii* show that although the scribe of Bodley 851 had access to "a very good archetype," there is "little reason to repose great trust" in this particular manuscript—it is a text that "has been subjected to the deterioration usual in textual transmission."[54] Indeed, the editors of the *Dissuasio Valerii* base their own text on another manuscript, judging the one in the *De nugis curialium* to be too corrupt. The *De nugis curialium* did have an audience who carefully, even invasively, read through Walter's work. This readership, however small, has had an outsized impact on Walter's reception. Their remnants, in the form of chapter titles and internalized glosses, are indications that Walter's medieval audience was trying to make sense of what was before them. We are now faced with the same task.

Some Conclusions: A Contrived Book

And so we arrive back where we began—with an imperfect text—only now it is clear that many of its imperfections are not Walter's. And the imperfections that remain show Walter to have been a diligent reviser whose work of revision remains incomplete. But what is this text we call *De nugis curialium*? The conclusions that follow here are based on the novel premise that Walter is a reasonably competent author. I have worked to show that the blame for the confused state of the *De nugis curialium* rests on two historical accidents. The first is that the extant text is plainly an unfinished work in the process of revision. The second is that the paratextual material found in the *De nugis curialium*, its chapter titles and numbers, are not authorial. Perhaps some fault can be laid at Walter's feet for the first: he may well have grown tired of the *De nugis curialium* and abandoned it. This scenario would indeed reflect poorly on Walter, but it is just as plausible that Walter died before he could finish his revision or that the completed work itself has not survived. Nonetheless, most of the evidence supporting a mercurial Walter does not withstand scrutiny.

On the contrary, plenty of evidence can be mustered to show that Walter could be a careful and conscientious writer. Certainly his revisions demonstrate that he labored over small details and that he attended to larger thematic concerns with prudence. The runaway success of the *Dissuasio Valerii*, which bristles with classical learning, should put any doubts to permanent rest about Walter's ability to plan and execute a literary work. *Distinctio* 3 also shows that Walter could write sustained, thematically unified pieces. As discussed in Chapter 1, this *distinctio* contains four polished romances, all of which concern loyalty and some form of a love triangle. With a clear introduction and a tidy ending, *distinctio* 3 again gives the impression of an accomplished and poised writer; as a stand-alone work, it is complete. Similar examples of consistent mini-works are found throughout the *De nugis curialium*. From its thoroughly revised introduction, *distinctio* 1 progresses logically and cleanly until chapter 25, which contains Walter's sustained anti-monastic satire. However, this satire, though it seems tacked on to *distinctio* 1, is itself internally consistent, refined, and ready for wider dissemination. Other sections of the *De nugis curialium* display similar unity. That these smaller pieces have been stitched together in Bodley 851 does not negate their own internal coherence, any more than the unfinished nature of *The Canterbury Tales* detracts from the charm and effect of individual tales or groups of tales. Given the presence of these smaller coherent movements and the fact that the text remains in the process of being revised, we can now return to Rigg's important exhortation: "We should be looking for Map's *plan*."[55]

Hinton thought the *De nugis curialium* to be a series of twenty or more disjointed fragments assembled together. Largely following James, Brooke and Mynors argue, with some hesitation, that the *De nugis curialium* is a once nearly finished book that has been broken apart and subjected to Walter's incessant meddling.[56] A courtly collage or the legacy of an untidy mind? Both of these theories, as Rigg has shown, too heavily emphasize the chronological order of composition, and neither addresses the presence of earlier draft material. To my mind, all the evidence suggests two plausible scenarios. In the first, the *De nugis curialium* as we have it represents a book that is, perhaps at best, half complete; what remains is Walter's work in progress toward a unified book that contains some of his best pieces of writing, the *Dissuasio Valerii* and the anti-monastic satire of *distinctio* 1, for example. The second scenario is more radical, but the one I favor: the *De nugis curialium* is a collection of

Walter's papers containing a few complete texts, earlier draft material, and some work in progress. It was never intended to be a complete book. This false impression has been created by later scribal interference.

Although Rigg suspects that Walter is attempting to make a single book, little in the work supports such overall unity. Along with the other chapter headings, the title for the entire work, "In libro Magistri Gauteri Mahap de nugis curialium distinctio prima" (The first distinction in the book of Master Walter Map, the Courtiers' Trifles), cannot be trusted. As discussed above, the presence of the form *Mahap* instead of *Map* strongly suggests the title is not authorial. Moreover, nowhere in the work is a title announced, nor does Walter ever use the word *nugae* in his text. That the title is not authorial explains why the perceived connection between Walter's *De nugis curialium* and the subtitle of John of Salisbury's *Policraticus, sive de nugis curialium et de vestigiis philosophorum* has always seemed somewhat slight.[57] The two works have little in common, though Walter's voracious appetite for modern stories has been described as a "pleasant antidote" to John's unrelenting conservatism.[58] It is perhaps likely that Walter occasionally has John's work in mind as he writes, but on the whole Walter's work does not systematically critique or parody the *Policraticus*, and thus, given the unreliableness of the chapter headings, it seems that the traditional title is not to be trusted. Rightly suspicious of the received title, Lewis Thorpe even proposed that contemporary evidence suggests that Walter was known for a work called something like *De facetis curialibus* (Concerning witty courtiers).[59] While his argument has more merit than blindly trusting the manuscript's headings, it is still impossible to tell if this title refers to the work in Bodley 851, either partly or wholly, or to some other lost work of Walter's.

More telling are the radically different narrators throughout the work. The first fifteen chapters of *distinctio* 1 present a harried Walter being forced to write at the hectic court at the urging of an unknown Geoffrey—the only time this addressee is named.[60] The overt concern with the court and the impossibility of literary pursuits in such disquiet only again appears in that section of *distinctio* 5 that, as has been demonstrated, is the earlier draft material of *distinctio* 1. The narrator of *distinctio* 2, however, shows an interest in collecting miracles and wonders. And the narrator of *distinctio* 3, though seemingly reluctant in typical *captatio benevolentiae* fashion, writes to soothe and nourish his addressee, who seems to be a secular cleric with a professional interest in law—there is no evidence that this is the same Geoffrey that is referenced in *distinctio* 1.[61] Moreover, the narrator who begins *distinctio* 4 dwells on moral instruction. And the narrator of *distinctio* 5 takes up the *moderni* and *antiqui* trope so common in the twelfth century. Few passages suggest a consistent narrative voice throughout the *De nugis curialium* as a whole. One of the few that do, however, is found in *distinctio* 4, where the narrator seems to echo concerns addressed in *distinctio* 1. Recently freed from the constraints of court, the narrator in *distinctio* 4 rejoices in his newfound *quies* (peace)— exactly what the narrator in *distinctio* 1 so desperately desires. (Ironically, though, this *quies* does not have the expected results.) However, the lack of progression—these narrative passages do not seem to tell the story of Walter's gradual retreat from court—and the chronological incoherence—Henry is dead in *distinctio* 4, alive in *distinctio* 1—make reading these two narrative voices as one difficult. Of course, this could all be due to the book's incomplete nature. It should also be said that many of the narrative voices in the *De nugis curialium* do have some similarities: they are witty, concerned with current events, and enjoy placing responsibility for drawing meaning out of their tales onto their readers. These similarities may point to the concerns of a larger, unified book. But they could just as easily be perennial interests of Walter himself.

Indeed, at no point in the *De nugis curialium* is there a clear reference to another part of the work. All explicit internal references are confined to their individual *distinctiones*: nothing in *distinctio* 1, for instance, refers to any of the other *distinctiones*. Nothing explicitly links these five *distinctiones* together. The only instance in which a *distinctio* explicitly references another is the very suspicious passage in *distinctio* 2, where the phrase "de quo superius" allegedly refers to a story of *distinctio* 4.[62] Not only is this reference incorrect, but as suggested above it may well be an internalized annotation. Without this phrase, which is untrustworthy in one way or another, no clear evidence shows that any *distinctio* is in conversation with another. Certainly, thematic similarities appear, but, as with similarities in narrative voice, these can be explained as general interests of Walter, and not evidence for a coherent project.

Furthermore, each *distinctio* represents a different genre. Although Walter is often described as a satirist, only *distinctio* 1 contains truly satirical writing, with the obvious exception of the draft material of the same section found in *distinctio* 5. *Distinctio* 2 is a different genre altogether. It largely contains the deeds of prodigious men, both sacred and secular. *Distinctio* 3, in turn, contains four refined romances. *Distinctio* 4 begins with the *Dissuasio Valerii*, itself the example par excellence of the school exercise of the same name. The rest of *distinctio* 4 contains more folktales and a good deal of supernatural stories. Were it not for the *Dissuasio*, *distinctiones* 2 and 4 would be quite similar. In addition to draft material, *distinctio* 5 contains a recent history of England, though, perhaps, *pseudohistory* is a better term. If Walter was making a single book, it was bound to be an eclectic one, so eclectic that one would be hard put to find another twelfth-century work that contains such disparity in tone, theme, and genre.

At some level, it is impossible to prove that the *De nugis curialium* was never intended to be a single work. Any evidence of disunity can be dismissed by claiming that Walter has not yet proceeded very far in his revisions. Nonetheless, if Walter was writing a single book, he still has much work to do. At any rate, even if the *De nugis curialium* was meant to be a unified work, Walter is constructing this intended book out of earlier projects, as the inclusion of the previously circulated *Dissuasio Valerii* and the revised version of the satire on the court verify. It is worthwhile, therefore, to consider the *De nugis curialium* as a collection of small pamphlets or tracts, some of which are complete and some of which are only half finished.[63] A new translation of the *De nugis curialium* might better be titled "On Courtiers' Trifles: The Works of Walter Map."

Distinctio 1, though incomplete, contains the highly polished revision of the satire on court that moves smoothly into criticizing contemporary monasticism. These smooth transitions come to a halt at chapter 25, Walter's well-known anti-monastic satire. This chapter definitely can stand alone as a cogent pamphlet. Indeed, Walter refers to it as a *libellus* in its own right.[64] This *libellus* seems to have been attached to the material in *distinctio* 1 because it too critiques the monastic orders. Either Walter planned to revise this pamphlet to fit neatly into *distinctio* 1, or a compiler has placed it there because of the similar subject matter. The lack of transition between chapters 24 and 25, along with the fact that the Order of Grandmont and the Carthusians are addressed twice, once in chapter 25 and once outside, gives away the unfinished nature of this *distinctio*. It should, however, be noted that the last chapter of *distinctio* 1 is not as out of place as some have thought.[65] Not only does it end with the same biblical reference as the tale that comes before it, but its story of three pious hermits serves as a clear exemplum for monastic behavior: the saintly Englishman who lives completely within the ambit of a seven-foot chain displays the literal restraint that the dissolute monks lack.

The coherence of *distinctio* 2, which deals with prodigious men and their miracles and wonders, though it is incomplete, is easily seen. And the finished state of *distinctio* 3, which contains four polished romances, has been mentioned above. On the other hand, *distinctio* 4, which contains the *Dissuasio Valerii*, presents challenges. Here, the rubricated chapter heading misleads us. The titles for the intrusive prologue and the nonsensically placed epilogue do not reflect the text at all. Little evidence suggests that either chapter is meant for "the whole work," as Brooke and Mynors claim.[66] Rather, I would suggest they act as new introductory material only for Walter's famous anti-matrimonial work, the *Dissuasio Valerii*. The prologue begins by extolling the moral virtues of instruction. Then, Walter praises an anonymous young man who remains ever attentive toward his elders' counsel. An eager learner, he now serves at the illustrious court of Philip of Alsace. Against this unknown man's exemplary behavior, Walter places one of the twelfth century's most famous examples of juvenile disobedience—the rebellion of the Young King Henry against his father, Henry II. Like a modern-day Absalom, the Young King charms and battles his way to popular acclaim. Sowing division and treachery wherever he goes, he does not follow his father's peaceful example. Even in death he remains impertinent: Walter gives his last words as "If I die, I will be peaceful; if not, I will fight."[67] Thus, the section titled "Prologus" comes to an end having provided both positive and negative exempla of the virtue of obedience and attentiveness to one's elders. There is little here to support the claim that this chapter was meant as a prologue for the whole work: every *distinctio* in the *De nugis curialium* begins with an introductory passage, and nothing sets the one in *distinctio* 4 apart as meant for the whole work. On the contrary, this chapter seems especially suited for the content that follows.

But the next chapter is titled, puzzlingly, "Epilogus" (Epilogue). Even Hinton, who first proposed the idea that the chapter headings are not Walter's, grants that this perplexing chapter title must have come from Walter: "what scribe," he asks, "would have been mad enough to designate 'Epilogus' a chapter in the very heart of the work?"[68] Furthermore, Hinton suggests that this "Epilogus" is in fact two separate sections placed together by a compiler. He terms them chapters "iia" and "iib."[69] He proposes the break because material before the *Dissuasio* seems to have been written in 1191, but after the *Dissuasio* ends, Walter seems to be writing in 1187.[70] And because Hinton places too much emphasis on chronological order, he assumes that there must be a clearly identifiable seam somewhere, and that Walter never intended to place these two sections together. Obviously, the break does not occur in the middle of the *Dissuasio*, since its integrity can be confirmed from its external survival, and he therefore chooses a sentence in the middle of chapter 2 as his seam: "incidencia, uero si notare fas est, incidit" (But if it is right to take note of such things—a chance event happened").[71] However, besides Hinton's mistaken belief that we must follow chronology as the key to composition, there is little here to warrant a break. Not only does the *uero* imply some connection with the preceding text, but Walter does on occasion make bald or sudden transitions.[72] Freed from the necessity of chopping up the text of the *De nugis curialium* into small, chronologically consistent fragments, there is little reason to propose a break here. If one ignores the incorrect heading, both chapters smoothly introduce the *Dissuasio Valerii*. Chapter 1, with its exempla explaining the importance of listening to the advice of one's elders, introduces the basic rhetorical gambit of the *Dissuasio*—a series of exempla to persuade Valerius not to marry. Chapter 2 introduces our narrator and contains the general circumstances of his writing and an address to the book's readers. What follows can only be called an anti-invocation of the Muses. The unruliness of the modern world means that standards have been lowered so much that Walter no longer fears to begin writing. Anticipating the use of classical exempla in the *Dissuasio*, famous figures from antiquity bring this last point home: the modern ages, for example, produce many who are more monstrous than Nero and Catiline. This invocation of the *antiqui* and *moderni* topos also looks forward to the revised conclusion of the *Dissuasio*, in which Walter admits that he has circulated the book under a classical pseudonym because nobody appreciates the work of a contemporary. After this newly written introduction, the *Dissuasio* begins in earnest. Only a rubricated chapter heading, which we have little reason to trust, occludes the integrity of these first chapters of *distinctio* 4.

Nonetheless, Hinton's question still remains: what scribe would be mad enough to write "Epilogus" in the margin of this section at the beginning of *distinctio* 4? It seems to me that our annotator, coming upon the *Dissuasio Valerii*, recognized that its style and form differed greatly from what he had read before, so much so that he assumed he was reading a different work altogether. Thus he assumed that the passage beginning "Hunc in curia regis" marked the end of the *De nugis curialium*, and so he dutifully wrote "Epilogus" in the margin. The mistaken note was not corrected and, like other marginal annotations, it later became the title for this chapter.

After the *Dissuasio* comes to an end, the work transitions in a seamless manner to the tale of Eudo. Thus, although he still has to reconcile some dates, Walter has finished the new packaging for his old work, the *Dissuasio*

Valerii. The continuity of this book progresses at least to chapter 13, "Nicholas Pipe, the Man of the Sea," and probably further. Moreover, *distinctio* 4 contains earlier versions of stories found in *distinctiones* 1 and 2. These revisions help us establish the relative chronology of these books. Walter has most recently worked on *distinctiones* 1 and 2. But a careful reading of *distinctio* 4 shows that the stories contained therein, even if they are earlier, fit their surrounding context and are complete in situ. Thus, *distinctio* 4 is not a collection of "raw" material set aside until needed, but a collection of stories designed to stand on their own in dialogue with their surrounds. What exactly Walter was aiming for in *distinctio* 4 is unclear, but it seems to be a collection of short tales united by their exemplariness.

Distinctio 5 is no great mystery: its introduction addresses the imbalance between the *moderni* and *antiqui*—a matter that Walter redresses by giving a rather whimsical and occasionally personal history of recent English kings. It should be noted that unlike *distinctio* 4 or *distinctio* 1, Walter defends the *moderni* against the *antiqui* in *distinctio* 5. "The exceptional deeds of modern heroes lie still," he complains, "and the fringes of an abject antiquity are raised up."[73] (This sharp difference in tone again points to the independence of the five *distinctiones*.) After introducing the mysterious king Appollonides, Walter describes how the fall of Jerusalem in 1187 was presaged by the crusaders' earlier victory in 1099 and the Norman conquest of England. Following Hinton, many have thought this passage at the beginning of chapter 3 is an interpolation.[74] Although it may well date from a later period in Walter's life, the invocation of the fall of Jerusalem does make sense as an introduction to recent events, especially since he explicitly links it with these two significant victories. Walter thus begins his history, such as it is, in the Anglo-Saxon past and works his way chronologically up to the present day. The only anomaly in *distinctio* 5 is its last chapter, which is titled "A Recapitulation of the Beginning of This Book, Differing in Expression but Not Substance."[75] As discussed in detail above, this section is merely the first draft of the first part of *distinctio* 1. As Rigg suggests, its position here is probably due to "its placement at the bottom of the pile as a now outdated draft."[76]

All of the *distinctiones* contain coherent stretches of passages. And even where a lack of transition exists, such as the anti-monastic satire in *distinctio* 1, the subject matter still remains relevant to its surroundings. I would suggest then, that unlike the chapter headings, these five *distinctiones* may actually reflect Walter's intentions. Perhaps they were originally separate stacks of unbound quires, collections of smaller works *in quaternis*. Whatever the case, my preferred explanation for the textual state of the *De nugis curialium* is that it reflects five separate works, and that only *distinctio* 3 seems truly finished. The rest of the material is in various states of completion, and the presence of revised passages shows that Walter was reworking earlier stories and using them in different ways in different works. These smaller works *in quaternis* were then gathered together, probably after Walter's death, and saved.[77] An earlier draft of the comparison of the court with hell, clearly detritus from Walter's process of revision, was included as well. The whole lot was then bound together, saving the collected works of Walter Map for the future. The practice of collecting an author's unfinished works was not unheard of in the Middle Ages: Alexander Hales and Thomas Aquinas both had incomplete works collected and edited after their deaths, and Jean Gerson's unfinished *Tractatus super Canta Canticorum* still found its way into circulation.[78] Somebody thought Walter's pile of works in progress was worth saving. The subsequent "book" received numerous marginal annotations and interlinear glosses. While the glosses became interpolated into the main text, many of the marginal annotations, which were originally a reader's notes on the contents of the work, were eventually turned into chapter headings and numbered in an attempt to make sense of the text. In effect, there was a collective effort to force a book out of disparate materials. Some form of this "book" was the exemplar that the scribe of Bodley 851 dutifully copied.

The textual history of the Roman poet Propertius provides an illustrative parallel to Walter Map's *De nugis curialium*.[79] Propertius, like Walter Map, has a critical reputation as a proto-modern: "he is regularly described as a difficult, idiosyncratic, and uniquely modern poet."[80] Moreover, the two seemingly share a stylistic preference for "abruptness, obscurity, lack of logic or even of clear meaning."[81] But this view of Propertius results from the same circular logic as found in evaluations of Walter: critics claim that Walter and Propertius are difficult and jarring authors because their manuscripts are difficult and jarring. In both cases, the modern evaluation is at odds with the contemporary judgments of the past: neither is described as difficult by his peers. Moreover, the manuscripts of Propertius are all derived from one single archetype, which has long been recognized to be highly corrupt; we can occasionally confirm the extent of the corruption thanks to ancient graffiti. Bodley 851 is likewise quite corrupt. I have, I hope, shown ample evidence for the presence of interpolated glosses. Nonetheless, for both authors scribal corruption has been mistaken for authorial intention. In the case of Propertius, "the casual scribal errors that created his 'incoherencies' have been accorded the exalted status of his most distinctive and admirable stylistic traits."[82] Thanks to two centuries of scribal interference, Walter Map has suffered the same fate. It is not without some irony that many of Walter's critical champions, those who praise him for his pioneering "metacritical" approach, have generally lauded aspects of his work that stem from the transmission of his manuscript rather than Walter himself.[83] The uncooperative nature of the *De nugis curialium*—its incompleteness, its disjointed sections, its eclecticism, and its invitation to readers to make order where there may be none—mainly results from the convoluted textual history of the work. Like Propertius, Walter only becomes truly postmodern when scribal interference is ignored. In place of a full-blown postmodern Walter, we now have a Walter whose barbed wit still stings, whose approach to writing still innovates, and whose anecdotes still entertain—but who now can be thought of as a meticulous reviser and a sober thinker.

Chapter 4

From Herlething to Herla

Although the confusing textual state of the *De nugis curialium* has certainly hindered our understanding of Walter Map's work, this same confusion has preserved a process that has profound importance for understanding how and why twelfth-century authors used the ancient British past to create one of the Middle Age's most enduring contributions to world literature—the Matter of Britain. Bodley 851's preservation of revised and unrevised versions of the same tale means that we can catch Walter in the act of writing a story set in the legendary world of British antiquity. Amid all the learned guesswork of how literary material from the Celtic West made its way into the wider European world, here we have an actual example of how one author created a piece of the Matter of Britain. This remarkable fact has long been obscured by the textual difficulties of the *De nugis curialium*. An analysis of Walter's process of composition casts just enough light on other narratives to suggest that medieval authors regularly created ersatz Celtic tales. Using Walter Map's tale of the wild hunt of King Herlething as a model, this chapter argues that the Matter of Britain owes a greater debt to the fertile minds of secular clerics and romancers than to the multilingual mouths of itinerant Welsh or Breton minstrels. Walter may not have been involved with the *Lancelot-Grail Cycle*, but he certainly had the literary tools necessary to create a work set in ancient Britain.

Understanding the composition of Walter Map's tale of King Herla reveals that the world of ancient Britain has a habit of appearing suddenly in medieval literature, sometimes where it had not been before. When it has been possible to glean some knowledge of how literature set in ancient Britain was composed—a possibility that is often lost given the vagaries of textual transmission—it becomes apparent that authors could bring preexisting narratives into the Matter of Britain with relative ease and with decided purpose.

Scholars have occasionally suspected that medieval authors purposely crafted tales to take on what we might call a Celtic appearance. As early as 1905, Lucien Foulet, arguing that the so-called anonymous lais plagiarized and poorly imitated Marie de France, suggested that any Celtic tradition in the anonymous lais occurs only because they were modeled on Marie's *Lais*.[1] That is, he claims that later authors produced tales that looked genuinely Celtic, but were actually modeled on Marie's own work. Foulet had no strong evidence in his favor, since the poor survival of medieval Breton literature makes it impossible to know for sure. This lack is why the testimony of the *De nugis curialium* is so important. As I will show, Walter's tale of Herla offers convincing evidence that medieval authors did drastically remodel their sources in an attempt to integrate them into the Matter of Britain, with one effect being that they appear Celtic to modern readers. Since no felicitous term for this process has been proposed, I will suggest an infelicitous one—"Britonicization," a term that in spite of its clunkiness gets to the heart of what medieval authors were doing: setting tales in the ancient British past.[2] A cursory overview of several texts suggests that Britonicization was relatively widespread.

Chrétien de Troyes, who probably had access to some genuine Celtic traditions, although at some remove, nonetheless adopted the same strategy as Walter Map when he wrote *Cligès*.[3] In this romance, Arthur's court figures as a destination for the aspiring Byzantine knight Alexander and his son Cligès. Although the Arthurian and British material provides the setting and continuity with Chrétien's other romances, the bulk of the narrative has little to do with them. Tellingly, *Cligès* is the only romance of Chrétien's "not to make use of Celtic mythical material."[4] While the exact origins of its plot are uncertain, its indebtedness to *Le Roman d'Enéas* and contemporary politics is clear.[5] Nonetheless, in reworking his sources Chrétien furnishes his protagonist with a Welsh name, and he incorporates Byzantine nobility into an Arthurian milieu, effectively making *Cligès* part of the Matter of Britain.[6] If the master of Arthurian romance saw fit to incorporate a preexisting narrative into the Matter of Britain, then surely others could too.

A less well-known example is Benedict of Gloucester's *Vita Dubricii*.[7] Writing at Gloucester in the mid-twelfth century, Benedict rewrote the Latin life of St. Dyfrig in order to place him more securely in the Arthurian world of ancient Britain. Dyfrig himself appears in Geoffrey of Monmouth's *History of the Kings of Britain*, although in a very different capacity than the earlier vita. Benedict combined these two sources in order help support Gloucester's own interests, and those of the diocese of Llandaf, where one of the abbey's own had recently become bishop. Benedict's vita benefited Gloucester on both of these fronts. However, the sudden vogue for the Matter of Britain must have also driven Benedict to offer a corrective to the portrait of Dyfrig found in Geoffrey of Monmouth's *History of the Kings of Britain*. The result is a harmonization of sorts. In Benedict's vita, Dyfrig becomes King Arthur's main spiritual support and is explicitly said to be responsible for Arthur's good fortune. The *Vita Dubricii* also reinforces the fact that the Matter of Britain is largely an Anglo-Norman invention and not a Welsh one, since Benedict still felt the need to incorporate Dyfrig into the ancient past imagined by Geoffrey, despite the fact that Dyfrig, for all Benedict knew, was himself a genuine character from the ancient British past. For Benedict and others, Geoffrey's *History* became the controlling text for the Matter of Britain.

The Middle English lay of *Sir Orfeo* also shows signs of Britonicization. Loosely based on the myth of Orpheus and Eurydice, *Sir Orfeo* departs drastically from classical versions of the tale, which was well known in the Middle Ages.[8] Lauded by critics, the Middle English lay almost certainly derives from an earlier version in French.[9] In it, the classical tradition was fused with "elements from a Celtic story of a very popular type."[10] The exact nature of the relationship between *Sir Orfeo* and its Celtic analogues remains subject to debate, but it is clear that the classical tale has been successfully made into what we now call a Breton lay. Moreover, manuscript evidence shows that this process was ongoing in the Middle Ages. The Auchinleck copy of *Sir Orfeo* specifically sets the story's action in Britain, instead of Thrace. At some point an inventive scribe must have felt that Thrace was an inappropriate setting for a Breton lay, so he invented an etymology that placed the action in Winchester, a town that does indeed figure in Arthurian legend.[11] His interpolation reads, "For Winchester was cleped þo / Traciens, wiþ-outen no."[12] This sleight of hand creates the "proper" setting for a tale that seems like it belongs to the Matter of Britain.

Chaucer's *Franklin's Tale* is probably the most conspicuous example of Britonicization. Set in ancient Brittany, this Breton lay seemingly has no Breton sources. Instead, Chaucer found his inspiration in one of his favorite authors, Boccaccio.[13] But in translating his sources to the ancient British past, he takes pains to get his setting correct. He chooses appropriate names for his protagonists, and his place-names reflect Breton geography (though perhaps a little inaccurately).[14] Indeed, he may have done so to comment on contemporary political affairs.[15] Whatever the case may be, Chaucer was not the first to transplant a story into the Matter of Britain.

Finally, the Welsh themselves could not resist the popular pull of the Matter of Britain. Not only was Geoffrey of Monmouth's work, including his fabrications, accepted as part of their own tradition, but the Welsh also inserted new tales into Geoffrey's version of the ancient past. *Cyfranc Lludd a Llefelys*, a story about two brothers who fight three oppressions over Britain, draws on native tradition and Geoffrey's own work.[16] The core of the tale seems to have preceded Geoffrey's work, but its present form results from a scribe fitting it snugly into a Welsh translation of Geoffrey's text. It occurs as an interpolated episode in some Welsh translations of Geoffrey's *History*, where it expands on the sons of Beli Fawr (Geoffrey's Heli). The interpolator has even made sure that the language of *Cyfranc Lludd a Llefelys* matches the peculiar Welsh that appears in translations from Latin.[17] The resulting tale is thus a literal insertion into the Matter of Britain.

Walter's tale of King Herla is yet another instance of placing a preexisting tale into the Matter of Britain. Although this tale is not the only time Walter uses the ancient British past as a setting, the evidence from the tale of King Herla is more extensive and more nuanced than in any other surviving medieval text.[18] Walter's tale also helps uncover another aspect to this understudied literary phenomenon. It shows that authors used the Matter of Britain to accomplish interesting literary work. Far from being a fad, the idea of ancient Britain could play an active, important role in carrying the intellectual import of medieval literature. In Walter's case, ancient Britain helps create brilliant literary satire—but that is only one of its possible uses.

A Supposedly Welsh Wild Hunt

Wales, or at least its Marches, loomed large in Walter Map's imagination. As discussed in Chapter 1, Walter comments upon the religious devotion of the Welsh, their hospitality, and their rage, and he recounts the deeds of Welsh princes, saints, thieves, and even supernatural beings. Accordingly, Walter Map is widely viewed as a skilled purveyor of Welsh anecdotes and even as an amateur, if somewhat misguided, ethnographer. Critics, especially earlier critics, have searched his work for reflexes of Celtic myth and folklore, often with the preconception that though the skin of Walter's writing may be courtly, its marrow remains deeply Welsh. Walter's "Welsh tales"—those stories that pertain to Wales or the Welsh—are often casually said to originate "from his Welsh homeland."[19] While many of these Welsh tales undoubtedly have their origins in the borderlands and betray a real and personal knowledge of Welsh mores and people, this chapter demonstrates that one of Walter's most celebrated "Welsh" tales, his account of King Herla, does not in fact derive from Welsh or Celtic folklore but is a continental tale outfitted in Celtic garb.

A summary of the tale of King Herla demonstrates just how many seemingly Celtic motifs it includes. The otherworldly visitor is no bigger than a monkey, has a fiery red face, a huge head, a long red beard, and legs that end in goat's feet. After informing Herla that he is the ruler of many kings and princes, the visitor states that he has admired Herla's fame and has come to honor him with his presence at Herla's wedding. The two then make a pact: after the dwarf king attends Herla's wedding, Herla must in turn attend his. At Herla's wedding, the dwarf king brings so many expensive supplies and servants that none of Herla's own preparations are touched and his servants rest leisurely. A year passes, and the dwarf king suddenly reappears to Herla, imploring him to keep their pact. Herla agrees and, after gathering his supplies and men, he follows the dwarf into a deep cave at the side of a cliff. Inside there is no sunlight—only a multitude of lamps. He travels until he reaches the opulent house of the dwarf king. After celebrating the nuptials, the king equips Herla and his men with hunting and birding supplies. Finally, the dwarf king gives Herla a small bloodhound, entreating him that none of his men should dismount before the dog does. Herla departs and emerges from the cave. He encounters a shepherd, whom he asks for information about his queen. Astonished, the shepherd replies that he can hardly understand his speech, for he is a Saxon and Herla a Briton. The shepherd then says that he has heard that queen's name in old stories. These old stories also tell of a certain King Herla who disappeared with a dwarf at this very cliff and was never seen on earth again. And that was two hundred years ago, he says. Understandably jarred, some of the company dismount, only to turn suddenly to dust. Afterward, Herla's wanderings continue "without stop or stay."[20] Only when Henry II is crowned king does the ghostly band disappear into the Wye at Hereford.

The tale of King Herla is often said to have been molded from Celtic elements. It does, after all, include several motifs that are commonly associated with Irish and Welsh literature: the visit from a fairy or dwarf; the making of a pact with this otherworldly visitor; entering the otherworld through the side of a mound or through a cave; the wealth and abundance of the otherworld; the curious way in which time operates differently there; and the taboo that the mortals must keep after they leave the otherworld. And to top it off, the action occurs in the Welsh Marches, and Herla is explicitly termed an ancient British (*Brito*)—that is, not English (*Saxo*)—king.

Scholars have long viewed the tale of Herla as Celtic, so much so that it has been employed as an analogue to prove the Celticity of other tales. Well over a century ago, George Kittredge found Herla's journey into the underworld similar to the one in *Sir Orfeo* and suggested that they both shared a Celtic source.[21] Roger Sherman Loomis, on numerous occasions, references Walter's tale of King Herla as some sort of Celtic analogue or source.[22] Vernon Harward, in his study of medieval Celtic dwarfs, considers the tale an especially valuable witness to the tradition of Welsh dwarfs, though he follows Loomis in agreeing that it "is ultimately a Breton tale which has been localized in Britain."[23] And in spite of subsequent criticism, Harward maintains "a Breton, if not a Welsh, provenance for Map's story of King Herla and the dwarf king."[24] For A. J. Bliss, the story of Herla also provides evidence for "the Celtic origin" of some episodes in *Sir Orfeo*.[25] Moreover, Marie-Thérèse Brouland finds in the story a number of Celtic elements, listing no fewer than seven specifically Celtic motifs in the tale, which, as she sees it, is a "Celtic tale mainly illustrating the problem of the flow of time."[26] Quotations like these could easily be multiplied. While Kittredge and Loomis, Harward, Bliss, and Brouland focus their attention on the Welshness or Celticity of the tale, other scholars, interested in different aspects of King Herla and the *De nugis curialium*, simply cite the tale as unproblematically Celtic and move on.

For all the attention paid to the story of King Herla, the *De nugis curialium* contains another, much shorter version of the tale, which is seldom discussed in scholarship. Last in a series of stories about phantoms and the supernatural, the shorter version tells of a troop of ghostly travelers that used to wander the countryside aimlessly. They were last seen in the first year of the reign of Henry II, in the March of Wales, where frightened but alert Welshmen attempted to attack the phantom band. The ghostly travelers, avoiding the battle, rose into the air and have not been seen since. As in the longer tale, the shorter version connects the infinite and pointless wandering of the troop with those poor saps like Walter who have to dash hither and thither as members of the peripatetic royal court. However, the shorter version lacks the fairy king, the journey to the underworld, and the encounter with the shepherd. Furthermore, there is no mention of Herla; instead the leader of the band is called "Herlething" (*Herlethingus*).[27] In other words, the shorter version lacks all those characteristics that make the longer piece seem so Celtic. Yet in this version the only element that can be called Celtic in any sense of the word is the location of the silent household's encounter with the Welshmen in the March of Wales. In comparison with the longer version's otherworldly visit, the shorter tale is a dull affair for those interested in discussing Welsh and Irish analogues.

Importantly, this shorter tale is found in *distinctio* 4 of the *De nugis curialium*, while the longer, more popular version appears in *distinctio* 1.[28] As I argued in Chapter 2, the doublets in the *De nugis curialium* result from Walter revising his work; the Herlething/Herla doublet is no exception. The story of King Herla, like the tales of Eadric the Wild and the militant monk of Cluny, has been revised from an earlier version found in *distinctio* 4. Thus, the shorter version of the tale of King Herla/Herlething is the earlier of the two, and it represents more faithfully the version of the story that Walter originally encountered. The longer version, on the other hand, has been thoroughly reworked, and its Celtic air largely results from Walter's own imagination. This is a boon for those examining the creation of the Matter of Britain, but a significant problem for those who use the tale as an authentic piece of folklore from the Welsh Marches.

Herla's spectral household has long been identified as a Welsh reflex of a widespread European folktale usually called "The Wild Hunt" or "The Ghostly Hunt," in which a band of ghostly hunters haunts the countryside, wailing and frightening the living. The leader's name is variously reported as Herlewin, Herlequin, Hellequin, or something similar. The story was in vogue during Walter's lifetime. Versions of the motif appear in the writings of Orderic Vitalis, William of Malmesbury, and Peter of Blois, the last of which refers to courtiers as "Herlequin's knights" (*milites Herlekini*).[29] The *De nugis curialium* contains a variant of this widely known tale, localized in or around Hereford, and Walter, whose purported homeland lies only some two dozen miles to the south, may have derived his vignette of Herlething from a version of the tale that he encountered there. Helaine Newstead, for example, remarks, "Walter Map may originally have heard the stories of King Herla and the Herlething in the neighborhood of Hereford, his early home, where he localizes them."[30] Indeed, folklorists claim, either tacitly or explicitly as Newstead does, that Walter collected two versions of this European folktale and recorded them both in the *De nugis curialium*.[31] In the same fashion, those scholars who rely on the tale of Herla to support their arguments about Celtic analogues or sources largely ignore the shorter tale, since it displays little if any Celtic character. The shorter version closely conforms to the standard motif, while the longer version with all its Celtic motifs differs greatly from the standard. This fact alone suggests that the longer version—the one with the much heralded and discussed King Herla—is more a creation of Walter's own than critics would like to admit. Our new understanding of the process of revision in the *De nugis curialium* makes this scenario all but certain.

Revising Herlething

Walter has so thoroughly reworked and expanded the story of King Herleth-ing that even though the stories are recognizably the same, few direct verbal echoes exist, primarily because Walter has added a great deal of material. Yet, enough remains to demonstrate that Walter had the earlier version directly before him as he wrote. The clearest example is "Ab illa die nusquam uisa est illa milicia, tanquam nobis insipientibus illi suos tradiderint errores" (From that day, the army has never been seen, as if they have passed down their wan-derings to us fools), which remains relatively intact as "Quieuit autem ab illa hora fantasitucs ille circuitus, tanquam nobis suos tradiderint errores, ad qui-etem sibi" (But from that time, that phantom circuit has been at peace, as if they have passed down their wanderings to us for their own peace).[32] The phrase beginning with *tanquam* is the crux of the both stories, as it makes explicit the comparison between the ghostly band and Henry's wandering court, a comparison that is elsewhere only implied. Walter has left this key phrase largely untouched. It is worthwhile to note that in both versions the syntax of this passage is almost identical, making it extremely unlikely that these two tales are two distinct versions of an oral folktale that Walter has recorded.

Other verbal similarities are likewise telling. In both versions the phan-tom band is called an *exercitus* (army); their travels, *errores* (wanderings); and their route, a *circuitus* (circuit). Moreover, in the early version, Herlething's troop travels "with carts and sumpter horses, pack-saddles and panniers, hawks and hounds, and a concourse of men and women."[33] This description is largely in accord with the other European occurrences of this myth—the troop is always equipped, usually for hunting, but sometimes for what appears to be a long journey. Walter not only keeps this detail, but provides an expla-nation for it as well, writing that the reason Herla's crew travels about so ap-pareled is because the dwarf king, in typical supernatural splendor, lavishly showered gifts upon him: "Herla departs laden with tributes and gifts of horses, dogs, hawks, and everything that seems the finest for hunting or fowling."[34] The setting, too, remains the March of Wales in the first year of Henry II's reign. Even without all the evidence for Walter's revisionary practice, all of these similarities and direct verbal echoes in such a small section of text would suggest that Walter has revised this passage.

But Walter has also made a small change in the portion of the story that otherwise remains intact. In accord with the common European folktale, in *distinctio* 4 Herlething's band is peopled by those who have died. This statement is omitted in the revised version, since Walter has just provided a detailed explanation of who Herla and his followers are and how they came to their fate. Herla and his band are not exactly dead but rather the unfortunate subjects of otherworldly temporal manipulation.

What on first glance appears to be another significant change to the core of the story results largely from mistranslation. In the earlier version, Welshmen in the March of Wales appear and harass the ghostly troop until it rises up into the air.

> Qui tunc primi uiderunt tibiis et clamoribus totam in eos uiciniam concitauerunt, et ut illius est mos uigilantissime gentis statim omnibus armis instructa multa manus aduenit, et quia uerbum ab eis extorquere non potuerunt uerbis, telis adigere responsa parabant. Illi autem eleuati sursum in aera subito disparuerunt.[35]

> (And those who first saw them roused the entire neighborhood against them by playing pipes and shouting, and as is the habit of that most vigilant people [i.e., the Welsh], a large band arrived at once equipped with every type of weapon, and since they could not wrench a word out of them with talk, they prepared to force a response with their spears. But they rose up into the air and immediately vanished.)

In the later version, this episode is condensed: "Tunc autem uisus fuit a multis Wallensibus immergi iuxta Waiam Herefordie flumen." All translations follow M. R. James, who writes, "In that year it was seen by many Welshmen to plunge into the Wye, the river of Hereford."[36] This would seem to be a significant difference—the Welsh do not take up arms, and the ghostly band disappears into the Wye rather than dissipating in the air above. However, the Welsh may be more active than previous translations suggest. As the editors point out, *iuxta Waiam* is an odd phrase in this context: surely Herla and his

men sink *into the Wye* and not *next to it*. However, there is an alternative reading that requires little textual finessing: taking *immergi* as the passive of "to
drown," rather than "to dip or to plunge," the sentence reads, "For at that
time he was seen being drowned by many Welshmen next to the river Wye in
Hereford."[37] Given that in the earlier version the Welshmen take up arms
against Herlething, it is not so far-fetched to think that Walter has them actually drowning Herla in the revision. Indeed, as I suggest below, this small
change has some important ramifications for the tale's view of the Welsh.

As is typical of Walter, the two tales both fit their immediate contexts
well. The earlier version of Herlething's ghostly troop falls at the end of a
string of tales describing supernatural events. Starting with the eighth chapter
of *distinctio* 4, one reads of a dead woman whose husband finds her in a fairy
band; of a man who takes a fairy as his lover; of a man who has captured a
fairy lover; of Gerbert who makes a pact with the devil; of the haunted shoe-
maker of Constantinople; of Nicholas Pipe who can live underwater; of a herd
of aerial goats in Le Mans; and finally of nocturnal bands of silent soldiers in
Brittany. Walter next introduces the story of Herlething and his followers as
another version of this preceding tale. The only real difference between this
tale in *distinctio* 4 and its European analogues is that it occurs "in the March
of Wales and Hereford in the first year of the reign of Henry II."[38] Local color
aside, the tale broadly conforms to the widely known ghostly troop legend.
The idea of aimless, joyless, and continuous wandering, however, piques Walter's attention, and he cannot resist a satirical comparison with the court of
Henry II. He ends the brief tale of Herlething with a snide remark: "From
that day that troop has nowhere been seen; they seem to have handed over
their wanderings to us poor fools."[39] After complaining about the harsh life of
the court, Walter then discusses a certain Salius who has avoided these same
errors. In *distinctio* 4, the story of Herlething pivots the plot from supernatural phenomena to a discussion of good kingship.

Walter seems to have thought the comparison of his frenzied court life
with the nocturnal flights of the ghostly hunt particularly apt and witty because he returned to it when he set out writing his satire of the court now
found in *distinctio* 1. In its new context, the tale serves as a climax to his dra-
matic, rancorous satire, in which he rages against the instability and unrest of
the court, compares it to hell, and discusses his own frantic household. The
story of Herlething complements this extended critique of the court and its
inquietude: not only does it reinforce the idea that courtiers are doomed to
endless wandering, but it also continues the eerie tone that dominates much

of the preceding matter. A ghostly band is good company for the inhabitants of hell, and with its sharp critique of Henry's wandering court, it is an excellent "cap to the foregoing dissertation."[40]

As mentioned above, Walter's contemporaries had already hit upon the joke of comparing the ceaseless travels of courtiers with the ghostly hunt. But in *distinctio* 1, Walter tells the joke better than any of them. Indeed, he elevates what seems to have been a courtier's wisecrack into a refined piece of literature. Walter has radically transformed the tale of Herlething to create a rhetorically unified story with a specific aim. One of the results of this radical transformation is that the revised tale appears to be a genuine piece of Celtic folklore or literature, though, as I hope to show, this is not Walter's immediate intention. In general, two major principles guide Walter's revision: First, in order to heighten the comparison between the ghostly hunt and Henry II's court, Walter creates a backstory for Herlething, in which he presides over a court strikingly similar to Henry II's. This backdrop allows for several pointed critiques of Henry's court. Second, Walter takes care to make the tale of King Herla fit into the Matter of Britain by invoking several of the most popular motifs of this newly popularized literary form. In doing so, Walter was so successful that, were it not his own earlier version, the tale of King Herla could easily pass for the genuine article.

Satirizing the Court

As many critics have remarked, the tale of King Herla satirizes Henry II's famous but, for Walter at least, too frenetic court.[41] Walter makes this point explicit by claiming that Henry II's court has inherited the aimless wandering of Herla and his band—a claim that is present in the earlier version of the tale as well. The revised version, too, acts as a clever etiological myth for the constant movement of the king and his court. However, the tale of King Herla satirizes more than just this single disreputable aspect of Henry II's court. A closer examination reveals many more correspondences between Herla's world and Henry's court.

The tale of King Herla opens with a narrator who is reluctant to narrate. To have the time to write well at court would be no less a miracle than for another Shadrach, Meshach, and Abednego to sing out from a blazing furnace.[42] "Nevertheless," he continues, "stories tell of one and only one court that was similar to our own, and they say that Herla, king of the most ancient

Britons, was called upon by another king, who from his small stature seemed to be a pygmy, no taller than an ape."[43] This is an evocative sentence, which, among other things, asks that readers remain alert to the similarities between the court of Herlething—whose name has been changed to Herla (more on this change later)—and that of Henry II. The comparison continues with what seems to be commonplace royal bootlicking. The dwarf king remarks, "I am certainly unknown to you, but I rejoice in the fame that lifts you above other kings, since you are both the noblest and the nearest to me in rank and blood."[44] For this reason, Herla is invited to attend the visitor's otherworldly marriage celebrations. Moreover, the dwarf king mentions that the king of France will soon offer his daughter as Herla's wife, an aside surely intended to refer to Eleanor of Aquitaine, daughter of William X, Duke of Aquitaine, and wife of Henry II. It must be no coincidence that both Herla and Henry take a French bride. Thus, the overt comparison with the contemporary court, which once only figured as the tale's conclusion, has now become the introduction to the revised tale, although as a good storyteller Walter leaves the true significance of this comparison for the end.

Activities of the royal court, both illicit and banal, lasted well into the night, and this unnatural wakefulness drew the ire of critics. William Rufus was said to hide his more disgraceful exertions under the cover of darkness; one of the reforms that Henry I undertook was to restore the practice of using lamps at night, which his predecessor had apparently forbidden.[45] Walter's contemporary John of Hauteville wrote of the court: "Sleep is infrequent there: the day, which will be spent grieving over weariness from remaining awake through the night, torments the eye of the knight."[46] Walter, too, addresses the court's late hours. In *distinctio* 1, Walter claims that the court attracts "creatures of the night" whose "eyes love the shadows and hate the light"—the justices, sheriffs, undersheriffs, and beadles that stalk and ambush their victims throughout the night.[47] Similarly, Herlething and his band also go abroad at night—a point intended to allude to the court's sleeplessness. However, in the reworked tale of King Herla, Walter opts for a subtler point of contact between Herla and the night: the dwarf kingdom into which Herla enters has "a light which seemed to proceed not from the sun or moon, but from a multitude of lamps."[48] Nicholas Vincent has astutely noted that one point of comparison "between Henry II's court and the wild hunt of Herla was that Herla and his court had been imprisoned for an eternity in darkness lit only by a multitude of lamps, and that they had thereafter hunted and travelled by night."[49] As Vincent points out, Henry's court used a "phenomenal quantity of wax" and appeared at times to be nocturnal.[50] Including the *lampades multae* and the odd light that the dwarf's kingdom emits serves to remind readers of the court's extravagant use of candles and its penchant for nighttime revelry or business—a luxury few people would have enjoyed in the twelfth century. Perhaps Walter even expunged the mention of Herla's band being *noctiuagus* (night wandering) in order to make the correspondence between Herla's band and Henry's court more realistic: the royal court did not travel during the night.

Another clear target of the tale's satire is hunting. As might be expected of any medieval aristocrat, Henry II deeply enjoyed hunting and falconry. Unsurprisingly, "hunting recurs as a constant theme in all of the sources for Henry's reign, be it in charters, pipe rolls or chronicles."[51] But Henry's fondness for the chase also led Gerald of Wales, among others, to censure him: "He derived a great deal of pleasure from the flight of birds of prey, and he enjoyed inordinately watching that breed of dogs which hunt down wild animals by using their keen scent because he delighted in their tuneful and harmonious barking coupled with their swift movements. If only he had been as devoted to religion as he was to hunting!"[52] Walter's pseudohistory in *distinctio* 5, in which Henry's defining traits are cataloged, likewise claims that the king "was always traveling on unbearable journeys, as if he enjoyed the privileges of a messenger who can travel posthaste, and in this respect he was exceedingly merciless to the household that followed him; he was an expert in hounds and hawks and could not get enough of that vain pastime."[53] Walter's distaste for Henry's passion for hunting also appears in the tale of King Herla. In the early version, Herlething's band, in accordance with widespread tradition, travels about with "sumpter horses, pack-saddles and panniers, hawks and hounds, and a concourse of men and women," as noted above. This motley contingent was largely kept in the revised version. However, the revised version carefully omits any mention of women and pack animals in order to focus on hunting: the dwarf king has supplied Herla and his men "with tributes and gifts of horses, dogs, hawks, and everything that seems the finest for hunting or fowling."[54] In *distinctio* 1, the band is no longer the undead hauling their belongings on an endless journey; they are now a courtly delegation splendidly equipped for a hunting expedition.

Moreover, one of the most memorable elements of the story concerns a hunting dog. As Herla and his followers are preparing to leave the otherworld, the dwarf gives the king "a small bloodhound" and absolutely forbids "anyone in his retinue from ever dismounting until that dog leaps down from the person carrying him."[55] True to narrative logic, some of the king's companions dismount before the bloodhound and instantly turn to dust. Realizing what has happened, King Herla warns that a similar death awaits anyone who dismounts, and he forbids "anyone from touching the ground before the dog descended."[56] With a sense of finality, we read that "the dog has not yet alighted."[57] The dry humor of this line is superb: a potent symbol of the royal hunt, the bloodhound—not the king—dictates when Herla's court will cease its wandering. They are powerless to stop the hunt. What should be a leisurely pursuit for the royal household has become a bar against any other activity. This jab at royal hunting would certainly have been well received among critics like Gerald of Wales

Finally, another parallel between the two courts occurs when Walter twice uses the word *circuitus* to describe Herla's wandering.[58] James translates this word as "course" and "journeying," and while those meanings are certainly present, such a translation misses the subtlety of the Latin word. *Circuitus* would have special significance for any courtier, as it can be used to describe the rounds of visits that the court, or especially justices, make.[59] Walter himself had served as a justice in eyre, and he elsewhere uses *circuitus* to describe the travels that such officials undertake.[60] Thus, not only does Herla's *circuitus* stand as a metaphor for the court's general unrest, but it also directly references the physical act of the court or courtiers moving from place to place in order to assert the king's authority throughout the land. Herla becomes a ghostly justice in eyre, or even a phantom king who "ceremoniously" visits his kingdom.[61] Herlething's aimless roaming has become Herla's courtly visitations.

Walter's revision of the short tale of Herlething slyly emphasizes that Herla and Henry have much in common. Herla's marriage with the daughter of the king of the Franks recalls Henry's marriage with Eleanor; the *lampades multae* of the otherworld evoke the court's use of candles and its long nights; the gift of hunting gear and the importance attached to the bloodhound call to mind Henry's devotion to hunting; Herla's wandering is described with the same language used to describe the court's official circuits; and Herla's court is explicitly said to be similar to Henry's at the beginning of the tale. On their own, these comparisons make for a fine piece of courtly satire. But Walter's most creative invention is setting this story in the ancient British past.

Making the Matter of Britain

This chapter's introduction unproblematically states that Walter has created a faux Celtic tale. That is not quite right. To modern readers, perhaps, the tale looks decidedly Celtic, with its otherworldly adventure, strange *geis*, and little people. *Celtic*, however, is a vexed term and expresses a concept that Walter and his contemporaries would not have recognized.[62] Until the invention of modern philology, the relationship between the Goidelic (Irish, Scots Gaelic, Manx) and the Brittonic (Welsh, Cornish, Breton) languages was not known. And pan-Celtic political and cultural aspirations are likewise foreign to the Middle Ages. Thus, although modern readers may well recognize shared motifs and telling analogues in Irish and Welsh literature, medieval readers would not necessarily think the two any more closely related than otherwise expected of geographically close cultures. While the term *Celtic* can be of some use to folklorists studying similarities among various literatures, it is not particularly helpful to the literary historian who is attempting to understand how twelfth-century English, Latin, and French writers received and transformed literature that dealt with the ancient British past. Not only is it anachronistic to assume that Walter transformed the short tale of Herlething into the Celtic tale of King Herla, but it is somewhat misleading. With very few exceptions, the "Celtic" literature that came into vogue in twelfth-century England and France had little to do with Irish characters, themes, or settings.[63] In the works of Béroul, Chrétien, and Marie—to name three conspicuous examples— Ireland appears merely as a nearby, ancillary locale. When scholars discuss the "Celtic" influence in twelfth-century literature, they almost always mean Welsh, Cornish, or Breton (that is, when the aspect in question can be identified with any certainty).[64]

Instead of trying to create a Celtic tale, what Walter actually does in revising the tale of King Herla is to set it in the ancient British past, in a mythical period before the arrival of Anglo-Saxons. This change of setting is extraordinarily consequential, for understanding both Walter Map and the place of ancient Britain in twelfth-century literature. Largely popularized by Geoffrey of Monmouth's *History of the Kings of Britain*, the ancient British past loomed large in the imagination of twelfth-century authors. Much of the *History* stems from Geoffrey's own fertile brain, but it does transmit some genuine Welsh traditions concerning the unity of Britain under the Welsh, its loss at the hands of the Saxons, and its future renewal with the aid of a national savior.[65] In addition to this geographical and temporal backdrop, Geoffrey's work also supplied a cast of characters from ancient Britain, which were often—but not always—centered around King Arthur. The explosive rise in popularity of stories set in the ancient British past, in particular those connected with King Arthur and his court, need not be recounted here.[66] But by the close of the twelfth century, medieval writers had developed a name for literature concerning the ancient British past—*la matière de Bretagne* (the Matter of Britain).[67] *Matière* (Lat. *materia*) roughly translates as the "subject matter of a story," and the term is frequently used by medieval writers to denote the topic they are to undertake. Walter is no exception.[68] *Bretagne*, however, is somewhat trickier, for it can refer to both Britain and Brittany.[69] In Geoffrey's *History*, and in actual fact, the Britons and Bretons are culturally linked, and their closeness in language and culture was recognized in the medieval era, which renders this apparent ambiguity more of a modern problem than a medieval one. Like the Matter of Rome or France, the Matter of Britain did ostensibly concern contemporary peoples or places, but also ancient ones. In sum, the Matter of Britain deals with ancient British characters in ancient British places; it is not so much a specific genre, as a setting. And it is into this setting that Walter places his tale of King Herla.

Because the *De nugis curialium* contains stories that Walter returned to over time, we can see just how a twelfth-century author goes about writing a tale meant for the Matter of Britain. First of all, Walter has transformed the folk character Herlething into a specifically Welsh king. The change of name from *Herlething* to *Herla* occurs for the simple reason that *Herla* sounds much more Welsh than *Herlething*.[70] Words ending in *-ing* are uncommon in Middle Welsh.[71] But more important is avoiding any associations with the Old English patronymic suffix *-ing* and the English word þing, "gathering, assembly." *Herla*, though not an actual Welsh name—Walter is no modern philologist after all—is reminiscent of the names "Heli," "*Hirel*glas," and "Helias," all of which are found in the *History of the Kings of Britain*. Moreover, Walter's familiarity with Welsh culture is well documented in the *De nugis curialium*, and with his time spent on the borders, and perhaps familial connections, he would have had a good feel for what sounded Welsh and what did not. Walter is not alone in his attention to detail here. Medieval authors took care to make sure their names "felt" right: Geoffrey of Monmouth, when not lifting his names from Welsh sources, fashioned names that sounded, to him at least, Welsh.[72] Conversely, Welsh translators puzzled over Geoffrey's made-up names, and they very often replaced them with something more appropriate or recognizable for their audience.[73] And Chrétien de Troyes went out of his way to find a Welsh name for the titular hero of *Cligès*.[74] Chaucer, too, carefully chose appropriate names for his ancient Breton characters in *The Franklin's Tale*.[75] Getting the right name was important to writers working with the Matter of Britain.

Of course, the revised tale unmistakably announces Herla's Welshness by claiming that he was "a king of the most ancient Britons." He also speaks Welsh. The shepherd who responds to Herla's question exclaims, "Sir, I can hardly understand your language, since I am a Saxon and you are a Briton."[76] Herlething, who is traditionally a continental figure, has undergone a rather extensive identity change. Carrying a Welsh-sounding name, ruling an ancient British kingdom, and speaking the Welsh language, Herla is unmistakably a character at home in the Matter of Britain.

The earlier tale already had a Welsh setting—the March of Wales and Hereford—which the revised version retains and clarifies. The location of Herla's disappearance becomes more detailed: he is last seen being drowned by Welshmen "next to the river Wye in Hereford," whereas the earlier version does not contain the river but only the "March of Wales and Hereford."[77] Furthermore, the revision explicitly states that Herla's band was seen "by the Welsh," whereas in the earlier version he merely says "that most alert race."[78] Both of these changes make Welsh presence and a Welsh setting explicit. These changes, however, may have more to do with Walter's satirical aims rather than cultivating the proper thematic air, as I suggest below.

While the Matter of Britain often contains elements of the marvelous or supernatural, they are not a defining feature. The same can be said for medieval romance in general: "although the marvelous plays a prominent role in medieval romance, it should not be considered *the* pre-eminent feature."[79] Nonetheless, a large part of Walter's revision concerns the marvelous journey of Herla into the otherworld. This too should be seen as a sign that Walter attempts to bend this tale toward the Matter of Britain, especially since the marvelous additions seem to mimic motifs found in Celtic literature. Scholars who have found in the tale of Herla a reserve of Celtic motifs have marshaled an impressive array of analogues. In this act, they are not wholly mistaken. Although they err in their explanation of the exact relationship between these analogues and Walter's tale of King Herla, they are right to see a relationship between Herla's tale and Celtic sources. In revising the tale, Walter draws on his knowledge of Celtic motifs, which he either picked up in the Welsh March or heard through the popular literature of Henry's court, in order to create a tale that would conform to the marvelous episodes that one expects to find in the Matter of Britain. Perhaps Walter loosely based Herla's journey to the otherworld on a specific Welsh tale he knew, but his systematic practice of drastic revision and the fact that nothing in the revised tale is without purpose should call into question any desire to see these tales as Celtic in the traditional, conservative sense, especially the sense used by folklorists. Indeed, such excellent use is made of the so-called Celtic material in the story that Walter either stumbled across a ready-made Celtic story perfect for his satiric purposes, or, as is almost certainly the case, he crafted a tale using his knowledge of Celtic motifs.

Walter's insertion of Herlething into the Matter of Britain is not an empty exercise in literary composition, nor is it merely an attempt to mimic a popular literary trend. It is, rather, a deliberately cultivated aspect of the story that adds an important layer to the tale's parodic aims. The fact that Walter has manufactured his own ancient British tale leads us to examine what specific literary effects the Matter of Britain brings about in this piece. This inquiry has some important consequences for literary historians.

In dealing with the "Celtic" elements of high medieval literature, literary scholars (and here and following, I mean those literary scholars who are not themselves Celticists) tend to follow one of two strategies. The first may be called the folkloric approach, which had its heyday in the mid-twentieth century. Analogues and source studies are the bread and butter of this methodology, and its ultimate goal seems to be to reconstruct earlier Celtic myths or folktales. This approach has not fared well, having recently been characterized as "the ancient and long-discredited attempts . . . to find a 'Celtic' hero lurking behind every knight, or a Welsh or Irish text behind every narrative element."[80] The results, however unsatisfying they may be to some, remain interesting for the light they shed on cultural interaction and shared narrative conventions. It is worth pointing out that those scholars pursuing this approach were almost never trained as Celticists, and they often had a poor grasp of the languages of their primary sources. Moreover, the last few generations of Celticists have shown little interest in the wider transmission and popularization of originally Celtic themes, characters, and motifs.[81]

The second approach literary scholars have adopted to the Celtic aspects of high medieval literature is best described as benign neglect. Perhaps distrustful of the extreme claims scholars such as R. S. Loomis took in studying Celtic analogues, many modern critics duly footnote the supposed Celticity of this motif, character, or setting, but do little else. And in footnotes they remain, paid no special attention, subsumed along with biblical quotes and classical references into that broad category of sources that authors are said to have drawn upon. Yet, unlike the case with scriptural or classical references, few have asked what specific resonances Celtic material might have had for a contemporary audience. Along these lines, Michael Faletra has observed, "it is not often acknowledged that the translation and adaptation of traditional Brythonic stories for Francophone audiences cannot be extricated from the power dynamic of Anglo-Norman expansion into Celtic territories—especially Wales—during precisely the same period."[82] Walter's creation of a Welsh Herla from a continental Herlething provides an opportunity to begin to explore what kind of literary work Celtic material could do for medieval audiences.

The exact nature of Henry II's cultivation of the Matter of Britain is still disputed. For example, although it is commonly assumed that Henry II specifically compared himself to the figure of Arthur for the purposes of propaganda, it seems that we have little actual evidence to support that view.[83] Nonetheless, the enthusiastic reception of the Matter of Britain among the Anglo-Normans arises, at least in part, from the fact that it supplies an illustrious past for Britain. And it is Geoffrey of Monmouth's *History* that provides the pseudohistorical background for this past. Many scholars explain the appeal of Geoffrey's work to the Anglo-Normans by claiming that it shows "how the Norman regime finds itself . . . in a position of dominance over the already-defeated Britons."[84] Doubtless there is some truth here. Regardless of how active Henry himself was in the creation and maintenance of the genre, the Matter of Britain provided the Anglo-Normans with a history of their territory that equaled or surpassed the foundation narratives of Charlemagne. First and foremost, literati like Walter would have viewed the Matter of Britain as a narrative of *inheritance*, explaining how they had come to hold land that had once been held by the ancient Britons. Inheritance is also the key to understanding why Walter sets the tale of Herla in ancient Britain.

The tale of King Herla contains a haunting portrait of the loss of inheritance by the Welsh. And though the English have clearly gained territory, they also gained something less desirable. Emerging from the dwarf's kingdom and discovering that some two hundred years have passed, Herla asks the shepherd about his queen. After explaining that the king's language is hard for him to understand, the shepherd continues: "However, I have not heard of that queen's name, except that they say a queen of the ancient Britons was called by this name some time ago, and she was the wife of King Herla who, as the story goes, is said to have disappeared with a pygmy at this cliff, and he never appeared on earth again. But the Saxons have held this kingdom for two hundred years now, and its inhabitants have been driven out."[85] This encounter with the shepherd, perhaps the most enigmatic part of the tale, captures the broad strokes of the *translatio imperii* motif commonly found in medieval literature. In Geoffrey's *History*, Trojan magnificence moves to Italy, then to France, and finally takes root in Britain, and by the end of Geoffrey's *History* the Anglo-Saxons have taken it for themselves. For the Normans, it was easy enough to claim that the *imperium* of the Anglo-Saxons had now passed to them. Walter invokes this view of history in his tale. For the Saxon shepherd, Herla, emblematic of the ancient British kings, has now become a thing of legend. With its use of *aiunt* (they say) and *fabulose dicitur* (the old story says), the tale confines Herla's past glories to the realm of storytelling. All that remains of his once glorious past has become stories on the lips of foreigners. And this transfer of Britons from their historical past into popular twelfth-century narratives is exactly what the Matter of Britain accomplishes.

The beginning of the tale conforms to the notion that the glories of the British past have passed to the court of Henry. Walter writes of "one, and only one court that was similar to our own."[86] As stated above, this comparison initially appears to be nothing but complimentary, justified by both Henry II's and Herla's reputations. The dwarf king praises Herla—and thus Henry—by mentioning his "fame that lifts [him] above other kings."[87] But it is neither Herla's courtliness nor his *imperium* that Henry II inherits. In a brilliant pun, Walter reverses the generic expectations of the Matter of Britain, wittily pointing out that after Herla's band has vanished, "as if they have passed down their *wanderings* to us for their own peace" (emphasis mine).[88] The word for "wanderings" here is *errores*, which can also mean "mistakes," as its descendant in Modern English does. Coupled with the verb *trado* (bequeath, hand over), it suddenly becomes clear that Henry II's court has not inherited the dominions or grandeur of the ancient British kings, but rather that Herla has left Henry's court with a string of bad habits, habits that Walter himself deplores: business and revelry that last through the night; an indulgence in hunting that, to courtiers at least, dictates the court's behavior; and, of course, the endless, erratic travels of the court. Walter has already stated in *distinctio* 1 that the knowledge of modern man is not his own, but has been passed down from the ancients.[89] It would seem that bad habits have come down to Walter's contemporaries as well. This is not the grand inheritance from the past that Walter's contemporaries had in mind.

According to the story's logic, Henry II is not at fault for this state of affairs, for as amusing and clever as Walter's manipulation of the motif of *translatio imperii* is, it also excuses the king.[90] This is of a piece with Walter's tone toward Henry II throughout *distinctio* 1, where the blame for the hectic state of the court falls mainly on courtiers—a fact emphasized in the story of the king of Portugal that follows.[91] In the tale of King Herla, however, the chaos of the court is an unavoidable inheritance. This idea is reinforced by the legal language that the dwarf king enforces upon Herla: *fedus eternum* (neverending pact), *Deo teste* (as God as your witness), *iuxta pactum nostrum* (in accordance with our agreement), *diffinicionis uestre* (your contract), *peti* (to be petitioned).[92] Herla unwittingly enters into a binding legal agreement, an agreement he seems to have had no say in negotiating. The same might hold, therefore, for Henry II, whose court has inherited the inquietude of the ancient British past.

If anyone besides the ancient Britons is to blame, it is their descendants— the Welsh. Much like the absurdity of ancient British knights abusing young Perceval for being Welsh in Chrétien's *Perceval*, this tale plays with temporality in a fascinating manner. That the English shepherd does not recognize Herla is understandable; that the Welsh at the river Wye do not recognize him is both tragic and, to an English audience at least, comic. Before the Welsh band stands Herla, an ancient, powerful British king—isn't this the moment that Welsh prophecy has foretold, a *mab darogan* (son of prophecy) come to restore the Welsh to their rightful place as rulers of Britain? The Welsh, however, indecorously drown this splendid king. Walter, here, is satirizing the Welsh obsession for messianic figures and their glorious past; he implies that if King Arthur himself were pulled out of the past and into the present, the Welsh would not recognize him, and likely even murder him. Their careless act sets King Henry's inheritance into motion.

The tale of King Herla, built upon the framework of a common folktale, is transformed into a sophisticated piece of courtly literature in Walter's hands. It satirizes both common targets of the court of Henry II and the internecine feuds of the Welsh. At the same time, it invokes the *translatio imperii* motif common to the Matter of Britain for a surprisingly innovative joke about inheritance. This story is Walter Map at his best. The tale of King Herla shows how the Matter of Britain can be manipulated for unexpected purposes. Even at the height of its popularity, it is more than just a literary ornament.

Moving Beyond Analogues

When medieval authors attempt to bring existing tales into the Matter of Britain, they invariably take on an aspect that appears Celtic to modern readers. This fact should give source and analogue hunters pause. If Walter Map could so drastically alter a tale that most modern commentators consider it genuinely Celtic, what hope is there of correctly identifying particular Celtic sources for other episodes in other medieval literature? I would suggest here that we follow Bliss, who long ago warned against the excesses of source hunting, but still maintained that some middle ground could be found. "The cause of scholarship," he writes, "would benefit more from a careful sifting out of the grain from the chaff than from the endless multiplication of improbable conjectures."[93] Here, I am not advocating a more careful type of source hunting, since the bulk of that work has already been completed. However, a reexamination of the Celtic elements—genuine or not—is timely, especially given recent interest in transnational and postcolonial approaches to medieval literature. Understanding the process of Britonicization in the high and late Middle Ages will work to this end. It provides a conceptual framework for approaching texts with Celtic material and guards against uncritical assumptions of Welsh or Irish sources.

In a way, what Walter Map's tale of King Herla reveals is nothing unexpected. P. Rickard probably speaks for most literary scholars, even today, when he claims that the majority of medieval French romances give the impression that their authors "used a vague and exotic 'British' setting which they had taken over from oral and written sources, and which conveyed nothing to them, since it corresponded to nothing in their own experience."[94] I would, however, disagree with the notion that ancient Britain had little significance to writers and readers, especially for the French and English, for whom the descendants of the ancient Britons were neighbors and, eventually, subjects. Perhaps some authors mindlessly applied the loose framework of the Matter of Britain to romances, but my reading of Walter Map suggests otherwise. The creation of the tale of Herla, with its reliance on what we today call "Celtic motifs," reminds modern scholars that medieval authors approached this material in a fundamentally different way. Of course, medieval authors and writers would have scarcely recognized the importance of, for example, the grail myth to a reconstructed Celtic mythology or appreciated the relationship between Gawain and Gwalchmai. As a result, those who have scoured medieval literature for the detritus of Celtic mythological or literary tradition have, by and large, underestimated the agency of medieval authors to adapt their source texts. They have failed to ask *why* medieval authors found certain Celtic motifs attractive, *how* medieval authors went about making Celtic material their own, and *what* the concept of ancient Britain accomplished for imaginative authors. The promise of satire clearly motivated Walter Map to incorporate Welsh motifs into his tale of King Herla. To excise this tale from its surroundings in an attempt to study its place in Celtic tradition misses this important point. The converse is also true, for when one ignores the Celtic motifs of the tale completely, the richness of Walter's parody and its relationship to the Matter of Britain remain obscured.

Or, to put it another way, only a naive reader would think that the portrayal of Native Americans in the novels of James Fenimore Cooper had little to do with contemporary politics and culture. And it would be a mad reader indeed who would sift through Cooper's work in the hopes of reconstructing genuine Native American myths and narratives. At the same time, however, it remains productive and exciting to see what kind of cultural work Cooper's "Matter of Native America" accomplishes. The same can be said of the uses and abuses of the Matter of Britain by French and English authors in the Middle Ages.

Chapter 5

The Welsh-Latin Sources of
the *De nugis curialium*

Walter Map's sources are typical of twelfth-century clerical literature: wide-ranging and diverse, with adventurous forays into what we would today call popular culture. He knew the usual suspects of classical and patristic authors like Horace, Virgil, Jerome, Augustine, and others.[1] The *De nugis curialium* also suggests that he was well acquainted with contemporary literature, including Geoffrey of Monmouth, Gerald of Wales, Hildebert of Le Mans, Bernard of Clairvaux, and perhaps even a version of *Amis and Amiloun*.[2] However, the bulk of the *De nugis curialium* consists of an original mixture of current events, personal reminiscences, and a good deal of curial gossip. With this eclectic medley of sources, Walter certainly lives up to his own self-description as a hunter seeking out wild narrative material for his hungry readers.[3] Tales that concern Wales or the Welsh were part of his quarry. Indeed, a few of these tales even show flashes of the same ethnographic spirit that animated his contemporary Gerald of Wales. In these tales, scholars have generally viewed Welsh folklore or oral tradition as lying behind Walter's Latin prose.[4] This is undoubtedly true in some cases. However, I believe that in at least two instances Walter took his stories not from Welsh folklore but from Latin documents that circulated throughout the ecclesiastical network of southeastern Wales and the southern Marches.

In addition to revealing more about Walter's sources and intellectual milieu, Walter's access to these documents demonstrates that Latin culture could act as a conduit for the transfer of Welsh traditions from Wales to the court of Henry II. Chapter 6 argues that it is precisely through this ecclesiastical network that early traditions about ancient Britain first made their way to the larger Anglo-Norman world. Arthurian romance, and the Matter of Britain in general, should be understood as ultimately a product of the antiquarian interests of enterprising and crafty twelfth-century clerics. And thus, the early distribution of the Matter of Britain is not—or at least not solely—the result of itinerant Breton minstrels, who have long been the preferred means of transmission. In spite of all the interest that the genesis of Arthurian romance has attracted, this ecclesiastical network of exchange remains underexplored, and Walter's participation in this network marks him out as someone who took an active interest in texts about ancient Britain, far more so than the lack of Arthur or his knights in the *De nugis curialium* would otherwise suggest. That the generation after Walter Map imagined him having access to Latin traditions about Arthurian legend is, therefore, not at all far-fetched.

Welsh Documents at St. Peter's, Gloucester

One ecclesiastical center that collected written Welsh material in the twelfth century was the Benedictine abbey of St. Peter's in Gloucester. It was there, I argue, that Walter Map read literary material that he would later revisit in the *De nugis curialium*. However, before exploring Walter's connections with the monastery and his use of its Welsh collection, the circumstances regarding the abbey's acquisition of these documents, as well as their content, should be reviewed.

Gloucester was a liminal place, as Geoffrey of Monmouth says, standing "beside the Severn between Wales and Loegria [i.e., England]."[5] This strategic position made Gloucester one of the major locations for launching military campaigns into Wales, but its position as a border town also begot cultural exchange between the Welsh and the English, ultimately allowing St. Peter's Abbey in Gloucester to gather one of the few demonstrable collections of Welsh literature outside of Wales. This Welsh material, in turn, can be traced from its composition in southern Wales, to its reception at St. Peter's Abbey, and finally to the court of Henry II.

The story of the abbey's collection of Welsh hagiography begins with the Norman colonization of Wales. While St. Peter's was a poor, unassuming Benedictine abbey at the time of the Norman Conquest, by the middle of the twelfth century it had become one of the most prosperous abbeys in England.[6] The abbey's growth was fueled both by the deft leadership of its first Norman abbot, Serlo (1072–1104) and by the extraordinary amount of patronage bestowed upon it. Gifts and donations came from all corners, but "it was the combination of the visiting royal court and the proximity of Wales that propelled Gloucester abbey into a position of distinction in post-Conquest England."[7] Soon after the conquest, Norman barons began eyeing Wales—southern Wales in particular. By fits and starts they pushed deeper into southern Wales, and as they consolidated their Welsh holdings, they donated many of their newly obtained church properties to monasteries in England and on the continent.[8] The reasons for doing so were complex, ranging from a desire to emulate or maintain Anglo-Saxon patterns of patronage to the simple fact that Gloucester Abbey had a good reputation for monastic discipline.[9] The abbots of Gloucester may have even been seen as effective agents for converting the *clas* churches of Wales into more orthodox establishments.[10] Regardless of the reasons for Gloucester's popularity, between 1080 and 1130 the disendowment of the churches of southern Wales was so sweeping and severe that, as R. R. Davies reminds us, "not until the Reformation was there to be a comparable sudden transfer of ecclesiastical wealth in Wales."[11]

St. Peter's could count itself among those houses that the Norman colonizers smiled upon.[12] In Abbot Serlo's time, Bernard Neufmarché (d. 1121–25?) granted the abbey the church of Glasbury, dedicated to St. Cynidr, along with other rights in Brycheiniog.[13] In 1093 William Rufus, as he lay gravely ill at Gloucester, supposedly granted the abbey St. Gwynllyw's in Newport—though this story may be an invention of later Gloucester monks; at any rate, it was held by St. Peter's in Abbot Serlo's time.[14] Furthermore, William de Londres (d. 1126) and his family acted as lavish benefactors for the abbey. William built a new church dedicated to St. Michael at Ewenny, which he gave to Gloucester, and in 1141 his son Maurice founded—or more likely affirmed his father's foundation of—Ewenny priory as a cell of Gloucester Abbey.[15] He also granted the Glamorgan churches of St. Michael's at Colwinston, St. Brides Major, and Colwinston, and Ogmore chapel to Gloucester, and in Carmarthenshire, he gave four churches to the monks of Gloucester (St. Elli's, Pembrey, St. Ismael's, and Llandyfaelog). The manor of Treguff likewise passed to Gloucester.[16]

Furthermore, Llancarfan, one of the most important ecclesiastical centers in southeastern Wales, fell into the hands of the monks of St. Peter's Abbey, thanks to a grant from Robert fitz Haimon.[17] The exact date of this important grant cannot be confirmed, but it seems to have occurred between 1095 and 1102. Although Gloucester later leased Llancarfan to the archdeacons of Llandaf, it guarded its interests there carefully.[18] A great deal of exchange must have occurred between Gloucester and Llancarfan, although the poor survival of Gloucester's own archive has made it difficult to discern the exact details.[19] Moreover, sometime after 1115, Gloucester was able to obtain another exceptionally important Welsh church, Llanbadarn Fawr in Ceredigion in the diocese of St. Davids.[20] A seat of great learning and home to an active scriptorium, Llanbadarn Fawr did not tolerate Gloucester control for long.[21] During the Anarchy the monks of Gloucester were driven out and they never regained possession of it.[22] All said, in the first quarter of the twelfth century, the monks of St. Peter's, Gloucester, could boast of a portfolio of Welsh properties that few could match.

One consequence of the abbey's Welsh holdings was a fair amount of cultural and literary exchange between Gloucester and its properties to the west. For example, Gloucester monks celebrated three Welsh saints, all of whom were associated with churches they held: the feasts of Teilo, Gwynllyw, and Padarn all appear in the abbey's calendar.[23] The monks also collected, and in one case wrote anew, vitae that concerned their Welsh interests.[24] The general explanation among scholars for this literary activity is that profit and a strict desire to document and safeguard holdings spurred Anglo-Norman monks on more than anything else.[25] This would be especially true if the monks of Gloucester behaved in a manner approaching R. R. Davies's estimation: "Towards the native church the Normans showed scant respect. Its practices and organization appeared bizarre at best, deplorable at worst; its patrons were a motley crowd of unfamiliar 'saints' sporting outlandish names."[26] But John Reuben Davies has recently argued that Anglo-Norman monks approached their new Welsh churches with some respect and that earlier accounts of degradation have been greatly exaggerated, especially claims that Normans rededicated churches to more acceptable saints.[27] Genuine curiosity about the history of these new acquisitions may thus have also driven the Gloucester monks to gather and read the lives of some important Welsh saints, and religious veneration of these new saints surely played a large role as well. Whatever the reason, Gloucester built up a collection of Welsh documents relating to its new holdings during the twelfth century.

Although compelling, evidence for Gloucester's Welsh collection is not altogether straightforward, since no Welsh-Latin texts are found in the surviving manuscripts from Gloucester Abbey. This lack, however, need not arouse inordinate suspicion, especially since the dissolution took a harsher toll at Gloucester than elsewhere: "Gloucester Abbey in view of its size, wealth and reputation, has been most unfortunate in the fate of its medieval library."[28]

Nonetheless, a significant portion of the abbey's twelfth-century library can be reconstructed, including its Welsh collection. MS Cotton Vespasian A.xiv provides the bulk of the evidence for the abbey's Welsh material. The first section of Vespasian A.xiv was originally an independent manuscript, containing the lives of several Welsh saints and a few Irish ones as well, along with extracts from a cartulary, a calendar, a glossary of Old Cornish, and two genealogical tracts.[29] The manuscript's importance to Welsh hagiography is paramount, as it is by far the most extensive collection of early Welsh vitae. The content of Vespasian A.xiv is eclectic: Some of the lives support the interests of the diocese of Llandaf, but others support the diocese of St. Davids. The calendar included in the manuscript betrays the influence of Monmouth, while the genealogical tract shows a Brecon interest. A number of saints from southeastern Wales (i.e., the diocese of Llandaf) appear in both the collection and the calendar. However, some extremely obscure saints from western Wales and Ireland are also found in this collection, and none of these shows any link with eastern Wales, where Vespasian A.xiv seems to have been compiled. Because of these peculiarities, a few different provenances for Vespasian A.xiv were proposed, but in 1958 Kathleen Hughes demonstrated that a strong case could be made that St. Peter's Abbey, Gloucester, first assembled much of the material that ultimately came to make up the manuscript.[30] Her argument has since received broad scholarly acceptance.[31]

As Hughes demonstrates, "the influence of Gloucester constantly intrudes on the composition of Vesp."[32] She explains all of the supposed inconsistencies in the manuscript collection by pointing out that Gloucester Abbey's possessions, scattered throughout two dioceses in southern Wales, account for the manuscript's seemingly odd confluence of vitae. Summarizing her evidence for Gloucester's influence on Vespasian, she writes:

> Gloucester influence on the Vespasian collection seems undeniable, though the manner in which it was exercised must be a matter of dispute. But it cannot be accidental that two very rare saints, Ailwin and Keneder, are connected with Gloucester and also appear in the Vespasian calendar. Gwynllyw was patron of an important church owned by Gloucester, the second *Life of Dyfrig* was indubitably composed by a St Peter's monk, and the Vespasian compilers could most readily have copied their Llancarfan charters with the cooperation of Gloucester. Gloucester's ownership of Llanbadarn Fawr accounts not only for the *Life of Padarn*, but for the definition of his

boundaries with which it concludes. Gloucester interests provide
the essential link between the eastern and western elements in the
Vespasian collection.[33]

To Hughes's evidence, we may also add the appearance of St. Ismael in the
Vespasian calendar, which may also be due to Gloucester influence. Churches
dedicated to St. Ismael are confined to Pembrokeshire, with the exception of
St. Ismael's near Kidwelly in Carmarthenshire, yet the date of his festival survives only in the Vespasian calendar.[34] Although Gloucester's own surviving
calendar omits the saint, the abbey did hold St. Ismael's near Kidwelly, and
the Vespasian calendar may again reflect Gloucester influence here.[35] In sum,
hagiography from all across southern Wales found its way to Gloucester, and
sometime before Vespasian A.xiv was assembled around 1200, the monks of
Gloucester sent some of their own collection of Welsh documents to their
counterparts at Monmouth.[36]

It is difficult to work out when exactly St. Peter's collected Welsh material. Hughes suggests that the abbey's Welsh collection dates to the 1130s.[37]
Gloucester received Llanbadarn Fawr soon after 1115, but it became independent again after the Welsh rebellion of 1136. Thus, Gloucester most readily
had access to the Llanbadarn Fawr material during these years.[38] Yet it is possible to provide a slightly narrower window for the importation of the Welsh
material: in 1122 the abbey suffered a destructive fire, and only three mass
vestments and a few books survived the blaze. Indeed, after the fire, most
scribal activity "seems to have involved copying borrowed texts."[39] The impe-
tus for the collection of the Welsh material may partly stem from the monks'
desire to replenish their library. Regardless, we can be fairly sure that the
Welsh material arrived after the 1122 fire, since no writing earlier than this
date survives from Gloucester.[40]

Comparison with the Book of Llandaf, a well-known collection of charters, vitae, and other material, can help establish a relative chronology. Three
of the vitae in Vespasian A.xiv also appear in the Book of Llandaf—the lives of
Dyfrig, Teilo, and Clydog—and it has been suggested that the Vespasian vitae
witness earlier versions of these lives and occasionally offer a superior reading
to their corresponding versions in the Book of Llandaf.[41] Moreover, although
it is not uncommon to find the Vespasian copyist misreading Welsh names,
evidence of more conservative orthography is sometimes preserved.[42] It seems
unlikely that Llandaf would have sent Gloucester earlier copies of the lives of
Dyfrig, Teilo, and Clydog when newer recensions, more clearly supporting a

Llandaf cause, were available. The Book of Llandaf has most recently been dated to a period between 1119 and 1134, which implies that these lives reached Gloucester at some point before 1134 at the latest, when the Book of Llandaf was being assembled.[43] However, if John Reuben Davies is correct in dating the *Vita Sancti Gundleii*, which was written for Gloucester, to the 1160s, then St. Peter's Abbey must have been soliciting Welsh material throughout the twelfth century.[44] This may be a minor point, but it shows that Gloucester's Welsh collection was not the fluke of a single transmission, but a decades-long process.

Vespasian A.xiv is not a perfect witness to Gloucester's collection of Welsh material. The criteria that Gloucester used when sending Welsh material to Monmouth remains unknown. Gloucester monks may have sent almost everything they had, or they could have sent only what Monmouth requested. Nonetheless, we can tentatively reconstruct at least some of Gloucester's Welsh collection by selecting the material in Vespasian A.xiv that better accords with Gloucester's temporal interests than with Monmouth's. Thus, it has been suggested the Vespasian A.xiv lives that issue from western Wales (those of Padarn, Brynach, Carannog, and Cybi), as well as the two Irish lives that were known in western Wales (Maedoc and Brendan) likely came from Gloucester.[45] These lives Gloucester seems to have gathered from the library of Llanbadarn Fawr and perhaps from its close associations with St. Davids.[46] Their presence at Monmouth is difficult to explain otherwise, since it is unlikely that Llancarfan—the other possible source for these vitae—would have distributed lives that explicitly promote the claims of a rival diocese. None of these lives show any trace of Llandaf influence. Without a doubt, Gloucester possessed the life of Dyfrig, as Benedict of Gloucester used it to create a new life of this saint.[47] Benedict's life also shows that Gloucester had a copy of the Llandaf text *De primo statu Landavensis ęcclesię*, which discusses the legend of King Lucius and the bishops Germanus and Lupus.[48] The same text also reveals that St. Peter's had quickly acquired a copy of Geoffrey of Monmouth's *History of the Kings of Britain*.[49]

Furthermore, Caradog of Llancarfan is believed to have written his life of St. Cadog for the Gloucester monks, and it is likely that he also composed the lives of Gwynllyw and Tatheus for the abbey, the latter possibly to aid the monks in a property dispute with Robert of Gloucester.[50] Evidence from the calendar of St. Peter's suggests that they had acquired the lives of Teilo, Gwynllyw, and Padarn.[51] The monks would need appropriate *lectiones* for these festivals, and extant vitae were one of the main sources for the creation of a saint's liturgy. That Gloucester actually held the churches of Gwynllyw and Padarn makes their possession of these two lives all the more likely. It is doubtful that the monks would have turned to *inventio* or oral tradition in order to create the appropriate liturgies when vitae were so readily available. It has also been suggested that the appearance in the Vespasian collection of the life of Clydog, a little-celebrated saint, may also be due to Gloucester's influence. Although Gloucester monks never held a church dedicated to Clydog, they did have significant interests in Ewyas Harold, only a few miles away from Merthyr Clydog (modern-day Clodock in Herefordshire).[52]

One further piece of evidence for Gloucester's Welsh collection has so far passed unnoticed. MS British Library, Egerton 2810 contains a late fourteenth-century copy of the *South English Legendary*.[53] Folios 94r–99r contain an unedited *Life of St. Teilo* in Middle English verse. Much of the manuscript, including the *Life of St. Teilo*, is written in a Gloucestershire dialect, and the manuscript seems to have moved from Gloucestershire to Cheshire, and finally to Lancashire, if the manuscript's dialects do indeed represent its movement.[54] From my examination of the Middle English *Life* in Egerton 2810, it is clear that the translator had in front of him the *Vita Sancti Teiliaui*, two copies of which are extant in the Book of Llandaf and Vespasian A.xiv.[55] The Middle English *Life* abridges its source, often omitting many of the details about the history of the early Welsh church; the miraculous episodes of the Latin life hold the translator's attention, not the ecclesiastical particulars that appealed to the *Vita*'s original audience of clergy in southeastern Wales. Nonetheless, the *Life* does follow the main events of the *Vita Sancti Teiliaui* fairly closely, and even if the Latin *Vita* had not survived, the fact that the Middle English *Life* insists on following the Latin original in calling St. Dyfrig "þe erchebissop" would still betray its ultimate provenance of Llandaf.[56] Since the Middle English *Life of St. Teilo* occurs in no other version of the *South English Legendary*, its presence in Egerton 2810 is almost certainly due to local interest. As far as I am aware, the only English ecclesiastical center where Teilo was venerated was St. Peter's Abbey, where he is one of three Welsh saints to appear in the surviving calendar.[57] Therefore, I think it is safe to assume that the Middle English *Life of St. Teilo* owes its creation to the monks of St. Peter's Abbey, which in turn provides valuable confirmation—outside of Cotton Vespasian A.xiv—that St. Peter's had been collecting Welsh vitae.

But the Middle English *Life* also raises interesting questions regarding the extent to which Vespasian A.xiv can be counted on to accurately reflect Gloucester's Welsh collection. The two surviving copies of the *Vita Sancti*

Teiliaui are not identical. The version of the *Vita* found in the Book of Llandaf is a later recension, with more propaganda reflecting Bishop Urban's grandiose claims for his diocese, while the copy found in Vespasian A.xiv is earlier. If Vespasian A.xiv broadly reflects texts that Gloucester held, one would assume that the Middle English *Life*, if it was in fact composed at the abbey, would represent the earlier *Vita Sancti Teiliaui* that appears in Vespasian A.xiv. Yet this is not the case. Instead, the copy that the Middle English translator was working from was the later recension, as witnessed by the copy in the Book of Llandaf.[58] There is a similar problem with the *Vita Sancti Cadoci*. An earlier version of the *Vita Sancti Cadoci* written by Lifris, and not Caradog's more recent version written especially for Gloucester, appears in Vespasian A.xiv. In the case of the *Vita Sancti Cadoci*, the monks at Monmouth might have preserved the earlier text because it was signficantly longer. Nonetheless, Vespasian A.xiv does include two lives of Dyfrig, which seems to suggest that if the Monmouth compiler had two versions of the *Vita Sancti Cadoci*, he might have included both. It could also be that the omission of Caradog's *Vita Cadoci* implies that the text was not yet available, and that it was written toward the later end of the circa 1120–50 window proposed by Brooke.[59] Yet the date of the life of St. Gwynllyw (ca. 1160s) implies that Gloucester sent material to Monmouth at some point after Caradog's *Vita Cadoci* was presumably complete.[60] Whatever the case may be, Vespasian A.xiv does not include the versions of the *Vita Sancti Cadoci* and the *Vita Sancti Teiliaui* that one would expect if they had come from St. Peter's, Gloucester. This incongruency reminds us how little we know about the circulation of texts in and around the ecclesiastical network of southern Welsh Marches, and it cautions us against placing too much faith in Vespasian A.xiv as a record of Gloucester's Welsh collection.

With this warning in mind, we can offer a tentative reconstruction of the collection of Welsh material at St. Peter's. Table 2 provides a list of all the Welsh documents that have been claimed to have been at Gloucester. On the right I have listed the strongest supporting evidence, and the list is ordered in what I perceive to be the strongest case to the weakest. The list errs on the side of inclusivity—it surely is faulty in one case or another. Gloucester may have held less Welsh material, or perhaps even more. In many instances, it is particularly difficult to tell Gloucester influence from Llandaf/Llancarfan. Nonetheless, the surviving evidence strongly suggests that the abbey amassed a sizable and varied collection of Welsh and possibly even Irish material. In style and purpose, the collection was diverse, encompassing ancient traditions and

Table 2. St. Peter's Collection of Welsh and Irish Material

Text	Evidence
Benedict's *Vita Dubricii*	Composed by Benedict, a monk of Gloucester
Vita S. Dubricii	One of Benedict's main sources
Historia regum Britanniae	Another of Benedict's sources
De primo statu Landavensis ecclesię	Another of Benedict's sources
Vita S. Paterni	Gloucester held Llanbadarn Fawr; Padarn appears in Gloucester's calendar
Lifris's *Vita S. Cadoci*	Gloucester held Llancarfan
Caradog's *Vita S. Cadoci*	Widely believed to have been written for Gloucester
Vita S. Teiliaui	Appears in Gloucester's calendar; a Middle English *Life of St. Teilo* probably comes from the abbey
Vita S. Gundleii	Believed to have been written for Gloucester; Gloucester held St. Gwynllyw's in Newport; Gwynllyw appears in Gloucester's calendar
Vita S. Tathei	Believed to have been written for Gloucester
De situ Brecheniauc	Gloucester had extensive interests in Brycheiniog (see below)
Vita S. Bernachii	Presence in Vespasian A.xiv best explained through Gloucester connections with Llanbadarn Fawr or St. Davids
Vita Prima S. Carantoci	" "
Vita Secunda S. Carantoci	" "
Vita S. Dauid	" "
Vita S. Maidoci	" "
Vita S. Brendani[1]	" "
Vita S. Clitauci	Gloucester held property near Merthyr Clydog

[1] Although called the *Vita Sancti Brendani* in Cotton Vespasian A.xiv, the text is actually the *Navigatio Sancti Brendani*. See J. S. Mackley, *The Legend of St. Brendan: A Comparative Study of the Latin and Anglo-Norman Versions* (Brill: Leiden, 2008), 64 n. 232; Giovani Orlandi, "Considerazioni sulla tradizione manoscritta della *Navigatio Sancti Brendani*," *Filogia mediolatina* 9 (2002): 51–75, at 58–59; *Navigatio Sancti Brendani Abbatis: From Early Latin Manuscripts*, ed. Carl Selmer (South Bend, IN: University of Notre Dame Press, 1959), xviii n. 10. Further complicating matters, I have found evidence that suggests that the *Navigatio* came to Vespasian A.xiv not from St. Davids but from England, which I will present in a forthcoming article.

those newly invented, and it contained a sizable amount of "secular" material, including references to Arthur and his knights.[61]

Gloucester was probably not unique in collecting Welsh vitae. There may have been other instances of Welsh literary material being appropriated by Anglo-Norman churches and monasteries.[62] Gerald of Wales provides an interesting anecdote in this regard. While discussing how Llanthony Prima was abused by its new priors, Gerald recounts the greed of Roger of Norwich, who was a prior of Llanthony in the latter twelfth century and, judging from his name, a transplant to Wales. Although Llanthony had suffered at the hands of other priors, Gerald singles out Roger, saying that he "damaged this place more than the others" and "altogether robbed the church of its books, decorations, and charters, flagrantly carrying away everything that had been left by the others."[63] We do not know where Roger absconded to with Llanthony's books, nor do we know if any of these books and charters contained Welsh material. This Augustinian house was a new church, dedicated in 1108 by the bishops of Llandaf and Hereford, and may not have had an extensive or particularly Welsh library. Nonetheless, Gerald's testimony reminds us that the literary transfer was not always a peaceful endeavor and that there was profit to be had from Welsh churches.

Although temporal concerns surely contributed to Gloucester's desire to collect Welsh documents, the abbey's rich spiritual and intellectual life suggests that they were received with more discernment than Roger of Norwich's plundering of Llanthony. The twelfth century was a vibrant and productive time for the monks of St. Peter's Abbey.[64] A string of effective abbots and a glut of patronage transformed this monastery into an animated intellectual center. Hamelin, abbot from 1148 to 1179, presided over an especially pronounced period of activity.[65] Gerald of Wales studied at St. Peter's during his abbacy.[66] The theologian Osbern Pinnuk was active at Gloucester and dedicated his *Liber deriuationum*, a collection of the lexical derivations of words, to Hamelin.[67] Furthermore, the abbey's scriptorium was at its most active during the "second quarter and middle of the century."[68] Of the abbey's once substantial library only perhaps one-quarter—around 110—of the volumes it contained are known to us, while the actual surviving works number far less.[69] The library's strength was its collection of Augustinian theology, but it included important recent works as well.[70] Moreover, Thomson has argued that the abbey's school left evidence of intensive use on at least two surviving manuscripts, giving us some "indication of the vigour of monastic culture at Gloucester around the middle of the twelfth century and later."[71] The abbey's school did attract at least a few men from Wales—Gerald of Wales among them—and around the time that St. Peter's began gathering Welsh hagiography there were likely more Welshmen at the abbey. As F. G. Cowley explains, "Before the advent of the Cistercians into the heart of Wales in the forties of the twelfth century there were very few opportunities open to Welshmen who were attracted to the monastic vocation. A few Welshmen favored by 'birth or brilliance' could find admittance to one of the larger abbeys along the border."[72] St. Peter's, Gloucester, was one such abbey. To sum up, the intellectual climate at the abbey around the middle of the twelfth century was dynamic. The abbey's school was well used and well attended, its scriptorium reached a high point, and its interest in Wales peaked. It was into this bustling community that hagiography from southern Wales was received. One would not expect this group of entertaining and, at times, quirky vitae to gather dust on the abbey shelves. Indeed, this collection of Welsh material was eagerly received by at least one monk—Benedict of Gloucester—and, I believe, Walter Map as well.

It is not particularly difficult to link Walter with St. Peter's, Gloucester. In fact, as many have noted, there is sufficient evidence to believe that Walter attended the abbey's school.[73] Particularly revealing is Walter's acquaintance with Gregory, a venerable and holy monk of the abbey. Walter begins *distinctio* 2 of the *De nugis curialium* by praising Gregory, who, sick with gout and suffering from painful ulcers in his legs, nevertheless remains faithful, cheerful, and devoted to the Lord. Walter recalls his own first journey across the English Channel—presumably to Paris to study—and tells how after his ship was beset by a great storm he prayed for Gregory's intercession. Miraculously, during the storm Walter has a vision of Gregory walking among the sailors, encouraging and aiding them, and when Walter awakes he finds the sea calm and silent. Walter then reports that he later told this story to Gregory's master, one Abbot Hamelin, who served as abbot of St. Peter's from 1148 to 1179.

Tellingly, Walter claims that he had met Gregory in person: he says that he "saw" Gregory and speaks as if he had often observed him in his suffering and daily routine.[74] If Gregory's ailments were as bad as Walter says they were, he probably could not have traveled much, meaning that Walter must have come to him at Gloucester. And since Gregory died in 1157 and Walter was a student in Paris by 1154, it would seem that Walter received the beginnings of his education at St. Peter's during the 1140s and early 1150s, which fits well with his assumed birth in the early to mid-1130s.[75] Chronology aside, it seems unlikely that Walter would pray to a local holy man if he had not met him in person. Gregory's fame was, as far as we can tell, of the local variety. Walter is one of only two sources for Gregory's spiritual prowess, the other being a Gloucester chronicle.[76] In addition to placing Walter at Gloucester, his acquaintance with the monk Gregory is noteworthy in another regard. Gregory was not only held in esteem for his ability to calm storms, but he was also one of the abbey's main scribes during this period.[77] Walter thus knew and admired a man who worked directly with the abbey's collection of Welsh material.

Moreover, it has been suggested that Walter may have first met his future patron and friend Gilbert Foliot at Gloucester, where the latter served as abbot from 1139 to 1148.[78] Before 1173, by which time Walter had become a royal clerk, he was apparently working as Gilbert's clerk during his tenure as bishop of London (1163–87).[79] Walter speaks very highly of Gilbert in the *De nugis curialium*, and he even recounts how Gilbert, while he served as bishop of Hereford (1148–63), helped deal with an evil, undead Welshman who harassed a village in his diocese.[80] Even without additional evidence that Walter first attended school at St. Peter's, Gloucester, his close relationship with Gilbert would put him at only one remove from one of the abbots who oversaw the abbey's growth and flourishing of its scriptorium.[81] Nonetheless, Walter's own career tracks so closely with Gilbert Foliot's—both men move from Hereford to London—that it seems reasonable to claim that Gilbert first met his future clerk at Gloucester at the abbey's school. Overall, Walter's association with the monk Gregory, Abbot Hamelin, and Gilbert Foliot suggests that Walter, like his contemporary Gerald of Wales, received his early education at Gloucester Abbey, not far from his supposed homeland in southwestern Herefordshire.

Walter, however, could have easily visited the abbey after his schoolboy days. Indeed, he implies as much when he says that he afterward told Abbot Hamelin about Gregory's intercession.[82] Clearly, Walter was grateful for his aid, and he made sure Hamelin knew about Gregory's miracle. Walter here all but states that he returned to St. Peter's to talk to Hamelin. He certainly was near St. Peter's Abbey sometime in the middle of the twelfth century, as he witnessed a charter to the priory of Llanthony Secunda, located some half a dozen miles to the south.[83] Walter also had lifelong interests in the area. Gunnar Stollberg suggests that Walter may have visited St. Peter's from the church at Westbury-on-Severn, which he held.[84] The two are separated by only ten miles. Unfortunately, we have no information that sheds light on when Walter obtained this benefice, though he seems to have resided there at times.[85]

He kept a close eye on Westbury, never forgiving the Cistercians of Flaxley Abbey for intruding upon his holdings there, an outrage that, according to Gerald of Wales, made Walter, when he acted as justice in eyre, swear to uphold justice for everyone except Jews and Cistercians.[86] Moreover, between 1165 and 1197 Walter witnessed several charters for Llanthony Abbey in Gloucestershire, another nearby center of learning and one that had close ties with St. Peter's.[87] He was also acquainted with Gilbert de Lacy, whose family had been great benefactors to the abbey.[88] Additional documentary evidence shows that Walter, or at least his name, was known to the monks of St. Peter's. In their record of a grant of lands from Walter Giffard, the monks of St. Peter's describe property in Hereford as extending "until Walter Map's oak."[89] Walter seems to have maintained a lifelong presence in the southern Marches. His colleagues and friends at St. Peter's, Gloucester, never would have been far away—nor would their collection of Welsh material.

Walter and the *Vita Sancti Cadoci*

The only story in the *De nugis curialium* that has a clearly identifiable Welsh textual tradition is Walter's short tale of Cadog. Crucially, this episode appears in the very same Welsh hagiographical material that St. Peter's collected. Coming at the end of a series of stories about hermits and saints in *distinctio* 2, the tale begins with Cadog—a king of Wales, according to Walter—forsaking the world and taking up a life of solitude. Walter's version of the story is as follows:

> Cadocus, Wallie rex, audiuit Dominum dicentem, "Qui non reliquerit omnia propter me non est me dignus," et relictis omnibus in heremo solitarius labore manuum suarum et sudore uultus sui panem quesitum iocunda et salubri deuocione comedit. Contigit autem post aliquot dies et annos, quod successor eius, sorte scilicet electus, faciens illac iter ad eum mitteret ut panem sibi militibusque suis acciperet. Qui respondit se modicum et quod tantis non sufficeret habere; si tamen pro Deo petere, se daturum. Remisit autem ad eum dicens, "Si miserit, recipiam; sin autem, mansionem eius et panem suum et ipsum flamma comburet." Cui Cadocus: "Malo ipse panem habeat, quam simul comburamur; sed maledicti qui comederint." Comedentibus autem illis, anathema scientibus nec

parcentibus, miles quidam Iltutus nomine, stans in medio eorum, abstinuit et dissuasit. At illi obstinati et deridentes eum casmate absorti perierunt; terra autem sub pedibus Iltuti mansit, et saluatus est. Hec de Cadoco Brenin.[90]

(Cadog, a king of Wales, heard the Lord saying, "He that leaveth not all things for me is not worthy," and after he had left all behind, as a hermit in the desert he ate bread obtained through the labor of his hands and the sweat of his brow with joyful and nourishing piety. But after some days and years it chanced that the one who had been chosen as his successor through drawing lots, as he was traveling that way, sent a messenger to him to seize bread for his soldiers and himself. And Cadog responded that he had only a little and not enough for so many men. Nevertheless, if he requested it for the sake of God, he would give it. He sent a message back to Cadog saying, "If he sends it, I will accept it. But if not, fire will reduce his dwelling and his bread and his own self to ashes." To this, Cadog replied, "I would prefer him having the bread than being burnt to ashes with it, but cursed are those who eat it." As they were eating, not even refraining though they were aware of the curse, a certain knight by the name of Illtud, as he stood in the middle of them, abstained and advised them against eating. But as they were defying and mocking him, they were swallowed up by the earth breaking open, and they died, yet the earth under Illtud's feet remained, and he was saved. But so much for Cadog Brenin.)

To the best of my knowledge, although the similarity of Walter's tale to the versions found in the Welsh vitae has often been acknowledged, no commentator has noticed the connection between Walter, St. Peter's Abbey, and these vitae.[91] Instead, Walter's knowledge of Illtud's conversion is commonly explained by making recourse to "oral tradition."[92]

Three Latin versions of Illtud's conversion exist. The *Vita Sancti Cadoci* and the *Vita Sancti Iltuti* both contain the episode, as does Caradog of Llancarfan's revision of the *Vita Sancti Cadoci*.[93] Overt textual borrowing frequently occurs in the Welsh-Latin vitae, so the fact that this episode appears in three lives is not particularly surprising. All of these vitae circulated in southeastern Wales in the twelfth century, and Gloucester almost certainly had at least one text that contained the episode. The case for Gloucester having the *Vita Sancti Iltuti* is less certain than for either version of the *Vita Sancti Cadoci*. Gloucester never held Llanilltud Fawr, Illtud's chief foundation, and there seems to be no overt reason for an interest in St. Illtud. However, the monks at Gloucester did maintain a close relationship with Llandaf, and it was in Llandaf's interest that the *Vita Sancti Iltuti* was written sometime after 1120.[94] The *Vita Sancti Iltuti* could have traveled to Gloucester Abbey along with other Llandaf material. Perhaps the Gloucester monks connected St. Illtud (whose name also appears as "Eltus," "Eltuth," and "Æltutus" in the Vespasian vitae) with St. Aldatus (Aldate), a local Gloucester saint whose feast day appears as a fourteenth-century addition in a Gloucester calendar.[95] St. Peter's may have sought out new traditions about this poorly known local saint when the *Vita Sancti Iltuti* appeared at some point after 1120.

Nonetheless, a Gloucester connection is more easily discernible for the *Vita Sancti Cadoci*. Llancarfan, the principle church of St. Cadog, had been in Gloucester's control from the beginning of the twelfth century, and it was a valuable possession. Indeed, the monks at Gloucester, just like those of Glastonbury, seemed to have "hired" Caradog of Llancarfan to compile lives of some of their most important Welsh saints.[96] To that end, Caradog seems to have written three lives for the monks of Gloucester: St. Cadog, St. Gwynllyw, and St. Tatheus.[97] These latter two saints are closely related to Cadog and would have held relevance for Gloucester. St. Peter's had the church of St. Gwynllyw, Cadog's father, in Newport. And Tatheus (called "Metheus" in the *Vita Sancti Cadoci*) plays an important role in the stories of Gwynllyw and Cadog:[98] Gwynllyw, before he settles on a more saintly way of life, steals Tathwy's cow, thus bringing Tathwy to his court, where he eventually becomes Cadog's teacher. Given their interest in Llancarfan and Newport, it is understandable that Gloucester monks would have an interest in these three vitae, all of which concern a close-knit family of saints.

Walter had clear connections to St. Peter's, Gloucester, whether as a young student or as an adult. If he had been a student there, or happened to visit on March 29, he could have even heard *lectiones* from the life of Gwynllyw, Cadog's father, as the abbey celebrated his feast day.[99] Moreover, all three of these vitae appear in Cotton Vespasian A.xiv, which was compiled at Monmouth. Monmouth, it should be remembered, was well within Walter's orbit. Either as a canon of Hereford or as the holder of Westbury-on-Severn, he would have been within a day's ride of two ecclesiastical centers where the *Vita Sancti Cadoci* is known to have been.

In addition to all the circumstantial evidence, there is one more clue that strongly suggests Walter obtained his knowledge of Cadog and Illtud from written Latin sources—the forms of the names *Cadocus* and *Iltutus*. Although the Welsh names in the *De nugis curialium* have received scant attention, their analysis can yield important information regarding the types of sources that Walter was using. The Latin orthography of proper names in medieval Wales often contains fossilized spellings from earlier orthographic systems.[100] Welsh scribes must have felt a certain affinity for this older orthography, since "there is a general tendency to keep a more archaic, sometimes a very ancient and Latin-looking, form in a Latin context."[101] The intricate, and sometimes controversial, details of early Welsh orthography needn't be rehearsed here, but for the present purposes two consequences of this conservatism are relevant.[102] First of all, correct archaic forms of names can help verify the antiquity of texts that only appear in late medieval manuscripts. For example, the orthography of a list of bishops for the ancient *clas* church at Glasbury found in a fourteenth-century manuscript points to an eleventh-century exemplar.[103] And second, the appearance of older orthography, which does not indicate contemporary pronunciation, can be a sign that authors and scribes have obtained the name from a textual source, as opposed to an oral source. Here, a useful analogy may be made with the conservative orthography of Modern French: If an English speaker writes that he has met a man named *Ahno* in Paris, his spelling reveals no knowledge of French orthography, and presumably he has only heard the name spoken. If however, *Arnaud* is written, then we can safely assume that our informant has some knowledge of written French. These differences would have been heightened in medieval society, where literacy was far less common than today. One well-known application of this principal is found in Bede's spelling of a Welsh abbot's name as *Dinoot*, a form that strongly suggests that Bede's source was at one remove or another oral tradition, which contrasts with other spellings that indicate textual transmission from a Welsh source, such as *Brocmail*.[104] Thus, in a Welsh context, the same name can be spelled quite differently in Latin as opposed to the vernacular.

The Welsh names of Walter's *De nugis curialium* can likewise yield valuable information about their provenance. In the case of the names *Cadocus* and *Iltutus*, both are Latin forms—not vernacular—which is highly indicative of Walter having access to a Latin source.[105] *Cadocus* represents the Middle Welsh name *Cadawc* (*Cadog* in Modern Welsh), which in Walter's day would have been pronounced something like /ˈkadaug/.[106] Importantly, the sequence

-ocus in *Cadocus* is a fossilized spelling of a common Welsh suffix, which can appear in names (e.g., *Petrocus* and *Carantocus*).[107] The ending *-ocus*, "an old stereotyped conventional form," contains archaic orthography that has been preserved in the fossilized Latin spelling of the name.[108] However, in Walter's contemporary Welsh, the vowel in this suffix would have been pronounced as a diphthong (/au/). The import of this is that if Walter had merely heard the name spoken aloud, he would have written *-auc*(*us*) or possibly *-aug*(*us*) instead of *-ocus*. It is instructive to compare the spelling *Cadocus* with a few other Welsh names in the *De nugis curialium*. The Welsh names from Walter's foray into the mythology of Brycheiniog provide a helpful contrast: *Wastiniauc, Brekeniauc, Madauc, Vagelauc*.[109] None of these names display the Latinate spelling *-o-* for *-au-* here. While the spelling *-auc* does not on its own indicate the oral transmission of these names (as will be discussed in full below), its use does however mark out *Cadocus* as a fossilized Latinate form. Furthermore, it also shows that Walter himself does not systematize his Welsh names; the variation must be a result of source material.

Similarly, the name *Iltutus* also suggests a Latinate background. Walter's Welsh contemporaries would have pronounced the name of this saint /ˈiɬtʉd/, which would have twisted the tongues of Old French or English speakers. Although *Iltutus* would be an unlikely spelling for someone who had only heard the name for several reasons, I will focus on two orthographic features.[110] The (in)famous Welsh sound /ɬ/, spelled *ll* or *l* in Middle Welsh and *ll* in contemporary Modern Welsh, is quite distinctive, and English speakers have wrestled with various ways to represent this sound for centuries. Just as Shakespeare approximated *Llywelyn* as *Fluellen*, medieval Anglo-Norman and English writers variously rendered /ɬ/ as *thl, lth, lh, sl,* and *tl*.[111] The Latin spelling *Iltutus* reflects an earlier period when this sound was either unmarked in orthography or had yet to fully contrast with /l/.[112] There are, moreover, a few examples where the *De nugis curialium* shows a distinctively non-Welsh spelling of the sound /ɬ/. These instances, in contrast, show Walter working to spell whatever his ear heard using "normal" Latin spelling. In the case of the sound /ɬ/, he seems to prefer the spelling *sl*: he spells *Gelligaer* as *Gesligair*, and he does so again for the Welsh name *Genillyn*, if that indeed is the name lying behind the manuscript's *Cheueslinus*.[113] However, when Walter uses a Welsh name that is widely known, either on account of Geoffrey of Monmouth or contemporary politics, he tends to use its common Latin form (and thus the sound /ɬ/ is left unmarked): *Luelinus* for *Llywelyn*; *Cadolanus* for *Cadwallan*; *Golenus* for *Gollwyn*.[114] In sum, the *De nugis curialium* displays two clear strategies for spelling the sound /ɬ/ in Welsh names. The first is to use the common Latin form in archaic or archaizing orthography (these names thus have attached to them standard Latin declensional endings, e.g., -*us*). The second is to try to approximate Welsh sounds as closely as possible in standard Latin orthography—the "Fluellen" strategy, as it were. Names formed by this strategy often, though not always, do not have Latin endings, and thus stick out as decidedly non-Welsh, for example, *Gesligair*.

The spelling *Iltutus* displays typical Welsh-Latin orthography in another way. The second *t* in *Iltutus* would have been voiced (/d/) in contemporary Welsh. Here again, the Latin spelling displays a fossilized form from an earlier orthographic system.[115] As with *Cadocus*, Walter's use of the form *Iltutus* betrays a knowledge of Welsh Latin. Tellingly, *Iltutus* and *Cadocus* do not represent the same type of Welsh-Latin spelling, as the second *t* in *Iltutus* retains a more conservative orthography than the *d* in *Cadocus*. Or, to put it another way, if these words were spelled using the exact same Welsh-Latin orthography, one would expect *Iltutus*/*Catocus* or *Iltudus*/*Cadocus*. That this is not the case is curious, yet it is easily explained: this same mixture of different strata of Welsh-Latin orthography, with *Cadog* as *Cadocus* and *Illtud* as *Iltutus*, appears in the *Vita Sancti Cadoci*.

The fact that Walter sometimes resorts to the "Fluellen" strategy shows that he does not always know the proper Latin form of Welsh names, bringing those instances in which he does know the correct Welsh-Latin orthography into sharp contrast. It would be curious indeed if Walter hit upon correct Welsh-Latin spellings *Cadocus* and *Iltutus*—both of which appear consistently in the vitae that circulated in and near Gloucester—without first having some sort of exposure to Welsh-Latin documents. Moreover, one more orthographic clue suggests that behind Walter's story of Cadog lies a written Welsh tradition: he closes the tale by writing "Hec de Cadoco Brenin" (But so much for King Cadog).[116] In addition to the pithy *hec de*, with which medieval Latin writers often announced the end of a section or topic, this succinct conclusion ends on the Welsh word *brenin* (king) for even greater effect. Had Walter obtained this story through an oral source, we may expect him to have indicated the lenition triggered by apposition, writing *Cadoco Vrenin* instead—though this point is not particularly telling.[117] In sum, all the orthographic evidence in Walter's conversion of Illtud suggests that he had access to written material from Wales. Or, to return to our French analogy, in this story Walter consistently uses the equivalent of *Arnaud* instead of *Ahno*. These spellings on their own do not indicate that Walter read the *Vita Sancti Cadoci*, but they do strongly suggest that Walter had encountered traditions about Cadog and Illtud in a nonvernacular source.

Whichever version of the *Vita Sancti Cadoci* that Walter encountered, he stayed close to his source. His tale of Cadog is a fairly accurate summary of the saint's renunciation of the world and the splitting of the earth episode as found in the various versions of the *Vita Sancti Cadoci*. Walter does, however, deviate from these sources in two ways. The first is quite understandable. Walter calls Cadog a king of Wales in both Latin and Welsh, even though he is never given that title in his vitae. Nonetheless, it is not difficult to see how Walter comes to that designation. According to Lifris's *Vita Sancti Cadoci*, Cadog's father Gwynllyw is king of the kingdom of Gwynlliog, and he grants his son his kingdom upon his death.[118] Moreover, Caradog of Llancarfan's revision of the *Vita Sancti Cadoci* styles him "the prince of Gwynlliog."[119] It is therefore only a small leap for Walter to call Cadog king.[120] This slight change could also be motivated by the content of *distinctio* 2, which in a large part contains vignettes of secular and sacred men. If Cadog is both a king and a hermit, the story better resonates with its immediate surroundings; he becomes similar to Elias, the Welsh hermit, and Llywelyn, the Welsh king.[121] Given Walter's ability to thoroughly rework his source material and earlier drafts, Cadog's promotion to king is a small alteration.

Walter's other change to the story of Cadog is likewise minor, but his motivation for doing so is more difficult to discern. In all versions of the *Vita Sancti Cadoci*, the passing king who harasses St. Cadog is his uncle, Paul Penychen. Walter does not name him but introduces him as follows: "Contigit autem post aliquot dies et annos, quod successor eius, sorte scilicet electus, faciens illac iter ad eum mitteret ut panem sibi militibusque suis acciperet" (But after some days and years it chanced that the one who had been chosen as his successor through drawing lots, as he was traveling that way, sent a messenger to him to seize bread for his soldiers and himself).[122] The phrase *sorte scilicet electus* is odd here—nowhere in the hagiographical legends is Paul Penychen designated king through drawing lots. Moreover, this detail seems to have no motivation whatsoever—it adds nothing to the narrative. Walter is often meticulous in his revisions, removing extraneous material with care, so it seems uncharacteristic of him to either insert or leave this unnecessary detail in his quite condensed story. One possible solution is that the phrase is another of the manuscript's many scribal interpolations.[123] The manuscript might have originally read "sorte faciens illac iter" (as fate would have it, he was traveling that way). A glossator may have incorrectly construed *sorte* as modifying *successor* and attempted to explain it by writing *scilicet electus*, which afterward became interpolated into the main text. This explanation has the added benefit of explaining the somewhat odd use of *scilicet* here. Nonetheless, the simplest explanation would be to assume a scribal error of *forte* for *sorte*, which would bring the passage more into line with the other known versions.[124] These two minor changes aside, Walter's version is a straightforward relation of the splitting of the earth episode.

Walter's Brycheiniog History

Immediately following the story of Cadog, Walter begins his tale of Gastin Gastiniog and his son Trunio Vaglog. The two stories are verbally linked by Walter's transition "Aliud non miraculum sed portentum nobis Walenses referunt" (The Welsh tell us of another thing—not a miracle, but a monstrosity).[125] The *portentum* in question is Trunio, who is another of Walter's half-fairy, half-human hybrids. The story is localized in Brycheiniog, an early medieval Welsh kingdom that roughly corresponds to the southern part of the historic county of Brecknockshire. Observing apparently supernatural bands of women dancing in the night, Gastin tries to catch one. Although for three straight nights they manage to scatter and sink into Llangorse Lake, on the fourth he is able to seize one. After this rape, the two wed, and the nameless fairy woman bears him many children. Gastin, however, eventually breaks his wife's commandment not to strike her with his bridle. After he does so, his wife flees back to the lake with his children, and Gastin only manages to save one, Trunio. Trunio, seeking to broaden his horizons, then travels to the king of Deheubarth and serves him. His new lord, however, haughtily boasts that his household is the finest and strongest under heaven. Trunio disagrees, which eventually leads the king of Deheubarth to attack Brychan, the king of Trunio's home territory of Brycheiniog. In the ensuing battle, Brychan routs his opponents and builds three cairns out of their dismembered limbs. Trunio, so people say, escaped such a fate and was rescued by his mother and still dwells with her in the lake. Walter, however, considers this a lie, since "an uncertainty of this sort could have been made up about a missing man."[126]

Outside of Walter's *De nugis curialium*, the story of Gastin and Trunio does not seem to have survived, although extant Welsh sources attest that Walter drew upon some body of Welsh knowledge for this fairy legend. Comparing Walter's tale with these Welsh sources, Brynley Roberts has attempted to reconstruct the early legend behind the fairy women of Llangorse Lake.[127] His analysis is probably the best possible given the evidence, although, as Chapters 2 and 4 have shown, Walter's ability to drastically alter his sources, or even his own earlier drafts, renders the testimony of the *De nugis curialium* particularly suspect in this regard. And although Roberts is not particularly interested in Walter's immediate sources, he, like many others, tends to subscribe to the vague notion that Walter picked up legends about Brecon through oral tradition.[128] However, rather than speculate about the ur-myth of the story of Gastin and his son, I will argue that the characters in the tale, as well as a few suggestive narrative details, provide strong evidence that Walter's source material lies in contemporary Welsh-Latin documents. Like Welsh vitae, it is also likely that these documents were available at Gloucester.

It is easy to see why St. Peter's Abbey would take an interest in Brycheiniog, as it had significant territorial holdings there. Bernard Neufmarché, who had invaded and colonized the region, in 1088 granted to St. Peter's Abbey

> Glasbury, with everything pertaining to it, free and quit of all secular service and custom, for perpetual alms; and church of Saint Cynidr in the same town, with everything pertaining to it. I also grant them, and I confirm it by my charter, a complete tithe of my entire lordship through all the land in Brycheiniog in woodland and in meadow, wherever people hold or cherish my lordship, that is, in grain, cattle, cheeses, hunting, and honey, and all other things from which a tithe should be granted.[129]

St. Cynidr appears in the calendar of Vespasian A.xiv, almost certainly from the influence of Gloucester monks.[130] And Bernard's gift of a tithe of the entire lordship ensured that the abbey scrutinized the region's affairs; indeed, Robert de Melun, the bishop of Hereford (1163–67) had to broker peace between the monks of Gloucester and Brecon Priory regarding tithes in the region.[131] The resulting arrangement leaves the monks of Gloucester holding the tithe of the lordship of Talgarth. They also held the tithe to Llanfaes, almost on the doorstep of Brecon Priory.[132] Earlier, in 1164, another argument with Brecon Priory reveals that the monks of Gloucester had claimed (apparently with some success) the parochial right of "Melianach" (Melinog), situated a few miles northwest of St. Cynidr's.[133] These wide-ranging interests throughout Brycheiniog made the area an especially valuable one for St. Peter's Abbey. As with its other Welsh holdings, the abbey seems to have collected documents concerning the history of its property, and the area of the ancient kingdom of Brycheiniog—which became the Norman lordship of Brecon—had much to say regarding its legendary past.

A few surviving sources hint at the extent of historical material concerning Brycheiniog that could have been available to the Gloucester monks. The small historical tract *De situ Brecheniauc* contains a brief account of the circumstances of the birth of Brychan, the eponymous founder of the kingdom of Brycheiniog, and it also lists his many sons and daughters.[134] The *De situ Brecheniauc* can be reasonably dated to the first third of the twelfth century and was probably composed at Brecon Priory or one of its dependent houses.[135] A document closely related to the *De situ Brecheniauc* has also survived to the modern day, however, just barely: Sir John Prise (1502–55) copied what is known as the *Cognacio Brychan* from an earlier medieval manuscript that was afterward lost or destroyed.[136] Additionally, two Middle Welsh genealogies derive some of their material from the *De situ Brecheniauc*.[137] The *De situ Brecheiniauc* is closest to the original composition, with the other three cognate documents showing signs of significant editing, glossing, and translation.[138] As the diocese of Llandaf grew in power and pretensions in the early twelfth century, the author(s) of the *De situ Brecheniauc* sought to counter rival claims by providing evidence for the antiquity and independence of their own churches.

The monks at St. Peter's Abbey would have found this document quite useful, since they held the church of St. Cynidr, who, after all, is said to be Brychan's grandson in *De situ Brecheniauc*, giving the saint an excellent local pedigree.[139] The *De situ Brecheniauc*, which survives only in the Vespasian manuscript, probably owes its presence there, and thus survival, to St. Peter's Abbey (its appearance in the manuscript is difficult to explain otherwise).[140] It could have come to Gloucester with other Llandaf or Llancarfan material, since the text was available to a genealogist who added material to the *Vita Sancti Cadoci*, which would have presumably happened at Llancarfan or Llandaf.[141] It is important to note that the monks of Gloucester were not merely interested in the lives of saints. They copied the text *De primo statu Landavensis ecclesie*, which details the history of the southern Welsh church, from Llandaf.[142] And they saw fit to document the properties of the canons of Llancarfan.[143] The *De situ Brecheniauc* would have made an attractive and useful addition to the abbey's Welsh collection.

Moreover, an odd genealogy relating to Brycheiniog, also unique to the Vespasian manuscript, is best explained as a Gloucester composition.[144] On the last folio of Vespasian's calendar of Welsh saints, in the section for December, a twenty-one-line note is found in the right-hand margin:

> Hec est generatio sancti Egweni, episcopi. Pater eius uocatur Gunleuus rex, et mater eius sancta Gladusa. Uilla, in qua genitus et natus fuit sanctus Egwenus, Brendlos uocatur. Frater eius beatus Keniderus, et ipse requiescat apud uillam, que dicitur Glesburia. Et sanctus Cadocus eiusdem sancti frater fuit. Isti tres sancti uiri, Egwinus, Keniderus, et sanctus Cadocus filii supradicti regis fuerunt.[145]

> (This is the genealogy of Saint Ecgwine the bishop. His father was called King Gwynllyw, and his mother was Gwladus. The town in which Saint Ecgwine was begotten and born is called *Brendlos*. Blessed Cynidr is his brother, and he lies at the town which is called Glasbury. And Saint Cadog was the brother of this same saint. These three saintly men, Ecgwine, Cynidr, and Saint Cadog, were sons of the king mentioned above.)

This curious genealogy has the fingerprints of a Gloucester monk all over it. That St. Ecgwine, bishop of Worcester (d. 717), is meant is confirmed by the note's placement in the month of December: the thirtieth of the month is his feast day.[146] The manifest purpose of this genealogy is to bring St. Ecgwine into the orbit of Welsh saints and to create a particularly close relationship between the English Ecgwine and the Welsh Cadog and Cynidr. Directly contradicting the genealogical information found elsewhere in the Vespasian manuscript, Ecgwine's genealogy seems to have sat uneasily with the scribe of the manuscript. While the *Generatio Sancti Egweni* remains in the margin, Ecgwine's festival looks to have been erased from the calendar.[147]

Silas Harris believed that this genealogy was composed at Monmouth.[148] But in light of Hughes's argument that a good deal of the material in the Vespasian manuscript came from Gloucester, a better case can be made for the *Generatio* having been composed for the benefit of St. Peter's.[149] As mentioned above, it was Gloucester that held the main churches of Cynidr (Glasbury) and Cadog (Llancarfan). Moreover, although Monmouth's interest in Ecgwine has been explained as the result of holding the benefice of Weston-sub-Edge—only a few miles away from the center of Ecgwine's cult at Evesham—or as the result of Ecgwine's increasing popularity in the twelfth century, the monks at Gloucester had a clearer connection to this Anglo-Saxon saint.[150] In the Middle Ages Gloucester lay in the diocese of Worcester, the heartland of St. Ecgwine and where his veneration was most intense. Liturgies throughout the diocese commemorated the feast of its most famous bishop, including the feast of his translation on September 10. Gloucester Abbey is no exception, as both feasts are found in its calendar.[151] The monks of St. Peter's Abbey also remembered St. Ecgwine in their *Historia*, where he consecrates Eadburh, sister of Cyneburh, as the abbey's second abbess (St. Peter's was originally a nunnery or a dual house).[152] In sum, the monks of St. Peter's had ample reason to unite their most famous bishop with Cadog and Cynidr.

Interestingly, the compiler of the *Generatio* appears to have taken advantage of the nominal similarity between the Welsh saint Eig(i)on, about whom nothing is known, and the Latin form of Ecgwine's name, *Egwinus/Egwenus*. The church of this Welsh saint is roughly three miles west of Glasbury (modern-day Llanigon), and the compiler of the *Generatio* may be implying a Gloucester claim for this church by sowing confusion between these two saints. Indeed, a century or so later it seems Eig(i)on and Ecgwine had been thoroughly confused in local documents.[153] The assertion that Ecgwine was born in *Brendlos*—which seems to have been a Norman spelling of *Bronllys*—may likewise connote the local aspirations of Gloucester monks.[154] In general, it should be remembered that St. Peter's excelled at creating documents to suit their immediate needs—a genealogy such as this would be a small matter for such seasoned forgers.[155] The *Generatio Sancti Egweni* neatly ties together Gloucester's holdings in Brycheiniog and southern Glamorgan with a powerful diocesan saint; in appropriating Welsh churches, Gloucester was therefore merely reuniting this long-separated saintly family.[156]

If the *Generatio Sancti Egweni* was written for the benefit of Gloucester, then it seems all the more likely that the presence of the *De situ Brecheniauc* in Vespasian A.xiv is also due to Gloucester, since both concern a region in which the abbey maintained substantial interests. Although Walter Map's immediate source for the story of Gastin and his son Trunio has not survived, I think it is possible that he drew upon a body of Brycheiniog lore and history that has much in common with the *De situ Brecheniauc*. Certainly, Walter's story of Gastin and Trunio differs greatly in plot, style, and tone from the *De situ Brecheniauc*, and it would be wrong to call this text a source in a traditional sense. Yet, Walter's story has the telltale signs of literary transmission, and it shares a few salient details with the genealogy. Walter could have used the *De situ Brecheniauc* in a manner approximating the previous generation's approach to Welsh sources—as a source for names, inspiration, and other authenticating details—and thus his tale may only vaguely resemble its source. Or Gloucester could have been in possession of another document from Brycheiniog that dealt with the region's history. Whatever the shape of Walter's immediate source or the manner of his adaptation, my aim is merely to show that the story of Gastin and Trunio comes from the same southern Welsh ecclesiastical milieu that produced Vespasian A.xiv, the Book of Llandaf, and Geoffrey's *History of the Kings of Britain*. As with Walter's story of Cadog, the following analysis is restricted largely to proper names, since Walter has been shown to alter his sources in quite radical ways.

The tale is explicitly localized on the shores of Llangorse Lake in Brycheiniog: "secus stagnum Brekeniauc" (beside the Lake of Brycheiniog).[157] The Llyfni (which through metathesis has become *Llynfi* in Modern Welsh) is a small river that flows into and then out of Llangorse Lake, until it joins the Wye at Glasbury, in sight of the church of St. Cynidr. The river plays a crucial role in Gastin's story. After he marries his fairy bride, she warns him, "I will serve you willingly, and I will obey you with complete devotion, until the day you strike me with your bridle while wanting to rush to the screams at the other side of the Llyfni."[158] Walter then explains that "the Llyfni is a river near the lake."[159] The form of the name in the manuscript calls for a brief explanation.[160] Its first appearance in Walter's manuscript reads *leuē*, with a suspension indicating a final nasal, while in the second instance the scribe has written *leueiii*, with three final minims. Wright's 1850 edition has *Lenem*, while James (and everyone following) has *Leuem*. However, the correct reading is clearly *Leueni*, a perfectly acceptable contemporary Welsh spelling of the river.[161] The testimony of Gerald of Wales, who also writes *Leueni*, confirms that a scribe at some point in transmission bungled the minims of this unfamiliar lake.[162] Similiar confusion is found in the treatment of *Brycheiniog*, which is spelled *brekeíiiauc, brekeiiiāc, brecheiiiauc*.[163] Either the first or the last preserves the underlying Welsh form *brekeinauc* or *brecheniauc*, both of which are attested, while the middle form shows that once again the minims of a foreign toponym led a scribe into error.[164] What is significant about *Leueni* and *Brecheniauc* is that both ultimately point to good twelfth-century Welsh spellings. Although they are not Welsh-Latin forms (like *Cadocus* and *Iltutus*), their use of vernacular Welsh orthography hints that Walter's immediate source was yet again literary and not oral: Walter, or anyone else unfamiliar with Welsh orthography, would probably not represent the /ł/ in *Leueni* with a simple *l*.[165] (Consider the spelling *Thleweny* in an inquest written in Edward II's time.)[166]

On its own, Walter's spelling of *Brycheiniog*, a well-known region whose name lived on in the lordship of *Brecon/Brecknock*, is not particularly telling.[167] That Walter spelled a minor local river using proper Welsh orthography, does, however, point toward a written source.

Another indication of Walter's access to a good Welsh source is his use of the word *Deheubarth*, which is the native word for another early medieval Welsh kingdom. Consisting roughly of southwestern Wales, nearby Deheubarth would be a logical place for Gastin's son Trunio to be fostered (if that is the relationship implied in the text). Here, too, a scribe has blundered a strange name, misreading an *h* as an *l* and thus rendering *Deheubarth* as *Deheulard*.[168] Adding to the confusion, at some point a marginal note incorrectly glossing *Deheubarth* as "North Wales" ("id est Norwallie") became interpolated into the main text of the *De nugis curialium*, just as many others did.[169] Walter's knowledge of this Welsh word is not particularly surprising: as a Marcher he would have had more than enough local knowledge of southern Wales to know this basic political term, or he could have extracted it from the *Itinerarium Kambriae* of Gerald of Wales.[170] That said, the political units described in this tale strongly imply that Walter was working from a Welsh historical source. In Walter's narrative, Brycheiniog is a separate political unit from Deheubarth: Deheubarth's independent, unnamed *rex* invades King Brychan's sovereign territory of Brycheiniog. Brycheiniog, however, ceased to exist as an independent kingdom sometime after 934, having been absorbed into greater Deheubarth.[171] Walter's story thus preserves an echo of Welsh dynastic politics some two hundred years before he was born.[172] Moreover, Walter's version of events roughly corresponds to the *De situ Brecheniauc*, which mentions that Clytguin, Brychan's son, invaded all of South Wales.[173] Therefore, both Walter's *De nugis curialium* and the *De situ Brecheniauc* imagine a battle between the king of Brycheiniog and Deheubarth, and both have Brycheiniog prevail. Walter, it seems, has been reading some Brycheiniog propaganda.

Two of the places in Walter's tale remain difficult to identify. The *monte cumeraic* where Brychan is bathing when told of the invading army is described as not being "terram suam" (his own land), but attempts to identify *cumeraic*, which has the feel of a Welsh word, have ventured no further than conjecture.[174] The best solution to date is that *monte cumeraic* is a scribal error for Montgomery.[175] In addition to being plausible, it fits the definition of being outside Brycheiniog. Furthermore, when King Brychan defeats the invaders from Deheubarth, he cuts off their right hands, penises, and right feet and orders cairns built up over each pile of dismembered limbs. Although Walter does not report the names of each of these cairns, this anecdote certainly looks like the onomastic lore that the medieval Welsh cherished.[176] The prevalence of the "right" feet and hands suggests a punning connecting with Deheubarth, which literally means "Right Part" in Welsh. (Rather than north, the medieval world oriented itself looking toward the east, which explains the equivalence of "right" with "south.") It is unclear if Walter was aware of this pun, but my sense is he was not. Walter took great delight in wordplay, and had he known, he might well have explained it to his audience, who he surely would not have been expected to know the etymology of this term (although it is transparent to a Welsh speaker). If such is the case, then Walter is passing on onomastic lore that he does not fully understand, which is again more suggestive of written, rather than oral, transmission.

The final toponym in Walter's account of the legendary history of Brycheiniog has suffered at the hands of scribes to a greater extent than the others. When a brave young man decides to risk his life by disturbing King Brychan's bath in order to bear the bad news of an invading army, the manuscript has him announce, "Vestra [*sic*] terre Reynos, id est Brecheniauc, non pugnent amodo quasi animalia desunt."[177] That is the entirety of his speech; it is also nonsensical and ungrammatical. A few attempts have been made to unravel this passage, though none are ideal.[178] If it originally read "Vestra [terra] . . . terre Reynos non pungent," an eye skip from *terra* to *terre*, and from apparently the beginning of the young man's speech to the very end, would explain the error. Regardless of the corruption of this passage, all commentators agree that *Reynuc* (Modern Welsh *Rheinwg*) lies behind the manuscript's *Reynos*.[179] The Welsh evidence suggests that *Rheinwg* is either another name for Brycheiniog, or a larger region encompassing it.[180] The phrase "id est Brecheniauc," as I argued in Chapter 3, is another of the manuscript's many interpolated glosses and is therefore not particularly trustworthy evidence for understanding the geography of Rheinwg: the glossator probably is using context to guess here. It is not difficult to imagine a scribe unfamiliar with this rare Welsh place-name confusing the letter *g* with a final round *s*, especially if his exemplar used the figure 8–shaped *g* typical of Anglicana.[181] This mistake, however, would presuppose an original spelling of *Reynug* or *Reynog*, which, while not impossible, is not an attested Middle Welsh spelling, nor would it fit the orthography of Walter's supposed exemplar, as he consistently writes *c* for final /g/.[182] Another possibility is that there has been no scribal error, and that *Reynos* displays the same pattern as the names *Caradawc* and *Meriadawc*,

which occur in French texts as *Caradues* and *Meriadus*.[183] Regardless of the
correct explanation for the corrupt form of this place-name, its presence in
the *De nugis curialium* again suggests that Walter had access to some very
specific local history—other than Walter's story and the *Vita Sancti Cadoci*
and *Vita Sancti Paterni* (both of which were at Gloucester), the name does not
appear to have traveled outside of Wales. Indeed, even within Wales it seems
to have been restricted to antiquarian texts or those that had local connections
to Brycheiniog.[184] Unless Walter himself traveled into Brycheiniog and consulted keepers of Welsh lore—and we have no evidence of that—he must have
picked up the name from some literary document.

The names of the tale's characters also show signs that Walter was working from a written document, and they also hint that he, or someone else, has
been creating new tales out of Brycheiniog myth. The appearance of a *Madauc*
(Modern Welsh *Madog*) at the court of the king of Deheubarth is not particularly helpful in this respect; this rather mundane Welsh name could have been
added by Walter or anyone else for local color.[185] The three remaining names,
however, are worth examination. I will begin with the least perplexing—
Brychan. The name appears three times and is spelled differently in our manuscript on each occasion: *breauc, brehein,* and *brechein*.[186] None of these
spellings is exactly as one would expect. The *De situ Brecheiniauc*, for example,
gives both the Latin *Brachanus* and, much more often, the Welsh form *Brachan*. The vitae in Vespasian A.xiv also have the Latin *Brachanus* and Welsh
Brachan. Walter's text seems to be aiming for a Welsh spelling. In particular I
would argue that *brechein* underlies these forms for a few reasons. First of all,
breauc looks suspect: it does not come close to any attested variant of *Brachan*.
This form is best explained as an error, with a scribe rendering the final *-kein,*
-chein, or *-hein* of this strange word as *-auc*, perhaps under the influence of the
several other Welsh names ending with *-auc* in this tale. The two other spellings, however, seem to result from invention of some sort. The forms *brehein*
and *brechein* appear to be back-formations from the name of the region,
brecheinawc.[187] In other words, someone has derived the name of the king
from the territory, and not the other way around as is philologically correct.[188]
Perhaps a scribe "corrected" *Brychan*, thinking that the name of this character
should more closely resemble his eponymous territory.[189] Or perhaps Walter
or Walter's source practiced some dubious etymology.

Bad etymology (by modern standards at least) also explains the mysterious character Wastinus Wastiniauc. John Rhys's suggestion that the Welsh
name behind this apparently ancient Latin form is *Gwestin Gwestiniog* has

been widely accepted.[190] It, however, is problematic in a few respects.[191] A better solution is found along the southwestern shore of Llangorse Lake, where Llangasty Tal-y-Llyn, an ancient church dedicated to a virtually unknown saint, lies. Roberts first suggested that Walter's (*G*)*wastinus* may have something to do with the mysterious saint Gastayn, to whom Llangasty is dedicated.[192] To add a few words in support of this view, Anglo-Norman orthography can again explain some peculiarities of the manuscript's spelling of Welsh names. The relatively free exchange of initial *g* and *w* (and indeed of *v* as well) in Anglo-Norman texts is well documented: it gives us the doublets *Gauvain* and *Wawayn*, Anglo-Norman *gages* and English *wages*, and even explains Marie de France's *garwuf* (werewolf, < Frankish **wari wulf*).[193] The form underlying Walter's text then is not *Gwastinus*, but rather *Gastinus*, which brings these two names into much closer alignment than Roberts suspects. The only other contemporary mention of this saint occurs in the Brychan documents during the baptism of St. Cynog, where the *Cognacio Brychan* has "ad sanctum Gastayn, cuius nunc ecclesia sita est iuxta Maram, qui baptizauit eum" but which the copyist of the *De situ Brecheniauc* has misconstrued as "ad castra baptizatus est."[194] Still, *Gastinus* does not seem quite right, since, given the rules of Welsh mutations, we should expect a *Casty* (< Latin *Castanius*?) to be the patron saint of Llangasty.[195] What has happened here? The simplest answer is that someone who knew that Welsh churches dedicated to a saint were named *llan* plus the saint's name, but who did not know Welsh, separated the two elements and incorrectly believed the patron saint of Llangasty to be someone named *Gasty*. He then duly Latinized the saint as *Gastinus*. Further evidence that the character is an invention of a later mind is found in his epithet *Wastiniauc*. As the *Vita Sancti Cadoci* helpfully explains, Welsh regions can be named after a founding figure by adding the suffix *-(i)auc* (Modern Welsh *-(i)og*): "Nam a Gundleio Gunliauc, a Brachano uero Brecheniauc uocatur" (For Gwynlliog is named from Gwynllyw, and Brycheiniog from Brychan).[196] However, no region named *Gastiniog, Gwestiniog, Wastiniog*, or the like is attested. The epithet *Wastinauc* seems to have been created as the putative territory for Gastin. Given that evidence of this naming strategy abounds in the *De situ Brecheniauc* and the Welsh vitae of Vespasian A.xiv, even a moderately clever Norman monk could use it to create ancient Welsh territories, no doubt to further the interests of his house.[197] Nonetheless, even as Walter's tale does not provide a clear cui bono for this snatch of the ancient traditions of Llangasty, the development of the legend of Gastin and the lake of Brycheiniog illustrates that someone took interest in the ancient history of

Llangasty and Llangorse Lake. In the twelfth century, that person would have almost certainly been a monk sifting through the legendary material of newly acquired territories.

By far the most problematic Welsh name in Walter's Brycheiniog history is Gastin's son Trunio Vagelauc.[198] The cognomen *Vagelauc* has a variety of meanings in Middle Welsh: "crooked," "carrying a (bishop's) crozier or a staff," or "lame."[199] The presence of *Vagelauc* has led to the identification of this character with Tynwedd/Tynwaed Vagloc, who is said to have raped Gwrgon, one of the daughters of Brychan.[200] Unfortunately, the veritable forest of minims in the manuscript's *t(r)iuuieuu* (consistently written as such four times), coupled with the unfamiliarity of this name, does not inspire complete confidence in accurate transmission, and it seems rash to identify Walter's character with another merely on the presence of an epithet. Orthographically, the name seems closest to *Truniaw* (Modern Welsh *Trunio*), the patron saint of Llandrinio.[201] The amount of minims aligns perfectly, and the only scribal error that must be assumed is misreading *a* as *e*. It is, however, difficult to explain how the name came to Walter, since Gloucester did not have any interest in Llandrinio, and the saint does not appear in Vespaisian A.xiv. Nonetheless, with a dozen or so Welsh names in the *De nugis curialium* and around two centuries of sloppy transmission between Walter's original text and Bodley 851, it is noteworthy that *Trunio* and *monte cumeraic* (if it is in fact Welsh) are the only Welsh names that remain unidentifiable in the *De nugis curialium*.

The characters, places, and politics in Walter's story of Gastin and his son Trunio show that he had access to a source dealing with Brycheiniog history. I have restricted my analysis to the tale's names because I am exceedingly wary of Walter's habit of radically altering his sources and rewriting his own work to serve some new purpose. In other words, the majority of the story's plot may well be Walter's own invention, pieced together from common folklore motifs, or radically adapted from a narrative like that found at the beginning of *De situ Brecheniauc*. This is the same author, after all, who attaches a similar fairy story to Eadric the Wild with no qualms whatsoever.[202] Nonetheless, not unlike Geoffrey of Monmouth raiding Welsh genealogies for lists of Welsh kings, Walter took at least the bare elements of his story from historical traditions gathered from Brycheiniog. The forms of the Welsh names witnessed in Bodley 851 point in the direction of a literary source, as do incidental details, such as the correct name of the river Llyfni and the aside that Llangorse Lake takes about two miles to walk around.[203] The latter is the type of unnecessary detail that looks to be an artifact from a source interested in property rights and land. Moreover, the appearance of both Welsh forms and Latin forms in the same story is likewise suggestive of Walter's use of a source. It has already been shown that Walter did not standardize his Welsh names, but that the *De nugis curialium* as a whole witnesses a mixture of Welsh-Latin orthography, proper vernacular Welsh forms, and Fluellen-like ear spellings. It is instructive that the latter type does not appear in the stories of Gastin Gastiniog. Instead, a few Latin forms sit comfortably alongside vernacular Welsh forms and some learned inventions. This is exactly the same intermixture that obtains through-out Vespasian A.xiv.[204] If Walter got his names for his Brycheiniog history from similar texts, we would expect that someone with a somewhat contrived Latinate name like *Gastinus* might have a son with the impeccably Welsh cog-nomen *Vagelauc*. Out of all of these, however, by far the most suggestive is the political situation describing an independent Brycheiniog triumphing over Deheubarth. A similar situation is only found in the *De situ Brecheniauc* and its related documents, and here it is a product of scholarly inventiveness, not folkloric confusion. Walter's immediate source(s) has not survived, as far as we can tell. It may well be that the *De situ Brecheniauc* was just one of many sources that Walter used to create his own Brycheiniog history. Whatever Walter was reading, it has every indication of belonging to the milieu of twelfth-century Norman monks in Wales—a preoccupation with ancient his-tory, an interest in the landscape, and the creation of new traditions about old figures.

Although Vespasian A.xiv provides ample testimony regarding the pres-ence of written traditions of Cadog and Brychan in southeastern Welsh eccle-siastical centers, two remarks from Gerald of Wales confirm that the manuscript was no anomaly. Gerald definitely took an interest in Welsh hagiography. He wrote the *Vita Sancti Davidis* and the no-longer-extant *Vita Caradoci*.[205] Ger-ald's tenure as archdeacon of Llanddew, just outside of Brecon, would have given him good access to local literary culture. His house at Llanddew was, as he rather forlornly puts it, "suitable for my studies and work in a pleasant, humdrum sort of way."[206] He clearly had read something like the *De situ Brech-eniauc*, if not the document itself, for he writes, "In ancient times the ruler of this region, which is called Brycheiniog, was a powerful and noble man named Brychan, and it is from him that this very land was given the name Brychein-iog. What seems to me noteworthy about him is that the British histories bear witness to the fact that he had twenty-four daughters."[207] The little that Gerald relates from these "British histories" (*historiae Britannicae*) closely agrees with the surviving Brychan documents.[208] Moreover, Gerald had also read an account of St. Illtud as well. In a brief list of the prodigies of Brycheiniog, he mentions that the saint's mare mated with a stag, and the resulting creature was a hybrid of both animals. Gerald's love of hybridity aside, he states that he gathered this fact from "the ancient and authentic documents of these parts."[209] Although the surviving *Vita Sancti Iltuti* does not contain this exact story, it does give an account of the saint's divinely tamed stag.[210] Gerald's testimony shows that alternative written accounts of the saint were in circulation, which accords well with the fact that Welsh vitae were redacted and copied with vigor in the century following the Norman invasion.[211] Like Walter Map, Gerald was able to read traditions about Brychan and Illtud with relative ease. His testimony explicitly mentions written sources, but it does so in a way that suggests that these documents were expected and commonplace. Gerald excels in expressing wonderment; it is revealing that the mere presence of written Welsh accounts of Brychan and Illtud draws none.

All the evidence points to a flurry of twelfth-century literary activity throughout southern Welsh ecclesiastical centers. The surviving Welsh vitae show clear signs of having been rewritten, excerpted, and "corrected" as they circulated throughout southern Wales and into England. The *Vita Dubricii*, for example, was first composed for Llandaf in support of Bishop Urban's diocesan claims, then it traveled to Gloucester where the monk Benedict rewrote it, and afterward both lives came to Monmouth. And the *Vita Sancti Cadoci*, first composed by Lifris, was later augmented with additional material, in addition to being rewritten by Caradog of Llancarfan. Much of the evidence for this flourishing literary culture was vanishing by the late Middle Ages. When John of Tynemouth (fl. ca. 1350) journeyed through Wales in search of hagiography, he found much (including Vespasian A.xiv), but his lament about material regarding St. Cynedd gives us a glimpse of what is lost: "I saw, in only one place in Wales, a great deal else written about this glorious confessor, which was not able to be read, since it had been erased, so to speak, by age."[212] The Welsh documents that Walter used for his own work would not have been rare or difficult to obtain; he could have found them at many churches in southern Wales and in interested English centers.

There is one final clue that Walter had access to written Welsh traditions: the tale of Gastin and Trunio immediately follows the story of Cadog. Although the rubricated chapter headings have marked the two out as distinct chapters, it is worth remembering that they are later scribal insertions and do not reflect Walter's intentions.[213] Indeed, the two tales are explicitly linked by the sentence "Aliud non miraculum sed portentum nobis Walenses referunt" (The Welsh tell us of another thing—not a miracle, but a monstrosity).[214] Walter also tells us that these stories share the same source—the Welsh. It is surely not a coincidence that the only two episodes in the *De nugis curialium* that reflect written Welsh traditions are found side by side. I would suggest that this present arrangement results from Walter copying a few select episodes from an anthology of historical material gathered from Wales, from a manuscript like Vespasian A.xiv. He was drawn to them on account of the organizing principle behind *distinctio* 2: secular and sacred wonders. Finding himself in need of a transition between the holy men at the *distinctio*'s beginning and a following series of *portenta* and *fantasmatae*, his mind would have naturally drifted to the Welsh vitae. The miracles of Welsh saints are as a whole more violent and, as it were, otherworldly than their English or French counterparts. In Walter's deft hands, the stories of Cadog and Gastin Gastiniog work as a thematic hinge that moves the narrative from traditional hagiography to secular supernatural phenomena. It is also no wonder that he chose a particularly vindictive scene from the *Vita Sancti Cadoci*, since Walter dwells on the reputed wrath of the Welsh several times in this *distinctio*. Walter seems to have selected these two stories from the available documents with particular care.

My present aim is not to show that Gloucester was, beyond the shadow of a doubt, the source for two of Walter's Welsh tales. Given the paucity of evidence from southeast Wales and Gloucester, it will probably remain impossible to know exactly where Walter obtained his written Welsh-Latin documents. Rather, the larger goal of this chapter is to show that Welsh-Latin material was easily available to Walter and his contemporaries. While I have built a case for Gloucester Abbey, Walter could have had similar documents from any number of places. For instance, it is also worth considering the possibility that Walter had the *De situ Brecheniauc*, or something like it, from Brecon itself. In 1202, King John confiscated the lands in Brecon and Llanddew held by St. Davids, and Walter Map was ordered to take possession of all the revenues to be had from Gerald's archdeaconry.[215] It is unclear whether Walter actually took possession of Gerald's beloved archdeaconry, but if he did, a visit to nearby Brecon would not be outside the realm of possibility.

The Sources of Walter's Other Welsh Tales

An examination of the other Welsh material in the *De nugis curialium* illustrates the contrast between the stories of Cadog and Gastin, which I have argued are based on written accounts, and those sections indebted to oral tradition or firsthand knowledge. According to Walter, three of his Welsh stories reached him through word of mouth, which usefully allows us to reconstruct his network of informants on Welsh matters. Unlike the stories of Cadog and Gastin, these stories do not display any deep knowledge of Welsh traditions, contemporary or ancient, but are rather interesting anecdotes from foreign observers.

The first informant brings us right back to Brycheiniog, where Walter had a powerful acquaintance: William de Briouze (d. 1211), a powerful Marcher baron who held the lordships of Brecon and Abergavenny, in addition to other territories. He furnished Walter with an anecdote about a noble Welshman who rises nude at dawn to pray, practices abstinence, and behaves with such self-control that you would consider him "close to the angels above men."[216] Nonetheless, this discipline does not carry over into other aspects of his life, as he still revels in battle and rejoices in murder and bloodshed. Walter uses this contradiction to illustrate the haphazard devotion of the Welsh, concluding, "These Welsh are by nature so strongly, one could even say innately, slow-witted in civility that if they seem restrained in one matter, they appear unruly and wild in many others."[217] Like Gerald of Wales, Walter could compliment the Welsh only to disparage them soon thereafter. While this story peddles common stereotypes about the Welsh found in many twelfth-century texts, it is uncommonly blunt about its provenance: "Cum domino Willelmo de Breusa, uiro armis eruditissimo, fuit, ut ipse michi retulit, Walensis quidam . . ." (There was with the lord William de Briouze, a man most experienced in warfare, as he himself told me, a certain Welshman . . .).[218] Surely, William de Briouze knew many Welshmen, especially nobles. After all, as lord of Brecon and Abergavenny either he or his deputies would have to deal with the Welsh on a regular basis. And Brecon was one of those lordships that by the mid-twelfth century had developed a pattern of "compromise and coexistence" rather than a continual state of war.[219] Furthermore, Walter's family may have had a connection with the Briouzes: Walter's nephew Philip appears as a clerk to Giles de Briouze, William's son and bishop of Hereford.[220] With

Walter's presence at court and border interests, the two men would have had no lack of opportunities to meet.

Walter claims two other figures from the borderlands as sources for Welsh tales, but unlike William de Briouze, nothing else is known about them. A certain Philip of Newton tells Walter a rather humorous story about three hermits that he encountered on a hunting trip in the Black Mountain: "The illustrious Philip of Newton told me that when he was going hunting on the Black Mountain . . ." (Philippus Neapolitanus, uir illustris, nobis retulit, quod cum in Nigra Montana uenatu uenisset . . .).[221] Several Newtons exist in Wales, but since the Black Mountain straddles the border between Hereford-shire and Wales, *Neapolitanus* probably refers to the town of Welsh Newton, sitting to the east of the Black Mountain in modern-day Herefordshire. While this story is set in the Welsh Marches, it does not, however, contain any Welsh characters. And although Philip's illustriousness has faded since Walter's days, the fact that he hunts shows that he was at least a minor aristocrat.

The third and final instance of Walter obtaining a Marcher tale through word of mouth is the ghoulish story about an evil Welshman who returns from the dead, bringing sickness and death to those whom he visits.[222] This medieval version of *The Night of the Living Dead* also shuffled to Walter through secondhand gossip: "William Laudun, an English knight mighty in strength and proven in valor, came to Gilbert Foliot, who was then bishop of Hereford, but now is bishop of London" to ask the bishop for advice on his undead Welsh problem.[223] Walter, in turn, must have heard this story from Gilbert, his longtime patron and friend. As an authority figure in a village with Welsh inhabitants, William Laudun (Landun/London?) though uniden-tified, seems to have been an Englishman of French extraction living some-where in the March, presumably a minor nobleman of the sort that Marcher lords employed to administer their lands.

Moreover, as bishop of Hereford, Gilbert controlled many areas where such a scenario would be likely. Not only was he responsible for the souls of Archenfield, where the Welsh were the majority, but he also held Bishop's Castle, a small borough near Lydbury—his manor—which had a small Welsh population as well.[224] Thus, William probably lived in one of those Welsh areas that were under the direction, spiritual or temporal, of the bishop of Hereford.

Walter's network of Welsh informants includes a powerful Marcher lord, an Anglo-Norman knight, a minor aristocrat, and a bishop. None of these is a

Welshman, and none of their stories show any deep knowledge of Welsh culture; they do not even provide their Welshmen with names. These are the stories of colonialists, and Walter's joy in recounting them says a great deal about his politics, or at least his political savviness.[225] Walter himself tells similar types of stories that he gathered firsthand: he speaks positively of the Welsh hermit Elias, whom he claims to have seen.[226] This short portrait of a Welshman is not the only time that Walter discusses the habits of those people he so ambiguously refers to as compatriots. A long section of *distinctio* 2 addresses the Welsh and has much in common with the work of Gerald of Wales, who stitches together his ethnographic passage with personal anecdotes, essentializing observations, and recent events.[227] Walter begins this section with his thoughts on the untrustworthiness of the Welsh, their hospitality, and their rage.[228] This introductory passage echoes the judgment of his English contemporaries—the Welsh can be pious and hospitable, but their uncouth rage controls them. Walter then moves to his study of the character of the Welsh king, Llywelyn ap Gruffudd.[229] Like Walter's other adventures in historical writing, this passage is a bewildering mixture of fact and fiction. Even if Walter created the bulk of his traditions about Llywelyn, the story shows that Walter seems to have a working knowledge of a few aspects of Welsh law.[230] And one Llywelyn story takes place beside Llangorse Lake, while another has Llywelyn and Edward the Confessor facing off across the Severn.[231] Walter then proudly recounts his conversation with Thomas Becket, in which Walter explains that the Welsh will only remain loyal under threat of force. Two further stories illustrate Walter's claim that "the glory of the Welsh is in plunder and theft."[232] The first tells of Cynan the Fearless, a bandit from Glamorgan, and his botched raid, which goes awry because he does not amply respect the custom of hospitality. The second describes Genillyn, a thief from North Wales in search of the mare of Cadwallon of Gelligaer. In a show of regional rivalry, Traer, a South Walian, boasts that he can do what Genillyn cannot, and he successfully steals the mare to the glory of his people. Next is the brief story of two Welshman who turn on one another in an unnecessary act of vengeance. "Behold," Walter interjects, "how foolish and unjust the wrath of the Welsh is and how eager they are for blood."[233] Walter closes his exposition on the Welsh with the story of the Welsh revenant told to him by William Laudun, making a smooth transition to the other prodigies of *distinctio* 2.

   No identifiable textual source exists for Walter's other Welsh tales. Moreover, the names Walter uses, with few exceptions, are given in their Latin forms and were in widespread circulation: *Luelinus*, *Griffinus*, *Gestinus* (for *Iestin*), *Meilerius*, *Hoelus*, *Traherius*, *Cadolanus*, *Resus*, and *Conanus* are some of the most common Welsh names and would have been easily familiar to anyone reading Geoffrey of Monmouth or with a passing interest in contemporary politics.[234] Twice in his Welsh excursus Walter uses uninflected vernacular forms: *Uther* and *Luarc* (for *Llywarch*). *Uther* is easily explained: Uther Pendragon, Arthur's father, would have been a familiar name by Walter's time. That *Luarc*, however, remains in the vernacular is more difficult to explain. It may be that this name was not as easily rendered into Latin as the others, or that Walter did not know the correct Latin form.[235] One victim of Llywelyn's rage bears the name *Rothericus*, a Latin form of *Rhodri*.[236] His nephew, on the other hand, is called *Meilinus*, an unknown Welsh name.[237] It could, however, easily be a scribal error for *Merlinus* or *Meylerius*. A *Golenus bard* appears in Llywelyn's cohort, and, as described above, *Golenus* is a Latin form of *Goll-wyn*. By far the rarest Welsh name that Walter uses in this section is *Theudus* (Modern Welsh *Tewdos/ Tewdus*), which has been glossed "quod Latine dicitur Theodosius" (which is *Theodosius* in Latin).[238] But here again is a possible Brycheiniog connection: one of Brycheinog's cantrefs is called Cantref Tewdos (also known as Cantref Mawr), and Walter may have deemed the name behind this cantref appropriate for a consort of a great southern Welsh king. It should be remembered that Walter's correct Latin forms of Welsh names only show that he read documents in Latin that dealt with Welsh matters—they are not indicative of his speaking Welsh. In contrast, two names from his story of Genillyn the Thief show him using nonnative orthography to spell two Welsh names: *Gesligair* for *Gelligaer* and *Cheneslinus* for *Genillyn*. As discussed above, the use of the spelling *sl* for the Welsh sound /ɬ/ arises from Walter trying to spell what his ear hears with standard Latin orthography. When it comes to names, Walter's Welsh excursus displays a quirky mix of good Latin and vernacular forms, alongside a few instances that clearly mark him as someone unfamiliar with Welsh orthography. This jumble of forms appears only in Walter's Welsh excursus—his English and French names always appear in their expected Latin forms.[239] This is exactly what one would expect from Walter, an interested observer but not a member of Welsh culture.

Overall, Walter's names in his Welsh stories (other than those in the two stories discussed above) are not particularly indicative of oral or literary transfer, especially since many of them would have been well known to a literate Englishmen in the twelfth century. Walter actually knows the proper Latin forms of several Welsh names, even if he adapts ad hoc spellings on a few occasions. Interestingly, while all Welsh characters remain nameless in the three stories explicitly identified as hearsay, Walter peppers his own stories with Welsh names. In doing so, he may be trying to add a modicum of realism to his stories by throwing in Welsh names that he had read or heard. Many, though not all, of the names in this section could be found in Geoffrey's *History* or anyone with a slight familiarity with Welsh Latin. This is perhaps why the Welsh names here often read like the twelfth-century Welsh equivalents of Tom, Dick, and Harry. Still, given the paucity of surviving materials, and Walter's penchant for drastic revision, it would be unwise to completely rule out the possibility that Walter based some of the stories in this section on Welsh documents. Be that as it may, the stories of Cadog and Gastin Gastiniog appear even more remarkable given their identifiable literary traditions.

Conclusion

The preceding discussion, in its search for evidence of written transmission, does occasionally draw too sharp a distinction between oral and literary culture. After all, these vitae and other documents that Gloucester Abbey gathered did not lie mute on their library shelves; they were altered, copied, and even read aloud on the feasts of Teilo, Gwynllyw, and Padarn. The ingenuity displayed in creating the *Generatio Sancti Egweni* surely required sly discussion of how best to justify Gloucester's consolidation of Welsh holdings. Indeed, I would suggest that a textual community—a microsociety "organized around the common understanding of a script"—developed around the Welsh vitae in twelfth-century Gloucester and elsewhere, such as Monmouth and Llandaf.[240] The common interpretative lens through which these ecclesiastical communities viewed their collections of Welsh vitae and other historic documents was one of property rights—who held what piece of land and why. The instability caused by the Norman invasion and the Anarchy gave these institutions an unparalleled chance to rewrite (or outright invent) traditions about ancient Welsh saints to support contemporary ecclesiastical aspirations. In this respect, the Book of Llandaf and Cotton Vespasian A.xiv are the two best surviving records of these textual communities. Any ecclesiastic in southeastern Wales or Gloucester would know how to "properly" interpret accounts of the Welsh past. Walter, it should be remembered, did not encounter stories of St. Cadog and the ancient inhabitants of Brycheiniog removed from this interpretative framework—a solitary clerk with a solitary manuscript. Indeed, his ability to bend his sources to suit his purposes is exactly what one would expect of the protégé of Gilbert Foliot, who throughout his life did not shy away from forgery and general legal chicanery.[241] This type of influence is best seen in Walter's outlandish story of Eadric the Wild, which explains that the bishop of Hereford came to hold the manor of Lydbury North through the offspring of a fairy and an Englishman.[242] Basing a property claim on a literal fairy story may strike modern readers as an outright farce, but audacious claims such as this one are consistent with how texts from this era function. Indeed, as much as this chapter has focused on Walter's use of written documents, we must also consider the possibility that Walter's knowledge of Welsh-Latin sources is, at least in part, from a spoken-Latin milieu. He may have known the proper spelling of *Cadog, Illtud,* and other names because he had heard them spoken aloud. Other evidence, however, seems to accord better with literary transfer: proper spelling of Welsh vernacular names, the creation of forms like *Gastinus, Gastiniog,* and *Brychein,* and the retention of small details, such as the circumference of Llangorse Lake and the dynastic conflict in the tale of Gastin and Trunio. Nonetheless, Walter knew well both the oral and literate sides of the culture that produced the *Vita Sancti Cadoci* and the *De situ Brecheniauc.*

Because Walter's account of Cadog and Brychan has been casually explained as a result of his knowledge of Welsh folklore, it is important to show that these tales most closely belong to an educated, Latin-speaking minority.[243] Gerald's acquaintance with written traditions, presumably in Latin, of Illtud and Brychan has already been mentioned, but the episode of the earth splitting before St. Cadog has a particularly literary pedigree. Christopher Brooke has studied this episode in detail, concluding that it was Lifris's own invention in his *Vita Cadoci,* written toward the end of the eleventh century.[244] Outside of Lifris's life, and the vitae dependent on it, the episode appears only in Walter's *De nugis curialium.* What Brooke says of Lifris holds for the rest of the Welsh lives composed in the beginning of the twelfth century: while some topographical explanations may be taken from local legends, "some, perhaps many of them, seem rather to be ingenious rationalizations of problems raised by local cults, especially by churches, chapels and wells dedicated to the saint."[245] The widespread appropriation of Welsh churches after the Norman invasion raised many more problems and called for many more ingenious rationalizations by a new generation of hagiographers. Indeed, the saints championed in southeastern Welsh hagiography do not appear in surviving vernacular Welsh poetry before 1300.[246] Although the small size of the extant corpus renders this point indecisive, it nonetheless agrees with the fact that much of the newly championed saints of the early twelfth century stem from a small circle of ecclesiastical writers, who invented at least as much as they drew on tradition. In this respect, Benedict of Gloucester unwittingly gives the game away when complaining that he can scarcely bear the fact that St. Dyfrig's illustrious deeds remained unknown; they were unknown because the account Benedict read was largely a recent creation of Llandaf.[247] When Walter encountered accounts of St. Cadog or Brychan Brycheiniog, he was not tapping into a stream of Welsh traditions as told by the *cyfarwyddiad*, Welsh storytellers. Instead, Latin texts and Anglo-Norman intermediaries brought Cadog and Brychan to Walter.

To summarize, St. Peter's, Gloucester, had interests throughout Wales, including Llancarfan, the seat of Cadog's cult, and Brycheiniog, the territory from which the tale of Gastin Gastiniog originates. Throughout the twelfth century, the monks at Gloucester collected vitae and other historical material concerning their new Welsh holdings, and Cotton Vespasian A.xiv, although ultimately assembled at Monmouth, provides us with a valuable glimpse into Gloucester's collection of Welsh literature. Several aspects in Walter Map's stories of Cadog and Gastin Gastiniog are best explained as arising from written sources similar to those Gloucester collected and not, as often suspected, from oral tradition. Walter may have first attended school at Gloucester, but at any rate he had close personal connections with the abbey, including two of its abbots and a resident holy man who himself may have worked as one of the abbey's main scribes. Indeed, Gilbert Foliot, the abbot from 1139 to 1148, was Walter's lifelong patron. Taken together, the evidence suggests that Walter Map copied, and later reworked and expanded, a few episodes from Gloucester's collection of Welsh material.

Chapter 6

Walter Map in the Archives and the Transmission of the Matter of Britain

In a lavishly illuminated manuscript containing the *Prose Lancelot*, the *Queste del Saint Graal*, and *La mort Artu*, Walter Map sits with a knowing smirk, pen in hand (Figure 1).[1] Opposing him rests an enthroned and sceptered king whose right index finger is raised in a commanding fashion and whose glance is turned not to Walter but to four courtiers standing to his left. A reader can easily be forgiven for passing over this reserved scene to proceed to the manuscript's more whimsical and gripping illustrations, perhaps hurrying along to a man laying eggs, determined knights locked in combat, or one of several misbehaving monkeys. But despite its relative banality, this particular miniature imagines a significant event in medieval literary history. It records the moment in which Henry II commands his clerk Walter Map to compose *La mort Artu*, thereby completing one of the five parts of the *Lancelot-Grail Cycle* (also known as the *Vulgate Cycle*), one of the most influential collections of Arthurian literature ever produced.[2] Directly below, a determined King Arthur leads four knights galloping out of a castle toward Winchester. The resemblance between Arthur below and Henry above could not be closer—their garments, beard, hair, and crown appear identical. Indeed, they seem to be the same figure. This symbolic doubling draws attention to Henry's literary patronage and the important role his court was believed to hold for the creation of Arthurian literature. Read together, these evocative images tell a story about the creation and the purpose of that wildly popular body of literature that concerns the pre-Saxon inhabitants of ancient Britain—the Matter of Britain. In these images, Arthur's deeds, written by the courtier Walter Map, ultimately glorify Henry II.

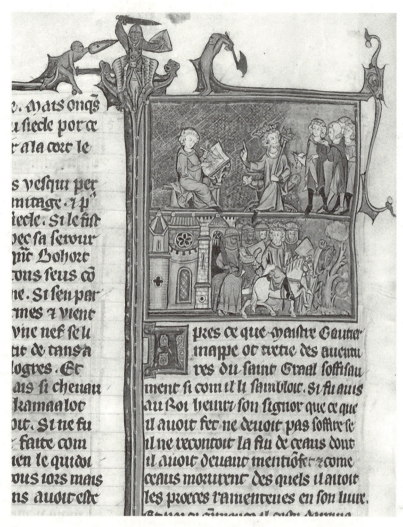

Figure 1. King Henry II commanding Walter Map to compose *La mort Artu* (top
panel). General Collection, Beinecke Rare Book and Manuscript Library,
Yale University, MS 229, fol. 272v.

The artist, however, was unlikely to have known that this emblematic scene could not have taken place. He was almost certainly unaware that the texts of the *Lancelot-Grail Cycle* were written after both Walter and Henry had died. Nonetheless, this illustrator, along with numerous thirteenth-century readers and writers, believed that Walter Map had played an important role in the transmission and creation of Arthurian literature. In addition to *La mort Artu*, the *Prose Lancelot* and the *Queste del Saint Graal* also claim to have their origins in Walter Map. Thus, Walter is given credit for the three earliest tales of the *Cycle*, a trilogy that often travels together in manuscripts, and his putative involvement is why the entire *Cycle* is sometimes known as the Pseudo-Map Cycle.[3] Although Walter has been summarily stripped of these works, the attributions, the earliest of which appears within a decade of his death, have never been satisfactorily explained.

Critical reactions to these attributions have varied. Most nineteenth-century scholars accepted the attributions to Walter Map without much question, as did, for example, the perceptive Welsh critic Thomas Stephens and the first editor of the *De nugis curialium*, Thomas Wright.[4] But Walter Map's astounding literary feat did not withstand scrutiny for long. By 1871, serious doubts had appeared,[5] and after Ferdinand Lot had established a more secure dating for the *Prose Lancelot*, it became quite apparent that Walter Map could not have been the author of any of the *Lancelot-Grail Cycle* in its present form.[6] However, it has still been possible to claim that Walter played *some* role in the *Cycle*'s history, either as a translator of an earlier Latin version or as an author of an earlier French romance that was later expanded.[7] A few have even proposed a connection between Walter and Chrétien de Troyes, which may have led to Walter being mistaken for an Arthurian author.[8] By far the most common explanation among recent scholars is that Walter's name serves to impart some historical veracity to the work: Walter Map, a clerk of Henry II who had gained some degree of fame in the late twelfth century, conjures up just the right amount of cultural and literary authority.[9] Others think the attribution a humility topos.[10] But to some the attribution makes little sense: Walter writes in Latin, while the *Lancelot-Grail Cycle* is a French work; Walter cannot write sustained narrative, while the *Lancelot-Grail Cycle* is nothing if not sustained; Walter has no interest in Arthurian material, while the *Lancelot-Grail Cycle* is a highlight of the genre.[11] In their eyes, so great is the disconnect between Walter and the *Cycle* that the attribution must be ironic.[12] On the other hand, many scholars echo Siân Echard's brief suggestion at the beginning of her seminal study of Arthurian Latin literature: "While Map did not write these vernacular romances, it is nevertheless probable that someone *like* him did."[13]

What Echard means here is that Walter Map is of the same milieu—educated, courtly, and associated with Henry II—as other Latin writers who were interested in Arthurian material. Walter Map, I will show, is exactly the type of author who would have been involved in the creation of the *Lancelot-Grail Cycle*. In particular, this chapter argues that Latin authors like Walter Map were instrumental in transmitting Welsh material to the rest of Europe. I argue that invoking the name Walter Map was not merely an attempt to create an imprimatur of literary authority, but a succinct expression of how the Matter of Britain passed outward from Wales into the rest of Europe. Whoever first hit upon the idea of claiming that Walter Map played an important role in the transmission of these French romances knew a bit more than has generally been assumed.

Walter Map in the *Lancelot-Grail Cycle*

In describing Walter Map's literary activities, the *Lancelot-Grail Cycle* is frustratingly inconsistent. At times, he is referred to not as the *Cycle*'s author but as its compiler. Yet elsewhere he is spoken of as if he is in fact the *Cycle*'s primary author. And still at other moments, he is said to be a translator. While these varying attributions may seem a hopeless hodgepodge, our knowledge of the composition of the *Lancelot-Grail Cycle* clarifies how Walter Map's reputation developed. Indeed, understanding the chronology of the *Cycle*'s composition strongly suggests that all the attributions to Walter Map draw upon a single early passage in which he is described as a compiler—an archivist even—and not as a translator or an author in his own right.

The fullest and earliest explanation of Walter's activities occurs in the *Queste del Saint Graal* (1220–25).[14] While the *Queste* is not the earliest text in the *Cycle*, either in terms of composition or narrative chronology, its author was nonetheless the first to bring Walter Map into the world of the *Cycle*. At the end of the *Queste*, when Sir Bors returns to Camelot, King Arthur holds a feast, during which a textual link between the Arthurian past and Henry II's court is imagined.

> After they had eaten, the king summoned the clerks who were putting into writing the adventures of the knights at court. When Bors

had recounted the adventures of the Holy Grail, as he had seen
them, they were recorded and kept in the archive at Salisbury. Master Walter Map withdrew them to write his book about the Holy
Grail, for the love of his lord King Henry, who had the story translated from Latin into French. But here the story stops and tells no
more about the adventures of the Holy Grail.[15]

The "archive of Salisbury" (l'almiere de Salebieres) is an appropriate place for
Arthur to deposit the records of the Grail quest, since Salisbury Plain is of
considerable importance in Arthurian myth. According to Geoffrey of Monmouth, Hengest and his men treacherously slew 460 British noblemen there,
and their bodies were later buried at a cemetery in Salisbury.[16] Merlin, in an
effort to commemorate their deaths, later removed Stonehenge from Ireland
and placed it on Salisbury Plain, on the "hill of Ambrius," as a memorial.[17]
Geoffrey also mentions a community of three hundred monks living on this
same hill.[18] While Geoffrey of Monmouth closely associates Salisbury and
Amesbury, later authors, such as Wace, collapse the distinction even more,
and by the time of the Stanzaic *Morte Arthur* and Sir Thomas Malory, the association of Amesbury with Arthurian legend has become traditional, since
both texts speak of Amesbury as the final retreat of Guinevere.[19] Moreover,
Henry II took a special interest in the religious life of Amesbury, dissolving
the ancient Benedictine abbey there in 1177 and founding in its place a double
priory of the Fontrevault order.[20] For all of these reasons, most scholars have
identified the "archive of Salisbury" as being held at Amesbury Priory.[21]

Walter Map, then, was imagined to have been rummaging through a monastic center dear to Henry when he found the marvelous records of Sir Bors.
The final detail that this passage provides is that Arthur had the Grail quest
recorded in Latin documents, and Walter "withdrew them to write his book"
(les trest a fere son livre). It is important to note that the passage claims that
Walter's own work was in Latin, which was only later translated into French at
the king's request, and judging from this passage at least, Walter does not
seem to have been the one who translated it. Although in many critical works
Walter Map is often spoken of as the "author" of the *Lancelot-Grail Cycle*, this
reference, which is the earliest in the *Cycle*, styles him as merely the compiler.[22] And here he works with monastic records in Latin, which, as Chapter
5 has shown, is an accurate representation of at least some aspects of Walter's
literary activity.

I would suggest that all other mentions of Walter Map in the *Lancelot-Grail*

Cycle are merely elaborations upon this passage in the *Queste* (1220–25). The next tale in the cycle, *La mort Artu* (1225–30), takes its cue from the *Queste*, as it begins by Walter picking up where he reportedly left off.

> After Walter Map had put into writing the *Adventures of the Holy Grail* as fully as he thought proper, his lord King Henry was of the opinion that his work would be left unfinished if he did not recount the rest of the lives of those about whom he had earlier spoken and the deaths of those whose feats of prowess he had recorded in his book. And for that reason he began this last part, and when he had composed it, he called it *The Death of King Arthur*, for the end tells how King Arthur was wounded in the battle at Salisbury and how he was separated from Girflet, who stayed with him so long that he was the last one to see Arthur alive. And in that way Master Walter begins this final part.[23]

The diction here remains somewhat ambiguous as to Walter's exact role in composition of the *Queste* and *La mort*. The phrases "put into writing" (*mis en escrit*) and "composed" (*ensemble mise*) both allow for the possibility described in the *Queste*—that Walter is merely compiling the story from extant Latin documents. But the manuscript tradition reflects uncertainty as to what role, exactly, Walter played in the composition of the *Queste*. For example, there are some interesting variants for the phrase *mis en escrit*: *traité* (treated, composed), *translaté* (translated), and *portraitié* (portrayed) are all attested alterations.[24] And a late thirteenth-century manuscript, MS Royal 19. C.xiii, which contains many interesting embellishments, here reads "si cum il les auoit truuees es anciens escritz & translate de latin en rumanz par la preere lo roi sun sein[g]neur" (when he had found them in ancient documents and translated them from Latin into French at the request of his lord the king).[25] This particular manuscript confronts the earlier ambiguity by making Walter responsible for both the discovery and the translation of the records of the Grail quest. Regardless of what exactly "mis en escrit" and "ensemble mise" mean at the beginning of *La mort*, its end again invokes Walter Map's involvement: "And now Master Walter Map has no more to say about the *Story of Lancelot*, for he has brought it to an end and has told everything that happened; his book ends here, and anything else that might be added would be a lie."[26] This colophon seems meant for the trilogy—the *Prose Lancelot*, the *Queste*, and *La mort*—since it references the entire *Story of Lancelot* and not simply *La mort*.

But even after the addition of the *Estoire del Saint Graal* and the *Estoire de Merlin* to the rest of the *Cycle*, it would remain a fitting ending for the entire work. MS Royal 19. C.xiii, the same manuscript that at the beginning of *La mort* has Walter discovering ancient documents and translating them, ends by recalling its beginning, adding "cum il le out trové en anciens esriz de almaire" (as he found it in the archive's ancient documents).[27] I mention this particular manuscript not because it has any special authority, but rather because it illustrates how traditions about Walter Map were altered as the *Cycle* grew in popularity and scribes and compilers reworked various elements.

To that end, scribal alteration is to thank for Walter's supposed authorship of the *Prose Lancelot*. Several manuscripts of the *Prose Lancelot* (1215–20) end by claiming "here Master Walter Map concludes his book and begins the *Grail*."[28] If one is reading the *Lancelot-Grail Cycle* in its narrative chronological order, from the first events to the last—as most modern readers do and many medieval readers did—this passage is the first mention of Walter Map's involvement with the *Cycle*. However, this passage is not in the earliest manuscripts; it is a later addition.[29] When all of the attributions are considered in order of composition, not narrative chronology, it becomes much easier to see how Walter Map's putative involvement with the *Lancelot-Grail Cycle* first took root.

The rough order of events must have been the following. Although the *Prose Lancelot* (1215–20) was the first of the *Cycle's* five works to have been composed, in its earliest form at least Walter Map is not mentioned. The next work composed in the *Cycle* was the *Queste* (1220–25), and it is here that Walter Map first appeared in any relation to Arthurian romance. Importantly, he is portrayed not as an author of French works or a translator into French but as an explorer of monastic libraries who extracts ancient Latin traditions about the Grail and compiles a book in Latin for Henry II's reading pleasure. In turn, it is Henry II who has Walter's Latin book translated into French, and so the *Queste* is born. The author of *La mort* (1225–30), the next text in the *Cycle* to be composed, merely follows the lead of the *Queste* in having Walter finish what he began. At some point after the *Prose Lancelot*, the *Queste*, and *La mort* had been drawn together to form a trilogy, a scribe made the easy decision to have Walter author the *Prose Lancelot* as well. After all, the end of the *Prose Lancelot* and the beginning of *La mort*, which relates Walter's discovery of the ancient documents at Salisbury, very often fall together in manuscript groupings of the *Cycle*—it is no wonder that several scribes gave in to the temptation to add Walter Map's name to the very end of the *Prose Lancelot*. After the entire *Cycle* had taken shape, Walter Map won himself another fan, as a unique fragmentary continuation of the *Merlin* proper regularly insists on Walter's involvement, claiming that he is responsible for translating Arthurian tales from Latin into French.[30] From one reference in the *Queste*, which has Walter acting as a Latin compiler, his reputation grew, and in later works he became a French translator and even an author in his own right.

That the earliest reference to Walter Map in the *Lancelot-Grail Cycle* depicts him as a Latin compiler should render the hand-wringing about whether Walter wrote French romances moot.[31] The notion that Walter translated or composed Arthurian prose works is a secondary development, an imaginative elaboration founded on a single passage in the *Queste*. Of course, it is certainly not out of the realm of possibility that Walter wrote French works, since he spoke French and since Latin clerical writers did not operate in a separate literary sphere, shut off from their vernacular counterparts.[32] Nonetheless, the only explicit claims that Walter wrote French romances are these later, secondary attributions. Although intriguing passages from Gerald of Wales and Hue de Rotelande are often presented in support of Walter having written French romances, neither is completely convincing in this regard.

In the midst of asking that someone translate his *Expugnatio Hibernica* into French, Gerald records Walter Map's estimation of his own work. Walter is supposed to have said:

> Multa, magister Giralde, scripsistis, et multum adhuc scribitis: et nos multa diximus. Vos scripta dedistis, et nos verba. Et quanquam scripta vestra longe laudabiliora sint, et longaeviora, quam dicta nostra, quia tamen haec aperta, communi quippe idiomate prolata, illa vero, quia Latina, paucioribus evidentia, nos de dictis nostris fructum aliquem reportavimus, vos autem de scriptis egregiis, principibus literatis nimirum et largis obsoletis olim, et ab orbe sublatis dignam minime retributionem consequi potuistis.[33]

> (You have written much, Master Gerald, and you are still writing a good deal, and I have talked of much. You have produced writing, and I words. And your writing is by far more praiseworthy and permanent than my words, although since my words are clear—by which I mean they are delivered in everyday language, while your writing is accessible to fewer because it is in Latin—I have gained some reward from my words, while for your excellent writing you have been able to secure scarcely appropriate compensation, since

exceedingly learned and generous princes have become forgotten
and have vanished from the earth.)

Much has been hung on this passage, especially Gerald's description of Walter's
activity as *dicta* (words) as opposed to Gerald's own *scripta* (writing). There is a
history, mistaken I believe, in taking this passage to refer to Walter's vernacular
French works by claiming that what Walter means by "nos multa diximus" (I
have talked of much) and "nos verba [dedimus]" (I have produced words) is
that he has composed French romances, either written or oral.[34] Yet the opposition important to Gerald is not one of genre, romance against his *Expugnatio*,
but rather of language, the easy familiarity of French against the more noble,
though less appreciated, Latin. Walter does not even have to compose anything
in French to gain reward—his witty words alone do the work for him. Gerald,
on the other hand, believes he has taken the high road of writing in Latin, and
it has cost him dearly. It is also important to remember that this passage is not
Walter's own description of his work, but Gerald's own self-serving presentation of a conversation that he and Walter apparently had on many occasions.[35]
Indeed, it is less about Walter and more about Gerald's belief that the deck is
always stacked against him. At any rate, Gerald is not telling the whole truth
here, since, as he well knows, Walter Map did write in Latin, both in poetry
and prose.[36] Walter never responded to this odd accusation, as he was dead by
the time Gerald wrote it—a convenient fact for Gerald.

Hue de Rotelande, another of Walter's contemporaries, and another man
from the Anglo-Welsh border, levies some sly criticism toward Walter in the
Ipomedon, one of his two surviving medieval romances:

> Ore entendez, seignurs, mut ben;
> Hue dit ke il n'i ment de ren.
> Ffors aukune feiz, neent mut,
> Nuls ne se pot garder par tut.
> En mendre afere mut suvent
> Un ben renablë hom mesprent.
> El mund nen ad un sul si sage
> Ki tuz jurs seit en un curage,
> Kar cist secles l'ad ore en sei,
> Nel metez mie tut sur mei!
> Sul ne sai pas de mentire l'art,
> Walter Map reset ben sa part.[37]

(Lords, listen now very well: Hue says that he lies about nothing
here, except in a few instances, but even then not much—nobody
can be careful everywhere. In small matters a quite sensible man
very often goes astray. There's no one in the world so wise that he is
always keeping watch. Because that's the nature of this world, don't
put it all on me! I am not alone in knowing the art of lying: Walter
Map also knows his part well.)

Earlier critics tended to see Hue's reference as confirmation that Walter
wrote French romances, especially since this authorial interjection occurs in
the context of a joust.[38] Romance, however, needn't be written in French,
and this passage says nothing about Walter's choice of language. Probably
for these reasons, recent readers have tended to restrict analyses of this passage to Hue's own relationship to fiction and truth, leaving aside speculation
regarding Walter's authorship of romance. Neil Cartlidge has recently argued that a comparison between Walter's and Hue's work reveals a surprising
similarity in their approach to irony: "Not only do both of them write fiction, but it is also characteristic of both of them to subject fiction to irony,
and specifically to that particular kind of irony exemplified by the peculiar
self-defeatingness of the assertions that Hue here pretends to make."[39] It is
relatively certain that the two knew one another, and they even had an acquaintance in common, Hugh of Hungary, who was also a canon of Lincoln, just as Walter himself was.[40] And whenever Walter visited Hereford
Cathedral, Hue would have been close by, since he lived at Credenhill, just
five miles to the north.[41]

For Cartlidge, the importance of this passage from the *Ipomedon* lies not
in any possible allusion to Walter writing romance, but in its playful recogni-
tion of literary kinship between the two men. To this insightful analysis I
would like to add that it is also possible that Hue may not be referencing
Walter's approach to irony in the *De nugis curialium* at all. Rather, he may
have had a few concrete examples of Walter's lying in mind. As I have argued
elsewhere, the *De nugis curialium* contains two stories in support of the rights
of the bishop of Hereford, both of which a skeptical contemporary could
rightly consider a lie: the fantastic story of Eadric the Wild whose son Alnoth
donated Lydbury North to Hereford and Edmund Ironside's gift of Ross to
the bishopric.[42] If Walter was in the habit of telling these same stories in and
around Hereford, or if they had gained any local currency, Hue easily could
have caught wind of his propensity to compose artful lies for the benefit of the

diocese. If this is the case, then Walter could have easily been perceived as a master in the art of lying.

Without the later expansion of Walter's reputation from Latin compiler to French translator, and finally to romancer in his own right, little in Gerald's and Hue's remarks would suggest Walter has been writing French romances. While Walter certainly *could have* written French romances, the same may be said for most of the secular clerics working in Henry's court. If the tradition of Walter as a French translator or author is a creation of the thirteenth century, what of the *Queste*'s description of Walter as a cleric working in a monastic archive to uncover traditions about the ancient British past—is there a glimmer of truth here? This portrait does, after all, better accord with our understanding of Walter's actual literary activity as witnessed in the *De nugis curialium*. But if Walter did compile, in some form or another, an earlier Latin version of the *Queste*, very little of Walter remains in the French romance. As many have remarked, it is highly unlikely that such a staunch opponent of the Cistercians would have authored a text that is infused with Cistercian thought.[43] Admittedly, the *De nugis curialium* and the *Queste* share a similar passage.[44] During Walter's Welsh excursus in *distinctio* 2, he remarks: "The glory of the Welsh is in plunder and theft, and they like both so much that it is an insult to a son if his father dies without a wound. For this reason few grow gray. There is a proverb there: 'Die young or beg old,' that is to say that every man should dash headlong into death so that he doesn't beg as an old man."[45] Contrasting Perceval's faith with that of his countrymen, the *Queste* remarks: "At that time people throughout Wales were so violent and disruptive that if a son found his father lying sick in bed, he would drag him out by the head or arms and kill him forthwith, for he would be dishonored if he allowed his father to die in bed."[46] The similarity is apparent, though not exact, but these anecdotes could easily reflect a popular Welsh stereotype, and they are certainly not indicative of common authorship. It is, at any rate, difficult to put any trust into a set of texts that insists that Arthur, Merlin, Sir Bors, and Christ himself are integral characters in its textual tradition.

Nonetheless, the *Estoire del Saint Graal* and the *Estoire de Merlin* also give credit to Robert de Boron, and here, at least, the attribution undoubtedly has some truth to it.[47] The remainder of this chapter will argue that the portrait of Walter Map from the *Queste* also contains a kernel of truth, though not regarding its author or compiler. While it tells us little about the thirteenth-century production of the *Lancelot-Grail Cycle*, the sketch of Walter working in Amesbury Abbey accurately depicts how material about ancient Britain made its

way from Wales to the rest of Europe—through an ecclesiastical network of
clerical authors writing in Latin.

The Problem of the First Transmission

To suggest that the educated classes of two neighboring yet linguistically distinct medieval peoples were able to exchange historical, literary, and legal material through the medium of Latin is on par with suggesting that medieval
people may have been familiar with cattle—it is so obvious as to need no
comment. Yet, in the case of Arthurian material moving from Wales to England and France scholars have been slow to recognize Latin as a possible
medium of transmission. There are some good reasons for this failure to credit
Latin clerical culture, alongside a host of poor ones, and I will revisit some of
the larger, disciplinary explanations for this neglect at the end of this chapter.
However, the most immediate cause is that two other vehicles for the distribution of the Matter of Britain have become firmly entrenched in scholarship—
traveling bilingual Breton minstrels and latimers, a professional class of
Anglo-Welsh translators. Both of these have, I believe, received too much emphasis in recent scholarship.

   Names in medieval literature can tell us a great deal. Indeed, they are the
best proof that some sort of cultural exchange occurred in early twelfth-
century Britain; Rachel Bromwich summarizes: "Irrefutable evidence for the
transmission of Celtic stories to the Normans at an early date is to be found in
the large number of personal names of Brythonic derivation which have come
down in the work of French and Latin writers."[48] A key word in this sentence
is *Brythonic* (recent scholarship tends to prefer the nearly synonymous term
Brittonic)—a term that may need some explanation.[49] A subset of Celtic languages, the Brittonic family consists of Welsh, Breton, Cornish, and Cum-
bric, the last spoken in Strathclyde or Cumbria until perhaps the twelfth
century. Importantly, Brittonic languages do not include Irish or its siblings
Scots Gaelic and Manx, which, while members of a larger Celtic family, were
so distinct that a medieval Irish speaker and his Welsh counterpart would not
have recognized that their own tongues were related.[50] I stress this last point
because in discussions of the first transmission of the Matter of Britain the
term *Celtic* obscures more often than it illuminates: elided are the differences
in Irish and Brittonic cultures and the particular ways their cultural material
was distributed and received into the larger Anglo-Norman world. And while

Irish literature could find a captive audience outside of its homeland—
especially Hiberno-Latin literature—it seems Ireland had little to do with the
initial creation and popularization of the Matter of Britain, though Irish influence on French-language literature becomes more discernable in the late
twelfth and early thirteenth centuries.[51] I will not, therefore, consider the possibility of Irish influence in the present study. Nor, for that matter, does Walter Map take a particular interest in the Irish.[52]

If the Irish are out, deciding on the best candidate for the Brittonic source
still remains troublesome. The slipperiness of the pairs *Bretaigne/Britannia* and
Bretun/Brito has been widely recognized: in the twelfth century they could
mean either Britain or Brittany, and Breton or Briton. Did Marie de France
intend Bretons or Britons when she claims "li Bretun" say that Lanval now resides on the isle of Avalon?[53] What would Marie's audience think? Although
medieval authors may not have cared too greatly about this distinction—
Britones everywhere spoke similar languages, after all, which was one of the
most important markers of medieval ethnicity—modern scholarship has
tended to focus on Bretons as the agents of textual exchange.[54] In particular,
the idea of the Breton minstrel or *conteur* as the agent of cultural exchange has
a certain romantic hold on this question. While earlier scholars like Joseph
Loth and Ferdinand Lot believed that the Normans picked up the Matter of
Britain from Welsh storytellers, this explanation was eclipsed, at least in
English-language scholarship, by the malleable figure of the Breton minstrel.[55]
First proposed in the Victorian era, the Breton minstrel was most vigorously
popularized by Roger Sherman Loomis in the mid-twentieth century.[56] Loom-
is's ideas have in general faired rather poorly, especially among Celticists. The
renowned Celticist Kenneth Jackson delivered the most well-known attack on
Loomis at a colloquium on the Grail romances held in 1954 at Strasbourg.[57]
And Loomis's ideas concerning the transfer of Celtic material to the rest of
Europe is one of many of the arguments that he singles out for censure.[58] In
spite of Loomis's counterarguments and his generally high standing in the
field, Celticists continued to remain highly skeptical of his theories. In 1964,
for example, Rachel Bromwich rebuked him for "mytholeg amheus, simsam, a
sigledig iawn" (doubtful, flimsy, and very shaky mythology) and, most important, for his poor grasp of Welsh and Irish.[59] Yet, Bromwich's admonitions
added little to the scholarly debate since they were in Welsh, and Loomis seems
not to have read much Modern Welsh—a point that is more than a little ironic.

Nonetheless, in a critical moment somewhat analogous to D. W. Robert-
son's insistence that patristic literature was relevant to the study of Chaucer,

Loomis's championing of Celtic literature sent eager scholars to Irish and Welsh texts, even if only as a backdrop for later stories. (A major difference between these two trends, however, was that patristic literature actually existed; many of these Celtic narratives had to be reconstructed, allowing for a significant amount of scholarly invention in the process.) For his unyielding belief that behind much of the best literature of the High Middle Ages lay Celtic origins—a fact that did not always sit well with scholars of a nationalistic bent—Loomis has been termed the "first modern postcolonial theorist of the British Isles."[60] While Loomis's interests ranged over a variety of Arthurian subjects, he typically argued that traveling, bilingual Breton *conteurs* carried out the original dissemination of Arthurian literature.

While this theory at first seems promising—Marie de France, after all, claims that some of her lais were first told by Bretons—Patrick Sims-Williams has persuasively argued that little if no evidence exists to show that Breton minstrels actually transmitted the Matter of Britain.[61] His arguments are clear and convincing and have so far gone unanswered. And Michael Faletra has recently remarked that the Breton minstrel theory overlooks important colonial dynamics and distracts us from instances of literary, as opposed to oral, transmission.[62] I have no desire to beat a horse that has lain dead for half a century, but the Breton minstrel theory is still very much with us. A few recent examples should suffice: A 2016 study on otherworldly motifs favorably cites Loomis's Breton minstrel theory, presumably unaware that other options are available.[63] And *The Medieval British Literature Handbook*, published in 2009, claims, "It is likely that Breton minstrels singing the legend to Norman lords in England, Sicily and Jerusalem popularized the cycle."[64] Such statements occur outside of Anglophone scholarship as well. A 2008 book on *The Song of Roland* evocatively writes that "one has to suppose that the *conteurs* who are going around the various Celtic regions, are inspired by several traditions which have merged and developed from Scottish (in particular Pictish), Welsh, Breton, and Cornish elements—perhaps even from ancient memories or from some oriental influences."[65] And in the standard German translation of the collection of Welsh prose tales known as the *Mabinogion*, a small section in the introduction is entirely devoted to "Mehrsprachige Erzähler" (Multilingual Narrators), who are, unsurprisingly, Breton *conteurs*: "That Brittany . . . played a significant role as the outpost of Arthurian tradition on the continent has been proven many times and is not astonishing."[66] If, as Sims-Williams argues, Breton minstrels were not as widespread as we have been led to believe, they have nonetheless managed to survive and even flourish in

modern scholarship as the preferred explanation for the early transmission of
the Matter of Britain.

Although the Breton *conteur* model of transmission has remained the
most popular, an alternative did appear in 1966 with Constance Bullock-
Davies's work on professional interpreters.[67] Using largely archival evidence,
Bullock-Davies shows that professional interpreters, *latimarii* in Latin, provided a valuable service for their lords and were well rewarded for their efforts
during the eleventh and twelfth centuries. Bullock-Davies views these interpreters as playing a crucial role in the transmission of Brittonic material: "*Cyf-
arwyddiaid* [Welsh storytellers], latimers, and French, Welsh and English
minstrels lived together in the same castles along the Welsh Marches from the
time of the Conquest. They could not have failed to impart to one another
something of each of their native literatures."[68] This model is appealing for a
few reasons. First of all, in contrast to Loomis's approach, Bullock-Davies is
able to find clear documentary evidence that latimers were widely used and
generously compensated. And second, she provides sufficient evidence to
show that latimers were at work during the eleventh and early twelfth century
and that they had access to important aristocratic circles. Thus they were in
the right place at the right time to facilitate literary exchange between the
Welsh and the Anglo-Normans. While this model is in some respects very
convincing, it does not, however, provide any direct evidence that professional
interpreters were the middlemen of the exchange. Undoubtedly they played
some role, but absolutely no evidence exists today to link a professional translator with any particular text, author, or motif.[69] Instead, the archival documents show *latimarii* operating primarily in a political rather than literary
sphere. Perhaps future proof will be uncovered, especially given that very little
is still known about the range and extent of professional interpreters and Bullock-Davies only scratched the surface of the available sources.

While professional translators and roving minstrels have an undoubtable
allure, the evidence from Walter's *De nugis curialium*, in contrast, suggests a
rather banal means of exchange—the Latin literature of the clerical class. In
this, I am proposing nothing particularly new. Sims-Williams, after rejecting
Breton *conteurs* as the medium of exchange, writes, "Another possibility,
which I would favour myself, is that the intermediaries were clerks, of the
same ilk as Geoffrey of Monmouth and Walter Map."[70] And the importance
of the clerical class to romance and Arthurian literature has been widely ex-
plored.[71] Moreover, Geoffrey of Monmouth, by far the most instrumental figure in the popularization of the Matter of Britain, wrote in Latin, in what he

humbly called an "agresti . . . stilo" (a rustic style).[72] Yet for all of this, the role that clerics like Walter and Geoffrey played in the transmission of the Matter of Britain from Wales to England and France has been greatly neglected, even though given the scarcity of surviving evidence they (and others like them) come as close as is possible to providing a smoking gun. Indeed, I would argue that in the *Queste* Walter Map's imagined use of Latin material found at an ecclesiastical center is a concise description of how textual material passed from Wales to Britain.

Latin Transmission of Ancient British Material in the Twelfth Century

In Chapter 5, I argued that scholars overlooked the possibility that Walter Map had textual sources for some of his Welsh tales, preferring instead to rely on oral tradition as the means of exchange. The same reluctance to credit Welsh-Latin documents as among Walter's many sources also extends to discussion of the Matter of Britain as a whole. The *De nugis curialium* shows us that Welsh traditions about ancient Britain could travel to the court of Henry II entirely in Latin. More evidence can be mustered for this scenario than for either Breton *conteurs* or professional translators as the agents of exchange. In addition to Walter Map's stories of Cadog and Gastin, there are other clear instances of Latin transmission from Wales to England in the twelfth century. In particular, I will discuss two other cases of Latin transmission, one virtually forgotten and the other extraordinarily well-known, though both come from the ecclesiastical milieu of southeastern Wales, just as do Walter's own stories of Cadog and Gastin. A brief examination of these two instances will show that Walter's transmission of Latin material into England was not a fluke.

The first of the two, Benedict of Gloucester's *Vita Dubricii*, also owes its creation to the collection of Welsh material at St. Peter's.[73] A monk at St. Peter's, Benedict took a particular interest in St. Dyfrig. At Gloucester Benedict read an earlier *Vita Dubricii*, which had been written for the diocese of Llandaf to give historical weight to its increasingly ambitious program of expansion.[74] He also knew that Dyfrig was one of the most important ecclesiastical figures in Geoffrey of Monmouth's *History of the Kings of Britain*. It was probably for the benefit of his friends and colleagues at Llandaf that Benedict decided to harmonize these two accounts of Dyfrig, forming an innovative mix of hagiography and Arthurian history.[75] Regardless of the text's politics, the fact that the original

Vita Dubricii found an eager audience at Gloucester again shows how easily Latin literature traveled across the border in the twelfth century and how easily Welsh material could be reworked and rewritten for a new audience.

The *nachleben* of Benedict's life of Dyfrig shares some striking similarities with the rest of the Matter of Britain, especially the figure of Arthur. It is well known that in England the figure of Arthur becomes less and less Welsh and more and more English as time passes. This transformation is unmistakable if one compares Geoffrey of Monmouth's Arthur with Mallory's. Benedict's version of Dyfrig, too, shows the same trajectory. In the fourteenth century, John of Tynemouth traveled around Britain collecting saints' lives and compiling them into his work the *Sanctilogium*, and one of the lives he acquired was Benedict's *Vita Dubricii*. He dutifully excerpted Benedict's work and copied it into his impressive compendium of vitae.[76] John of Tynemouth's work was itself later revised, and in 1516 it was published by Wynkin de Worde as *Nova Legenda Anglie*, which was promptly translated into English as the *Kalendre of the Newe Legende of England*. The version of Benedict's *Vita Dubricii* therein is a highly abridged account of the saint's birth and miracles, acknowledging that in this "Legende be dyuerse goodly thynges of Kynge arthur, of Stonthynges, and of dyuerse Myracles here omyttyd."[77] The Galfridian sections of Benedict's *Vita Dubricii* must not have inspired a pious reaction in the English translator. However, it is not the vita itself but its packaging that is of interest here. In this collection, Dyfrig is one of many saints from the Celtic fringe—Ireland, Scotland, and Wales—that have been subsumed as English. Indeed, the prologue announces this English hagiographical colonization explicitly. The work declares its topic as "the most parte of tho sayntes that be in the sayd legende & in this kalender were eyther borne in this Realme or were abydynge therin & that theyse other countreys Irelande Scotlande and Wales of veray ryght owe to be subiecte & obedyent to this Realme of Englonde as it semyth this lytyll treatyce maye conuenyentlye be callyd the kalender of the newe Legende of Englonde."[78] Dyfrig, like the other saints of Wales, Ireland, and Scotland, has become a good English subject by the close of the medieval era. And thus, although literary traditions about this somewhat obscure Welsh saint are not as glamorous or as influential as the more familiar narratives of the Matter of Britain, literary traditions of Dyfrig did leave Wales and did find their way into the vernacular, and, like the legends of King Arthur, they were employed in rhetoric aimed against the Welsh. Like Arthur, Dyfrig was created by a twelfth-century clerical writer from a few hints of earlier tradition. Like Arthur, Dyfrig became known outside of Wales. And like Arthur,

Dyfrig was eventually appropriated by the English. When one wonders how legends of Arthur initially spread from Wales to the rest of Europe, one could do worse than look to Dyfrig as an example.

At last we come to Geoffrey of Monmouth. Undeniably, his *Prophetiae* and *History of the Kings of Britain* first ignited enthusiasm for narratives of ancient Britain in lands outside of Wales (his other surviving work, the *Vita Merlini* seems to have had a smaller impact). In spite of his obvious importance, Geoffrey's work has generally not been held up as a model of literary transfer from Wales to England. First of all, discussion of Geoffrey's sources has tended to center on the existence of the very old book written in the British language (*Britanici sermonis*).[79] It has for some time been de rigueur to dismiss this claim as a bald-faced lie—which it almost certainly is—while adding that Geoffrey did have access to some Welsh traditions without offering any specifics, perhaps aside from the *Historia Brittonum* and Gildas.[80] Besides these well-known Welsh sources, Geoffrey's fertile mind is typically said to account for most of his facts about Welsh history. Thus, the overall impression is that Geoffrey's text is not particularly helpful when it comes to the question of the first transmission—he seems to have been making up the majority of it as he wrote. Second, Geoffrey had little direct influence on the first generation of romancers: Béroul, Thomas of Britain, Chrétien de Troyes, and Marie de France. If these authors knew Geoffrey, it may have been through Wace's French translation, but aside from the general atmosphere of ancient Britain, they drew little directly from Geoffrey's Latin text. Transmission of British material should thus be best approached through these vernacular French sources in the opinion of Loomis and others. To be sure, both of these reasons for omitting Geoffrey (and thus Latin) from the question of the first transmission contain some truth: Geoffrey does take the general medieval allowance for creative liberties in historical writing to a new extreme, and the first generation of romancers does have a wide variety of sources not present in Geoffrey's work. Furthermore, Geoffrey can easily be brought into line with theories of vernacular transmission by claiming that he had access to oral traditions of Arthur, Merlin, and others, which he then translated into Latin.[81] Nonetheless, in spite of these objections, the *History of the Kings of Britain* does have a good deal to tell us about the transmission of Welsh material, and it, like Benedict's *Vita Dubricii*, agrees with the evidence found in Walter Map's *De nugis curialium*.

Although little discussed outside of Welsh scholarship, Geoffrey clearly made use of the same network of Latin documents that has been detailed in Chapter 5. As a Monmouth man who would dedicate his *History of the Kings of Britain* to Robert, Earl of Gloucester, himself a patron of St. Peter's Abbey, Geoffrey's participation in this textual network is rather unsurprising. A quick overview of Geoffrey's interest in Welsh-Latin texts will show that Geoffrey, like Walter and Benedict, adapted material from this textual network for his own purposes.

It has long been known that Geoffrey used Welsh genealogies to create the lineages of many of the earliest British kings in his *History*.[82] Although it is a commonplace to say that the Welsh took (and still take) a greater interest in genealogy than their immediate neighbors, the Normans who invaded southern Wales found them useful and interesting as well. As has already been discussed, the *De situ Brecheniauc* and the *Cognacio Brychan* owe their survival to Norman antiquarians.[83] The vitae in Vespasian A.xiv, also a Norman compilation, often contain genealogies of their respective saints. While the exact genealogy that Geoffrey used does not survive, it was closely related to that found in Harley 3859 (ca. 1100), a manuscript that also contains important copies of the *Annales Cambriae* and the *Historia Brittonum*.[84] These texts derive from St. Davids, and another version was in circulation in southern Wales in the twelfth century. [85] What is important at present, however, is the fact that Geoffrey's essential Welsh sources traveled together in a Latin manuscript context.

More to the point, Geoffrey knew exactly what his contemporaries in southern Wales and the borderlands were doing as they "discovered" and promulgated their new historical works about the ancient British past. So great was his interest in this new historical writing that earlier critics thought he may have authored the Book of Llandaf, since Geoffrey's *History*, which usually spends little time on saintly matters, includes the saints Dyfrig, Teilo, and Samson in some detail; all three are instrumental in the Book of Llandaf's grand vision of the diocese of Llandaf.[86] It is difficult to say whether Geoffrey knew the Book of Llandaf itself, or whether he had read the source material that the Book of Llandaf drew upon. But his familiarity with its more brazen concoctions does not mean he believed them. Geoffrey, though he had read these texts in one form or another, did not use them as sources in the same way as he used other Latin accounts of the ancient British past. Indeed, in many ways Geoffrey's *History* can be read as a tongue-in-cheek reaction against the new historical writing of the likes of the Book of Llandaf or the vitae of Vespasian A.xiv. Whereas the obscure saint Dyfrig had been elevated to the status of the bishop of Llandaf in the Llandaf material, Geoffrey makes him the archbishop of the invented archbishopric of Caerleon, in direct contradiction of what Llandaf and even St. Davids were claiming in Geoffrey's day. Again and again Geoffrey thumbs his nose at the historical investigations of his colleagues in southern Wales.[87] Although the point cannot be pressed here, Geoffrey's presentation of Arthur in all his glory can be read as a reaction against the rather boorish and rapacious Arthur of the vitae of Vespasian A.xiv. Geoffrey also made use of a short history of the establishment of the British church that circulated widely in southern Wales and that Gloucester had also acquired as part of its Welsh collection—the *De primo statu Landavuensis ęcclesię*.[88] Finally, Geoffrey may have even had access to the Brychan documents, judging from the forms of some of his names.[89] In sum, whenever Geoffrey's Welsh sources can be identified with any confidence, they are Welsh-Latin texts that circulated throughout southern Wales in the early twelfth century.[90]

Even Breton lays, which are typically put forward as the best evidence of oral transmission, occasionally suggest that Latin was used as a medium between ancient Britain and the modern day.[91] The prologue to *Tyolet* imagines the following chain of transmission from Arthur's court to a contemporary Breton lay:

> The adventures were recounted at court,
> Just as they had been found.
> Worthy clerics of the time
> Had them all written down.
> They were put into Latin
> And written down on parchment,
> So that when the time was right
> They would be listened to with pleasure.
> Now they are told and recounted,
> Translated from Latin into the vernacular;
> The Bretons composed a number of lays about them[92]

Moreover, the *Lai de l'Espine*, though it does not explicitly invoke Latin as does *Tyolet*, envisions an ecclesiastical chain of transmission:

> I am making known the stories
> which are still in Caerleon
> In the church of Saint Aaron,
> And they are known in Brittany
> And have been witnessed in many places.
> Because I have found them in writing.[93]

Whether or not this writing (*estoire*) was in Latin, this passage still describes a literate chain of transmission, all while stressing the connection with an ecclesiastical site in southern Wales (which admittedly has strong Arthurian connections). While these claims are difficult to substantiate in the case of these two lays, they at least demonstrate that composers of Breton lays believed Latin ecclesiastical transmission took place.[94]

Walter Map was not the only person writing in twelfth-century England to use Welsh-Latin documents for information about ancient Britain. The monks of Gloucester had gathered their own collection, which Benedict of Gloucester then used to write his *Vita Dubricii*. Geoffrey of Monmouth worked from several Welsh-Latin documents to compile his *History*. Other instances are not difficult to find. The monks at Glastonbury acquired genealogical materials ultimately stemming from St. Davids.[95] And Gerald of Wales, although he tends to focus more on contemporary matters, does occasionally indicate that he had read Latin texts about the British past, especially when it suited his own immediate goals.[96] Finally, a textual path, established almost certainly by Cistercians, connected Wales and northern England in the late twelfth and early thirteenth centuries.[97] Future research may well uncover more such instances in the twelfth century.

But the twelfth century is no anomaly. Latin textual exchange between Anglo-Saxon England and Wales is also well documented.[98] In particular, St. Augustine's, Canterbury, acquired a significant amount of texts from Wales, and the monastery's own style of English Square minuscule script shows considerable Brittonic influence. All the details of this earlier textual exchange between England and Wales have yet to be established, but it is clear that influx of Welsh-Latin material into England in the early twelfth century continues an earlier, and in some ways rather unremarkable, pattern of textual exchange between English and Welsh ecclesiastic centers. In this regard, a comparison with Ireland is also instructive. While Irish vernacular influence is difficult to trace outside of the Gaelic-speaking realms, "the whole of Europe felt the influence of *Latin* works written in Ireland, such as biblical commentaries, saints' Lives, canon law texts, penitentials, and the *Navigatio Sancti Brendani*."[99] As one scholar has remarked, "Even the tiny quantity of surviving manuscripts makes it clear that Celtic books were widely available in Anglo-Saxon England."[100] Thus, although the Norman presence in Wales incited a vogue for traditions about ancient Britain, the mechanism through which these traditions spread into England and beyond was nothing new.

Conclusion: A Minimalist Approach to the First Transmission

Why has abundant evidence for the Latin transmission of narratives of ancient Britain from Wales to England been ignored in favor of theories that have little convincing evidence in their favor? Disciplinary considerations and some long-held prejudices have both contributed to the neglect of the Latin evidence. First (and perhaps foremost), Celticists, those best prepared to critique the Breton minstrel theory and to offer an alternative, have generally paid little heed to Arthurian literature outside of Wales, a few notable exceptions aside.[101] Discussing those scholars who have argued for the Celtic origins of the Holy Grail, John Carey has, for example, noted, "More surprising, and far more damaging to their position, is the circumstance that almost none of the *advocates* of a Celtic origin for the Grail have been Celticists."[102] The same can be said for many of those who seek out Welsh sources for Arthurian literature in general. With a robust vernacular literature of their own to edit and examine, Welsh scholars have typically given little professional thought to Arthurian literature outside of Wales. An unfortunate and unintended consequence has been that the scholars best equipped to study the transmission of Brittonic material have generally remained uninterested, allowing those with less command of Celtic literatures and languages to fill the scholarly void. The resulting work, which strives to reconstruct ancient Celtic myths, has generally appalled Celticists. Kenneth Jackson described Celtic scholars being "put off by the mass of what seems to them unbridled speculation" in the scholarship of those he bitingly terms mere Celtic enthusiasts.[103] Ceridwen Lloyd-Morgan's exasperation probably speaks for most: "The ancient and long-discredited attempts of R. S. Loomis and his followers to find a 'Celtic' hero lurking behind every knight, or a Welsh or Irish text behind every narrative element, have not, apparently, lost their attraction."[104] This vicious circle of scholarly retrenchment has continued largely unimpeded to the present day.

There is also a problem of scope. The myopic focus on the figure of Arthur that has driven much of the inquiry into the first transmission has meant that material that does not directly address Arthur has often been overlooked. Although Arthur is the organizing principle for most literature dealing with the Matter of Britain, especially after the twelfth century, Arthurian literature and the Matter of Britain are not necessarily coterminous. The famous first occurrence of the term *Matter of Britain* dates from the early thirteenth-century in the work of Jehan Bodel, who uses it somewhat derisively to describe one of three literary matters, or subjects.[105] In Bodel the term is already retrospective, encompassing a literary phenomenon that is half a century old. Yet even here Arthur is not the defining feature, since Bodel does not mention him (though it is entirely possible that by his time readers would expect Arthur in any romance dealing with ancient Britain). Scholars of the first transmission have taken their cue from the first generation of romancers, for whom Arthur was the sine qua non of the ancient British past. But this first generation of romancers had themselves taken their own cue from the renaissance in ancient British historical research that flourished in the first half of the twelfth century. In this period, Welsh vitae, histories, and various other documents like genealogies and charters were all part of the same process of historical recovery and invention. The ancient British past exercised the minds of William of Malmesbury, Caradog of Llancarfan, Geoffrey of Monmouth, the archbishops of both St. Davids and of Llandaf, Benedict of Gloucester, and the Brycheiniog author of the *De situ Brecheniauc*. While Arthur does appear, sometimes gloriously, in this corpus of work, it is a mistake to sift out Arthurian lore, treating it as somehow distinct. To separate the figure of Arthur from the context of his early creation is to miss this point and to miss rather important evidence for the transmission of Arthurian material.

The third reason for the popularity of the Breton minstrel thesis is that it speaks to some long-held prejudices about Welsh literary culture and the "supposed Celtic preference for oral rather than written transmission."[106] Reading through the body of scholarship that argues for oral transmission, it is not uncommon to encounter quotes about Welsh literature in the following spirit: "In short, it was Chrétien who gave absolute clarity to Dark Ages folk tales that can often seem like childlike gibberish to the modern reader, even after sympathetic translation."[107] In addition to disparaging Welsh literary traditions, Loomis and others are guilty of an a priori dismissal of written, especially Latin, transmission, while at the same time postulating lost French manuscripts with ease.[108] Although much of medieval Welsh literary culture has been lost—one estimate puts the survival rate of vernacular manuscripts at one in five and Latin manuscripts at one in a hundred—enough remains to show that it was vigorous, extensive, and in touch with the larger European world.[109]

Finally, the last reason why the Breton minstrel has been such a popular candidate for the medium of Anglo-Welsh exchange is that it enables scholars to practice a certain type of folkloric or mythological methodology. In short, Breton *conteurs*, with their emphasis on the vernacular and orality, allow

scholars to quickly write off the substantial literary culture of Wales, both in
the vernacular and in Latin. Loomis and others preferred to invoke oral tradition because a large part of their project was piecing together the detritus of
Celtic mythology by comparing this source with that analogue. Underlying
this methodology was the assumption that the minstrels and later poets, like
Chrétien or Marie, did not really understand their source material, and, be-
wildered, they preserved much of it unchanged. For Loomis, educated Latin
authors, those who like Walter Map would turn a Welsh saint into a king to
fit the narrative context, who like Benedict of Gloucester would combine two
diametrically opposed versions of a vita for political purposes, or who like
Geoffrey of Monmouth would use Welsh historical documents as the fertile
soil in which to plant his fanciful creations—writers like these would have
been far too clever for Loomis. Instead, inert, artless transmitters, bumbling
about with half-understood stories, are necessary for reconstructing ancient
ur-myths and Celtic sun gods. But this approach greatly underestimates both
how little so-called Celtic material was necessary to create a new tale of the
Matter of Britain and how French and English authors deployed Celtic material for their own artistic ends. The seeds of this misconception are found in
Matthew Arnold's *On the Study of Celtic Literature*, where he claims that "the
mediaeval story-teller is pillaging an antiquity of which he does not fully possess the secret; he is like a peasant building his hut on the site of Halicarnassus
or Ephesus; he builds, but what he builds is full of materials of which he
knows not the history or knows by a glimmering tradition merely; stones 'not
of this building,' but of an older architecture, greater, cunninger, more majes-
tical."[110] A model of transmission that envisions an oral culture trading in
ancient, corrupted tales meant that modern scholars could, with the right effort, rebuild the grand temple that Arnold imagines.

In place of a Breton minstrel or a professional translator, the surviving
evidence suggests the following scenario, which I will call the minimalist theory of the first transmission of the Matter of Britain. The first half of the
twelfth century witnessed a renaissance in historical writing in southern
Wales, largely, though not solely, instigated by the Norman Conquest. The
fruits of this scholarship, written in Latin, were easily disseminated to places
like Gloucester. Now the minimalism. We have every reason to believe that
authors needed only a small touch of ancient British tradition on which to
build their larger creations. Geoffrey of Monmouth used a small array of
Welsh-Latin documents to create a sprawling history; Walter Map took a European folktale and created an entire story set in the British past; he also may

have invented much of the story of Gastin and Trunio from a short account; even Chrétien de Troyes dressed an entire preexisting story up in ancient British trappings by adding a few elements that he had gleaned from some place or another.[111] In short, scholars have seriously overestimated how much narrative material was needed by medieval authors to create a passable narrative set in ancient Britain. A few may have had access to longer texts, but it seems a list of names and a few minor details may have been enough for most. Moreover, Sims-Williams points out that shorter Latin texts like Walter's stories of Cadog, Herla, and Gastin may have existed in greater quantity: "Such Latin material could have formed the basis for French vernacular poems in the fifties and the sixties of the twelfth century, and these may in turn have been superseded and eclipsed by the masterpieces of Thomas, Chrétien, and Marie in the seventies and eighties, with successive vernacular poets amplifying, refashioning, and embellishing the works of their Latin and French predecessors."[112] This minimalist theory does, however, shift much of the responsibility for the creation of Arthurian literature away from the Welsh and toward the first generation of romance authors working in French and Latin. This may well be a small concession if we are to move the study of "Celtic elements" in romance past the steady accumulation of analogues, reconstructed stories, and ur-myths.

Walter Map took an interest in written traditions about ancient Britain, which he had access to through the medium of Latin. A courtier to Henry II, Walter shows how easily historical traditions from a small Welsh kingdom could move to one of the most important cultural centers in Europe. Given all this, it seems much easier to understand how a decade after Walter's death, when the author of *La mort* was pressed to imagine how narratives of ancient Britain passed into French, he imagined a clerical writer discovering Latin documents in an ecclesiastical center with Arthurian connections. He did so because that was the model of transmission that, when looking back over the twelfth century, simply made sense.

Epilogue

This entire book, not unfairly, could be summarized as one expansive gloss on a single passage from the *Queste del Saint Graal*:

> When Bors had recounted the adventures of the Holy Grail, as he had seen them, they were recorded and kept in the archive at Salisbury. Master Walter Map withdrew them to write his book about the Holy Grail, for the love of his lord King Henry, who had the story translated from Latin into French.[1]

With the exceptions of Sir Bors and the Holy Grail (sadly), everything here has some element of truth to it. Indeed, this passage describes a paradigm of textual transmission that, as I have argued, is the best explanation for how literary material moved out of Wales and into the rest of Europe, forming the collection of romances, histories, and other texts that make up the Matter of Britain. This paradigm emphasizes literary transmission rather than oral: "recorded and kept." It credits ecclesiastical networks for their role in preserving and circulating narratives about ancient Britain: "the archive at Salisbury." It gives primacy to Latin and not to a vernacular: "translated from Latin into French." And it imagines "Master Walter Map" as the nexus between past and present, between the Latin archives and the French romances. Walter's fluency with romance, his self-designation as a Marcher, his involvement with Henry II's court, his own interest in imagining the ancient British past, and his use of Welsh-Latin documents from a network of ecclesiastical sites—all of this marks him as a man who very well could have done what the author of the *Queste* said he did. Walter's involvement in the *Queste* is not an enigma, or a parody, or an outlandish invention on par with Wolfram von Eschenbach's invocation of the mysterious Kyot and the Arabic sources that he allegedly accessed. In my view, the anonymous author of the *Queste del Saint Graal*, when pressed to invent a plausible source for his Arthurian narrative, could have done no better than Walter Map.

In explaining why Walter Map became attached to the *Lancelot-Grail Cycle*, this book opens up two further areas of research. First of all, I hope that it can help reinvigorate the study of Walter Map. The Walter Map I have argued for is a competent, yet still biting and original, writer—an author who was a meticulous reviser and a clear thinker. Treating the document known as *De nugis curialium* as a collection of five disparate texts in various states of revision, all of which represent a different genre, seems preferable, and a much better working hypothesis, than laying the blame for the text's difficulties solely at Walter's feet. If readers, led astray by rubrics and modern paratext, can resist the temptation to cherry-pick individual stories and can instead read the episodes in each *distinctio* as in close dialogue with one another, I am certain that much more about Walter's literary artistry will become apparent. As I mentioned in the beginning of this book, I have intentionally focused on the parts of the *De nugis curialium* that concern Walter's reputation as an Arthurian author. Walter Map still awaits those astute readers who will approach each *distinctio* as a work unto itself and who will give his texts the time and patience that they so strongly deserve.

At this point, I also hope it is clear that this book contains an implicit argument about methodology. It demonstrates that there is much to gain from an interdisciplinary perspective that puts Celtic studies into dialogue with the rest of medieval studies. It shows that the Latin literary culture of southern Wales elucidates the creation and spread of the Matter of Britain. Perhaps what sets this particular proposal apart from the general din of interdisciplinary calls to action is that there are few scholarly fields as close, yet at the same time so frustratingly detached, as Celtic studies and English studies. The institutionalization of literary studies under the rubric of national blocks has meant that Welsh, Irish, and the other Celtic languages are seldom studied alongside medieval English and French. There are, of course, notable exceptions, but it is fair to say Celtic studies do remain marginalized in academia, particularly in North America. At present, medievalists are more likely to look to the Mediterranean—justly so—to bolster our claim that the Middle Ages did indeed foster transnational and transcultural literature. Looking to the west can yield similar critical benefits, yet we still understand less than we should about the multilingual intellectual culture of Wales and the borderlands. We still do not fully know the extent of French, English, and Latin writing in medieval Wales. The Celtic West still has much to offer.

Emblematic of this disciplinary divide is an odd gloss in Cotton Vespasian A.xiv. In its copy of the *De situ Brecheniauc*, the perplexing Welsh name

Windouith has been glossed by the equally perplexing ".i. eurus de uent."[2] Commentators have been especially puzzled by the word *eurus*, and they have generally preferred to view it as a Latin gloss, reading *eurus* as "East Wind" and *de uent.* as some shortened version of *de uento* (about/from wind).[3] Still, this forced gloss makes little sense: "East Wind from wind"? It is better to recognize this marginal phrase as one of the manuscript's French glosses, and the puzzling *eurus* as a common Old French spelling of the word that has become Modern French *heureux*.[4] Everything now clicks into place. The glossator thought the Welsh name *Windouith* meant "blessed with wind." Only through a transcultural and transnational perspective does his reading become clear. I would contend that our scholarship will be enriched if we follow the lead of this intrepid glossator who did not stay in his disciplinary boundaries: a French speaker, reading Welsh Latin, working in a border area, who thought a text about the Welsh past might repay careful reading.

Appendix

A Preliminary List
of Suspected Interpolated Glosses
in the *De nugis curialium*

The first column refers to the distinction and chapter number, followed by the page number, in Brook and Mynor's edition of the *De nugis curialium*. An asterisk indicates that the notes in Brooke and Mynor's edition suggest the passage is a gloss.

1.10, p. 20	Sciebam autem quod illi simile consilium darent, id est, ad suam utilitatem, mea neclecta
1.10, p. 24	cuius ignorat cogitaciones aut linguam, id est, quicquid eorum corda loquantur
1.25, p. 84	Hos alliciunt, et ad camineas suas a strepitu seorsum ab hospitibus caritatis, id est pulicibus [MS publicibus] longe
1.25, p. 98	inuicem, id est inter se*
1.25, p. 106	confusi ut solent, id est ioculantes
1.25, p. 112	de hiis, id est de Hebreis
1.26, p 114	Noster dominus, id est, rex Henricus secundus
2.11, p. 150	Deheubard [MS Deheulard], id est Noruuallie*
2.11, p. 152	Vestra terre Reynos, id est Brecheniauc*
2.17, p. 166	Hic insulam nostram, id est Angliam
2.18, p. 176	regnum Parthis, id est Turchis*
2.19, p. 178	nomen ei Gillescop, id est episcopus
2.23, pp. 188–90	processit [MS processus] igitur inde arbitratus se nubeculam, id est paruulum, a mari, i. Wallia, que semper in

motu est, natum, regem futurum, quod ei postea detexit euentus

2.23, p. 194 Quesiuit a me, qui marchio sum Walensibus, que fides, id est fidelitas, eorum, et quomodo credi possint

2.26, p. 200 brachanum, id est tapetum optimum

4.1, p. 280 qui omnes misericordias Dauid fidelis domino nostro patri suo compleuerit, id est illas quas ipse fideli suo Dauid habuit

4.3, p. 304 neutra tamen defraudata est fine fraudis feminee proprio, id est malo

4.11, p. 358 et quibuscunque modis ipsam ille temptauerat, id est omnibus

4.15, p. 376 Alanus Rebrit, id est rex Britonum

5.3, p. 414 nefrendem, id est adolescentem et uirginem suem

5.6, p. 482 Set ut ad materiam unde digressus sum, id est ad regem Henricum secundum reuertar

5.7, p. 504 Nunquid non ego sum in curia Ticius, et forsan alius aliquis, cuius cupido cordi uultures apponuntur, id est affectus nigri, diuellentes ipsum

5.7, p. 504 cribro quod a paleis grana secernit, id est, discrecione, uasa complere pertusa laboramus, id est, animos insaciabiles, quorum adulterauit ambicio fundum

5.7, pp. 506–8 "Nec in persona propria neque per nuncium uisitauit nos neque respexit," id est, non dedit

5.7, p. 508 Hi sortes in urnam mittere uidentur, id est, causarum casus in inuolucrum

Notes

INTRODUCTION

1. *DNC*, xviii n. 4.

2. Max Manitius, *Geschichte der Lateinischen Literatur des Mittelalters*, vol. 3 (Munich: C. H. Beck, 1931), 264–74; Gunnar Stollberg, *Die soziale Stellung der intellektuellen Oberschicht im England des 12. Jahrhunderts* (Lübeck: Matthiesen, 1973), 70–81 and 168–71; Egbert Türk, *Nugae curialium: La règne d'Henri II Plantegenêt (1145–1189) et l'éthique politique* (Geneva: Librairie Droz, 1977), 158–77; *DNC*, xiii–xix; Walter Map, *Svaghi di Corte*, trans. Fortunata Latella (Parma: Pratiche Editrice, 1990), 1:27–31; Alberto Várvaro, *Apparizioni fantastiche: Tradizioni folcoriche e letteratura nel medioevo—Walter Map* (Bologna: Il Mulino, 1994), 217–27; *CPGC*, 5–14.

3. See Chapter 1, this volume.

4. *DNC*, 5.6, p. 494: "fideles et necessarii."

5. *GCO*, 4:219–22, at 219.

6. John's appointment of Giles de Braose as bishop of Hereford instead of Walter, whom the chapter had proposed, had more to do with pleasing William, Giles's father, than with any particular dislike of Walter. See Julia Barrow, "Athelstan to Aigueblanche, 1056–1268," in *Hereford Cathedral: A History*, ed. Gerald Aylmer and John Tiller (London: Hambledon Press, 2000), 21–47, at 30.

7. *GCO*, 3:200–201.

8. Julia Barrow, "A Twelfth-Century Bishop and Literary Patron: William de Vere," *Viator* 18 (1987): 175–90.

9. The response of W. Bothewald, subprior of St. Frideswide's in Oxford, preserves one line of Walter's satirical attack. It is edited in *The Latin Poems Commonly Attributed to Walter Mapes*, ed. Thomas Wright (London: Printed for the Camden Society by J. B. Nichols and Son, 1841), xxxv–xxxvii.

10. Alfred Lord Tennyson, *The Works of Alfred Lord Tennyson, Poet Laureate*, vol. 6 (Boston: Houghton, Mifflin, 1892), 67.

11. A. G. Rigg, "Golias and Other Pseudonyms," *Studi Medievali* 18 (1977): 65–109. For false attributions in general, see Pascale Bourgain, "The Circulation of Texts in Manuscript Culture," in *The Medieval Manuscript Book: Cultural Approaches*, ed. Michael Johnston and Michael van Dussen (Cambridge: Cambridge University Press, 2015), 140–59, at 154.

12. Joshua Byron Smith, "'The First Writer in the Welsh Language': Walter Map's Reception in Nineteenth-Century Wales," *National Library of Wales Journal* 36, no. 2 (2015): 183–97. See also *CPGC*, 15 n. 6.

13. Hieronymus, *Epistolae*, ed. Johannes Andreas (Rome: Conradus Sweynheym and Arnoldus Pannartz, 1468). See E. Ph. Goldschmidt, *Medieval Texts and Their First Appearance in Print*, Supplement to the Bibliographical Society's Transactions, no. 16 (London: Printed for the Bibliographical Society at Oxford University Press, 1943), 40. I have found nothing to contradict Goldschmidt's claim.

14. For the genuine list of Walter's work and verse, see Manitius, *Geschichte der Lateinischen Literatur*, 264–74; Paul Lehmann, *Mittellateinische Verse in "Distinctiones monasticae et morales" vom Anfang des 13. Jahrhunderts*, Sitzungsberichte der Bayerischen Akademie der Wissenschaften, Philosophisch-Philologische und Historische Klasse, Jhrg. 1922, Abh. 2 (Munich: Bayerischen Akademie der Wissenschaften, 1922), 12–15; Rigg, "Golias and Other Pseudonyms," 84–85. For the *ex dictis W. Map*, two short anecdotes attributed to Walter in MS Corpus Christi College 32, fol. 94v, see *DNC*, 515–16. For the unsubstantiated claim of five manuscripts containing some of Walter's histories, see *CPGC*, 42 n. 1.

15. *DNC*, 5.6, pp. 496–97: "Gallicum Merleburge."

16. *DNC*, 4.5, pp. 312–13: "Cum enim putuerim, tum primo sal accipiet, totusque sibi supplebitur decessu meo defectus, et in remotissima posteritate michi faciet auctoritatem antiquitas, quia tunc ut nunc uetustum cuprum preferetur auro nouello."

17. *DNC*, xxx.

18. Várvaro, *Apparizioni fantastiche*. This work, though not widely cited in English-language scholarship, argues that the *De nugis curialium* is indicative of twelfth-century Europe's newfound interest in folk traditions and narrative. According to Várvaro, conservative clerics generally repressed traditional, nonecclesiastical beliefs and lore until the twelfth century, when writers like Walter worked to legitimize folklore to create an exciting intermingling of different cultural sources: "L'uso letterario, sia pur volgare, dei materiali della narrativa folclorica ha creato una nuova opposizione, si é risolto non nello schiacciamento del livello culturale alto su quello basso ma nella formazione di un nuovo livello alto, che lentamente sarà accettato anche da chi gestiva la cultura latina" (211; the literary use of material from folkloric narrative, although in the vernacular, has created a new opposition, as it has resulted not in the crushing of the high cultural standard under the low one, but in the formation of a new high cultural standard, which would slowly be accepted even by someone who had been in charge of Latin culture).

19. First suggested in A. G. Rigg, review of *De nugis curialium: Courtiers' Trifles*, by Walter Map, ed. and trans. M. R. James, rev. C. N. L. Brooke and R. A. B. Mynors, *Speculum* 60, no. 1 (1985): 177–82, at 182.

CHAPTER 1

1. See Chapter 6, this volume.

2. It made sense for the Welsh present to be linked with their glorious British past. For example, Geoffrey of Monmouth cites a very old book in the British language (*Britanici sermonis*), while dismissing his contemporaries for not knowing about the Arthurian past. *HRB* §1, p. 5; §208, p. 281. Elsewhere, as in Wace's *Roman de Brut*, Layamon's *Brut*, and some of the lais of Marie de France, the Welsh present is explicitly linked with the Arthurian past.

3. *GCO*, 1:306.

4. *GCO*, 1:306: "Medicum enim animarum quaerimus non effunerarium, nec canem mutum habere volumus, nec pastorem elinguem."

5. *GCO*, 1:306–7.

6. *DNC*, 2.23, p. 196: "In rapina et furto gloria Walensium"; 2.20, p. 182: "omnino sint infideles ad omnes."

7. For Gerald's complex identity, see Robert Bartlett, *Gerald of Wales, 1146–1223* (Oxford: Oxford University Press, 1982), esp. 16–29; Jeffrey Jerome Cohen, *Hybridity, Identity, and Monstrosity in Medieval Britain: On Difficult Middles* (New York: Palgrave Macmillan, 2006), 77–108.

8. Gianni Mombello, "Les avatars d'une facétie de Cicéron," in *Grant risee? The Medieval Comic Presence*, ed. Adrian P. Tudor and Alan Hindley (Turnhout: Brepols, 2006), 225–46, at 230 ("né au pays de Galles"); Albert Hughes Williams, *An Introduction to the History of Wales* (Cardiff: University of Wales, 1941–48), 2:50.

9. Gilda Caiti-Russo, "Situation actuelle de Gautier Map, écrivain fantastique," *Revue des Langues Romanes* 101, no. 2 (1997): 125–43, at 125; Michel Rubellin, "Au temps où Valdès n'était pas hérétique: Hypothèses sur les rôle de Valdès à Lyon (1170–1183)," in *Inventer l'hérésie? Discours polémiques et pouvoirs avant l'Inquisition*, ed. Monique Zerner (Nice: Centre d'Études Médiévales, 1998), 193–217, at 199.

10. R. T. Jenkins, "Map, Walter," in *Y Bywgraffiadur Cymreig hyd 1940*, ed. John Edward Lloyd and R. T. Jenkins (London: Honourable Society of Cymmrodorion, 1953), 578: "Rhaid ymwrthod â'r syniad ei fod yn Gymro." No entry for Walter exists in the English-language version, published as *The Dictionary of Welsh Biography down to 1940* (London: Honourable Society of Cymmrodorion, 1959). Both the English- and the Welsh-language versions are available online, accessed July 8, 2016, http://yba.llgc.org.uk/en/index.html. For Walter's reception in nineteenth-century Wales, see Smith, " 'The First Writer in the Welsh Language.' "

11. For the later variants of *Map*, such as *Mapes* and *Mahap*, see Chapter 3, this volume.

12. First proposed in H. L. D. Ward and J. A. Herbert, *Catalogue of Romances in the Department of Manuscripts in the British Museum* (London: Trustees of the British Museum, 1883–1910), 1:736. For a recent discussion of the name, see David E. Thornton, "Hey, Mac! The Name *Maccus*, Tenth to Fifteenth Centuries," *Nomina* 20 (1997): 67–94, at 82–83.

13. Thornton, "The Name *Maccus*."

14. For Godric Map in the Bodmin Gospels (MS British Library Add. 9381, fol. 8), see Ward and Herbert, *Catalogue of Romances*, 1:736; Paul Russell, *Read It in a Glossary: Glossaries and Learned Discourse in Medieval Ireland* (Cambridge: Hughes Hall and Department of Anglo-Saxon, Norse, and Celtic, University of Cambridge, 2008), 12.

15. *DNC*, 5.6, p. 494: "quidam clericus, qui uobis hec scripsit, cui agnomen Map"; *DMLBS*, s.v. "agnomen."

16. *DNC*, xvi, esp. n. 4.

17. For the connotations of *Sais*, see *Gwaith Meilyr Brydydd a'i Ddisgynyddion*, ed. J. E. Caerwyn Williams, Peredur I. Lynch, and R. Geraint Gruffydd (Cardiff: University of Wales Press,, 1994), 317–18. See also the discussion of Rhys Sais in Frederick C. Suppe, "Interpreter Families and Anglo-Welsh Relations in the Shropshire-Powys Marches in the Twelfth Century," *Anglo-Norman Studies* 30 (2007): 196–212, at 196–97.

18. R. R. Davies, *The Age of Conquest: Wales, 1063–1415*, rev. ed. (Oxford: Oxford University Press, 2000), 103.

19. Davies, *Age of Conquest*, 103.

20. *DNC*, xiv and the following pages.

21. *DNC*, xiv, n. 3

22. Jenkins, "Map, Walter," 578; *CPGC*, 6–8.

23. *CPGC*, 7–8. See also Gösta Tengvik, *Old English Bynames* (Uppsala: Almqvist & Wiksells Boktryckeri-A.-B., 1938), 378. The Worcestershire place-names *Mapnors*, *Mappenor(e)*,

Mappenouer point to a possible Old English personal name **Mappa*. A. Mawer and F. M. Stenton, *The Place-Names of Worcestershire* (Cambridge: Cambridge University Press, 1927), 148. It is of course possible that there are two separate etyma here, one English, and one Welsh. Also worth noting in this discussion is the odd "on Ælfrices maphappes" found in the Leofric Missals. Tengvik, *Old English Bynames*, 378.

24. *CPGC*, 7–8.

25. Although Bate and others do not explore this possibility, one could surmise that the Latin word *mappa* has been interpreted as a weak Old English noun, many of which indicate agency (e.g., *hunta*, "hunter"). Given the lack of other similar developments and the absence of documentation for an administrative position called a *mappa*, this possibility seems farfetched. Moreover, Latin *măppa* has a short *a*, while Walter's agnomen contains a long *a*, according to metrical evidence from Gerald of Wales. See Chapter 3, this volume.

26. Final /a/ in Old English is reduced to /ə/ in early Middle English and was written *-e*. There is, however, the possibility, remote though it seems to me, that the form "Map" witnesses the loss of final *-e*. See Donka Minkova, *The History of Final Vowels in English: The Sound of Muting* (Berlin: Mouton de Gruyter, 1991), 45–55.

27. T. J. Morgan and Prys Morgan, *Welsh Surnames* (Cardiff: University of Wales Press, 1985), 155; Thornton, "The Name *Maccus*," 82. The fact that the name is sometimes lenited (e.g., *Walt[erus] Vab*) shows that it was understood as an epithet. In Wales the name seems to appear primarily in the south. For the Breton surnames *Le Mab*, *Le Maby*, *Le Map*, and *Le Mapp*, see Marcel Divanach, *5000 patronymes bretons francisés* (Brest: Éditions du Vieux meunier breton, 1975), 74 and 76.

28. *Welsh Genealogies, A.D. 300–1400*, ed. Peter C. Bartrum (Cardiff: University of Wales Press for the Board of Celtic Studies, 1974): 4:798, s.v. "Rhys ap Tewdwr 23"; 1:115, s.v. "Bleddyn ap Maenyrch 31."

29. *DMLBS*, s.v. "filius," def. 1d.

30. Thornton, "The Name *Maccus*," 83.

31. *DNC*, 1.24, p. 72; 1.32, p. 130.

32. *DNC*, 5.4, p. 192; 1.25, p. 106; 2.23, p. 192; 2.9, p. 146 and 2.23, p. 196; 2.9, p. 146.

33. The lordships in the vicinity are Ewyas Lacy, the northernmost parts of Monmouth and Hay, Abergavenny, Blaenllyfni, and Brecon.

34. *DNC*, 2.26, pp. 200–202.

35. Barrow, "Athelstan to Aigueblanche," 38.

36. *DNC*, xiv.

37. Simon Meecham-Jones, "Where Was Wales? The Erasure of Wales in Medieval English Culture," in *Authority and Subjugation in Writing of Medieval Wales*, ed. Ruth Kennedy and Simon Meecham-Jones (New York: Palgrave Macmillan, 2008), 27–57, at 31–32; Llinos Beverley Smith, "The Welsh and English Languages in Late-Medieval Wales," in *Multilingualism in Later Medieval Britain*, ed. David Trotter (Cambridge: D. S. Brewer, 2000), 7–21, at 12; B. G. Charles, "The Welsh, Their Language and Place-Names in Archenfield and Oswestry," in *Angles and Britons: O'Donnell Lectures*, ed. Henry Lewis (Cardiff: University of Wales Press, 1963), 85–110.

38. R. R. Davies, *Lordship and Society in the March of Wales, 1282–1400* (Oxford: Clarendon Press, 1978), 17.

39. Bartlett, *Gerald of Wales*, 22–24.

40. *DNC*, 5.6, p. 494.

41. Huw Pryce, "British or Welsh? National Identity in Twelfth-Century Wales," *English Historical Review* 116, no. 468 (2001): 775–801.

42. *DNC*, 2.20, p. 182: "compatriote nostri Walenses."

43. *DMLBS*, s.v. "compatriota." The only other use of *compatriota* in the *De nugis curialium* also occurs in the context of regional, not ethnic, identity; see *DNC*, 1.30, p. 120.

44. *DNC*, 4.1, p. 278.

45. *DNC*, 4.1, p. 278.

46. For *brycan* and *brenhin*, see Chapter 3, this volume.

47. See Chapter 5, this volume.

48. See Chapter 5, this volume.

49. *GCO*, 1:306: "Verumtamen si de Anglia oriundus nobis urgenter praefici debet antistes, in duorum alterutrum, ut capiat contentio finem." When Gerald returns to this event years later in 1218 as he is writing the *De iure et statu Meneuensis ecclesiasiae*, he provides a somewhat different account: "Archidiaconus autem tunc ei duos, decanum scilicet Lincolniae Rogerum et archidiaconum Oxoniensem Walterum Map, nominavit, quos ipse viros bonos et honestos esse dicebat; sed aliquos, qui de Anglia essent oriundi et Walliae tamen magis intimi, morum gentis utriusque non ignari ipsum nominare suadebat" (*GCO*, 3:321; At that time the archdeacon [i.e., Gerald] proposed to him two men, who he said were good and honest people: Roger, deacon of Lincoln, and Walter Map, archdeacon of Oxford, but he kept urging him to propose others who were born in England, yet nevertheless quite close to Wales and knowledgeable of the mores of both people of the land). See also Lewis Thorpe, "Walter Map and Gerald of Wales," *Medium Aevum* 47 (1978): 6–21, at 20 n. 59. For the date of the *De iure et statu*, see Bartlett, *Gerald of Wales*, 178–79.

50. *GCO*, 1:306.

51. *GCO*, 1:306–7: "vel in archidiaconum Oxoniensem, virum liberalitate conspicuum, copiosa litteratura, et urbana eloquentia praeditum, morumque gentis utriusque terrae tam ex vicinitate locorum quam frequentia non ignarum."

52. For Gerald's perceptive comments on language, see Bartlett, *Gerald of Wales*, 170–71.

53. Bartlett, *Gerald of Wales*, 155–56.

54. *DNC*, 2.23, p. 194.

55. *DNC*, 2.23, p. 194.

56. For a possible meeting in Paris, see *DNC*, xv n. 4.

57. *DNC*, 2.23, p. 194: "Quesiuit a me, qui marchio sum Walensibus, que fides, [id est fidelitas,] eorum et quomodo credi possint." For the interpolation "id est fidelitas," see Chapter 3, this volume.

58. *DNC*, 2.23, p. 194: " 'Refer' inquit 'lapidem in locum suum.' "

59. *DNC*, 2.23, p. 194: "Et ego uobis ex hoc facto notifico fidem Walensium, quod dum tenebitis ensem supplicabunt, cum ipsi tenuerint imperabunt."

60. *GCO*, 3:145–46.

61. *DNC*, 2.20, p. 182.

62. *DNC*, 2.21, p. 184.

63. *DNC*, 2.23, p. 196: "Iuuenis mortuus aut senex pauper."

64. *DNC*, 2.26, p. 202.

65. Bartlett, *Gerald of Wales*, 20–21. See also the discussion of Gerald as a Marcher in Georgia Henley, "Gerald of Wales and Welsh Society," in *A Handbook on Medieval Wales*, ed. Emma Cavell and Kathryn Hurlock (Leiden: Brill, forthcoming 2018). I would like to thank Georgia for allowing me to read her chapter prior to publication. Also useful is the discussion of Gerald's motivations in Huw Pryce, "Gerald's Journey through Wales," *Journal of Welsh Ecclesiastical History* 6 (1989): 17–34.

66. *GCO*, 1:57: "in Marchiae finibus ad Walliam pacificandam."

67. Bartlett, *Gerald of Wales*, 25–29.

68. *GCO*, 3:200–201.

69. *GCO*, 1:307.

70. See Chapter 5, this volume.

71. *DNC*, 5.5, p. 450; 1.31, p. 124; 1.23, p. 70.

72. For a life of the secular cleric, see John Cotts, *The Clerical Dilemma: Peter of Blois and the Literate Culture in the Twelfth Century* (Washington, DC: Catholic University of America Press, 2009).

73. *DNC*, 2.23, pp. 194–97: "Et ut aliquid sciatis quo Franco deuenerit, rex a suis inuentus statim retinuit eum pauidum et fugientem cum magna laude, suis referens quam probe quamque facete coegisset eum referre lapidem, et dedit eum Crespium in Valesio in hereditatem."

74. I have only listed three of the many variant spellings given in *The Anglo-Norman Dictionary*, accessed July 12, 2016, http://www.anglo-norman.net/D/Galeis.

75. W. L. Warren, *Henry II* (Berkeley: University of California Press, 1973), 161–69; Davies, *Age of Conquest*, 290–92.

76. *DNC*, 2.24, p. 196: "super Sabrinam . . . in Glanmorgan"; "uirum strenuum et habundantem."

77. Frederick C. Suppe, *Military Institutions on the Welsh Marches: Shropshire, A.D. 1066–1300* (Woodbridge: Boydell Press, 1994), esp. 7–33.

78. Suppe, *Military Institutions*, 20–21.

79. *DNC*, 2.24, p. 196: "egressus est solus nemus quod toti eminet prouincie, multa manu in memore abscondita struxitque innocenti nociuas insidias."

80. *DNC*, 2.24, p. 196.

81. Frederick Suppe also suggests that Walter may have observed raids in person, citing his tenure as a canon of Hereford Cathedral and as an itinerant justice in Gloucestershire in 1173 (*Military Institutions*, 11 n. 18).

82. It is relevant to point out that the Annals of Margam mention a series of particularly devastating Welsh raids in 1185 after Earl William of Gloucester had died, and during or just after the period in which Walter composed the bulk of *DNC*: "Hic etiam Walenses pagum Glamorganensem incendiis atque rapinis hostiliter vastare coeperunt; tunc ab eis inter alias et villa Kerdiviae incendio est tradita, villaque de Kenefegiam vice secunda. Castellum quoque de Neth secundo obsessum et fortiter aliquamdiu oppugnatum, donec ab Anglia veniens exercitus Francigenarum fugavit agmen hostile Walensium, machina quam fecerant igne cremata" (Also in this year, the Welsh began to violently ravage the district of Glamorgan with fire and raids; at that time, among others, both the town of Cardiff and the town of Kenefeg (for a second time) were burned by them. The castle at Neath was also besieged a second time and for a while it boldly suffered the assault, until the army of the French [or of men of French descent] came from England and put the hostile Welsh troop to flight, after the seige engine that they had built had been burned). *Annales de Margan*, in *Annales Monastici*, vol. 1, ed. Henry Richards Luard (London: Longman, Green, Longman, Roberts, and Green, 1864), 17–18.

83. *DNC*, 2.24, p. 196

84. Gen. 18.

85. *DNC*, 2.24, p. 196: "Quam recte sine pauore dicitur!"

86. *DNC*, 2.24, p. 198: "Sciebam Deum intus esse; scio eciam Iudam Machabeum Dei fortissimum atletam dixisse. 'Non in multitudine exercitus uictoria belli, sed de celo fortitudo

est.' Ideo timebam hunc insultum producere, nec est oblitus Dominus in nepotes meos ulcisci superbiam obiurgacionis."

87. *DNC*, 2.23, p. 188: "Luelinus iste, cum esset iuuenis, uiuente Griffino patre suo."

88. See, for example, *DNC*, 2.22, p. 186 n. 1.

89. For Gruffudd ap Llywelyn, see Michael Davies and Sean Davies, *The Last King of Wales: Gruffudd ap Llywelyn, c. 1013–1063* (Stroud: History Press, 2012); and T. M. Charles-Edwards, *Wales and the Britons, 350–1064* (Oxford: University of Oxford Press, 2013), 561–68.

90. *Brut y Tywysogyon; or, The Chronicle of the Princes: Red Book of Hergest Version*, ed. Thomas Jones (Cardiff: University of Wales Press, 1955), 26–27, sub anno 1063: "pen a tharyan ac amdiffnwr y Brytanyeit."

91. Lindy Brady, *Writing the Welsh Borderlands in Anglo-Saxon Literature* (Manchester: University of Manchester Press, forthcoming 2017), 115–24. I would like to thank Lindy for allowing me to read her book prior to publication.

92. *DNC*, 2.22, p. 186: "uir infidus ut fere omnes decessores eius et posteri."

93. *The Anglo-Saxon Chronicle*, ed. and trans. Michael Swanton (New York: Routledge, 1998), 184–87. See also Simon Keynes, "Diocese and Cathedral before 1056," in *Hereford Cathedral: A History*, 4–20, at 18–20; Barrow, "Athelstan to Aigueblanche," 22–23.

94. Davies, *Age of Conquest*, 25; *The Anglo-Saxon Chronicle: A Collaborative Edition*, vol. 5, *MS C*, ed. Katherine O'Brien O'Keeffe (Cambridge: D. S. Brewer, 2001), 115, sub anno 1053.

95. For an introductory overview of Welsh law, see Davies, *Age of Conquest*, 115–38; T. M. Charles-Edwards, *The Welsh Laws* (Cardiff: University of Wales Press, 1989). For some of the peculiarities of law in the Welsh March, see Sara Elin Roberts, "Legal Practice in Fifteenth-Century Brycheiniog," *Studia Celtica* 35 (2001): 307–23.

96. *DNC*, 2.22, p. 186: "Delusum se dicit rex, et quasi de re ueraciter acta stomacatur."

97. *DNC*, 2.22, pp. 186–88: "Iudicia terre nostre sequi oportet, et que statuerunt patres precepta longaque consuetudine firmata sunt, nulla possumus racione destruere. Sequamur eos, et antequam in contrarium decreta dictent publica nichil nouum proferamus. Ab antiquissimis promulgatum est institutis, ut qui regis Wallie reginam adulterio deturpauerit, mille solutis regi uaccis cetera indempnis liber abibit. De uxoribus similiter principium et magnatum quorumcunque secundum singulorum dignitates constituta est pena sub certo numero. Iste acusatur de sompnio concubitus cum regina, nec inficiatur. De ueritate criminis confessa certum est quod mille uacce darentur."

98. See Robin Chapman Stacey, "King, Queen, and *Edling* in the Laws of Court," in *The Welsh King and His Court*, ed. T. M. Charles-Edwards, Morfydd E. Owen, and Paul Russell (Cardiff: University of Wales Press, 2000), 29–62, at 37.

99. *Cyfreithiau Hywel Dda yn ôl Llyfr Blegywryd*, ed. Stephen J. Williams and J. Enoch Powell, 2nd ed. (Cardiff: University of Wales Press, 1961), 3–4. Walter could have also had access to a Latin version. See *The Latin Texts of the Welsh Laws*, ed. Hywel David Emanuel (Cardiff: University of Wales Press, 1967), 110.

100. *DNC*, 2.23, p. 188: "paterni concessor cineris."

101. *DNC*, 2.23, p. 188.

102. *DNC*, 2.23, p. 190: "Vnum admirabile frustum inter alia hic repperi, nam illud pessundo semper et sub aliis pono subiciens, et statim apparet super omnia alia."

103. *DNC*, 2.23, p. 190: "fur argutissimus et uehementissimus in alienas irruptor opes."

104. *GCO*, 6:216: "praedicant, et confidentissime jactant, toto quod mirum est in hac spe populo manente, quoniam in brevi cives in insulam revertentur; et juxta Merlini sui vaticinia,

exterorum tam natione pereunte quam nuncupatione, antiquo in insula tam nomine quam omine Britones exultabunt." Cf. *GCO*, 4:48–49.

105. *DNC*, 4.2, p. 282.

106. *DNC*, 2.23, p. 190: "in pace, excepta quam ipse suis faciebat persecucione."

107. *DNC*, 2.23, p. 190: "Neminem occido, sed obtundo cornua Wallie, ne possint ledere matrem."

108. For an overview of Welsh political violence, see Davies, *Age of Conquest*, 56–81.

109. See Davies and Davies, *Last King of Wales*, 65–68; Charles-Edwards, *Wales and the Britons*, 565–66.

110. *DNC*, 2.23, p. 192: "Allegabat maioritatem Luelinus, parietatem Eduuardus; Luelinus quod sui totam Angliam cum Cornubia, Scocia et Wallia conquisissent a gigantibus, et se affirmabat in rectissimo descensu heredem, Eduuardus quod a conquisitoribus suis eam sui obtinuissent antecessores."

111. *HRB* §21.453–60, pp. 26–29: "Erat tunc nomen insulae Albion; quae a nemine, exceptis paucis gigantibus, inhabitabatur. Amoeno tamen situ locorum et copia piscosorum fluminum nemoribusque praeelecta, affectum habitandi Bruto sociisque inferebat. Peragratis ergo quibusque prouinciis, repertos gigantes ad cauernas montium fugant, patriam donante duce sorciuntur, agros incipiunt colere, domos aedificare, ita ut in breui tempore terram ab aeuo inhabitatam censeres. Denique Brutus de nomine suo insulam Britanniam appellat sociosque suos Britones."

112. *HRB*, §21.467–69, pp. 28–29: "Delectabat enim eum contra gigantes dimicare, quorum copia plus ibidem habundabat quam in ulla prouinciarum quae consociis suis distributae fuerant." For Cornwall's unique place in Geoffrey's work, see Oliver Padel, "Geoffrey of Monmouth and Cornwall," *Cambridge Medieval Celtic Studies* 8 (1984): 1–28.

113. For the biblical origin of the name *Goemagog* and the insular myth of aboriginal giants, see Jeffrey Jerome Cohen, *Of Giants: Sex, Monsters, and the Middle Ages* (Minneapolis: University of Minnesota Press, 1999), 35–36.

114. For a survey of Geoffrey's British geography, see John S. P. Tatlock, *The Legendary History of Britain: Geoffrey of Monmouth's "Historia Regum Britanniae" and Its Early Vernacular Versions* (Berkeley: University of California Press, 1950; repr., New York: Gordian, 1974), 7–84.

115. *HRB*, §23.1–14, pp. 30–31.

116. *HRB* §208.598–600, pp. 280–81: "Degenerati autem a Britannica nobilitate Gualenses numquam postea monarchiam insulae recuperauerunt; immo nunc sibi, interdum Saxonibus ingrati consurgentes externas ac domesticas clades incessanter agebant."

117. *DNC*, 2.23, p. 194: "more Walensium obseruatum est usque ad potestatem nocendi."

118. Joshua Byron Smith, "Gerald of Wales, Walter Map, and the Anglo-Saxon Past of Lydbury North," in *New Perspectives on Gerald of Wales: Texts and Contexts*, ed. Georgia Henley and Joseph McMullen (Cardiff: University of Wales Press, forthcoming).

119. See Chapter 6, this volume.

120. *DNC*, 3.1, p. 210: "a philosophice uel diuine pagine senatu." See Chapter 3, this volume.

121. *DNC*, 3.1, p. 210.

122. *DNC*, 3.1, p. 210: "innobiles et exangues inepcias." In reading *innobiles* (i.e., *ignobiles*) for MS *innolibiles*, I follow Rigg, review of *De nugis curialium: Courtiers' Trifles*, 179.

123. For an overview of the importance of the reader in Walter's work, see Robert R. Edwards, "Walter Map: Authorship and the Space of Writing," *New Literary History: A Journal of Theory and Interpretation* 38 (2007): 273–92, esp. 282–83; Siân Echard, "Map's Metafiction:

Author, Narrator and Reader in *De nugis curialium*," *Exemplaria: A Journal of Theory in Medieval and Renaissance Studies* 8 (1996): 287–314.

124. James Wade, *Fairies in Medieval Romance* (New York: Palgrave Macmillan, 2011), 91–93; Echard, "Map's Metafiction," esp. 306–13; Keith Bate, "La littérature latine d'imagination à la cour d'Henri II d'Angleterre," *Cahiers de civilisation médiévale* 34 (1991): 3–21, at 10–17; Kathryn Hume, "The Composition of a Medieval Romance: Walter Map's *Sadius and Galo*," *Neuphilologische Mitteilungen* 76 (1975): 415–23; R. E. Bennett, "Walter Map's *Sadius and Galo*," *Speculum* 16 (1941): 34–56.

125. *DNC*, 3.2, p. 214: "cum omnia possit a mulieribus euincere, uacuum se penitus fatetur ab opere, sed michi soli."

126. *DNC*, 3.2, p. 214: "quo possit in Galonis amplexus illabi, nudamque se nudo iungere, manum iubet inicere pudendis, et ut casta referat utrum possit an non."

127. *DNC*, 3.2, p. 222: "et placui fere, sensique uirum integrum et promptum, si te sensisset. Sed ut a<d>uertit quod minor, quod minus habilis, quod non idonea fui sicut tu, statim eiecta sum."

128. For *Gawain and Bran de Liz* and *Guerehés* (both episodes in the First Continuation to *Perceval*), see Bennett, "Walter Map's *Sadius and Galo*." For *Amis and Amiloun*, see primarily Hume, "Composition of a Medieval Romance." For *Eger and Grime*, see Wade, *Fairies in Medieval Romance*, 91–93. For *Tristan and Isolde* and the *Lai de Graelent*, see Bate, "La littérature latine," 18–20. For *Petronius Rediuiuus*, see *"Petronius Rediuiuus" et Helias Tripolanensis*, ed. Marvin L. Colker (Leiden: Brill, 2007), 5–6. For the possibility that Walter and Chrétien shared some of the same sources, see John Carey, *Ireland and the Grail* (Aberystwyth: Celtic Studies Publications, 2007), 347–49.

129. Tony Davenport, "Sex, Ghosts, and Dreams: Walter Map (1135?–1210?) and Gerald of Wales (1146–1223)," in *Writers of the Reign of Henry II: Twelve Essays*, ed. Ruth Kennedy and Simon Meecham-Jones (New York: Palgrave Macmillan, 2006), 133–50, at 147. See also *DNC*, xxi.

130. *DNC*, 3.2, p. 218: "Ego michi fraus, ego proditrix, ego michi laqueus facta sum."

131. Also noted by Jill Mann in *Feminizing Chaucer*, 2nd ed. (Woodbridge: D. S. Brewer, 2002), 165–66.

132. For this story as an example of the importance Walter places on controlling one's emotions, see Scott Waugh, "Histoire, hagiographie et le souverain idéal à la cour des Plantagenêt," in *Plantagenêts et Capétiens: Confrontations et héritages*, ed. Martin Aurell and Noël-Yves Tonnerre (Turnhout: Brepols, 2006), 429–46, at 431–33.

133. *DNC*, 3.3, p. 250.

134. *DNC*, 3.3, p. 246.

135. *DNC*, 3.3, p. 250: "Hec superbe solium babilonis ingressa latenter."

136. *DNC*, 3.3, p. 250.

137. *DNC*, 4.3, p. 306.

138. *DNC*, 3.4, p. 264: "Soluit igitur a freno iumentum, ut quocunque fames iusserit pabula querat, ultroneam extollens ad astra pudiciciam."

139. *DNC*, 3.4, p. 266.

140. *DNC*, 3.4, p. 266: "Non tamen admirabilis, non uxoris, non eorum que tulerunt, sed solius equi iacturam intemperate plangit, nec filii nec familie consolacione leuatur."

141. *DNC*, 3.4, p. 266.

142. *DNC*, 3.4, p. 268: "Illis iam prope agentibus, equs Rasonis non assuetus in congressu quiescere, leuato capite hinnit, et pedibus arenam terens dominum suum a morte premunit."

143. *DNC*, 3.4, p. 270: "Raso equi sui celeritate quocunque uult transfertur."

144. *DNC*, 3.4, p. 264: "Soluit igitur a freno iumentum, ut quocunque fames iusserit pabula querat."

145. See Davenport, "Sex, Ghosts, and Dreams," 145–46.

146. This small section, in which a young Welshman gains martial prowess, generally parallels Chretién's *Perceval*, in which a young, dullard Welshman slowly becomes a knight. The two stories also defer revealing the young Welshman's name until he has gained significant knightly skills. The name *Resus*, it should be noted, is the common Latin form of the Welsh name *Rhys*.

147. *DNC*, 3.5, p. 274: "Rollo causa fuit."

148. *DNC*, 3.5, p. 274: "Nunquam a Reso Rolloni pro benignitate retribuetur inuria; inurbanum enim est ut ei thorum uiolem, quem michi totus negauit orbis et ipse prestitit."

149. C. Stephen Jaeger, *Ennobling Love: In Search of a Lost Sensibility* (Philadelphia: University of Pennsylvania Press, 1999).

150. *DNC*, 3.5, p. 272: "Vincit ferratas acies, muros et turres, et qui transuehit ipsum animus ad omnes uictorias a seipso effeminatur, sed infeminatur, quoniam in femineam transit impotenciam, ut earum instar sine respectu post uota currat, ouis intus et leo foris, et qui castra subuertit exterorum, a domesticis curis castratus emollescit, plangit, precatur et plorat. Illa non ut uirgo uel uirago, sed ut uir deuouet et spernit, et quibuscunque potest modis in desperacionem trudit." As the editors note, the Latin of the first half of this passage is somewhat problematic, especially the phrase *sed infeminatur*.

151. Davenport, "Sex, Ghosts, and Dreams," 146.

152. See esp. *DNC*, xxi–xxiii, where it is claimed that "no surviving romance can be attributed to [Walter]; he may well have written none." The editors here clearly mean French-language romances; there is a marked hesitation to grant Walter's Latin works the designation of romance in their introduction.

153. Bate, "La littérature latine," 21.

154. See, for example, Siân Echard, *Arthurian Narrative in the Latin Tradition* (Cambridge: Cambridge University Press, 1998); and *Latin Arthurian Literature*, ed. and trans. Mildred Leake Day (Cambridge: D. S. Brewer, 2005). See also the discussion of Latinity in Chapter 6, this volume.

155. For a reassessment of Henry's patronage of Arthurian literature, see Martin Aurell, "Henry II and Arthurian Legend," in *Henry II: New Interpretations*, ed. Christopher Harper-Bill and Nicholas Vincent (Woodbridge: Boydell Press, 2007), 362–94. For an overview of the literary culture at Henry II's court, see Ian Short, "Literary Culture at the Court of Henry II," in Harper-Bill and Vincent, *Henry II*, 335–61; and John Gillingham, "The Cultivation of History, Legend and Courtesy at the Court of Henry II," in Kennedy and Meecham-Jones, *Writers of the Reign of Henry II*, 25–52.

156. *La Queste del Saint Graal: Roman du XIIIe siècle*, ed. Albert Pauphilet (Paris: Champion, 1923), 279–80; *La Mort le Roi Artu: Roman du XIIIe siècle*, ed. Jean Frappier (Paris: Droz, 1936), 3.

CHAPTER 2

1. *DNC*, 2.13, p. 160: "Britonum, de quo superius."

2. *DNC*, 5.7, p. 498: "Recapitulacio principii huius libri ob diuersitatem litere et non sentencie."

3. James Hinton, "Walter Map's *De nugis curialium*: Its Plan and Composition," *PMLA* 32 (1917): 81–132, at 125; Davenport, "Sex, Ghosts, and Dreams," 136; Walter Map, *Svaghi di corte*, trans. Fortunata Latella (Parma: Pratiche Editrice, 1990), 1:19: "farraginoso ed asistematico nella sua struttura."

4. *DNC*, 4.2, p. 282: "Hunc in curia regis Henrici libellum raptim annotaui scedulis." However, see below for a better translation of this passage.

5. Hinton, "Walter Map's *De nugis curialium*," 81–82. The first edition of Walter's work carries the same warning: "His Latin is very unequal; but we are perhaps not entirely competent to pronounce judgment in this respect, as the text in the unique manuscript of his prose Latin work which has come down to us is extremely corrupt" (*Gualteri Mapes "De nugis curialium": Dinstinctiones quinque*, ed. Thomas Wright [London: J. B. Nichols and Son, 1850], viii).

6. One notable exception is the more measured approach taken by Siân Echard in "Map's Metafiction," esp. 289–92.

7. Robert Levine, "How to Read Walter Map," *Mittellateinisches Jahrbuch* 23 (1988): 91–105, at 92. Positive evaluations of Walter's artistic skill can be found in Latella's translation of Walter Map, *Svaghi di corte*, esp. 1:20–21; *Gautier Map: Contes de courtisans*, trans. Marylene Perez (third cycle doctorate's thesis, Lille, 1982), esp. viii–ix; Ronald E. Pepin, *Literature of Satire in the Twelfth Century: A Neglected Mediaeval Genre* (Lewiston, NY: Edwin Mellen Press, 1988), esp. 1–24 passim.

8. *Master Walter Map's Book: "De nugis curialium" (Courtiers' Trifles)*, trans. Frederick Tupper and Marbury Bladen Ogle (London: Chatto and Windus, 1924), xxiii.

9. Montague Rhodes James, ed., *Walter Map: De Nugis Curialium* (Oxford: Clarendon Press, 1914), xxiv.

10. *Walter Map's "De Nugis Curialium,"* trans. Montague Rhodes James, with historical notes by John Edward Lloyd, ed. E. Sidney Hartland (London: Honourable Society of Cymmrodorion, 1923), ix. James, however, did not have the benefit of our current lexicographical resources, and many of Walter's "mistakes" are actually fairly widespread Medieval Latinisms. For example, two of the exemplary words James cites here are *simultas* and *infrunitus*, but Walter's use of the two conforms to contemporary practice. See *DMLBS*, s.vv. "3 simultas"; "infrunitus."

11. Sebastian Coxon, "Wit, Laughter, and Authority in Walter Map's *De nugis curialium* (Courtiers' Trifles)," in *Author, Reader, Book: Medieval Authorship in Theory and Practice*, ed. Stephen Partridge and Erik Kwakkel (Toronto: University of Toronto Press, 2012), 38–55, at 39.

12. Türk, *Nugae curialium*, 177: "Ses histoires, où le pays de Galles joue un grand role et où l'influence de la littérature française se fait jour, nous révèlent un Map critique et crédule, divisé entre la raison et l'irrationnel."

13. Short, "Literary Culture at the Court of Henry II," 341.

14. David Knowles, *The Monastic Order in England, 940–1216*, 2nd ed. (Cambridge: Cambridge University Press, 1963), 676.

15. *DNC*, xlv.

16. Hinton, "Walter Map's *De nugis curialium*."

17. Hinton, "Walter Map's *De nugis curialium*," 116.

18. *DNC*, 4.2, p. 282.

19. *DMLBS*, s.v. "raptim"; *OLD*, s.v. "raptim."

20. Also critical of Hinton's breaking up and recording of fragments is Ferdinand Seibt, "Über den Plan der Schrift 'De nugis curialium' des Magisters Walter Map," *Archiv für Kulturgeschichte* 37 (1955): 183–203, at 185–86.

21. *DNC*, xxvi.

22. *DNC*, xxix–xxx.

23. *DNC*, xxvii.

24. *DNC*, xxix. The quote continues, "perhaps it is more likely to have been placed there by a careless scribe."

25. Rigg, review of *De nugis curialium*, 182. Seibt, who critiqued Hinton's obsession with chronology, nonetheless himself places far too much emphasis on trying to divine the original date of composition of certain episodes. For example, his dating of one section to after Christmas in 1182 but before the death of the Young King Henry in June of 1183 relies on positing the presence of later interpolations. Yet, he never asks *who* made those "interpolations." Rather, in my view the inconsistencies in question are not interpolations but evidence that Walter was revising his text. See Seibt, "Über den Plan der Schrift," 192–93.

26. However, earlier critics generally realized that the version of the satire on court found in *DNC* 5.7 was an earlier draft of the version found at the work's beginning; see James, *Walter Map*, xxvii; Hinton, "Walter Map's *De nugis curialium*," 88; Seibt "Über den Plan der Schrift," 187; *DNC*, xxv, xxix, and 5.7, p. 498 n. 3.

27. Rigg, review of *De nugis curialium*, 182.

28. Rigg, review of *De nugis curialium*, 182.

29. Rigg's remarks in full are:

The revised tales (1.1–9 revised from 5.7, 1.11 from 4.13, 1.14 from 4.7, 2.12 from 4.10, 2.13 from 4.8) show that Map was gradually reworking earlier material. I believe that 1–3 are in nearly final state: each episode or topic is linked to the next (only 2.18 is really intrusive). For example, the list of disasters in 1.15 demonstrates the inefficacy of the prayers of monks and nuns (48/20ff.) and so leads to the antimonastic section. 1–3 lacks only the elimination of conflicting dates (*nunc, hodie*, etc.) to be in final shape. 4, however, was still being used, with the old versions of tales still in place and the fate of the remainder not yet decided; 4.2a looks very much like an epilogue intended for the whole *De nugis*. 5.1–6 (the pseudohistory) was probably nearly complete. 5.7 was simply put at the bottom of the pile as a now outdated draft. We can suppose that Map then took the whole pile of material with him to Oxford in 1197, where it lay until a fourteenth-century editor copied it all out.

Rigg, review of *De nugis curialium*, 182.

30. *DNC*, 5.7, p. 502; 1.4, p. 8.

31. *DNC*, 5.7, p. 510; 1.10, p.14.

32. *DNC*, 4.10, p. 350; 2.12, p. 158.

33. *DNC*, 5.7, p. 506; 1.9, p. 10. The revised version of this passage is somewhat problematic as it falls immediately after the loss of (apparently) one folio. From what survives, it seems that Walter has drastically reimagined the function of the judges in his work. Whatever the case may be, these alliterative adjectives do not appear in the earlier version where the passage is complete; thus, they are a product of revision.

34. *DNC*, 5.7, p. 502; 1.4, p. 8.

35. *DNC*, 4.7, p. 343; 1.14, p. 40.

36. *DNC*, 5.7, p. 502; 1.4, p. 8.

37. *DNC*, 4.7, p. 342; 1.14, p. 40.

38. *DNC*, 4.7, p. 500; 1.1, p.2.

39. *DMLBS*, s.v. "definire," def. 2 and 3. In the High Middle Ages, *diffinire* is commonly

found for *definire*; see *LSM* 7:222.1, §14.5. For Walter's mock scholasticism, see A. G. Rigg, "Walter Map, the Shaggy Dog Story, and the *Quaesitio Disputata*," in *Roma, Magistra Mundi: Itineraria Culturae Medievalis;* Mélanges offerts au Père L.E. Boyle à l'occasion de son 75e anniversaire, ed. Jacqueline Hamesse (Louvain-la-Neuve: Fédération des Instituts d'Études Médiévales, 1998), 723–35; Monika Otter, *Inventiones: Fiction and Referentiality in Twelfth-Century English Historical Writing* (Chapel Hill: University of North Carolina Press, 1996), 114–15.

40. *DNC*, 1.2, p. 8.

41. *DNC*, 1.9, p. 10.

42. *DNC,* 5.7, p. 510; 1.10, p. 14.

43. *DNC*, 5.7, p. 502: "Yxion ibi uoluitur in rota, sibi sepe dissimilis, super subter, hinc et illinc"; 1.5, p. 8: "Sibi sepe dissimilis, super, subter, ultra, citra." Notice, too, that in this passage Walter has changed the syntax in order to bring the alliteration to a more prominent position.

44. *DNC*, 5.5, p. 504; 1.5, p. 10.

45. *DNC*, 5.7, pp. 498–500; 1.1, p. 2.

46. 2 Cor. 12:2.

47. *DNC*, 1.1, p. 2: "Centimanus gigas est, qui totus mutilatus totus est idem et centimanus, ydra multorum capitum." Unlike James and other translators, I have translated *mutilatus* not as "maimed" but rather as "having had a body part cut off," which gives much better sense here. See *DMLBS*, s.v. "mutilare," def. 3. Cf. Johannes de Hauvilla, *Architrenius*, ed. and trans. Winthrop Wetherbee (Cambridge: Cambridge University Press, 1994), 1.10.312–13, pp. 20–21; 8.2.20–21, pp. 198–99.

48. *DNC,* 1.1, p. 2.

49. *DNC,* 1.1, p. 2.

50. For an overview of this popular comparison, see Laurence Harf-Lancner, "L'Enfer de la cour: La cour d'Henri II Plantagenet et la Mesnie Hellequin (dans l'œuvre de J. de Salisbury, de Gautier Map, de Pierre de Blois et de Giraud de Barri," in *L'État et les aristocraties: France, Angleterre, Ecosse, XIIᵉ–XVIIᵉ siècle; Actes de la table ronde*, ed. Philippe Contamine (Paris: Presses de l'École normale supérieure, 1989), 27–50.

51. *DNC,* 5.7, p. 500.

52. *DNC*, 1.2, p. 8.

53. *DNC*, 1.5, p. 8.

54. *DNC*, 5.7, p. 502.

55. *DNC,* 5.7, p. 504; 1.5, p. 10.

56. For Herla, see Chapter 4. For Eadric the Wild, see Smith, "Gerald of Wales, Walter Map."

57. *DNC*, 1.1, p. 4.

58. Brian Stock, "Antiqui and Moderni as 'Giants' and 'Dwarfs': A Reflection of Popular Culture?," *Modern Philology* 76 (1979): 370–74.

59. *DNC,* 1.1, p. 6.

60. C. Stephen Jaeger, "Pessimism in the Twelfth-Century 'Renaissance,'" *Speculum* 78 (2003): 1151–83, at 1180.

61. M. T. Clanchy, "*Moderni* in Education and Government in England," *Speculum* 50 (1975): 671–88.

62. *DNC*, 1.1, p. 30. See Chapter 4, this volume.

63. *DNC*, 1.1, pp. 6–8.

64. Hinton, "Walter Map's De nugis curialium," 130; Otter, *Inventiones*, 113. Hinton does, it should be said, find this aspect of Walter "charming."

65. Horace, *Ars Poetica*, lines 1–5.

66. Quoted in *Medieval Grammar and Rhetoric: Language Arts and Literary Theory, AD 300–1475*, ed. Rita Copeland and Ineke Sluiter (Oxford: Oxford University Press, 2009), 598.

67. *CPGC,* 54–57.

68. *CPGC,* 55–56.

69. *DNC,* 1.1, p. 2.

70. *DNC,* 5.7, p. 510: "Rex autem huius, si bene nouit eam, non est a calumpnia liber, quia qui rector est tenetur esse corrector."

71. *DNC,* 5.7, p. 510: "Hic autem rex in curia sua marito similis est qui nouit ultimus errorem uxoris."

72. *DNC,* 1.10, p. 16: "Nec possumus in dominum et rectorem nostrum culpam refundere, cum nichil in mundo quietum sit, nec ulla possit quispiam diu tranquillitate letari."

73. *DNC,* 1.10, p. 24: "Hec omnia pro rege nostro."

74. *DNC,* 1.10, p. 24: "Hec omnia pro rege nostro: quomodo compescet milia milium et ad pacem gubernabit, cum nos modici patres moderari paucos nequeamus?"

75. For the argument that these two versions display two different kinds of discursive strategies—*Sprache der Nähe* and *Sprache der Distanz* (roughly corresponding to private and public)—see Andreas Bihrer, "Selbstvergewisserung am Hof: Eine Interpretation von Walter Maps *De nugis curialium* I, 1–12," *Jahrbuch für Internationale Germanistik* 34, no. 1 (2002): 227–58.

76. *DNC,* 4.7, pp. 340–44.

77. *DNC,* 4.8, p. 344: "de mortibus quarum iudicia dubia sunt."

78. *DNC,* 4.8, p. 344.

79. *DNC,* 4.7, p. 340: "Lector et auditor disputent si miles rectum habuit zelum."

80. *DNC,* 4.7, p. 344: "Decessit autem monachus in fide Christi, et bona spe feruentique penitencie zelo."

81. *DNC,* 4.7, p. 340: "Queri eciam potest de salute monachi Cluniacensis."

82. *DNC,* 1.11, p. 30: "Libetne nuper actis aurem dare parumper?"

83. *DNC,* 1.14, p. 38: "At aliter alii; longeque miserabilius contigit uiro nobili et strenuo, qui similiter eiusdem loci monachus simili modo casu eodem necessario reuocatus ad arma."

84. *DNC,* 1.14, p. 38: "multa bellorum infortunia magnifice fortique perpessus animo, a fractura semper nouus renascebatur ad prelium et, quasi rediuiuo furore succensus."

85. *DNC,* 1.10, p. 16: "cum nichil in mundo quietum sit, nec ulla possit quispiam diu tranquillitate letari."

86. *DNC,* 1.11, p. 30: "Quieuit autem ab illa hora fantasticus ille circuitus, tanquam nobis suos tradiderint errores, ad quietem sibi."

87. *DNC,* 1.15, pp. 44–46: "et in summa ibi pace<m> stabilissimo sancxerunt obtentu, sic autem ut iam fiat uoluntas eorum sicut in inferno sic et in terra."

88. *DNC,* 1.10, p. 24: "Quiete mentis est et ad unum simul collecte poetari. Totam uolunt et tutam cum assiduitate residenciam poete, et non prodest optimus corporis et rerum status, si non fuerit interna pace tranquillus animus; unde non minus a me poscis miraculum, hinc scilicet hominem ydiotam et imperitum scribere, quam si ab alterius Nabugodonosor fornace nouos pueros cantare iubeas." Walter uses *poeta* and *poetari* in the loose senses of "writer" and "to write literature"; see James, *Walter Map,* xxiv; Hinton, "Walter Map's *De nugis curialium,*" 127–29.

89. *DNC,* 1.12, p. 34: "Et tu, cum nostra procellosa <sit> pre ceteris mater affliccionum et irarum nutrix, inter has precipis poetari discordias?"

90. *DNC,* 1.12, p. 36: "Hii temporis huius philosopi, quibus nichil deest, qui omni plenitudine refertam habent residenciam et pacem fori<s>, recte ceperunt, finemque bonum consequentur. Sed quo michi portus, qui uix uaco uiuere?"

91. *DNC*, 1.15, p. 48; Luke 10:38–42.

92. *DNC*, 1.10, p. 24: "religatum et . . . relegatum."

93. Cotts, *The Clerical Dilemma*, 15.

94. *DNC*, 1.13, p. 38: "distractumque prius, tempore scilicet milicie secularis, animum, co-piam adeptus et iam quietem, adegit in unum collectis uiribus; se subito poetam persensit, suo-que modo—lingua scilicet Gallica—preciosus effulgens, laicorum Homerus fuit. He michi utinam inducie, ne per multos diffuse mentis radios error soloecismum faciat."

95. *DNC*, 1.14, p. 40: "In memoriam hic reuocentur uerba misericordie que ait 'In quacun-que hora ingemuerit peccator, saluus erit.' " It is difficult to say if Walter knew this phrase from a liturgical source, a biblical source, or both. See Marbury B. Ogle, "Bible Text or Liturgy," *Harvard Theological Review* 33 (1940): 194–224, at 218–21.

96. *DNC*, 1.15, p. 40: "annos scilicet remissionis et gracie, securitatis et pacis, exultacionis et uenie, laudis et leticie."

97. *Opera S. Bernardi,* ed. J. Leclercq and H. M. Rochais (Rome: Editiones Cistercienses, 1977), 8:435.

98. Smith, "Gerald of Wales, Walter Map."

99. *DNC*, 2.13, p. 160; 4.8, p. 344.

100. For Gastin Gastiniog, see Chapter 5, this volume.

101. Laurence Harf-Lancner, "Des fées et des morts: La légende des fils de la morte dans le *De nugis curialium* de Gautier Map," in *"Furent les merveilles pruvees et les aventures truvees": Hommage à Francis Dubost*, ed. Francis Gingras et al. (Paris: Champion, 2005), 321–31.

102. *DNC*, 2.13, p. 160: "qui manent et bona se successione perpetuant, ut hic Alnodi et ille Britonum de quo superius, in quo dicitur miles quidam uxorem suam sepellisse reuera mor-tuam, et a chorea redibuisse raptam, et postmodum ex ea filios et nepotes suscepisse, et perdu-rare sobolem in diem istum, et eos qui traxerunt inde originem in multitudinem factos, qui omnes ideo 'filii mortue' dicuntur."

103. *DNC*, 4.8, p. 344.

104. *DNC*, 2.13, p. 160: "ut hic Aldnodi et ille Britonum de quo superius, in quo dicitur miles quidam uxorem suam sepellisse reuera mortuam."

105. *DNC*, 1.12, pp. 34–36.

106. A. Boutémy, "Giraud de Barri et Pierre le Chantre: Une source de la *Gemma ecclesias-tica*," *Revue du moyen âge latin* 2 (1946): 45–62; E. M. Sanford, "Giraldus Cambrensis' Debt to Petrus Cantor," *Medievalia et humanistica* 3 (1945): 16–32.

107. *DNC*, 5.3, p. 416. See Oleg Bychkov, "The Use of the *De officiis* I in Walter Map's *De nugis curialium*," *Notes and Queries* 240 (1995): 157–59.

108. Bennett, "Walter Map's *Sadius and Galo*."

109. *CPGC*, 36: "Si on compare la version de Map avec celle, anonyme, des *Analecta Dub-linensia*, on constate qu'en général Map a raconté une histoire plus cohérente et plus satisfaisante."

110. Ralph Hanna III and Traugott Lawler, eds., *Jankyn's Book of Wikked Wyves*, 2 vols. (Athens: University of Georgia Press, 1997–2014), 1:100–110.

111. For the beta family, see Ralph Hanna, "Another Manuscript of Walter Map's '*Dissuasio Valerii*,' " *Journal of Medieval Latin* 24 (2014): 277–83. In a forthcoming article, Ralph Hanna also suggests that the alpha and beta families represent two different promulgations of the text and that the beta version witnesses a revised text, one in which Walter drops his act of pretend-ing to be a classical author. See Ralph Hanna, "Walter Map's *Dissuasio Valerii*: Newly Identified Copies and Their Clarification of the Text's Transmission," *Mittellateinisches Jahrbuch* 52

(forthcoming 2017). I would like to thank Prof. Hanna for sharing his work with me before publication and for his other insightful comments about the *Dissuasio*.

112. Hanna and Lawler, *Jankyn's Book of Wikked Wyves*, 1:107 n. 183.

113. *DNC*, xlviii. The identification of Walter is in a later hand. See Hanna and Lawler, *Jankyn's Book of Wikked Wyves*, 1:60 n. 118 and the textual note at 1:123. I have checked several, though by no means all, of the continental (alpha) manuscripts, and none betrays knowledge of Walter's authorship.

114. Hanna, "Walter Map's *Dissuasio Valerii*."

115. Amelia Borrego Sargent, "Gerald of Wales's *Topographia Hibernica*: Dates, Versions, Readers," *Viator* 43 (2012): 241–61.

116. Cotts, *The Clerical Dilemma*, 269–88.

117. *Nigel de Longchamp's Speculum Stultorum*, ed. John H. Mozley and Robert R. Raymo (Berkeley: University of California Press, 1960), 16–27.

CHAPTER 3

1. Seibt cites Hinton's argument approvingly; see Seibt, "Über den Plan der Schrift," 185.

2. *DNC*, xxvii.

3. Hinton, "Walter Map's *De nugis curialium*," 82.

4. Hinton, "Walter Map's *De nugis curialium*," 82 n. 11

5. For the importance of this manuscript, see Chapter 2, this volume.

6. *GCO* 1:362: "Versibus ornatum bis senis accipe munus, / Et de tot gemmis elige, Mape, duos."

7. *The Vulgate Version of the Arthurian Romances*, ed. H. Oskar Sommer, 8 vols. (Washington, DC: Carnegie Institution of Washington, 1908–16), vol. 8, *Index of Names and Places to Volumes I–VII*, 60.

8. Lehmann, *Mittellateinische Verse*, 12–15; Rigg, "Golias and Other Pseudonyms," 85.

9. Only two such spellings appear in Rigg's survey in "Golias and Other Pseudonyms," 89–99.

10. The spelling *Mahap*, I would venture, is the result of a two-step process: First, a scribe indicated the long vowel in *Map* by doubling the *a*—not an uncommon scribal practice. (Again, we know the vowel is long thanks to Gerald's verse.) Then, erroneously believing the strange name *Maap* to be disyllabic, another scribe inserted an *h* to mark vowel hiatus. For *h* indicating hiatus, see *LSM*, 7:162, §121.1; Ian Short, *A Manual of Anglo-Norman*, 2nd ed. (Oxford: Anglo-Norman Text Society, 2013), §19.3, p. 100. Other Welsh names have suffered the same fate: See *Kehingayr* and *Mahelgun* for *Keingayr* and *Maelgun* in *Vitae Sanctorum Britanniae et Genealogiae*, ed. and trans. A. W. Wade-Evans (Cardiff: University of Wales Press, 1944); new ed., ed. Scott Lloyd (Cardiff: Welsh Academic Press, 2013), 314, 315. See also *Mahello* for *Mael* in *Cartularium Prioratus S. Johannis Evangelistae de Brecon*, ed. R. W. Banks (London: Whiting, 1884), 44. The spelling *luhyn* for *llwyn*, "grove," appears in Wendy Davies "Braint Teilo," *Bulletin of the Board of Celtic Studies* 26 (1974–76): 123–37, at 134; reprinted with the same pagination in her *Welsh History in the Early Middle Ages* (Farnham: Ashgate, 2009), chap. 3. Finally, *Traherius* for *Traer* occurs in *DNC*, 2.25, p. 198.

11. The following poems in Bodley 851 have, at one time or another, been attributed to Walter: *Convocacio sacerdotum* (fols. 75a–76rb); *De coniuge non ducenda* (fols. 80va–81va); *Debate Between Heart and Eye* (81va); and the *Apocolypsis Goliae* (fols. 118va–120vb). For a short

bibliography of these poems, see A. G. Rigg, "Medieval Latin Poetic Anthologies (II)," *Mediaeval Studies* 40 (1978): 387–407, at 397–401.

12. MS Bodley 851, fol. 118va.

13. Rigg, "Medieval Latin Poetic Anthologies (II)," 389–90. Hand X wrote the rubricated headings in parts 1 and 2 of Bodley 851.

14. *DNC*, 5.4, p. 420.

15. *DNC*, 1.13, p. 36; 2.3, p. 134; 5.5, pp. 436–56. Once, however, the body has "Ludouuicus" (442). Although Brooke and Mynors have printed "Ludowicus" here, the manuscript in fact reads "Ludouuicus." See Christopher McDonough, review of *De nugis curialium: Courtiers' Trifles*, by Walter Map, ed. and trans. M. R. James, rev. C. N. L. Brooke and R. A. B. Mynors, *Mittellateinisches Jahrbuch* 20 (1985): 294–302, at 297.

16. Rigg, "Medieval Latin Poetic Anthologies (II)," 389–90.

17. One inconsistency suggests scribe A may be behind the differing orthography. Scribe A has written "Chnutus" in the body of the text, but "Cnutone" in the table of contents. Perhaps scribe A preferred to have the letter *h* follow stops in vernacular names and adapted names as he went along but failed to insert one at the very end. Scribe X, meanwhile, simply followed his exemplar, ignoring scribe A's innovations. At any rate, it is probably not of much consequence for the present discussion.

18. On fol. 7v, the manuscript reads: "Det Dominus cor curialibus carneum, ut in aliquo moncium pausare possit. Sibi sepe dissimilis, super, subter, ultra, citra, De yxione .v, Yxion ibi uoliuitur . . ." Compare this with the earlier draft, ". . . ut in aliquo moncium pausare possint. Yxion ibi uoluitur in rota, sibi sepe dissimilis, super subter, hinc et illinc" (*DNC*, 5.7, p. 502). The phrase beginning *sibi sepe* clearly describes Yxion.

19. *DNC*, 5.5, p. 436

20. *DNC*, 5.7, p. 498.

21. See Chapter 2, this volume.

22. Hinton, "Walter Map's *De nugis curialium*," 87.

23. *DNC*, 4.4, p. 310 n. *c*; "Walter Map's 'Dissuasio Valerii,'" in *Jankyn's Book of Wikked Wyves*, vol. 1, *The Primary Texts*, ed. Ralph Hanna III and Traugott Lawler (Athens: University of Georgia Press, 1997), 121–48, at 144–47.

24. *DNC*, 2.6, p. 140.

25. *DNC*, xxvii.

26. *DNC*, xxvii.

27. Rigg, "Medieval Latin Poetic Anthologies (II)," 390–91.

28. For example, on folios 8ra, 13va, 15rb, and 16ra.

29. Cf. the discussion of the skipped fitt number in *Beowulf* in *Klaeber's Beowulf and the Fight at Finnsburg*, 4th ed., ed. R. D. Fulk, Robert E. Bjork, and John D. Niles (Toronto: University of Toronto Press, 2008), xxxiv–xxxv.

30. I have provided a list of these *id est* interpolations in the Appendix.

31. *DNC*, 2.25, p. 200; *GPC*, s.v. "brycan."

32. *GCO*, 6:184: "Pannus durus et asper, quem patria parit, qui et vulgari vocabaulo Brachan dicitur."

33. On this word, see Chapter 5, this volume.

34. *DNC*, 2.11, p. 150. Henry Bradley, "Notes on Walter Map's *De Nugis Curialium*," *English Historical Review* 32 (1917): 393–400, at 395, suggests that Walter may here be referring to Rhodri Mawr's rule over Deheubarth, and thus implying that Deheubarth is to be considered part of Rhodri's northern kingdom. See also Chapter 5.

35. *DNC*, 2.11, p. 152.

36. *DNC*, 1.26, p. 114; 2.17, p. 166.

37. *DNC*, 5.3, p. 414.

38. *DNC*, 2.23, p. 194: "Quesiuit a me, qui marchio sum Walensibus, que fides, id est fidelitas, eorum . . ." See *DMLBS*, s.v. "fides," def. 4a. See also *DNC*, 2.23, p. 194 ("fidem Walensium") and 3.2, p. 218 ("sed et fides eum tenebat").

39. *DNC*, 2.18, p. 176. See *DMLBS*, s.v. "Parthus," def. b.

40. *DNC*, 5.7, p. 504.

41. *DNC*, 5.7, p. 504.

42. *DNC*, 2.23, p. 188: "Vidi hodie mane nubeculam a mari ascendere, et facta est in nubem maximam, ita ut totum operiretur mare."

43. *DNC*, 2.23, pp. 188–90.

44. *DNC*, 1.10, p. 24: "nemo preualeat ad plenum temperare familiam cuius ignorat cogitaciones aut linguam, id est, quicquid eorum corda loquuntur."

45. *DNC*, 1.10, p. 24. Cf. Gen. 1.6 ("dividat aquas ab aquis"); Gen. 11.8 ("atque ita divisit eos Dominus ex illo loco in universas terras"); and Deut. 32.8 ("quando dividebat Altissimus gentes").

46. *DNC* 1.25, p. 112: "Ego autem de hiis, id est de Hebreis, quod scio et quod ecclesia flet . . . loquor."

47. *DNC*, 5.6, p. 482.

48. *DNC*, 1.25, p. 84.

49. *DNC*, 1.25, p. 84; *Walter Map's "De Nugis Curialium,"* trans. James, 45 n. 2.

50. *DNC*, 1.24, p. 78; 2.23, p. 194; 5.5, p. 448.

51. *DNC*, 5.4, p. 414 n. 1.

52. For writers glossing their own work, see Mark Kauntze, *Authority and Imitation: A Study of the "Cosmographia" of Bernard Silvestris* (Leiden: Brill, 2014), 137–39.

53. For the glosses in Bodley 851, see Rigg, "Medieval Latin Poetic Anthologies (II)," 395; William Langland, *Piers Plowman: The Z Version*, ed. A. G. Rigg and Charlotte Brewer, Texts and Studies 59 (Toronto: Pontifical Institute, 1983), 1–5; Hanna and Lawler, *Jankyn's Book of Wikked Wyves*, 1:102 n. 172.

54. Hanna and Lawler, *Jankyn's Book of Wikked Wyves*, 1:101–2.

55. Rigg, review of *De nugis curialium*, 182.

56. In general, M. R. James did not approach medieval manuscripts with the same passion for codicology that a modern bibliographer might. As Paul Needham has pointed out, he "was not deeply interested in questions of book structure and his own collations in later catalogues show many signs of haste, carelessness, and inconsistency." When it came to codicological descriptions, his "heart was not in it." Had James been more attuned to codicological matters, he might well have been willing to explore alternative explanations for the textual state of the *De nugis curialium*. See Paul Needham, *The Bradshaw Method: Henry Bradshaw's Contribution to Bibliography*, Seventh Hanes Lecture Presented by the Hanes Foundation for the Study of the Origin and Development of the Book (Chapel Hill: Hanes Foundation, Rare Book Collection, University Library, University of North Carolina at Chapel Hill, 1988), 29–30.

57. The best evidence for a connection between the two texts is summarized in A. G. Rigg, *A History of Anglo-Latin Literature, 1066–1422* (Cambridge: Cambridge University Press, 1992), 347–48 n. 91.

58. Rigg, *History of Anglo-Latin Literature*, 92.

59. Thorpe, "Walter Map and Gerald of Wales."

60. Seibt, "Über den Plan der Schrift," 188–91, argues that Geoffrey is the addressee of most of the work in the *De nugis curialium*, but, during the ten years of its composition, Geoffrey became less important, and he eventually changed the dedication to Henry II. Overall, I see litte to support Seibt's assumption.

61. André Boutemy, however, argues that the addressee of *distinctio* 3 is indeed the same Geoffrey, citing what sees as similarities between the two: both desire appealing stories containing a moral (*Gautier Map, conteur anglais: Extraits du "De Nugis Curialium"* [Brussels: Office de Publicité, 1945], 19). But this topos is so common as to render the conflation unconvincing. See also Chapter 1, this volume.

62. *DNC*, 2.13, p. 160; see Chapter 2, this volume.

63. Bate has also suggested that the *De nugis curialium* contains works that were originally separate. He identifies three pamphlets: the *Dissuasio Valerii*; *distinctio* 3, which he claims was written for "a young knight" (*un jeune chevalier*); the anti-monastic pamphlet that is now chapter 25 of *distinctio* 1. He makes no suggestions as to the rest of the *De nugis curialium*. See *CPGC*, 20–21. Similarly, Boutemy has argued that the *De nugis curialium* as it is represents the fragments of two originally distinct books, one addressed to Geoffrey and the other to Henry II. See Boutemy, *Gautier Map*, 20.

64. *DNC*, 1.25, p. 110: "Olfecerunt iam hunc Hebrei [i.e., the Cistercians] libellum." See also Hinton "Walter Map's *De nugis curialium*," 100–101; Seibt, "Über den Plan der Schrift," 190 n. 29.

65. James, *Walter Map*, xxviii; Hinton, "Walter Map's *De nugis curialium*," 101–2; *DNC*, xxvii.

66. *DNC*, xxviii.

67. *DNC*, 4.2, p. 282: "Si decessero, quiescam; si non, impugnabo."

68. Hinton, "Walter Map's *De nugis curialium*," 92.

69. Hinton, "Walter Map's *De nugis curialium*," 108–9.

70. Hinton, "Walter Map's *De nugis curialium*," 85–86.

71. *DNC*, 4.2, p. 286.

72. E.g., *DNC*, 1.11, p. 30: "Libetne nuper actis aurem dare parumper" (Would you like to turn your ear to recent events for a moment?); 4.8, p. 344: "Quia de mortibus quarum iudicia dubia sunt incidit oracio" (Since our discussion falls on deaths in which God's judgment is uncertain).

73. *DNC*, 5.1, p. 404: "Iacent tamen egregia modernorum nobilium, et attolluntur fimbrie uetustatis abiecte." This difference in the treatment of *antiqui* and *moderni* also leads Boutemy to view *distinctio* 5 as separate from the rest of the *De nugis curialium*; see Boutemy, *Gautier Map*, 20.

74. Hinton, "Walter Map's *De nugis curialium*," 112; Boutemy, *Gautier Map*, 20.

75. *DNC*, 5.7, p. 498: "Recapitulacio principii huius libri ob diuersitatem litere et non sentencie."

76. Rigg, review of *De nugis curialium*, 182.

77. For authorial copies being kept and stored away, see Bourgain, "Circulation of Texts," 151.

78. For Hales and Aquinas, see Alain Boureau, "Peut-on parler d'auteurs scolastiques?," in *Auctor et auctoritas: Invention et conformisme dans l'écriture médiévale*, ed. Michel Zimmerman (Paris: École des Chartes, 2001), 267–79, at 273 and 271. For Gerson, see André Combes, *La théologie mystique de Gerson: Profil de son évolution*, 2 vols. (Rome: Desclée, 1963–64), 2:650–56. See also Daniel Hobbins, *Authorship and Publicity Before Print: Jean Gerson and the*

Transformation of Late Medieval Learning (Philadelphia: University of Pennsylvania Press, 2010), 2, 62, and 276 n. 63. I would like to thank Daniel Hobbins for bringing these references to my attention.

79. J. L. Butrica, "Editing Propertius," *Classical Quarterly* 47, no. 1 (1997): 176–208. I would like to thank Mark Kauntze for bringing this article to my attention.

80. Butrica, "Editing Propertius," 176.

81. Butrica, "Editing Propertius," 180.

82. Butrica, "Editing Propertius," 180–81.

83. The useful distinction between "metacritical" and "anecdotal" approaches to Walter is formulated in Edwards, "Walter Map." To varying degrees, the following works all discuss Walter's metacritical elements: Levine, "How to Read Walter Map"; Echard, "Map's Metafiction"; Coxon, "Wit, Laughter and Authority."

CHAPTER 4

1. Lucien Foulet, "Marie de France et les lais bretons," *Zeitschrift für romanische Philologie* 29 (1905): 19–56, at 56: "Ou en tout cas si une telle tradition existe, les lais anonymes ne l'ont pas connue: si nous écartons les affirmations de convention de leurs prologues, nous verrons que nulle part ils ne s'y réfèrent réellement" (Or in any case, if such a tradition [i.e., Breton] may have existed, the anonymous lais did not know it: if we rule out the conventional assertions of their prologues, we see that nowhere do they really refer to it).

2. Although our analyses are quite different, Patrick Joseph Schwieterman and I have arrived at the same conclusion independently and roughly at the same time. In his dissertation, "Fairies, Kingship, and the British Past in Walter Map's *De Nugis Curialium* and *Sir Orfeo*" (Ph.D. diss., University of California, Berkeley, 2010), 21, Schwieterman uses the term "Briticize" with reference to Walter's transformation of this folktale.

3. For a recent review of Chrétien's possible Irish and Welsh sources, see Carey, *Ireland and the Grail*.

4. Lucie Polak, *Chrétien de Troyes: Cligés*, Critical Guides to French Texts 23 (London: Grant and Cutler, 1982), 9.

5. Polak, *Chrétien de Troyes*, 9–21.

6. Patrick Sims-Williams, "A Turkish-Celtic Problem in Chrétien de Troyes: The Name Cligés," in *Ildánach Ildírech: A Festschrift for Proinsias Mac Cana*, ed. John Carey, John T. Koch, and Pierre-Yves Lambert (Andover, MA: Celtic Studies Publications, 1999), 215–30.

7. Joshua Byron Smith, "An Edition, Translation, and Introduction to Benedict of Gloucester's *Vita Dubricii*," *Arthurian Literature* 29 (2012): 53–100.

8. Aside from vernacular adaptations, medieval readers could find the story in Virgil, *Georgics* 4; Ovid, *Metamorphoses* 10–11; Boethius, *De consolatione philosophiae* 3.12.

9. *Sir Orfeo*, ed. A. J. Bliss (Oxford: Clarendon Press, 1966), xl–xli.

10. *Sir Orfeo*, xxxiii. For the extensive debate on the nature of *Sir Orfeo*'s claimed Celtic sources see George Lyman Kittredge, "Sir Orfeo," *American Journal of Philology* 7 (1886): 176–202; Roger Sherman Loomis, "*Sir Orfeo* and Walter Map's *De Nugis*," *Modern Language Notes* 51, no. 1 (1936): 28–30; Constance Davies, "*Sir Orfeo* and *De Nugis*," *Modern Language Notes* 51, no. 7 (1936): 492; Constance Davies, "Notes on the Sources of 'Sir Orfeo,'" *Modern Language Review* 31, no. 3 (1936): 354–57; Constance Davies, "Classical Threads in 'Orfeo,'" *Modern Language Review* 56, no. 2 (1961): 161–66; J. Burke Severs "The Antecedents of Sir Orfeo," in *Studies*

in Medieval Literature: In Honor of Professor Albert Croll Baugh, ed. MacEdward Leach (Philadelphia: University of Pennsylvania Press, 1961), 187–207; Dorena Allen, "Orpheus and Orfeo: The Dead and the Taken," *Medium Aevum* 33 (1964): 102–11; Patrizia Grimaldi, "Sir Orfeo as Celtic Folk-Hero, Christian Pilgrim, and Medieval King," in *Allegory, Myth, and Symbol*, ed. Morton W. Bloomfield (Cambridge, MA: Harvard University Press, 1981), 147–61; Marie-Thérèse Brouland, *Sir Orfeo: Le substrat celtique du lai breton anglais* (Paris: Didier Érudition, 1990).

11. *Sir Orfeo*, xv. For Winchester in Arthurian legend, see Tatlock, *Legendary History of Britain*, 36–39.

12. *Sir Orfeo*, p. 6, lines 49–50.

13. N. R. Havely, *Chaucer's Boccaccio: Sources for "Troilus" and the "Knight's" and "Franklin's Tales"; Translations from the "Filostrato," "Teseida" and "Filocolo"* (Woodbridge: D. S. Brewer, 1980). On the difficulty of establishing Chaucer's use of Boccaccio for *The Franklin's Tale*, see Dominique Battles, "Chaucer's *Franklin's Tale* and Boccaccio's *Filocolo* Reconsidered," *Chaucer Review* 34, no. 1 (1999): 38–59.

14. John S. P. Tatlock, *The Scene of the Franklin's Tale Visited* (London: Published for the Chaucer Society by Kegan Paul, Trench, Trübner, 1914); William Henry Schofield, "Chaucer's *Franklin's Tale*," *PMLA* 16 (1901): 405–49; Peter Lucas, "Chaucer's Franklin's Dorigen: Her Name," *Notes and Queries* 37 (1990): 398–400; Andrew Breeze, "The Name of Kayrrud in the *Franklin's Tale*," *Chaucer Review* 37, no. 1 (2002): 95–99.

15. Shannon Godlove, " 'Engelond' and 'Armorik Briteyne': Reading Brittany in Chaucer's *Franklin's Tale*," *Chaucer Review* 51, no. 3 (2016): 269–94. I would like to thank Shannon for allowing me to see a version of this paper prior to publication.

16. *Cyfranc Lludd a Llefelys*, ed. Brynley F. Roberts (Dublin: Dublin Institute for Advanced Studies, 1975).

17. See *Cyfranc Lludd a Llefelys*, xxviii. An analysis of "translation style" in Middle Welsh remains a desideratum.

18. See, for example, the tale of Gado in *DNC*, 2.17, pp. 166–74, a story whose setting is inspired by Geoffrey of Monmouth's *History of the Kings of Britain*.

19. See, for example, Reto Radulf Bezzola, *Les origines et la formation de la littérature courtoise en Occident (500–1200)*, 3 vols. (Paris: Champion, 1944–63), 3:94: "La seconde partie du *De nugis* est toute remplie d'histoires de fees et de fantômes, qui lui proviennent pour la plupart de sa patrie galloise."

20. *DNC*, 2.11, p. 30: "sine quiete uel residencia."

21. Kittredge, "Sir Orfeo," 194. However, Kittredge does continue, "I am aware that most of the cases so far cited may be challenged as either not pure Celtic or not quite to the point"— but context makes clear that he is mainly worried about geography (195).

22. See the following works by Roger Sherman Loomis: "*Sir Orfeo* and Walter Map's *De Nugis*"; "The Spoils of Annwn: An Early Arthurian Poem," *PMLA* 56 (1941): 887–936, at 917; "King Arthur and the Antipodes," *Modern Philology* 38 (1941): 298–304, at 301 and the following pages; and *Arthurian Tradition and Chrétien de Troyes* (New York: Columbia University Press, 1949; reprint, 1961), 166–67.

23. Vernon J. Harward, *The Dwarfs of Arthurian Romance and Celtic Tradition* (Leiden: Brill, 1958), 9 et passim.

24. Vernon J. Harward, " 'Celtic Myth and Arthurian Romance': A Reply," *Medium Aevum* 31 (1962): 43–44, at 43 n. 4. Harward is replying to A. J. Bliss, "Celtic Myth and Arthurian Romance," *Medium Aevum* 30 (1961): 19–25. Bliss is off the mark when he claims that the story is not of Welsh provenance because it takes place in England: only the last part of the story

explicitly mentions a setting, the river Wye at Hereford, which was hardly a place devoid of Welsh influence or culture in the Middle Ages. Nonetheless, I do ultimately agree with Bliss's skepticism, though our reasons differ.

25. *Sir Orfeo*, xxxvii and the following pages.

26. Brouland, *Sir Orfeo*, 172: "C'est un conte celtique illustrant principalement le problème de l'écoulement du temps pour le héros ayant séjourné dans l'Autre Monde."

27. Some scholars call the wandering band "the Herlething" or "Herlethingi." This trend likely derives from a casual misreading of the Latin: "Cetus eciam et phalanges noctiuage quas Herlethingi dicebant . . ." (*DNC*, 4.13, p. 370). *Herlethingi* is thus incorrectly treated as a predicate accusative. We would expect an accusative plural, likely in some adjectival form, for this reading to be correct. Rather, *Herlethingi* here is a genitive of the name *Herlethingus*; this is confirmed a few sentences later in a similar phrase: "Hec huius Herlethingi uisa est ultimo familia." Thus, James's translation is correct, although awkward: "The nocturnal companies and squadrons, too, which were called of Herlethingus." Perhaps "which were said to belong to Herlething" is better.

28. *DNC*, 1.11, pp. 26–30; 4.13, pp. 370–72.

29. For a good summary of scholarship, see Brouland, *Sir Orfeo*, 163–74. See also Orderic Vitalis, *Ecclesiastical History*, ed. Marjorie Chibnall (Oxford: Clarendon Press, 1973), 4:xxxviii and the following pages. The best edition of Epistle 14 of Peter of Blois is found in Lena Wahlgren's *The Letter Collections of Peter of Blois* (Göteborg, Sweden: Acta Universitas Gothoburgensis, 1993), 140–65, quote at 147, line 50. See also Cotts, *The Clerical Dilemma*, 155–56.

30. Helaine Newstead, "Some Observations on King Herla and the Herlething," in *Medieval Literature and Folklore Studies: Essays in Honor of Francis Lee Utley*, ed. Jerome Mandel and Bruce A. Rosenberg (New Brunswick, NJ: Rutgers University Press, 1971), 105–10, at 110.

31. E.g., Newstead, "Some Observations," 110; Juliette Wood, "Walter Map: The Contents and Context of *De Nugis Curialium*," *Transactions of the Honourable Society of Cymmrodorion* (1985): 91–103.

32. *DNC*, 4.13, p. 370; 1.11, p. 30.

33. *DNC*, 4.13, p. 370: "cum bigis et summariis, cum clitellis et panariolis, auibus et canibus, concurrentibus uiris et mulieribus."

34. *DNC*, 1.11, p. 28: "recedit Herla muneribus onustus et xenniis equorum, canum, accipitrum, et omnium que uenati uel aucupio prestanciora uidentur."

35. *DNC*, 4.13, p. 370.

36. *DNC*, 1.12, p. 31. Cf. *Master Walter Map's Book*, trans. Tupper and Ogle, 18 ("And then it was seen by many Welsh sinking into the river Wye at Hereford"); *Storïau Gwallter Map*, trans. R. T. Jenkins (Llandybie: Llyfrau'r Dryw, 1941), 14 ("Yn wir, dywedir bod rhyw Gymry wedi gweled Herla Frenin a'i fintai yn nedio i mewn i afon Gŵy, yn Sir Henffordd, ac na ddaethant byth allan"); *Gautier Map, conteur Anglais*, trans. Boutemy, 39 ("Mais alors de nombreux Gallois le virent disparaitre dans la rivière Wye á Hereford"); *Gautier Map: Contes de courtisans*, trans. Perez, 23 ("Car à ce moment-là bien des Gallois l'ont vu s'engloutir dans la rivière Wye à Hereford"); Walter Map, *Svaghi di corte*, trans. Latella, 1:69 ("Proprio allora, infatti, é stato visto da molti Gallesi tuffarsi nei pressi di Wye, fiume della contea di Hereford"); *CPGC*, 93 ("Puis maints Gallois l'ont vue se plonger dans la rivière Wye à côté de Hereford").

37. *DMLBS*, s.v. "immergere," def. 2.

38. *DNC*, 4.13, pp. 370–71: "in marchia walliarum et Herefordie anno primo rengi Henrici secundi."

39. *DNC*, 4.13, p. 370: "Ab illa die nusquam uisa est illa milicia, tanquam nobis insipientibus illi suos tradiderint errores."

40. Hinton, "Walter Map's *De nugis curialium*," 95.

41. For a studies of Walter's use of satire, see Margaret Sinex, "Echoic Irony in Walter Map's Satire Against the Cistercians," *Comparative Literature* 54 (2002): 275–90; Stephen Gordon, "Parody, Sarcasm, and Invective in the *Nugae* of Walter Map," *Journal of English and Germanic Studies* 116 (forthcoming 2017). I would like to thank Stephen for letting me read his article prior to publication.

42. *DNC*, 1.10, p. 24. Cf. Dan. 3.

43. *DNC*, 1.11, p. 26: "Vnam tamen et solam huic nostre curie similem fuisse fabule dederunt, que dicunt Herlam regem antiquissimorum Britonum positum ad racionem ab altero rege, qui pigmeus uidebatur modicitate stature, que non excedebat simiam."

44. *DNC*, 1.11, p. 26: "tibi quidem ignotus, sed de fama que te super alios reges extulit exultans, quoniam et optimus es et loco michi proximus et sanguine."

45. Frank Barlow, *William Rufus* (Berkeley: University of California Press, 1983), 103–4.

46. "Rarus ibi sompnus. vigilate tedia noctis / Indolitura dies equitantis vexat ocellum" (Johannes de Hauvilla, *Architrenius*, 6.13.416–17, p. 166).

47. *DNC*, 1.10, p. 12: "Sunt et ibi germina noctis, noctua, nicticorax, uultur et bubo, quorum oculi tenebras amant, oderunt lucem."

48. *DNC*, 1.11, p. 28: "in lumine, quod non uidebatur solis aut lune sed lampadarum multarum."

49. Nicholas Vincent, "The Court of Henry II," in *Henry II: New Interpretations*, ed. Christopher Harper-Bill and Nicholas Vincent (Woodbridge: Boydell Press, 2007), 278–334, at 331. Vincent here falls into the trap of equating the two versions of the story, for the revised tale makes no mention of Herla traveling during the night.

50. Vincent, "Court of Henry II," 330.

51. Vincent, "Court of Henry II," 321.

52. *GCO*, 5:304: "Avium, quarum victus ex preda, volatu plurimum; canumque, feras narium sagacitate persequentium, tam voce sonora et consona, quam cursu veloci, ultra modum delectatus. Et utinam tam devocioni deditus quam venacioni."

53. *DNC*, 5.6, p. 476: "semper itinerans erat dietis intolerabilibus quasi duplomate <utens>, et in hoc familie sequenti nimis immisericors; canum et auium peritissimus et illusionis illius auidissimus."

54. *DNC*, 1.11, p. 28: "recedit Herla muneribus onustus et xenniis equorum, canum, accipitrum, et omnium que uenati uel aucupio prestanciora uidentur."

55. *DNC*, 1.11, p. 28: "et canem modicum sanguinarium portatilem presentat, omnibus modis interdicens ne quis de toto comitatu suo descendat usquam, donec ille canis a portatore suo prosiliat."

56. *DNC*, 1.11, p. 30: "Rex uero racionem eius intelligens resolucionis, prohibuit sub interminacione mortis consimilis ne quis ante canis descensum terram contingeret."

57. *DNC*, 1.11, p. 30: "Canis autem nondum descendit."

58. *DNC*, 1.11, p. 30: "Vnde fabula dat illum Herlam regem errore semper infinito circuitus cum exercitu suo tenere uesanos" and "Quieuit . . . fantasticus ille circuitus."

59. *DMLBS*, s.v. "circuitus," def. B.

60. *DNC*, 1.10, p. 14.

61. *DNC*, 1.11, p. 30: "cessauit regnum nostrum celebriter ut ante uisitare." James translates *celebriter* as "in force," doubtlessly connecting the adverb to *celeber*. However, this meaning is not attested, and "ceremoniously" gives better sense. See *DMLBS*, s.v. "celebriter."

62. Patrick Sims-Williams, "Celtic Civilization: Continuity or Coincidence?," *Cambrian*

Medieval Celtic Studies 64 (2012): 1–45; *Irish Influence on Medieval Welsh Literature* (Oxford: Oxford University Press, 2011), 4–8; "Celtomania and Celtoscepticism," *Cambrian Medieval Celtic Studies* 36 (1998): 1–35, at 12–16. See also Chapter 6, this volume.

63. Two thirteenth-century romances that uncharacteristically take place in Ireland are *Les Merveilles de Rigomer* and *Durmars li Galois*.

64. Rachel Bromwich, "First Transmission to England and France," in *The Arthur of the Welsh*, ed. Rachel Bromwich, A. O. H. Jarman, and Brynley F. Roberts (Cardiff: University of Wales Press, 1991), 273–98; Rachel Bromwich, "Celtic Elements in Arthurian Romance: A General Survey," in *The Legend of Arthur in the Middle Ages: Studies Presented to Armel H. Diverres*, ed. P. B. Grout et al. (Cambridge: D. S. Brewer, 1983), 41–55.

65. Brynley F. Roberts, "Geoffrey of Monmouth and Welsh Historical Tradition," *Nottingham Medieval Studies* 20 (1976): 29–40. See also Chapter 6, this volume.

66. For a good recent overview (although limited to the French tradition), see Caroline Jewers, "Myth and the *matière de Bretagne*," in *The Cambridge History of French Literature*, ed. William Burgwinkle, Nicholas Hammond, and Emma Wilson (Cambridge: Cambridge University Press, 2011), 47–56. A somewhat dated though still helpful study is P. Rickard, *Britain in Medieval French Literature, 1100–1500* (Cambridge: Cambridge University Press, 1956). For initial responses to the historicity of the Matter of Britain, see D. H. Green, *The Beginnings of Medieval Romance: Fact and Fiction, 1150–1220* (Cambridge: Cambridge University Press, 2002), 168–87.

67. The first extant appearance of this term is Jehan Bodel, *La Chanson des Saisnes*, ed. Annette Brasseur (Geneva: Librairie Droz, 1989), 1:2, lines 6–7: "N'en sont que trois materes a nul home vivant: / De France et de Bretaigne et de Ronme la grant."

68. *DNC*, 1.13, p. 36: "Materiam michi tam copiosam eligis, ut nullo possit opere superari, nullis equari laboribus"; 2.32, p. 208: "Siluam uobis et materiam, non dico fabularum sed faminum appono"; 5.2, p. 408: "Hoc ercle dictum et factum stilo dignum Homeri censeo, et me tam eleganti materia indignum."

69. J. E. Caerwyn Williams, "Brittany and the Arthurian Legend," in Bromwich, Jarman, and Roberts, *The Arthur of the Welsh*, 249–72, at 259–60.

70. For the etymology of *Herlething*, see Leo Spitzer, "Anglo-French Etymologies," *Studies in Philology* 41 (1944): 521–43; Charles H. Livingston, "Old French Herluin," *Modern Language Notes* 60, no. 3 (1945): 178–80.

71. Words ending in *-ing* (/iŋ/) are rare in Middle Welsh, occurring primarily as loanwords from Old or Middle English, e.g., *edling* < OE æðeling, "prince"; *ffyrling, ffyrdling* < ME *farthing*; *resing* < ME *raising(e)*, "grape"; and *lloring* < OE *lærig*, "shield boss, shield," although in the latter case the *-ing* arose from orthographic confusion and not directly from borrowing. See *GPC*, s.vv. "edling," "ffyrling," "rhesin"; Thomas Jones, "Lloring," *Bulletin of the Board of Celtic Studies* 13 (1948–50): 75; Idris Foster, "Lloring," *Bulletin of the Board of Celtic Studies* 8 (1935–37): 21–23. Cf. *ffaling* < Middle Irish *fallaing*, "cloak" (*GPC*, s.v. "ffaling"). Other borrowings into Welsh originally ending with *-in* seem to have undergone hyperforeignization, with Welsh speakers sometimes changing *-in* to *-ing* in foreign words: *vring* < ME *urin*, "urine"; *rosing* < ME *resin*, "resin"; *Llading* < Lat. *Latina*, "Latin"; *dwsing* < ME *doseine*, "dozen." If this is the case, then words ending in *-ing* (/iŋ/) truly did seem foreign to Welsh speakers. However, a native explanation of this phenomenon is possible. See John Morris Jones, *A Welsh Grammar: Historical and Comparative* (Oxford: Clarendon Press, 1913), §106.1.2.

72. For Geoffrey's names, see Tatlock, *Legendary History of Britain*, 116–70; Brynley F. Roberts, "The Treatment of Personal Names in the Early Welsh Versions of *Historia Regum Britanniae*," *Bulletin of the Board of Celtic Studies* 25 (1973): 274–90; A. E. Hutson, *British Personal*

Names in the "Historia regum Britanniae" (Berkeley: University of California Press, 1940). See also Chapter 5, this volume.

73. Roberts, "Treatment of Personal Names."

74. Sims-Williams, "A Turkish-Celtic Problem."

75. *Arveragus*, a Latinized form of a Celtic name, and *Aurelius*, a Roman name used by the British were likely taken from Geoffrey of Monmouth's *Historia*, which Chaucer knew. See Schofield, "Chaucer's *Franklin's Tale.*" The name *Dorigen*, although its provenance remains murky, is nonetheless meant to be a Breton name. See Tatlock, *Scene of the Franklin's Tale Visited*, 37–41; Lucas, "Chaucer's Franklin's Dorigen."

76. *DNC*, 1.11, p. 26: "Herlam regem antiquissimorum Britonum"; pp. 28–30: "Domine, linguam tuam uix intelligo, cum sim Saxo, tu Brito."

77. *DNC*, 1.11, p. 30: "immergi iuxta Waiam Herefordie flumen"; 4.13, p. 370: "in marchia Walliarum et Herefordie."

78. *DNC*, 1.11, pp. 30–31: "a multis Wallensibus"; 4.13, pp. 370–71:"uigilantissime gentis."

79. K. S. Whetter, *Understanding Genre and Medieval Romance* (Burlington, VT: Ashgate, 2008), 96.

80. Ceridwen Lloyd-Morgan, "Crossing the Borders: Literary Borrowing in Medieval Wales and England," in *Authority and Subjugation in Writing of Medieval Wales*, ed. Ruth Kennedy and Simon Meecham-Jones (New York: Palgrave Macmillan, 2008), 159–73, at 159.

81. A welcome recent exception is Carey, *Ireland and the Grail*. Rachel Bromwich's work often concerned these matters as well. See, for example, "Chwedlau'r Greal," *Llên Cymru* 8 (1964–65): 48–57; and "First Transmission." See also Chapter 6, this volume.

82. Michael Faletra, "Chivalric Identity at the Frontier: Marie's Welsh Lais," *Le Cygne: Journal of the International Marie de France Society* 4 (2006): 27–41, at 27.

83. Instead, his sons—especially Geoffrey, who named his own son Arthur—seem to have eagerly taken up the mythical figure of Arthur in their own propaganda (Aurell, "Henry II and Arthurian Legend").

84. Michael Faletra, "Narrating the Matter of Britain: Geoffrey of Monmouth and the Norman Colonization of Wales," *Chaucer Review* 35, no. 1 (2000): 60–85, at 63.

85. *DNC*, 1.12, p. 30: "nomen autem illius non audiui regine, nisi quod aiunt hoc nomine dudum dictam reginam antiquissimorum Britonum que fuit uxor Herle Regis, qui fabulose dicitur cum pigmeo quodam ad hanc rupem disparuisse, nusquam autem postea super terram apparuisse. Saxones uero iam ducentis annis hoc regnum possiderunt, expulsis incolis."

86. *DNC* 1.11, p. 26: "Vnam tamen et solam huic nostre curie similem fuisse fabule dederunt, que dicunt Herlam regem antiquissimorum Britonum positum ad racionem ab altero rege."

87. *DNC*, 1.11, p. 26: "fama que te super alios reges extulit."

88. *DNC*, 1.11, p. 30: "tanquam nobis suos tradiderint errores, ad quietem sibi."

89. *DNC*, 1.1, p. 6.

90. Andreas Bihrer also argues that this tale excuses Herla, though with emphasis on the mythological function of the story and not its status as a part of the Matter of Britain: "Damit wird den Zwergen als einer mythischen Gruppe die Schuld am Umherziehen des Königshofes gegeben" ("Selbstvergewisserung am Hof," 241; That is to say that the blame for the wandering of the king's court is ascribed to the dwarves as a mythical group).

91. See Chapter 2, this volume.

92. *DNC*, 1.11, p. 26: "Sitque fedus eternum inter nos"; p. 28: "Rex optime, Deo teste uobis assum iuxta pactum nostrum in nupciis uestris; si quid autem diffinicionis uestre potest amplius a me peti quam quod cernitis, accurate supplebo libens."

93. Bliss, "Celtic Myth and Arthurian Romance," 25.

94. Rickard, *Britain in Medieval French Literature*, 120.

CHAPTER 5

1. For Walter's quotes and allusions, see *DNC*, 524–26.

2. For Walter's possible use of a version of *Amis and Amiloun*, see Hume, "Composition of a Medieval Romance."

3. *DNC*, 2.32, p. 208.

4. Much has been written about Walter's use of folklore, but the most thorough study is Várvaro, *Apparizioni fantastiche*. Also useful is Wood, "Walter Map: The Contents and Context of *De Nugis Curialium*."

5. *HRB* §68.335–36, p. 84: "id est Gloucestria, nuncupata usque in hodiernum diem in confinio Kambriae et Loegriae super ripam Sabrinae sita est."

6. For the postconquest history of St. Peter's Abbey, see David Bates, "The Building of a Great Church: The Abbey of St Peter's, Gloucester, and Its Early Norman Benefactors," *Transactions of the Bristol and Gloucestershire Archaeological Society* 102 (1984): 129–32; Rodney Thomson, "Books and Learning at Gloucester Abbey in the Twelfth and Thirteenth Centuries," in *Books and Collectors, 1200–1700*, ed. James P. Carley and Colin G. C. Tite (London: British Library, 1997), 3–26; *The Original Acta of St. Peter's Abbey, Gloucester, c. 1122 to 1263*, ed. Robert B. Patterson, Gloucestershire Record Series (Gloucestershire: Bristol and Gloucestershire Archaeological Society, 1998), xxi–xxxii; Christopher Brooke, "St Peter of Gloucester and St Cadoc of Llancarfan," in *Celt and Saxon: Studies in the Early British Border*, ed. Nora Chadwick (Cambridge: Cambridge University Press, 1963), 258–332; reprinted with revisions in Christopher N. L. Brooke, *The Church and the Welsh Border in the Central Middle Ages*, ed. D. N. Dumville and C. N. L. Brooke, Studies in Celtic History, 8 (Woodbridge: Boydell Press, 1986), 50–94.

7. Emma Cownie, *Religious Patronage in Anglo-Norman England, 1066–1135* (Woodbridge: Boydell, 1998), 65.

8. For an overview of Anglo-Norman attitudes toward Welsh holdings, see John Reuben Davies, "The Cult of Saints in the Early Welsh March," in *The English Isles: Cultural Transmission and Political Conflict in Britain and Ireland, 1100–1500*, ed. Seán Duffy and Susan Foran (Dublin: Four Courts Press, 2013): 37–55; Emma Cownie, "Gloucester Abbey, 1066–1135: An Illustration of Religious Patronage in Anglo-Norman England," in *England and Normandy in the Middle Ages*, ed. David Bates and Anne Curry (London: Hambledon Press, 1994), 143–58; Cownie, *Religious Patronage*, 54–65; Brian Golding, "Trans-Border Transactions: Patterns of Patronage in Anglo-Norman Wales," *Haskins Society Journal* 16 (2005): 27–46.

9. For Gloucester's good reputation, see William of Malmesbury, *Gesta Pontificum Anglorum*, vol. 1, *Text and Translation*, ed. and trans. M. Winterbottom (Oxford: Clarendon Press, 2007), 4.155, pp. 446–49.

10. In this regard, Gerald of Wales reminisces about how well St. Peter's governed Llanbadarn Fawr. See *GCO*, 6:121.

11. R. R. Davies, *Age of Conquest*, 181.

12. For the Welsh estates and rights granted to St. Peter's, see Cownie, *Religious Patronage*, 54–65; Kathleen Hughes, "British Library MS. Cotton Vespasian A. xiv (*Vitae Sanctorum Wallensium*): Its Purpose and Provenance," in *Celtic Britain in the Early Middle Ages: Studies in Scottish and Welsh Sources*, ed. David. N. Dumville (Woodbridge: Boydell, 1980), 53–66, at 58–61

(an earlier version of the same chapter appears in *Studies in the Early British Church*, ed. Nora K. Chadwick [New York: Cambridge University Press, 1958], 183–200).

13. *Historia et cartularium monasterii Sancti Petri Gloucestriae*, ed. William Henry Hart (London: Longman, Green, Longman, Roberts, and Green, 1863–67), 1:314, 222; I. W. Rolands, "William de Braose and the Lordship of Brecon," *Bulletin of the Board of Celtic Studies* 30 (1982–83): 123–33; John Reuben Davies, "Cult of Saints," 40–41. For an analysis of the trustworthiness of Gloucester's *Historia* and *Cartularium*, see Brooke, "St Peter of Gloucester and St Cadoc of Llancarfan" (1986), 50–65.

14. *Historia et cartularium monasterii Sancti Petri Gloucestriae*, 1:102; Brooke, "St Peter of Gloucester and St Cadoc of Llancarfan" (1963), 261–62; Jeremy K. Knight, "St. Tatheus of Caerwent: An Analysis of the Vespasian Life," *Monmouthshire Antiquary* 3 (1970–71): 29–36, at 34.

15. *Historia et cartularium monasterii Sancti Petri Gloucestriae*, 1:75–76; J. Conway Davies, "Ewenny Priory: Some Recently-Found Records," *National Library of Wales Journal* 3 (1944): 107–37.

16. *Historia et cartularium monasterii Sancti Petri Gloucestriae*, 1:115.

17. *Historia et cartularium monasterii Sancti Petri Gloucestriae*, 1:115, 223, 226; Golding, "Trans-Border Transactions," 35–36; Brooke, "St Peter of Gloucester and St Cadoc of Llancarfan" (1986), 64–65.

18. For example, between 1175 and 1180 Gloucester successfully reasserted its rights to Llancarfan against the claims of Archbishop William. See *Historia et cartularium monasterii Sancti Petri Gloucestriae*, 2:12–14; *Episcopal Acts and Cognate Documents Relating to Welsh Dioceses, 1066–1272*, ed. J. Conway Davies (Cardiff: Historical Society of the Church in Wales, 1946–48), 2:660–61 and 64–65; John Reuben Davies, *The Book of Llandaf and the Norman Church in Wales* (Woodbridge: Boydell, 2003), 107–8.

19. John Reuben Davies, *Book of Llandaf*, 105–8.

20. *Historia et cartularium Monasterii Sancti Petri Gloucestriae*, 1:106.

21. Michael Lapidge, "The Welsh-Latin Poetry of Sulien's Family," *Studia Celtica* 8–9 (1973–74): 68–106; Charles-Edwards, *Wales and the Britons*, 648–50.

22. *GCO*, 6:121.

23. *English Benedictine Kalendars After A.D. 1000*, ed. Francis Wormwald, 2 vols. (London: Harrison and Sons, 1939), 2:39–55.

24. A monk of St. Peter's named Benedict redacted an earlier life of St. Dyfrig. See Smith, "An Edition, Translation, and Introduction to Benedict of Gloucester's *Vita Dubricii*."

25. For the importance of preconquest vitae to ecclesiastical property, see Wendy Davies, "Property Rights and Property Claims in Welsh *Vitae* of the Eleventh Century," in *Hagiographie, cultures et sociétés, IVᵉ–XIIᵉ siècles*, ed. E. Patlagean and P. Riché (Paris: Études Augustiniennes, 1981), 515–53; repr. with the same pagination in Davies, *Welsh History in the Early Middle Ages*, chap. 14.

26. R. R. Davies, *Age of Conquest*, 181.

27. John Reuben Davies, "Cult of Saints."

28. Thomson, "Books and Learning at Gloucester Abbey," 3.

29. Most of the lives are published and translated in *Vitae Sanctorum Britanniae et Genealogiae*; references are to the revised edition. For the life of St. Dyfrig, see Smith, "An Edition, Translation, and Introduction." For the life of St. Padarn, see " 'Vita Sancti Paterni': The Life of Saint Padarn and the Original 'Miniu,' " ed. and trans. Charles Thomas and David Howlett, *Trivium* 33 (2003); for the life of St. David, see "Rhygyfarch's *Life* of St David," ed. and trans. Richard Sharpe and John Reuben Davies, in *St David of Wales: Cult, Church and Nation*, ed. J.

Wyn Evans and Jonathan M. Wooding (Woodbridge: Boydell and Brewer, 2007), 107–55. For the Cornish glossary, see Alderik Blom, "The Welsh Glosses in the Vocabularium," *Cambrian Medieval Celtic Studies* 57 (2009): 23–40; Oliver Padel "The Nature and Date of the Old Cornish Vocabulary," *Zeitschrift für celtische Philologie* 61 (2014): 173–99. For the calendar, see Silas M. Harris, "The Kalendar of the *Vitae Sanctorum Wallensium*," *Journal of the Historical Society of the Church in Wales* 3 (1953): 3–53. For the genealogical tract, see Ben Guy, "*De situ Brecheniauc* and Related Texts" (forthcoming). I would like to thank Ben for making a copy of his work available to me prior to publication. For some of the textual problems posed by the manuscript see Hywel D. Emanuel, "An Analysis of the Composition of the 'Vita Cadoci,'" *National Library of Wales Journal* 7 (1951–52): 217–27.

30. Hughes, "British Library MS. Cotton Vespasian A. xiv." For an earlier discussion of the provenance of Cotton Vespasian A.xiv, see Harris, "Kalendar of the *Vitae Sanctorum Wallensium*"; and the description of the manuscript by Robin Flower in *Vitae Sanctorum Britanniae et Genealogiae*, viii–xi. Flower preferred Brecon, while Harris showed that the manuscript was ultimately compiled in Monmouth, though he noted extensive Gloucester influence.

31. John Reuben Davies, *Book of Llandaf*, 133 n. 9; Sims-Williams, "A Turkish-Celtic Problem," 224 n. 39; R. R. Davies, *Age of Conquest*, 106. Sims-Williams and R. R. Davies qualify their support for Hughes's theory by adding "probably" and "possibly." References of this type could be multiplied.

32. Hughes, "British Library MS. Cotton Vespasian A. xiv," 58.

33. Hughes, "British Library MS. Cotton Vespasian A. xiv," 60.

34. Harris, "Kalendar," 34–36. Harris identified a set of six saints, Ismael included, whose appearance in the Vespasian calendar derives ultimately from a calendar from St. Davids. He suggests that Monmouth may have obtained these festivals from the same center as their copy of the *Vita Sancti Dauid*. Hughes, moreover, notes that Gloucester and St. Davids were on friendly terms during this period (see "British Library MS. Cotton Vespasian A. xiv," 58–59). Therefore, it is possible that not only Ismael but the five other saints owe their presence in the Vespasian calendar to Gloucester. It is, however, worth noting that St. Ismael was also known at Llandaf (see John Reuben Davies, *Book of Llandaf*, 88, 118).

35. *Historia et cartularium monasterii Sancti Petri Gloucestriae*, 1:75–76.

36. For the close relationship of Monmouth and Gloucester monks in this period, see Harris, "Kalendar," 24–25.

37. Hughes, "British Library MS. Cotton Vespasian A. xiv," 61.

38. Hughes, "British Library MS. Cotton Vespasian A. xiv," 61.

39. *Original Acta of St. Peter's Abbey*, xxiv.

40. Thomson, "Books and Learning at Gloucester Abbey," 6.

41. Hughes, "British Library MS. Cotton Vespasian A. xiv," 61–63; John Reuben Davies, *Book of Llandaf*, 118–19, 124; Patrick Sims-Williams, "The Emergence of Old Welsh, Cornish and Breton Orthography, 600–800: The Evidence of Archaic Old Welsh," *Bulletin of the Board of Celtic Studies* 38 (1991): 20–86, at 30 et passim.

42. E.g., the Book of Llandaf's *Arthbodu* versus Vespasian's *Artbodv* (*The Text of the Book of Llan Dâv*, ed. J. Gwenogvryn Evans, with the cooperation of John Rhys [Oxford, 1893], 359). For *th* as a modernization of *t*, see "Sims-Williams, "Emergence of Old Welsh, Cornish and Breton Orthography," 73.

43. On the date of the Book of Llandaf, see John Reuben Davies, "*Liber Landavensis*: Its Date and the Identity of Its Editor," *Cambrian Medieval Celtic Studies* 35 (1998): 1–11; revising

this earlier study, Davies, in *Book of Llandaf*, 132–42, argues that Caradog of Llancarfan is responsible for the Book of Llandaf.

44. John Reuben Davies, *Book of Llandaf*, 13.

45. Hughes, "British Library MS. Cotton Vespasian A. xiv," 58–59.

46. However, the *Vita Sancti Dauid* and the *Vita Sancti Maidoci* were both known to have been at Llandaf, and Gloucester could have obtained these lives, and perhaps others, from Llandaf. For a reconstruction of Llandaf's library, see John Reuben Davies, *Book of Llandaf*, 129–31.

47. Smith, "An Edition, Translation, and Introduction"; Benedict says that he "wears the habit of the monastery of St. Peter's Gloucester" (73–74). It would be highly unusual for a monk to exit his cloister in order to compose a vita.

48. Benedict of Gloucester used this text in writing his new life of Dyfrig: compare "Super omnes autem britannos dextralis partis britannię beatum Dubricium summum doctorem a rege & ab omni parrochia electum archiepiscopum consecrauerunt" (*Text of the Book of Llan Dâv*, 69); and Benedict's "Super omnes utique dextralis britannie fines beatum Dubricium metropolitanum archipresulem ab ambrosio aurelio rege totius brittonum monarchie filio constantino fratre quoque Vther patris arthurii magni, necnon et ab omni clero et populo illius Archidioceseos canonice delectum consecrauerunt" (Smith, "An Edition, Translation, and Introduction," §7, pp. 78–81). This text seems to have been in vogue in twelfth-century Wales. See John Reuben Davies, *Book of Llandaf*, 110–11.

49. Benedict's *Vita Dubricii* is essentially a harmony of the Dyfrig promoted by Llandaf and the Dyfrig found in Geoffrey's *Historia*. Benedict's exemplar of the *Historia* belongs to a group of manuscripts that circulated in and around the southern March and southwestern England. See Smith, "An Edition, Translation, and Introduction," 66–71.

50. For Caradog writing for Gloucester Abbey, see John Reuben Davies, *Book of Llandaf*, 142; Brooke, "St Peter of Gloucester and St Cadoc of Llancarfan" (1963), 283–322; Knight, "St. Tatheus of Caerwent," 33–35.

51. *English Benedictine Kalendars*, 2:39–55.

52. *Historia et cartularium monasterii Sancti Petri Gloucestriae*, 1:285–86; Hughes, "British Library MS. Cotton Vespasian A. xiv," 63.

53. "London, British Library, Egerton 2810," *Manuscripts of the West Midlands: A Catalogue of Vernacular Manuscript Books of the English West Midlands, c. 1300–c. 1475*, accessed April 1, 2015, http://www.hrionline.ac.uk/mwm/browse?type=ms&id=58#biblio. See also Manfred Görlach, *The Textual Tradition of the "South English Legendary"* (Leeds: University of Leeds, School of English, 1974), 90–92; and John Reuben Davies, *Book of Llandaf*, 121. I would like to thank Erik Kooper and David Callander, who are preparing an edition and translation of the Middle English *Life of Teilo*, for sharing their research with me.

54. Görlach, *The Textual Tradition*, 91. The *Life of St. Teilo* is in the hand of scribes A(1) and C(3), whose Gloucestershire dialects are identified in Angus McIntosh, M. L. Samuels, and Michael Benskin, *A Linguistic Atlas of Late Medieval English: County Dictionary* (Aberdeen: Aberdeen University Press, 1986), 4:196, LP 7110. Kooper and Callander, in their forthcoming edition of the *Life*, argue that the scribes had a Middle English exemplar that contained traces of a southeastern English dialect.

55. Edited in *The Text of the Book of Llan Dâv*, 97–117. Although the *Vita Sancti Teiliaui* in Cotton Vespasian A.xiv remains unedited, a full collation is provided in *The Text of the Book of Llan Dâv*, 360–62.

56. Fol. 94v et passim.

57. *English Benedictine Kalendars*, 2:40, 45.

58. The Middle English *Life* has Teilo consecrated bishop at the same point in the narrative as the Book of Llandaf version, while the Vespasian version does not have this episode. See fol. 96v, lines 11–18; *Text of the Book of Llan Dâv*, 107, 361. The Middle English *Life* also contains two miracles that are not found in the Vespasian version, but present in the Book of Llandaf: the healing of a paralytic and a king who goes mad from violating the church of Llandeilo. See fol. 98r, line 37, to fol. 98v, line 4; *Text of the Book of Llan Dâv*, 116–17, 361.

59. Brooke, "St Peter of Gloucester and St Cadoc of Llancarfan" (1986), 92.

60. John Reuben Davies, *Book of Llandaf*, 134.

61. For a review of Arthurian material in Welsh vitae, see Andrew Breeze, "Arthur in Early Saints' Lives," in *The Arthur of Medieval Latin Literature*, ed. Siân Echard (Cardiff: University of Wales Press, 2011), 26–41.

62. Battle Abbey and Tewkesbury Abbey, as well as Hereford and Worcester, may reward further study in this regard. Although the comparison does not align in all the details, Jocelin of Furness wrote a new life of St. Patrick at the behest of John de Courcy. Here, too, colonial expansion provoked Celtic hagiography. See Seán Duffy, "The First Ulster Plantation: John de Courcy and the Men of Cumbria," in *Colony and Frontier in Medieval Ireland: Essays Presented to J. F. Lydon*, ed. T. B. Barry, Robin Frame, and Katharine Simms (London: Hambledon Press, 1995), 1–28, at 8–9.

63. *GCO*, 6:39: "Rogerus autem, qui plus ceteris locum infestans, et cuncta quae ab aliis relicta videbantur palam asportans libris, ornamentis, et privilegiis ecclesiam ex toto privavit."

64. Thomson, "Books and Learning at Gloucester Abbey," provides the best overview. Unfortunately, no book catalog survives for Gloucester Abbey for this period. For partial lists from the later Middle Ages, see *English Benedictine Libraries: The Shorter Catalogues*, ed. R. Sharpe et al., Corpus of British Medieval Library Catalogues 4 (London: British Library in association with the British Academy, 1996), 245–55.

65. Thomson, "Books and Learning at Gloucester Abbey," 7 et passim.

66. *GCO*, 4:107.

67. Osbern's unpublished theological works are found in MS British Library, Royal 6 D.ix. For the most recent edition of the *Liber deriuationum*, see Osbern Claudianus, *Derivazioni*, ed. P. Busdraghi et al., 2 vols. (Spoleto: Centro italiano di studi sull'Alto Medioevo, 1996).

68. Thomson, "Books and Learning at Gloucester Abbey," 6.

69. Thomson, "Books and Learning at Gloucester Abbey."

70. *Original Acta of St. Peter's Abbey*, xxiv–xxv. See also *Registrum Anglie de libris doctorum et auctorum veterum*, ed. Richard H. Rouse and Mary A. Rouse (London: British Library, 1991), 292–93.

71. Thomson, "Books and Learning at Gloucester Abbey," 12–14.

72. F. G. Cowley, *The Monastic Order in South Wales, 1066–1349* (Cardiff: University of Wales Press, 1977), 46.

73. *DNC*, xv n. 3; Stollberg, *Die soziale Stellung*, 72; Thomson, "Books and Learning at Gloucester Abbey," 4.

74. *DNC*, 2.2, p. 132: "Gregorium Gloucestrie monachum uidi . . ."

75. *DNC*, xv, esp. n. 3.

76. Outside of Walter Map, the only other mention of Gregory comes from Gregory of Caerwent (fl. 1237), a monk who partially compiled the annals of Gloucester Abbey. While a medieval version of Gregory of Caerwent's work does not survive, Laurence Nowell made a copy in the mid-sixteenth century that is still extant (MS British Library, Cotton Vespasian A.v, fols.

195r–203v). Under the year 1157 (fol. 199v) is written, "Obiit piae memoriae Gregorius Monacus Glocestriae cuius sancti exercitii testes sunt multi libri in ecclesia sua manu scripti" (Here died Gregory monk of Gloucester, of pious memory; the witnesses of his holy toil are the many books in the church written by his hand). See also Adrian Morey and C. N. L. Brooke, *Gilbert Foliot and His Letters* (Cambridge: Cambridge University Press, 1965), 80; and Michael Hare, "The Chronicle of Gregory of Caerwent: A Preliminary Account," *Glevensis: The Gloucester and District Archaeological Research Group Review* 27 (1993): 42–44.

77. Thomson, "Books and Learning at Gloucester Abbey," 9 et passim. This identification assumes that the two Gregories—Walter's and Gregory of Caerwent's—are one and the same.

78. Stollberg, *Die soziale Stellung*, 72: "Möglich ist ferner, daß Walter auch Gilbert Foliot, der ihn um 1173 in das Londoner Kapitel aufnahm, bereits aus Gloucester oder Hereford kannte und sogar bereits seit frühen Zeiten Gilberts protégé war, was aber gleichfalls nicht zu belegen ist" (Moreover, it is possible that Walter also already knew Gilbert Foliot, who received him into the London chapter around 1173, from Gloucester or Hereford and that he had perhaps already been Gilbert's protégé since an earlier time; this likewise cannot be proven). See also *DNC*, xv–xvi.

79. *The Letters and Charters of Gilbert Foliot*, ed. Z. N. Brooke, Adrian Morey, and C. N. L. Brooke (Cambridge: Cambridge University Press, 1967), no. 439, p. 475.

80. *DNC*, 1.12, p. 36; 1.24, p. 80; 2.27, p. 202; 4.5, pp. 312–14.

81. Thomson, "Books and Learning at Gloucester Abbey," 4.

82. *DNC*, 1.2, p. 134: "Hoc de ipso postmodum abbati suo Hamelino retuli" (I afterward told Hamelin, his abbot, about his deed).

83. London, The National Archives, C115/K2/6683/sec. viii, no. 12, fol. 141v, cited in *DNC*, xv n. 3. The charter is dated 1148x74.

84. Stollberg, *Die soziale Stellung*, 74: "jedoch sind auch Besuche in Gloucester etwa von Westbury aus in späterer Zeit denkbar, ohne daß Walter in Gloucester die Schule besucht hatte" (however, visits to Gloucester at a later time, perhaps from Westbury, are also possible without Walter having attended the school in Gloucester).

85. *GCO*, 4:222–25.

86. *GCO*, 4:219.

87. Stollberg, *Die soziale Stellung*, 72 n. 10.

88. *DNC*, 2.3, p. 134.

89. *Historia et cartularium monasterii Sancti Petri Gloucestriae*, 2:156.

90. *DNC*, 2.10, p. 148.

91. For example, Walter's most recent editors recognize this tale as a "developed version" of the same episode found in Welsh hagiography. See *DNC*, 2.10, p. 148 n. 1. However, they do not make the connection with St. Peter's Abbey, nor do they speculate on how Walter obtained this story. See also Brooke, "St Peter of Gloucester and St Cadoc of Llancarfan" (1963), 303 n. 2.

92. E.g., Elissa R. Henken, *Traditions of the Welsh Saints* (Woodbridge: D. S. Brewer, 1987), 93–94.

93. The two earlier lives are edited and translated in *Vitae Sanctorum Britanniae et Genealogiae*, 24–141 (*Vita Sancti Cadoci*); 194–233 (*Vita Sancti Iltuti*); see 62–64 and 196–97 for the episodes in question. Caradog's life is edited in "Vie de Saint Cadoc par Caradoc de Llancarfan," ed. P. Grosjean, *Analecta Bollandiana* 60 (1942): 35–67, with the splitting of the earth episode occuring at 53.

94. For the connections between Llandaf and St. Peter's, see Smith, "An Edition, Translation, and Introduction" 61–62; John Reuben Davies, *Book of Llandaf,* 105–8; Hughes, "British

Library MS. Cotton Vespasian A. xiv," 63–64. The surviving *Vita Sancti Iltuti* was written after 1120, though it was likely reworked from an older source with the intention of discrediting earlier tradition of St. Illtud in order to support the interests of the diocese of Llandaf. See Davies, *Book of Llandaf,* 133–34.

95. *English Benedictine Kalendars*, 2:40, 45.

96. Caradog's *Vita Sancti Cadoci* reworks a late eleventh-century life written by Lifris. See Emanuel, "Analysis of the Composition of the 'Vita Cadoci'"; Brooke, "St Peter of Gloucester and St Cadoc of Llancarfan" (1963), 283–322; Wendy Davies, "Property Rights and Property Claims," 519–24. Emanuel argues that Lifris's life as we have it in Vespasian contains later interpolations, while Brooke claims that most of these interpolations actually stem from Lifris himself. For the dating of Lifris's life, see John Reuben Davies, *Book of Llandaf,* 76 n. 2.

97. John Reuben Davies, *Book of Llandaf,* 108, 133–34; Brooke, "St Peter of Gloucester and St Cadoc of Llancarfan" (1963), 310–15; Hughes, "British Library MS. Cotton Vespasian A. xiv," 59–60; Knight, "St. Tatheus of Caerwent," 33–35.

98. For the conflation of *Tathwy* and *Metheus*, see Knight, "St. Tatheus of Caerwent," 32.

99. It is uncertain when the monks at Gloucester added Gwynllyw to their calendar: in the only surviving twelfth-century calendar, "Sancti Gundley" appears as a later thirteenth- or fourteenth-century addition. See *English Benedictine Kalendars*, 2:46. However, given the poor survival rate of Gloucester manuscripts, it is difficult to draw any firm conclusions from this.

100. For some of the difficulties in interpreting archaic British names, especially in the early Middle Ages, see Paul Russell, "Old Welsh *Dinacat, Cunedag, Tutagual*: Fossilised Phonology in Brittonic Personal Names," in *Indo-European Perspectives in Honour of Anna Morpurgo Davies*, ed. J. H. W. Penney (Oxford: Oxford University Press 2004), 447–60.

101. Kenneth Jackson, *Language and History in Early Britain: A Chronological Survey of the Brittonic Languages, First to Twelfth Century A.D.* (Edinburgh: Edinburgh University Press, 1953), 297.

102. For the orthography of early British Latin and Old Welsh, see, inter alia, Jackson, *Language and History in Early Britain*; Sims-Williams, "Emergence of Old Welsh, Cornish and Breton Orthography"; Charles-Edwards, *Wales and the Britons*, 75–173; Alexander Falileyev, *Llawlyfr Hen Gymraeg* (Caerfyrddin: Y Coleg Cymraeg Cenedlaethol, 2016), 7–9.

103. The list is published in Léon Fleuriot, "Les évêques de la 'Clas Kenedyr,' évêché disparu de la région de Hereford," *Études Celtiques* 15 (1976–78): 225–26. For an analysis, see John Reuben Davies, "The Archbishoprics of St Davids and the Bishops of *Clas Cynidr*," in *St David of Wales: Cult, Church and Nation*, ed. J. Wyn Evans and Jonathan M. Wooding (Woodbridge: Boydell Press, 2007), 296–304.

104. Most recently in John Koch, *Cunedda, Cynan, Cadwallon, Cynddylan: Four Welsh Poems and Britain, 383–655* (Aberystwyth: University of Wales Centre for Advanced Welsh and Celtic Studies, 2013), 107–9. See also Sims-Williams, "Emergence of Old Welsh, Cornish and Breton Orthography," 25; Jackson, *Language and History in Early Britain*, 295; and Russell, "Old Welsh *Dinacat, Cunedag, Tutagual*," 453.

105. Juliette Wood very briefly noted the Latinate forms of a few of Walter's Welsh names in "Walter Map: The Contents and Context of *De Nugis Curialium*," 94.

106. See, e.g., *Brut y Tywysogyon*, 186 ("Llangadawc"); *Trioedd Ynys Prydein: The Welsh Triads*, ed. and trans. Rachel Bromwich, 2nd ed. (Cardiff: University of Wales Press, 1978), 251 ("Cadawc ap Gwynlliw Varvoc").

107. Jackson, *Language and History in Early Britain*, 296–99; Sims-Williams, "Emergence of Old Welsh, Cornish and Breton Orthography," 63–71. For an analysis of this suffix, see Paul

Russell, *Celtic Word-Formation: The Velar Suffixes* (Dublin: School of Celtic Studies, Dublin Institute of Advanced Studies, 1990), 16–28, 32–60; and Russell, "Old Welsh *Dinacat, Cunedag, Tutagual*," 457.

108. Jackson, *Language and History in Early Britain*, 298.

109. *DNC*, 2.11, pp. 148–54. The names in this tale are the only other examples of the Latin forms of the Welsh suffix *-(i)og* in the *De nugis curialium*.

110. It is unlikely, for example, that Walter would have represented the sound /ʉ/ as *u*, since *i* or *y* would perhaps be expected in an Anglo-Norman context (cf. Bede's *Dinoot* for Old Welsh /dʉːˈnaud/).

111. Jackson, *Language and History in Early Britain*, 479–80; Paul Russell, "Some Neglected Sources for Middle Welsh Phonology," *Études Celtiques* 29 (1992): 383–90, at 386.

112. Jackson, *Language and History in Early Britain*, 473–80.

113. *DNC*, 2.25, p. 198. J. E. Lloyd first identified *Cheueslinus* as *Genillyn* in *Walter Map's "De Nugis Curialium,"* 107 n. 2. This identification seems probable for two reasons. First of all, confusion between a majuscule *c* and *g* is easy to understand: a similar error seems to have occurred with *Clotguin* being read as *Gloitguin* in the Harleian genealogies. See Ben Guy, "A Second Witness to the Welsh Material in Harley 3859," *Quaestio Insularis* 15 (2014): 72–91. I would like to thank Ben for making his article available to me prior to its publication. Second, *ch* for *c* (/k/) occurs in Anglo-Norman environments and elsewhere in Medieval Latin. See Short, *Manual of Anglo-Norman*, §27.1, p. 123; *LSM*, 7:169–71, §131. Another instance of this latter phenomenon in the *De nugis curialium* is the spelling of *Chnut* for *Cnut* at *DNC*, 5.4, p. 422 and the following pages. *Chenedre* for *Cynidr* likely witnesses the same process. See Fleuriot, "Les évêques de la "Clas Kenedyr," 15.

114. *DNC*, 2.22, p. 186 et passim; 2.25, p. 198; 2.23, p. 189. Although unidentified in all the translations of the *De nugis curialium*, the name *Golenus* is clearly the Latin form of the not-uncommon Welsh name *Gollwyn* (note that in Welsh-Latin orthography, the letter *e* can represent the diphthong /uɨ/, spelled *wy* in Modern Welsh; cf. *Oudoceus* for *Euddogwy*). See also Sims-Williams, "Emergence of Old Welsh, Cornish and Breton Orthography," 49–59; Russell, "Old Welsh *Dinacat, Cunedag, Tutagual*," 457. Because Walter calls this character "Golenus bard" (Golenus the poet), a relationship between Golenus and the "Gellan telynyaur penkerd" that appears in the *Historia Gruffud vab Kenan* has been tentatively suggested. See *Historia Gruffud vab Kenan*, ed. D. Simon Evans (Cardiff: University of Wales Press, 1997), 21, 87 n. 21.13–14. However, aside from their poetic associations, there seems to be no compelling reason to link them, especially since *Gellan* is a poorly attested name, though it could have been known among the non-Welsh in southeastern Wales, as the name does appear in the Book of Llandaf. See *Text of the Book of Llan Dâv*, 146, 154, 157, 202.

115. Cf. "et sanctus Iltuit, inter Walenses famosissimus" in John Scott, *The Early History of Glastonbury: An Edition, Translation and Study of William of Malmesbury's "De antiquitate Glastonie Ecclesie"* (Woodbridge: Boydell Press, 1981), §22, p. 70.

116. *DNC*, 2.10, p. 148. In Old and Middle Welsh, *brenin* is often spelled *brenhin*.

117. Examples of unlenited nouns in apposition are easy to come by in Middle Welsh, especially with the word *brenin* (king). See T. J. Morgan, *Y Treigladau a'u Cystrawen* (Cardiff: University of Wales Press, 1952), §50.2, pp. 122–23. Conversely, it is not difficult to imagine that a courtier and Marcher like Walter knew the Welsh word for "king"; perhaps Walter simply attached the name to Cadog and the unmarked lenition signifies nothing but Walter's ignorance of Welsh grammar. Cf. the unmarked or absent mutation in "Golenus bard" at *DNC*, 2.23, p. 188.

118. *Vitae Sanctorum Britanniae et Genealogiae*, 90.

119. "Vie de Saint Cadoc par Caradoc de Llancarfan," 58: "princeps super Gunluniat [*sic*]."

120. Brooke, "St Peter of Gloucester and St Cadoc of Llancarfan" (1986), 83–84 n. 145.

121. *DNC*, 2.9, p. 146; 2.22–23, pp. 187–97.

122. *DNC*, 2.11, p. 148.

123. See Chapter 2, this volume.

124. I would like to thank Paul Russell for this suggestion.

125. *DNC*, 2.11, p. 148.

126. *DNC*, 2.11, p. 154: "quod de non inuento fingi potuit error huiusmodi."

127. Brynley Roberts, "Melusina: Medieval Welsh and English Analogues," in *Mélusines continentales et insulaires: Actes du colloque international tenu les 27 et 28 mars 1997 à l'Université Paris XII et au Collège des Irlandais*, ed. Jeanne-Marie Boivin and Proinsias MacCana (Paris: Champion, 1999), 281–96.

128. Speaking of the name *Wastinus Wastaniauc*, Roberts writes, "This might be acceptable if we believed that Map's legend had a written source which preserved archaic forms, but it appears more likely that his source was oral, whether directly in Welsh or at least one remove, in Latin." Roberts, "Melusina," 285–86.

129. *Historia et cartularium monasterii Sancti Petri Gloucestriae*, 1:314: "Glesburiam, cum omnibus ad eam pertinentibus, liberam et quietam ab omni saeculari servitio et consuetudine, in perpetuam elemosinam; et ecclesiam Sancti Kenedri in eadem villa cum omnibus pertinentiis suis. Concedo etiam eis, et carta mea confirm, totam decimam totius dominii mei per totam terram in Brecheinauc in bosco et in plano, quicunque dominium meum habuerint vel coluerint, scilicet annonae, pecorum, caseorum, venationis, et mellis, et de omnibus aliis rebus de quibus decimae dari debent."

130. Harris, "Kalendar."

131. *Cartularium Prioratus S. Johannis Evangelistae de Brecon*, 35–36; *Historia et cartularium monasterii Sancti Petri Gloucestriae*, 1:315. For another dispute between the priory and the abbey regarding tithes in Talgarth, see *Cartularium Prioratus*, 102–3.

132. *Historia et cartularium monasterii Sancti Petri Gloucestriae*, 1:315.

133. *Cartularium Prioratus*, 34–35.

134. Edited in *Vitae Sanctorum Britanniae et Genealogiae*, 313–15; and in *Early Welsh Genealogical Tracts*, ed. P. C. Bartrum (Cardiff: University of Wales Press, 1966), 14–16. A translation and historical analysis of the tract is found in Charles Thomas, *And Shall These Mute Stones Speak? Post-Roman Inscriptions in Western Britain* (Cardiff: University of Wales Press, 1994), 131–62. However, Ben Guy has recently reevaluated and redited the *De situ Brecheniauc* as well as its related documents in "*De situ Brecheniauc* and Related Texts."

135. Guy, "*De situ Brecheniauc* and Related Texts." Thomas has argued that the *De situ Brecheniauc* contains much earlier material, dating from perhaps the sixth century (*And Shall These Mute Stones Speak*, 131–35). Patrick Sims-Williams agrees that the tracts were put in their current form in the early postconquest period, though he cautions that "several religious centres in this small area played a part in the development of the Brychan legends," in "The Provenance of the Llywarch Hen Poems: A Case for Llan-gors, Brycheiniog" *Cambrian Medieval Celtic Studies* 26 (1993): 27–63, at 58. Overall, Guy's analysis is the most thorough and convincing.

136. Edited in *Vitae Sanctorum Britanniae et Genealogiae*, 315–18; and in *Early Welsh Genealogical Tracts*, 17–19. For the relationship with the *De situ Brecheniauc*, see Thomas, *And Shall These Mute Stones Speak*, 131–62. The *Cognacio Brychan* has also been reedited in Guy, "*De situ Brecheniauc* and Related Texts."

137. Guy, "*De situ Brecheniauc* and Related Texts."

138. Guy, "*De situ Brecheniauc* and Related Texts."

139. "Kehingayr filia Brachan, mater sancti Kenider de Glesbyri" (*Early Welsh Genealogical Tracts*, 15).

140. Hughes, "British Library MS. Cotton Vespasian A. xiv," 59.

141. Guy, "*De situ Brecheniauc* and Related Texts."

142. See note 48 above.

143. Hughes, "British Library MS. Cotton Vespasian A. xiv," 59–60.

144. Harris, "Kalendar," 42–44.

145. Edited in *Vitae Sanctorum Britanniae et Genealogiae*, 319; *Early Welsh Genealogical Tracts*, 21; Harris, "Kalendar," 43. The manuscript is damaged here and around half of the text of the *Generatio* is missing. However, a transcript made by Sir John Price (Cotton MS Domitian i, fol. 160r) contains the full version.

146. Harris, "Kalendar," 42–43.

147. Harris, "Kalendar," 43 n. 128.

148. Harris, "Kalendar," 42–44. Monmouth held the benefice of Weston-sub-Edge, a few miles from Evesham Abbey, the seat of Ecgwine's cult, and they had ample reason to be interested in Cadog. Moreover, two churches dedicated to Cynidr were nearby. Harris, however, was writing before Hughes claimed a Gloucester provenance for much of the material in the Vespasian manuscript. Nonetheless, it may well be that Monmouth found the *Generatio Sancti Egweni* attractive for these exact reasons and therefore requested a copy from Gloucester. As Harris notes, Vespasian contains enough blank pages that the compiler could have easily included the *Generatio Sancti Egweni* without difficulty. The scribe, therefore, seems to have copied this genealogy from another document after the completion of the manuscript in order to add more information about St. Ecgwine.

149. First suggested in passing by Hughes, "British Library MS. Cotton Vespasian A. xiv," 59.

150. Michael Lapidge, for example, sees the *Generatio* as merely evidence of Ecgwine's popularity in "The Medieval Hagiography of St. Ecgwine," *Research Papers: The Vale of Evesham Historical Society* 6 (1977): 77–93, at 82.

151. *English Benedictine Kalendars*, 2:42, 52, 55.

152. *Historia et cartularium monasterii Sancti Petri Gloucestriae*, 1:6.

153. Two thirteenth-century taxation lists in the Cartulary of St. John's Priory (Brecon) consistently spell the name of the patron saint of Llanigon as *Eguino*. See *Cartularium Prioratus*, 18–21.

154. Richard Morgan and R. F. Peter Powell, *A Study of Breconshire Place-Names* (Llanrwst: Gwasg Carreg Gwalch, 1999), 46. The spelling of *-dlos* for *-llys* seems to be another attempt to indicate the sound /ɬ/ by those not literate in Welsh. Cf. *Gundleus* for *Gwynllyw* throughout his vita in *Vitae Sanctorum Britanniae et Genealogiae*, 172–93.

155. Morey and Brooke, *Gilbert Foliot and His Letters*, 124–46; Brooke, "St Peter of Gloucester and St Cadoc of Llancarfan" (1986), 60–64.

156. A Gloucester provenance allows for a somewhat more precise dating of the *Generatio Sancti Egweni*. Obviously, the *Generatio* does not represent (even in a distorted manner) any ancient traditions: Ecgwine was almost completely unknown until Byrhtferth of Ramsey composed his life (ca. 1016), and the *Generatio* stands alone in making Cadog and Cynidr brothers. Gloucester had acquired Glasbury by 1088 and Llancarfan by 1102. A *terminus ante quem*, however, is more difficult to discern. Although St. Peter's traded Glasbury manor for the manor of Eastleach Martin in Gloucestershire in 1144, it retained the church of St. Cynidr. For the details of this odd arrangement, see *Historia et cartularium monasterii Sancti Petri Gloucestriae*, 1:311–14;

Brooke, "St Peter of Gloucester and St Cadoc of Llancarfan" (1963), 282–83; Golding, "Trans-Border Transactions," 39. Similarly, St. Peter's kept a close watch on Llancarfan, even after it leased the property to the archdeacons of Llandaf. Therefore, the *Generatio* could have feasibly been composed sometime between 1102 and sometime shortly after 1200, when it was copied into the Monmouth calendar.

157. *DNC*, 2.11, p. 148. Walter's preference for *stagnum Brekeniauc* does not indicate vagueness about the lake's actual name; rather, he follows the early practice as referring to Llangorse Lake as "The Mere/Lake of Brycheiniog." See *GCO*, 6:33 ("lacus ille de Brecheniauc magnus et famosus, quem et Clamosum dicunt"); *Vitae Sanctorum Britanniae et Genealogiae*, 316 ("ad sanctum Gastayn, cuius nunc ecclesia [i.e., Llangasty Tal-y-llyn] sita est iuxta Maram"); *Cartularium Prioratus*, 26 ("Mara"); *Anglo-Saxon Chronicle: A Collaborative Edition*, 5:76 sub anno 916 ("Brecenanmere"). The *cors* of *Llangorse*, a name first attested in the modern era, merely means "swamp, bog, marsh." The Welsh name for the lake is *Llyn Syfaddan*. For further discussion, see R. F. Peter Powell, "Llyn Llan-gors," *Brycheiniog* 22 (1986–87): 39–41.

158. *DNC*, 2.11, p. 150: "Libens tibi seruiam, et tota obediam deuocione usque in diem illum quo prosilire uolens ad clamores ultra Leuem [rect. *Leueni*] me freno tuo percusseris."

159. *DNC*, 2.11, p. 150: "Est autem Leuem [rect. *Leueni*] aqua uicina stagno."

160. Fol. 26r.

161. The presence of a "silent" *e* may be an Anglo-Normanism. See Russell, "Some Neglected Sources," 386.

162. *GCO*, 6:21: "lacus ille magnus, qui fluvium Leveni ex se transmittit."

163. Fol. 26r–v.

164. If the spellings of the Vespasian manuscript are closest to Walter's source, then *brecheniauc* may be the form that Walter encountered, although it is quite possible that a scribe has scrambled the minims here. However, *brekeíuauc* could perfectly well represent *brekeinawc* (Modern Welsh *Brycheinog*), an alternative form, probably southern in origin (Russell, *Celtic Word-Formation*, 48). If, however, *Reynos* stands for *Reinuc* (Modern Welsh *Rheinwg*), then perhaps *brekeinauc* is more appropriate, since both would show *-og* instead of *-iog*. It is interesting to note that the *Historia et cartularium* of St. Peter's Abbey never once uses an *-iog* form, but has *Breuheynauc, Breyhenoc,* and *Brecheinauc* in addition to other Latinized and bastardized forms. See *Historia et cartularium monasterii Sancti Petri Gloucestriae*, 3:339. It is even possible that Vespasian A.xiv is itself ambiguous here and that Wade-Evans has been misled by relying on the familiar modern form of the word with the *-iog* suffix.

165. It is also doubtful that he would choose *e* for the schwa-like sound of the first syllable of both words: while *e* could certainly represent a schwa in both the Anglo-Norman French and the English of the twelfth century, it does so only in final syllables.

166. *Calendar of Inquisitions Post Mortem and Other Analogous Documents*, vol. 5, *Edward II* (London: Printed for His Majesty's Stationery Office by Mackie, 1908), no. 538, p. 334.

167. However, it may be worthwhile noting that Walter does not use a Latin form of *Brycheiniog* common in contemporary documents, but, like Gerald of Wales, he (or more likely his source) prefers the vernacular form. See *GCO*, 6:20, 31, 32, et passim.

168. The difference between *Deheubard* and *Deheubarth* is of little consequence and could result from variation in native Welsh orthography or Anglo-Norman influence. Cf. *Talgard* in place of *Talgarth* in *Historia et cartularium monasterii Sancti Petri Gloucestriae*, 1:315; *Vitae Sanctorum Britanniae et Genealogiae*, 26, 319; and the common variations on *Iorwert/Iorwerth/Iorwerd* and *Mareduth/Maredud*. Ample instances of these last two sets, sometimes within the same

document, can be found in *The Acts of Welsh Rulers, 1120–1283*, ed. Huw Pryce (Cardiff: University of Wales Press, 2005).

169. For the interpolated glosses of the *De nugis curialium*, see Chapter 3, this volume.

170. In particular *GCO*, 6:20–36.

171. Charles-Edwards, *Wales and the Britons*, 548–49.

172. It may be worthwhile considering a possible anachronism in Walter's text. As has been noted, Deheubarth was established by Hywel Dda in the tenth century, and thus did not exist in the putative time of Brychan. See Thomas, *And Shall These Mute Stones Speak*, 150; Roberts, "Melusina," 291. It could be significant that *De situ Brecheniauc* imagines the same anachronistic scenario in an attempt to nourish grandiose claims for the region's past. That Walter, who has no discernable reason to show partiality to Brycheiniog, retains this peculiar detail would thus be solid evidence that he was using the *De situ Brecheniauc* or a similar document as a source. However, it is entirely possible that Deheubarth here is being used in the generic sense of South Wales, with little regard to strict political definitions, and therefore the apparent shared anachronism reflects nothing more than a common broad understanding of Deheubarth as simply a synonym for South Wales.

173. *Vitae Sanctorum Britanniae et Genealogiae*, 314; *Early Welsh Genealogical Tracts*, 15: "Clytguin filius Brachan, qui invasit totam terram Sudgwalliae. Clydouc sanctus et Dedyu sanctus filii illius Clytguein." Cf. the corresponding passage in the *Cognacio Brychan* (in *Vitae Sanctorum Britanniae et Genealogiae*, 317; *Early Welsh Genealogical Tracts*, 18): "Clytwyn, a oresgynnaud Deheubarth, qui pater erat sanctorum Clydauc et Dettu" (Clytwyn, who conquered Deheubarth, who was the father of Saints Clydauc and Dettu).

174. M. R. James leaves it untranslated in his 1923 translation, as do Tupper and Ogle in their 1924 rendition; Brooke and Mynors have without comment altered James's translation, supplying "Montgomery" (*DNC*, 2.11, p. 153), followed by Bate (*CPGC*, 147). Roberts suggests the *cum mouric/mouruc* in Archenfield, attested in the Book of Llandaf ("Melusina," 290 n. 23).

175. Confusion between a majuscule *c* and *g* would account for the greatest difference, since the normal Latin word for Montgomery is *Mons Gumeri* or *Gumericii*.

176. Roberts has identified these as the Tri Chrugiau, on the ridge of Mynydd Epynt, a location that suits a battle between Deheubarth and Brycheiniog. See Roberts, "Melusina," 290–91.

177. *DNC*, 2.11, p. 152.

178. James, identifying this passage as corrupt, translates as "Your land of Rheinwg (i.e., Brycheiniog) can fight no more from this moment, for there are no beasts left." *DNC*, 2.11, p. 153. I suspect that Bradley, "Notes on Walter Map's *De Nugis Curialium*," 396, is correct when he suggests that "animalia desunt" may have at one time read "nonnulla desunt." In light of my earlier discussion in Chapter 3 of the presence of interpolated glosses in the manuscript, this suggestion seems particularly compelling. Thus, "amodo quasi nonnulla desunt" (from henceforth it is as if something is missing) was once a scribe's interlinear gloss that, like many others in the *De nugis curialium*, eventually became incorporated into the main text before another scribe, not recognizing this passage as containing an interpolated interlinear gloss, attempted—unsuccessfully—to make sense of this clearly corrupt passage by changing *nonnulla* to *animalia*.

179. First suggested by John Rhys in James's notes to *Walter Map: De nugis curialium*, 265; and echoed by J. E. Lloyd in James's translation *Walter Map's "De Nugis Curialium*," 81, and the present editors. See also Roberts, "Melusina," 289–90.

180. P. C. Bartrum, "Rhieinwg and Reinwg," *Bulletin of the Board of Celtic Studies* 24 (1970): 23–27.

181. Albert Derolez, *The Paleography of Gothic Manuscript Books: From the Twelfth to the Early Sixteenth Century* (Cambridge: Cambridge University Press, 2003), 137.

182. Bartrum, "Rhieinwg and Reinwg," 26–27.

183. J. R. F. Piette, "Yr Agwedd Lydewig ar y Chwedlau Arthuraidd," *Llên Cymru* 8 (1965): 183–90, at 186–87. Piette claims that the occurence of names that originally ended in a velar stop but that have a final /s/ in French texts suggests a "benthyciad ysgrifenedig" (written borrowing). Unfortunately, Piette never fully explains his logic here. However, it seems to me that these names have been brought into the Old French declensional system and that the normal masculine nominative singular ending *-s* has been added, producing the expected phonological result: cf. *le coc* (oblique singular) and *li cos* (nominative singular). Contrary to Piette's opinion, forms like *Meriadus* seem to have undergone some type of Gallicization, which, I would think, is more suggestive of oral transmission. If Old French morphology is to blame for the manuscript's *reynos*, then it could have occurred at several points in transmission: the nonnative scribe who drew together the legend in Brycheiniog, scribes at, say, Monmouth, Brecon, or Gloucester, or even Walter Map himself (who spoke French with native fluency).

184. All extant references are gathered in Bartrum, "Rhieinwg and Reinwg," 26–27. Aside from the two vitae, the name appears in the *Annales Cambriae* (MS C), the genealogical tracts *Bonedd y Saint* and *Plant Brychan*, the Welsh laws (Peniarth 32 and Peniarth 278), the early Welsh poetry of Llywarch Hen (who may have been of Brycheiniog extraction), and a poem to Hywel ap Goronwy (d. 1106), whose territorial interests lay in Buellt and Rhwng Gwy a Hafren, exactly where this archaic term may be expected to maintain some currency.

185. *DNC*, 2.11, p. 150.

186. *DNC*, 2.11, pp. 150, 152.

187. First suggested by Roberts, "Melusina," 289.

188. The *-ei-* in *brechein*, is only explicable as a back-formation, since all other instances of *Brychan* have the vowel *a* in the final syllable. Interestingly, if *brechein* is indeed a back-formation, then it again is more evidence that the form behind the scribe's *brecheiniauc* is *brecheinauc* and not *brecheniauc*. The variant forms *brehein* and *brekeinauc* where one may expect a spelling of *-ch-* suggest Anglo-Norman interference: alteration between the letters *h* and *ch* to indicate the sound /x/ are common occurrences in Latin and French documents in England, and interchange between *ch* and *k* in early French texts also occurs. Additionally, Medieval Latin in general, not only that found in an Anglo-Norman context, allows for *c* (and thus *k* in an Anglo-Norman environment) for *ch* and *h* for *ch*. Thus, from an original *ch* in a foreign word, a scribe could easily substitute either *k* or *h*, depending on what sound he believed *ch* to represent. It seems that one instance of each has occurred: *brehein* and *brekeinauc*. For the relevant orthographical developments in early French, Anglo-Norman, and Medieval Latin, see Mildred K. Pope, *From Latin to Modern French with Especial Consideration of Anglo-Norman: Phonology and Morphology* (Manchester: Manchester University Press, 1934), §1216, p. 456; §694.a, p. 277; *LSM*, 7:168–69, §128; 169, §130.

189. One sentence seems to call out for deriving the king's name from his territory: "Annuit rex, ingressique regnum Brehein a Brekeniauc [rect. *Brekeinauc*] predam multam collegerunt" (*DNC*, 2.11, p. 152; The king agreed, and after they had invaded Brychan's kingdom, they gathered a great deal of plunder from Brycheiniog). Incorrectly construing *a Brekeniauc* as dependent on *Brehein* instead of *collegerunt* could lead to the phrase *regnum Brehein a Brekeniauc* (the kingdom of Brychan from/of Brekeniauc). If this seems like a stretch, consider that all translations of Walter's text have been misled in exactly this manner, e.g., "Brychan of Brycheiniog"

and "Brychan de Brycheiniog" (*DNC*, 2.11, p. 153; *CPGC*, 147). Cf. the beginning of the *Vita Sancti Cadoci*, where personal names are generated from the terms for different cantrefs (*Vitae Sanctorum Britanniae et Genealogiae*, 25–26).

190. *Walter Map's "De Nugis Curialium,"* 77 n. 2.

191. Roberts, "Melusina," 286: "This is correct phonetically but it assumes that Map's names represent old, pre-vowel affection, forms, not contemporary ones."

192. Roberts, "Melusina," 286.

193. Short, *Manual of Anglo-Norman*, §28, pp. 124–25. Cf. the *g* in place of *w* in Germanic words borrowed into Medieval Latin (*LSM*, 7:152–53, §115). Roberts, like Rhys before him, assumes that the name displays the common variation between initial *gw-* and *w-* in Anglicized Welsh names. See Morgan and Morgan, *Welsh Surnames*, 8. The Brycheiniog setting and the similarity with Llangasty, however, suggests that the intended name is *Gastinus* and not *Gwastinus*. For another possible example of *g/w* alternation in the *De nugis curialium*, see the editors' suggestion that Walter's *Gado* stands for Old English *Wada* at *DNC*, xl. Cf. *Waleranius* for *Galeran* at *DNC*, 5.5, p. 446 and the following pages, if the identification in James Hinton, "Notes on Walter Map's 'De Nugis Curialium,'" *Studies in Philology*, 20 (1923): 448–68, at 462, is correct.

194. *Vitae Sanctorum Britanniae et Genealogiae*, 316, 314.

195. Thomas, *And Shall These Mute Stones Speak*, 132. Moreover, the *ad castra* of the *De situ Brecheniauc* suggests an earlier name beginning with the letter *c*. For later medieval spellings of *Llangasty* that suggest a name beginning with the letter *c*, see Morgan and Powell, *Study of Breconshire Place-Names*, 104.

196. *Vitae Sanctorum Britanniae et Genealogiae*, 28.

197. Although it is a slight point, the use of the suffix *-iog* in *Wastiniauc* may also indicate that name belongs to a different textual layer. If I am correct above in my argument that *brekeinauc* and *reynuc* are the forms that Walter encountered in his source, and that both witness the less common southern variant of this suffix (*-og*), then *Wastiniauc* would stick out as a different dialectical form. This may be a relic of the invention of this name; someone has created this word using the much more common variant *-iog* without noticing that it breaks the dialectical pattern for the rest of the document. Of course, it is possible that two different dialectical forms could appear in the same source.

198. *DNC*, 2.11, p. 150.

199. *GPC*, s.v. "baglog."

200. *Early Welsh Genealogical Tracts*, 82. Cf. "a Dinavt Vagloc" and its variants "dinawaed," "a chinawed," and "a Thinwaed," in *Trioedd Ynys Prydein*, no. 16, p. 28.

201. First proposed in S. Baring Gould and John Fisher, *Lives of the British Saints* (London: Published for the Honourable Society of Cymmrodorion by C. J. Clark, 1907–13), 4:265.

202. See Smith, "Gerald of Wales, Walter Map."

203. *DNC*, 2.11, p. 148: "stagnum Brekeniauc [rect. *Brekeinauc*], quod in circuitu duo miliaria tenet." James translates this passage as "which is two miles broad," but *circuitus* more properly applies to making a circuit around the lake. It takes over three modern miles to walk around the lake, and its present breadth is right at a mile at the broadest.

204. On the mixing of Welsh and Latin forms, see Jackson, *Language and History in Early Britain*, 296–98.

205. The *Vita Sancti Davidis* is edited in *GCO*, 3:377–404, 431–34. The *Vita Caradoci*, which celebrated a twelfth-century recluse from Brycheiniog, appears in abbreviated form in John of Tynemouth's massive fourteenth-century compilation of saints. It is edited in *Nova Legenda Anglie*, ed. Carl Horstman (Oxford: Clarendon Press, 1901), 1:174–76.

206. *GCO*, 6:47: "domicilium, felici quadam mediocritate studiis idoneum atque labori."

207. *GCO*, 6:31: "Erat autem antiquitus regionis illius, quae Brecheniauc dicitur, domina-tor vir potens et nobilis, cui nomen Brechanus; a quo et terra Brecheniauc denominata. De quo mihi notabile videtur, quod ipsum viginti quator habuisse filias historiae Britannicae testantur."

208. The *De situ Brecheniauc* claims that Brychan had twenty-five daughters, while the *Cognacio Brychan* gives twenty-four.

209. *GCO*, 6:28: "antiquis et authenticis partium istarum scriptis." Gerald added this sec-tion on Illtud during his second revision of the *Itinerarium*. See Amelia Borrego Sargent, "Vi-sions and Revisions: Gerald of Wales, Authorship, and the Construction of Political, Religious, and Legal Geographies in Twelfth and Thirteenth Century Britain" (Ph.D. diss., University of California, Berkeley, 2011), 258.

210. *Vitae Sanctorum Britanniae et Genealogiae*, 204–5.

211. For the opinion that the surviving *Vita Sancti Iltuti* was reworked from an earlier life to support the interests of Llandaf, see John Reuben Davies, *Book of Llandaf*, 133–34.

212. *Nova Legenda Anglie*, 2:109: "Multa alia de confessore isto glorioso in uno solo loco Wallie scripta vidi, que vetustate quasi deleta legi non poterant."

213. See Chapter 3, this volume.

214. *DNC,* 2.11, p. 148. Unfortunately, Walter's use of *referre* offers no clues as to the man-ner of transmission, since the word can refer to both written and oral narration. See *DMLBS*, s.v. "referre." It does not prove that Walter attributes this story to "tradizione orale gallese" (Welsh oral tradition) as Várvaro claims in *Apparizioni fantastiche*, 69.

215. *GCO*, 3:200–201.

216. *DNC,* 2.8, p. 146: "supra hominem angelis putares proximum."

217. *DNC,* 2.8, p. 146: "adeo firmiter et tanquam naturaliter inest eis Walensibus hebetudo mansuetudinis, ut si in aliquo uideantur modesti, in multis appareant discoli et siluestres."

218. *DNC,* 2.8, p. 146.

219. R. R. Davies, *Lordship and Society in the March of Wales*, 101.

220. See Ralph V. Turner, "Briouze, William (III) de (*d.* 1211)," in the *Oxford Dictionary of National Biography*. Confusingly, there are two William de Briouzes that could have told Walter this story—William II and his son William III. The editors of *DNC,* assume him to be William III, a favorite of King John. See *DNC,* 2.8, p. 146 n. 2. However, I see no particular reason to choose the son. The elder was closer in age to Walter, and he served as sheriff of Hereford from Easter 1173 to 1175.

221. *DNC,* 1.32, p. 130.

222. For an analysis of this tale, see Stephen Gordon, "Monstrous Words, Monstrous Bod-ies: Irony and the Walking Dead in Walter Map's *De nugis curialium*," *English Studies* 96, no. 4 (2015): 379–402.

223. *DNC,* 2.27, p. 202: "Willelmus Laudun, miles Anglicus, fortis uiribus et audacie pro-bate, uenit ad Gillebertum Foliot, tunc episcopum Herefordensem, nunc autem Lundoniensem."

224. Brock Holden, *Lords of the Central Marches: English Aristocracy and Frontier Society, 1087–1265* (Oxford: Oxford University Press, 2008), 47.

225. For Walter's views on the Welsh, see Chapter 1, this volume.

226. *DNC,* 2.9, p. 146: "Vidi Helyam heremitam Walensem, preclare fidei et uite probablis hominem."

227. *DNC,* 2.20–26, pp. 182–202.

228. *DNC,* 2.20–21, pp. 182–84. The chapter headings divide this coherent introduction to the habits of the Welsh into two separate chapters.

229. *DNC*, 2.22–24, pp. 186–96. That Llywelyn ap Gruffudd is the king's name is clear: "Luelinus iste, cum esset iuuenis, uiuente Griffino patre suo . . ." (*DNC*,2.23, p. 188). See also Chapter 1, this volume.

230. See Chapter 1, this volume.

231. The manuscript reads "super ripam stagni de Behthenio" (*DNC*, 2.22, p. 188). *Behthenio* is almost certainly a scribal error for *Brechenio*, a common Latin form of *Brycheiniog*. *Brechenio* may well represent the form Walter is most familiar with, thus making the appearance of the Welsh form *Brekeinauc* in the story of Gastin even more indicative of a written source.

232. *DNC*, 2.23, p. 196: "In rapina et furto Gloria Walensium." See also Chapter 1, this volume.

233. *DNC*, 2.26, p. 202: "Ecce quam stulta quamque iniusta est ira Walensium, et quam in sanguine<m> proni sunt."

234. For *Gestin* in place of *Iestyn*, see *Annales de Margan*, 12. For *Gistinus*, see *The Text of the Book of Llan Dâv*, 271–72. For *Resus* (Rhys), see Chapter 1, this volume.

235. For example, every time *Llywarch* appears in the surviving charters of the Welsh kings, it remains in the vernacular. See *Acts of Welsh Rulers*, nos. 63, 84, 121, 180, 229, 346, 504. And the *Annales Cambriae* entries of the twelfth century strongly prefer the vernacular form of the name, though one instance of *Lewarchi* does occur, but even then MS C has *Lyvarch*. See *Annales Cambriae*, ed. John Williams ab Ithel (London: Longman, Green, Longman, and Roberts, 1860), 52 and n. 17. On the other hand, the *Vita Griffini Filii Conani* unproblematically has *Lywarchus*. See *Vita Griffini Filii Conani: The Medieval Life of Gruffudd ap Cynan*, ed. and trans. Paul Russell (Cardiff: University of Wales Press, 2005), 60, 184. Nonetheless, as already mentioned, the mix of Welsh and Latin forms is to be expected in Medieval Latin documents produced in Wales. Gerald of Wales, for example, consistently employs Latin forms, yet he still uses the vernacular *Anaraut*, *Angharat*, *Cadelh*, and *Meuric*.

236. The equivalence of *Rhodri* and *Rothericus* has passed unnoticed in all editions and translations of the *De nugis curialium*. For a few examples, see *Acts of Welsh Rulers*, no. 405; and *GCO*, 6:126 et passim.

237. The manuscript reads *melıtıııı* with no suspension mark (fol. 32r). For *r*/*i* confusion in Welsh names, see also the discussion of *Cimmeired* (from the Book of Llandaf) and *Cimerred* (from Cotton Vespasian A.xiv) in Sims-Williams, "Emergence of Old Welsh, Cornish and Breton Orthography," 33, esp. n. 2.

238. *DNC*, 2.23, p. 188.

239. The French forms are too many to list, but the English/Germanic forms are as follows: *Edricus Wilde* (Eadric the Wild), *Aldnodus* (Alnoth), *Epelbertus*/*Edelbertus* (Ethelbert), *Edgarus* (Edgar), *Edwwardus* (Edward), *Edelredus* (Æthelred), *Eluredus* (Ælfred), *Godwinus* (Godwine), and *Chnutus* (Cnut). The one exception seems to be *Walenfreit* at *DNC*, 2.9, p. 146.

240. Brian Stock, *Listen for the Text: On the Uses of the Past* (Baltimore: Johns Hopkins University Press, 1990), 23.

241. For an account of his forgeries on Gloucester's behalf, see Morey and Brooke, *Gilbert Foliot and His Letters*, 124–46.

242. Smith, "Gerald of Wales, Walter Map."

243. For example, Henken, *Traditions of the Welsh Saints*, 93–94; Várvaro, *Apparizioni fantastiche*, 69; *CPGC*, 29–30. See also Rigg, *History of Anglo-Latin Literature*, 92.

244. Brooke, "St Peter of Gloucester and St Cadoc of Llancarfan" (1963), 303–4.

245. Brooke, "St Peter of Gloucester and St Cadoc of Llancarfan" (1963), 303.

246. Nerys Ann Jones and Morfydd E. Owen, "Twelfth-Century Welsh Hagiography: The

Gogynfeirdd Poems to the Saints," in *Celtic Hagiography*, ed. Jane Cartwright (Cardiff: University of Wales Press, 2003), 45–67.

247. Smith, "An Edition, Translation, and Introduction," §1, pp. 73–74.

CHAPTER 6

1. Yale MS 229 (image on fol. 272v), which dates to the late thirteenth century. For the image, see Elizabeth Morrison and Anne D. Hedeman, eds., *Imagining the Past in France: History in Manuscript Painting, 1250–1500* (Los Angeles: J. Paul Getty Museum, 2010), 111–14. For other examples of this iconography, which is sometimes identified as "Arthur and his scribe," see Martine Meuwese, "Crossing Borders: Text and Image in Arthurian Manuscripts," *Arthurian Literature* 24 (2007): 157–77, at 160, esp. n. 10. For the possibility that the images of Walter Map in the *Lancelot-Grail Cycle* do not actually represent Walter, see Richard Trachsler, "Gautier Map, une vieille connaissance," in *Façonner son personnage au Moyen Âge*, ed. Chantal Connochie-Bourgne (Aix-en-Provence: Presses universitaires de Provence, 2007), 319–28.

2. The complex history of transmission, expansion, and redaction of the *Lancelot-Grail Cycle* requires some explanation of terminology. Following many recent critics, I use the term to refer to the collection of five texts: the *Estoire del Saint Graal*, the *Estoire de Merlin*, the *Prose Lancelot*, the *Queste del Saint Graal*, and *La mort Artu*.

3. E. Jane Burns, "Introduction," in *The History of the Holy Grail*, trans. Carol J. Chase, vol. 1 of *Lancelot-Grail: The Old French Arthurian Vulgate and Post-Vulgate in Translation*, ed. Norris J. Lacy (Cambridge: D. S. Brewer, 2010; first published by Garland, 1992–96), xix–xx.

4. Thomas Stephens, *The Literature of the Kymry*, 2nd ed. (London: Longman, Green, 1876), 311; *Latin Poems Commonly Attributed to Walter Mapes*, viii.

5. Adolf Birch-Hirschfeld, *Die Sage vom Gral: Ihre Entwicklung und dichterische Ausbildung in Frankreich und Deutschland im 12. und 13. Jarhundert* (Leipzig: Vogel, 1877), 227–42.

6. Ferdinand Lot, *Étude sur le Lancelot en prose* (Paris: É. Champion, 1918), 127–29.

7. In favor of an earlier Latin version is Ronald E. Pepin, "Walter Map and Yale MS 229," in *Essays on the "Lancelot" of Yale 229*, ed. Elizabeth M. Willingham (Turnhout: Brepols, 2007), 15–17, at 16. See C. L. K.'s review of Lot's book in *English Historical Review* 35, no. 137 (1920): 304–6, which suggests that the *Queste* could be based on a lost romance by Walter. (My thanks to an anonymous reader for suggesting that C. L. K. is C. L. Kingsford [1862–1926].) J. Neale Carman suggests that Walter may have collaborated with Eleanor of Aquitaine in the initial stages of the *Prose Lancelot*. See J. Neale Carman, *A Study of the Pseudo-Map Cycle of Arthurian Romance* (Lawrence: University Press of Kansas), 109–11. A few scholars have suggested that Walter Map wrote the Anglo-Norman romance on which Ulrich von Zatzikhoven based his *Lanzelet*. See K. G. T. Webster, "Walter Map's French Things," *Speculum* (1940): 272–79, at 276.

8. Walter visited Marie de Champagne and her husband, Henry I, Count of Champagne, at their chateau in Troyes, shortly before Henry set out on crusade in 1179 (*DNC*, 5.5, p. 450). June Hall McCash tantalizingly suggests that Walter may have met Chrétien de Troyes during his stay in Troyes in "Chrétien's Patrons," in *A Companion to Chrétien de Troyes*, ed. Norris J. Lacy and Joan Tasker Grimbert (Cambridge: D. S. Brewer, 2005), 26–42, at 20–21. See also Carey, *Ireland and the Grail*, 347–48.

9. Lot also thought him a good choice because of Walter's associations with the Welsh (see *Étude sur le Lancelot*, 128–29). R. E. Bennett suggested that Walter's romance of Sadius and

Galo, which he saw as "the finest, if not the finest of Latin chivalric romances," shows that Walter could write sustained romances ("Walter Map's *Sadius and Galo,*" 56). Bate also believed that the Sadius and Galo romance demonstrates Walter's facility with the genre (*CPGC*, 58–70). Walter's recent editors see the ascriptions both as ironic and as evidence that Walter must have done something to render his reputation such as it is (see *DNC*, xxi–xxiii). Similar explanations are found in Jean Frappier, *Étude sur "La Mort le Roi Artu,"* 2nd ed. (Geneva: Droz, 1961), 21.

10. Frappier, *Étude sur "La Mort le Roi Artu,"* 21.

11. M. R. James believed the attributions to be "unsolved enigmas" (*Walter Map's "De Nugis Curialium,"* xvi). Boutemy thought Walter's lack of organization was an "argument décisif" against his having any hand in the *Prose Lancelot,* though he remained cautiously optimistic that Walter may have written some romance, in Latin or in French, that has not survived (*Gautier Map, conteur anglais,* 18–19, 29–30). The attributions are "unexplained and wanting further study," according to Frank Brandsma, *The Interlace Structure of the Third Part of the Prose "Lancelot"* (Cambridge: D. S. Brewer, 2010), 10.

12. Pauline Matarasso, *The Redemption of Chivalry: A Study of the "Queste del Saint Grail"* (Geneva: Droz, 1979), 236–37.

13. Echard, *Arthurian Narrative in the Latin Tradition,* 1. Virginie Greene suggests that someone in Walter's milieu may have written *La mort Artu,* and she quite tentatively puts forth Gerald of Wales as a plausible candidate; see Virginie Greene, *Le sujet et la mort dans "La Mort Artu"* (Saint-Genouph: Nizet, 2002), 84.

14. For the dating of the texts in the *Cycle,* see Ferdinand Lot, *Étude sur le Lancelot en prose,* 126–40; Lot, "Sur la date du *Lancelot* en prose," *Romania* 57 (1931): 137–46; *L'Estoire del Saint Graal,* ed. Jean-Paul Ponceau, 2 vols. (Paris: H. Champion, 1997), 1: x–xlv. Although there is a wide scholarly consensus concerning the order in which they were composed, the dating of each text can vary slightly depending on the secondary source consulted. For the sake of consistency, I have followed the dates given in Burns, "Introduction," xiii–xiv. For a description of attempts to harmonize these once-independent narratives, see Elspeth Kennedy, "The Making of the *Lancelot-Grail Cycle,*" in *A Companion to the "Lancelot-Grail Cycle,"* ed. Carol Dover (Cambridge: D. S. Brewer, 2003), 13–22.

15. *The Quest for the Holy Grail,* trans. E. Jane Burns, vol. 6 of *Lancelot-Grail,* ed. Lacy, 171; *La Queste del Saint Graal,* ed. Pauphilet, 279–80: "Quant il orent mengié, li rois fist avant venir les clers qui metoient en escrit les aventures aus chevaliers de laienz. Et quant Boorz ot contees les aventures del Seint Graal telles come il les avoit veues, si furent mises en escrit et gardees en l'almiere de Salebieres, dont Mestre Gautier Map les trest a fere son livre del Seint Graal par l'amour del roi Henri son seignor, qui fist l'estoire translater de latin en François. Si se test a tant li contes, que plus n'en dist des Aventures del Seint Graal."

16. *HRB* §104, p. 135.

17. *HRB* §§127–30, pp. 171–75.

18. *HRB* §127, p. 170.

19. Carman, *A Study of the Pseudo-Map Cycle,* 122–25.

20. Carman, *A Study of the Pseudo-Map Cycle,* 122–25.

21. Carman, *A Study of the Pseudo-Map Cycle,* 122–25; Lot, *Étude sur le Lancelot,* 196 n. 1; Frappier, *Étude sur "La Mort le Roi Artu,"* 175 n. 3.

22. E.g. *DNC,* xx. Cf. Lot, *Étude sur le Lancelot,* 127.

23. *The Death of Arthur,* trans. Norris J. Lacy (Cambridge: D. S. Brewer, 1993–96), 3; *La Mort le Roi Artu,* 3:

Aprés ce que mestres Gautiers Map ot mis en escrit des *Aventures del Seint Graal*
assez soufisanment si com li sembloit, si fu avis au roi Henri son seigneur que ce
qu'il avoit fet ne devoit pas soufire, s'il ne ramentevoit la fin de ceus dont il avoit fet
devant mention et conment cil morurent dont il avoit amenteües les proesces en son
livre; et por ce commença il ceste derrienne partie. Et quant il l'ot ensemble mise, si
l'apela *La Mort le Roi Artu*, por ce que en la fin est escrit conment li rois Artus fu
navrez en la bataille de Salebieres et conment il se parti de Girflet qui si longuement
li fist compaignie que aprés luis ne fu nus hom qui le veïst vivant. Si commence
mestres Gautiers en tel maniere ceste derrienne partie.

24. *La Mort le Roi Artu*, 3 n. 1.2

25. Variants of this manuscript (designated *R*) are given in *The Vulgate Version of the Arthu-*
rian Romances, ed. H. Oskar Sommer, vol. 6, *La Mort le Roi Artus*, 203 n. 2. For a description of
the manuscript, see *La Mort le Roi Artu*, xxvi, l–li.

26. Lacy's trans., *Death of Arthur*, 136; *La Mort le Roi Artu*, 238: "Si se test ore atant mestre
Gautiers Map de l'*Estoire de Lancelot*, car bien a tout mené a fin selonc les choses qui en avin-
drent, et fenist ci son livre si outreement que après ce n'en porroit nus riens conter qui ne'en
mentist de toutes choses."

27. *La Mort le Roi Artu*, 238 n. 204.10.

28. *Lancelot: Roman en prose du XIIIᵉ siècle*, ed. Alexandre Micha, 9 vols. (Geneva: Droz,
1978–83), 6:244; translation from *Lancelot: Parts V and VI*, trans. William W. Kibler and Carleton W. Carroll, vol. 5 of *Lancelot-Grail*, ed. Lacy, 437. See also the variants in Sommer's *Vulgate*
Version, vol. 5, *Le Livre de Lancelot del Lac III*, 409 n. 4.

29. For this passage as a later addition, see Elspeth Kennedy, "Variations in the Patterns of
Interlace in the Lancelot-Grail," in *The Lancelot-Grail Cycle: Text and Transformations*, ed. Wil-
liam W. Kibler (Austin: University of Texas Press, 1994), 31–50, at 47–48, esp. n. 11; Carman,
Study of the Pseudo-Map Cycle, 110.

30. The text is edited under the title of *Livre d'Artus* in Sommer's *Vulgate Version*, vol. 7,
Supplement: Le Livre d'Artus, 69, 127, 141, 145, 149.

31. See, inter alia, Webster, "Walter Map's French Things"; and *DNC*, xx–xxiii.

32. Addressing the commingling of Latin and French literary culture with specific reference
to Walter Map is Neil Cartlidge, "Masters in the Art of Lying: The Literary Relationship Between Hugh of Rhuddlan and Walter Map," *Modern Language Review* 106 (2011): 1–16, at 4.

33. *GCO*, 5:410–11.

34. Webster, "Walter Map's French Things," 275–76; *DNC*, xxii.

35. *GCO*, 5:410: "dicere pluries, et nos in hunc modum convenire solebat."

36. See Chapter 1, this volume. A. G. Rigg remarks that Gerald's comments do not reflect
what Walter says about himself in *A History of Anglo-Latin Literature*, 91–92.

37. *Ipomedon: Poème de Hue de Rotelande, fin du XIIᵉ siècle*, ed. A. J. Holden (Paris: Klincksieck, 1979), 379–80, lines 7175–86.

38. Dominica Legge, *Anglo-Norman Literature and Its Background* (Oxford: Clarendon
Press, 1963), 86–87.

39. Cartlidge, "Masters in the Art of Lying," 7.

40. Cartildge, "Masters in the Art of Lying," 6–7.

41. For Walter's Hereford interests, see Chapter 1, this volume.

42. Smith, "Gerald of Wales, Walter Map."

43. See, for example, Richard Barber, "Chivalry, Cistercianism and the Grail," in Dover, *Companion to the "Lancelot-Grail Cycle,"* 3–12.

44. Lot, *Étude sur le Lancelot*, 128–29 n. 3.

45. *DNC*, 2.23, p. 196: "In rapina et furto gloria Walensium, et adeo eis utrumque placet, ut inproperium sit filio si pater sine uulnere decesserit. Vnde fit ut pauci canescant. Prouerbium ibi est 'Iuuenis mortuus aut senex pauper,' scilicet ut cito quisque in mortem irruat, ne senex mendicet."

46. *Quest for the Holy Grail*, 60; *La Queste del Saint Graal*, 95: "a cel tens estoient si desreez genz et si sanz mesure par tout le roiaume de Gales que se li filz trovast le pere gisant en son lit par achaison d'enfermeté, il le tresist hors par la teste ou par les braz et l'oceist errannment, car a viltance li fust atorné se ses peres moreust en son lit."

47. For a discussion of the use of Robert de Boron as an authoritative/authorial figure, see Rupert T. Pickens, "Autobiography and History in the Vulgate *Estoire* and in the *Prose Merlin*," in Kibler, *The Lancelot-Grail Cycle*, 98–116.

48. Bromwich, "First Transmission to England and France," 276.

49. For an overview of the uses of these two mostly synonymous terms, see Koch, *Cunedda, Cynan, Cadwallon, Cynddylan*, 17–18.

50. For the distinctiveness of the Welsh and the Irish in the medieval mind, and the tendency of the modern term *Celtic* to mask real cultural differences, see Patrick Sims-Williams, "Celtic Civilization: Continuity or Coincidence?," *Cambrian Medieval Celtic Studies* 64 (2012): 1–45; Sims-Williams, *Irish Influence on Medieval Welsh Literature* (Oxford: Oxford University Press, 2011), 4–8; Sims-Williams, "Celtomania and Celtoscepticism," *Cambrian Medieval Celtic Studies* 36 (1998): 12–16.

51. For the possibility of a somewhat later influx of Irish material, see Matthieu Boyd, "Melion and the Wolves of Ireland," *Neophilologus* 93 (2009): 555–70. Two recent studies in favor of early Irish influence are Carey, *Ireland and the Grail*; and K. Sarah-Jane Murray, *From Plato to Lancelot: A Preface to Chrétien de Troyes* (Syracuse, NY: Syracuse University Press, 2008), esp. 87–170. Like Carey, Rachel Bromwich postulates Irish influence only through the medium of Welsh in "Celtic Dynastic Themes and Breton Lays," *Études Celtiques* 9 (1961): 439–74, at 470. For Irish-language literature in Wales, see Sims-Williams, *Irish Influence on Medieval Welsh Literature*.

52. Bennett, however, argues that Walter's tale of Sadius and Galo uses a source closely resembling the Irish story *Fingal Ronain* ("Walter Map's *Sadius and Galo*," 50–53).

53. Marie de France, *Lais*, ed. Alfred Ewert, with an introduction and bibliography by Glyn S. Burgess (London: Bristol Classical Press, 1995), 74, line 642.

54. J. R. F. Piette, however, doubted that Breton influence was as great as his contemporaries claimed ("Yr Agwedd Lydewig ar y Chwedlau Arthuraidd"). For an overview of the study of the first transmission, see Gerald Morgan, "Welsh Arthurian Literature," in *A History of Arthurian Scholarship*, ed. Norris J. Lacy (Cambridge: D. S. Brewer, 2006), 77–94, at 86–87. For a recent summary of scholarly responses to the Breton/Briton question, see Williams, "Brittany and the Arthurian Legend," 259–63.

55. Joseph Loth, "Des nouvelles theories sur l'origine des romans arthuriens," *Revue Celtique* 13 (1892): 475–503; Loth, *Contributions à l'étude des romans de la Table Ronde* (Paris: H. Champion, 1912); Ferdinand Lot, "Études sur la provenance du cycle arthurien," *Romania* 24 (1895): 497–528; Lot, "Provenance du cycle arthurien," *Romania* 28 (1899): 1–48; Lot, "Nouvelles études sur la provenance du cycle arthurien," *Romania* 28 (1899): 321–47; and 30 (1901): 1–21.

56. R. S. Loomis, *The Grail: From Celtic Myth to Christian Symbol* (Cardiff: University of Wales Press, 1963); Loomis, "The Oral Diffusion of the Arthurian Legend," in *Arthurian Literature in the Middle Ages: A Collaborative History*, ed. Roger Sherman Loomis (Oxford: Oxford University Press, 1959), 52–63. See also Léon Fleuriot and Auguste-Pierre Ségalen, *Héritage celtique et captation française*, Histoire littéraire et culturelle de la Bretagne, vol. 1 (Paris: Champion, 1997), 148–52;

57. Kenneth Jackson, "Les sources celtiques du roman du Graal," in *Les romans du Graal aux XIIᵉ et XIIIᵉ siècles, Strasbourg, 29 mars–3 avril 1954* (Paris: Centre national de la recherché scientifique, 1956), 213–31. Loomis replied in "Objections to the Celtic Origin of the 'Matière de Bretagne,' " *Romania* 78 (1958): 47–77. For a discussion of the reception of Jackson's paper and the ensuing controversy, see Raymond J. Cormier, "Tradition and Sources: The Jackson-Loomis Controversy Re-examined," *Folklore* 83, no. 2 (1972): 101–21.

58. Jackson, "Les sources celtiques du roman du Graal," 224–26.

59. Bromwich, "Chwedlau'r Greal," 51. For another early critique of Loomis's methodology, see Bliss, "Celtic Myth and Arthurian Romance."

60. Jeffrey Jerome Cohen, "Introduction: Infinite Realms," in *Cultural Diversity in the British Middle Ages: Archipelago, Island, England*, ed. Jeffrey Jerome Cohen (New York: Palgrave Macmillan, 2008), 1–16, at 6–7. Simon Meecham-Jones has also drawn attention to the positive effect that Loomis had in directing scholars toward Celtic literature in "Where Was Wales?," 35.

61. Patrick Sims-Williams, "Did Itinerant Breton *Conteurs* Transmit the *Matière de Bretagne*?," *Romania* 116 (1998): 72–111.

62. Michael Faletra, *Wales and the Medieval Colonial Imagination: The Matters of Britain in the Twelfth Century* (New York: Palgrave Macmillan, 2014), 11–14.

63. Muriel A. Whitaker, "Otherworld Castles in Middle English Arthurian Romance," in *Late Medieval Castles*, ed. Robert Liddiard (Woodbridge: Boydell Press, 2016), 393–408, at 397.

64. Julia Bolton and Daniel T. Kline, "Literary and Cultural Contexts: Major Figures, Institutions, Topics, Events, Movements," in *The Medieval British Literature Handbook*, ed. Daniel Kline (London: Continuum, 2009), 49–81, at 55.

65. Aline Laradjii, *La légende de Roland: De la genèse française à l'épuisement de la figure du héros en Italie* (Paris: Harmattan, 2008), 84: "Il faut bien s'imaginer que les conteurs, qui circulent dans les différentes régions celtes, s'inspirent de diverses traditions, qui ont fusionné et qui sont contituées d'éléments écossais (et, plus particulièrement, pictes), gallois, bretons, corniques, voire de souvenirs antiques ou de quelques influences orientales." Laradjii does, however, suggest that a literary route is possible (77).

66. Helmut Birkhan, *Keltische Erzählungen vom Kaiser Arthur, Teil 1*, 2nd ed. (Vienna: LIT Verlag, 2004), 43: "Daß die Bretagne, im 6. Jahrhundert von Cornwall aus besiedelt, als keltischer Vorposten der Arthurtradition auf dem Festland eine bedeutende Rolle spielte, ist vielfach belegt und nimmt nicht wunder."

67. Constance Bullock-Davies, *Professional Interpreters and the Matter of Britain* (Cardiff: University of Wales Press, 1966). See also Rachel Bromwich's important review of *Bullock-Davies's* book in, *Llên Cymru* 9 (1967): 249–51; and Constance Bullock-Davies, "Welsh Minstrels at the Courts of Edward I and Edward II" (paper presented at the Transactions of the Honourable Society of Cymmrodorion, Session 1972–73, London, 1972 and 1973).

68. Bullock-Davies, *Professional Interpreters and the Matter of Britain*, 18.

69. Rachel Bromwich also noted the lack of direct evidence in her review of *Professional Interpreters and the Matter of Britain*, 250: "Felly y mae'r dystiolaeth anuniongyrchol yn ategu damcaniaeth y Dr. Bullock-Davies yn gryf: yr oedd gan y lladmeryddion uchel eu gwaed a'u

haddysg gyfleusterau di-ail i gwpláu'r gwaith cyfieithu. Er hynny, rhaid inni gydnabod nad oes yn aros i'n hoes ni y mymryn lleiaf o dystiolaeth uniongyrchol fod y fath beth wedi digwydd" (Therefore, indirect evidence strongly supports Dr. Bullock-Davies's theory: The latimers of noble blood and education had unrivaled opportunities to accomplish the work of translating. However, we must acknowledge that not the least bit of direct evidence remains in our age that this sort of thing has happened).

70. Sims-Williams, "Did Itinerant Breton *Conteurs* Transmit," 111. With some hesistation, Bromwich arrives at the same conclusion in "First Transmission to England and France," 289: "These ecclesiastical collectors and writers were a very important medium—perhaps, in the last resort, the most important of all—for the collection and transmission of early secular Arthurian material to England and to the European Continent."

71. For the Latin tradition of Arthur and the Matter of Britain, see the essays in Siân Echard, ed., *The Arthur of Medieval Latin Literature: The Development and Dissemination of the Arthurian Legend in Medieval Latin* (Cardiff: University of Wales Press, 2011); and Echard, *Arthurian Narrative in the Latin Tradition*. For the importance of clerics to early vernacular romance, see Stephen Jaeger, "Patrons and the Beginnings of Courtly Romance," in *The Medieval Opus: Imitation, Rewriting and Transmission in the French Tradition: Proceedings of the Symposium Held at the Institute for Research in the Humanities, October 5–7, 1995, at the University of Wisconsin–Madison*, ed. Douglas Kelly (Amsterdam: Rodopi, 1996), 45–58; Cartlidge, "Masters in the Art of Lying"; M. T. Clanchy *From Memory to Written Record, England, 1066–1307* (Cambridge, MA: Harvard University Press, 1979), 215.

72. *HRB* §2.14, p. 5.

73. Smith, "An Edition, Translation, and Introduction to Benedict of Gloucester's *Vita Dubricii*"; see also Chapter 4, this volume.

74. John Reuben Davies, *Book of Llandaf*, 84–86.

75. Smith, "An Edition, Translation, and Introduction," 55–58.

76. *Nova Legenda Anglie*, 1:267–71.

77. *The Kalendre of the Newe Legende of England* (London, 1516), 24.

78. *Kalendre of the Newe Legende*, ii; the prologue is also reprinted in *Nova Legenda Anglie*, xxi–xxiv, citation at xxi–xxii.

79. *HRB* §1, p. 5.

80. For example, Karen Jankulak, *Geoffrey of Monmouth* (Cardiff: University of Wales Press, 2010), 13–14.

81. E. M. R. Ditmas, "Geoffrey of Monmouth and the Breton Families in Cornwall," *Welsh History Review* 6 (1972): 451–61.

82. Edmond Faral, *La légende arthurienne: Études et documents*, 3 vols. (Paris: H. Champion, 1929), 2:137–39; Hutson, *British Personal Names*, 89; Stuart Piggott, "The Sources of Geoffrey of Monmouth I: The 'Pre-Roman' King-List," *Antiquity* 15 (1941): 269–86; Tatlock, *Legendary History of Britain*, 163 n. 254; Guy, "A Second Witness." See also P. C. Bartrum, "Was There a British 'Book of Conquests'?," *Bulletin of the Board of Celtic Studies* 23 (1968): 1–6.

83. See Chapter 5, this volume.

84. According to Guy, "A Second Witness," Geoffrey's collection of genealogies derives from a mid-tenth-century exemplar at St. Davids.

85. *Annales Cambriae, A.D. 682–954: Texts A–C in Parallel*, ed. and trans. David N. Dumville (Cambridge: University of Cambridge Press, 2002), vi; Guy, "A Second Witness."

86. *Text of the Book of Llan Dâv*, xviii–xxvii. See also Christopher Brooke, "The Archbishops of St Davids, Llandaff, and Caerleon-on-Usk," in *Church and the Welsh Border*, 16–49.

87. An overview of the "hash" that Geoffrey has made of his colleagues' "precious claims" is found in Brooke, "Archbishops of St Davids, Llandaff, and Caerleon-on-Usk," 16–24, quote at 23.

88. Brooke, "Archbishops of St Davids, Llandaff, and Caerleon-on-Usk," 21–23; John Reuben Davies, *Book of Llandaf*, 110–11. For Gloucester's possession of this document, not noted by Brooke or Davies, see Chapter 5, note 48, above.

89. Hutson, *British Personal Names*, 16.

90. How exactly Geoffrey obtained these documents requires further study. Ben Guy has recently suggested that Caradog of Llancarfan may have sent Geoffrey some written materials ("*De situ Brecheniauc*").

91. I would like to thank Lindsey Panxhi for bringing these two instances to my attention.

92. *Tyolet*, in *"Doon" and "Tyolet": Two Old French Narrative Lays*, ed. and trans. Glyn S. Burgess and Leslie C. Brook, Liverpool Online Series: Critical Editions of French Texts 9 (Liverpool: University of Liverpool, 2005), 76–77, lines 25–35.

> A la cort erent racontees,
> Si comme elles erent trovees.
> Li preude clerc qui donc estoient
> Totes escrire les fesoient.
> Mises estoient en latin
> Et en escrit em parchemin,
> Por ce qu'encor tel tens seroit
> Que l'en volentiers les orroit.
> Or sont dites et racontees,
> De latin en romanz trovees;
> Bretons en firent lais plusors.

93. *Lai de l'Espine*, in *French Arthurian Literature IV: Eleven Old French Narrative Lays*, ed. and trans. Glyn S. Burgess and Leslie C. Brook (Cambridge: D. S. Brewer, 2007), 216–17, lines 6–11.

> Les estoires en trai avant
> Qui encor sont a Carlion,
> Enz el mostier saint Aaron,
> Et en Bretaingne conneües
> Et en pluseurs leus son veües,
> Por ce que les truis en estoire.

94. For the *Lai de l'Espine*, see Glyn S. Burgess, *The Lais of Marie de France: Text and Context* (Athens: University of Georgia Press, 1987), 24–25.

95. Guy, "*De situ Brecheniauc*"; Scott, *Early History of Glastonbury*, 187–88 n. 22.

96. See Chapter 5, this volume.

97. David N. Dumville, "The Origin of the *C*-Text of the Variant Version of the *Historia Regum Britannie*," *Bulletin of the Board of Celtic Studies* 26 (1975): 315–22; Dumville, "Celtic-Latin Texts in Northern England, c. 1150–1250," *Celtica* 12 (1977): 19–49.

98. Christine Voth, "Irish Pilgrims, Welsh Manuscripts and Anglo-Saxon Monasteries: Was Script Change in Tenth-Century England a Legacy of the Celtic World?," in *Select Proceedings from the International Society of Anglo-Saxonists, Dublin 2013* (forthcoming); Guy, "A Second

Witness"; Helen McKee, *The Cambridge Juvencus Manuscript Glossed in Latin, Old Welsh and Old Irish: Text and Commentary* (Aberystwyth: CMCS Publications, 2000); McKee, "The Circulation of Books Between England and the Celtic Realms," in *The Cambridge History of the Book in Britain*, vol. 1, *c. 400–1100*, ed. Richard Gameson (Cambridge: Cambridge University Press, 2012), 338–43; McKee, "St Augustine's, Canterbury: Book Production in the Tenth and Eleventh Centuries" (Ph.D. thesis, University of Cambridge, 1997); David N. Dumville, "English Square Minuscule Script: The Mid-Century Phases," *Anglo-Saxon England* 23 (1994): 133–64; Dumville, "English Square Minuscule Script: The Background and Earliest Phases," *Anglo-Saxon England* 16 (1987): 147–79. I would like to thank Chris Voth and Ben Guy for making their work available to me prior to publication.

99. Sims-Williams, *Irish Influence*, 1.

100. McKee, "Circulation of Books," 339.

101. John Carey's *Ireland and the Grail* argues that a group of ultimately Irish tales made their way to Chrétien. Although evidence for this textual exchange is much thinner than that outlined above, Carey's theory nonetheless argues for a primarily textual route as opposed to oral. Rachel Bromwich has also devoted significant effort to the Welsh elements in Arthurian literature; see Bromwich, "First Transmission"; Bromwich, "Celtic Elements, 41–55; Bromwich, "Chwedlau'r Greal." See also Ceridwen Lloyd-Morgan, "Nodiadau Ychwanegol ar Achau Arthuriaidd a'u Ffynonellau Ffrangeg," *National Library of Wales Journal* 21 (1980): 329–39.

102. Carey, *Ireland and the Grail*, xv.

103. Jackson, "*Les sources celtiques*," 214: "ils sont rebutés par la masse de ce qui leur paraît être de la speculation débridée."

104. Ceridwen Lloyd-Morgan, "Crossing the Borders: Literary Borrowing in Medieval Wales and England," in *Authority and Subjugation*, 159–74, at 159.

105. Bodel, *La Chanson des Saisnes*, 1:2: "N'en sont que trois materes a nul home vivant: / De France et de Bretaigne et de Ronme la grant" (lines 6–7).

106. Sims-Williams, "Celtomania and Celtoscepticism," 9.

107. William Farina, *Chrétien de Troyes and the Dawn of Arthurian Romance* (Jefferson, NC: McFarland, 2010), 32. Although a journalist by training, Farina has read his scholarly sources with care—his sentiment here merely distills his bibliography in less guarded terms than his academic counterparts.

108. Sims-Williams, "Did Itinerant Breton *Conteurs* Transmit," 74–76.

109. For the survival rate of Welsh vernacular and Latin manuscripts, see Daniel Huws, "The Medieval Manuscript in Wales," in *Medieval Welsh Manuscripts*, ed. Daniel Huws (Aberystwyth: University of Wales Press and the National Library of Wales, 2000), 1–23, at 3–4. For a recent overview of Welsh literary culture before the twelfth century, see Charles-Edwards, *Wales and the Britons*, 625–79.

110. Matthew Arnold, *On the Study of Celtic* Literature (London: Smith, Elder, 1867), 61.

111. See Chapters 4 and 5, this volume; Sims-Williams, "A Turkish-Celtic Problem."

112. Sims-Williams, "Did Itinerant Breton *Conteurs* Transmit," 111.

EPILOGUE

1. *The Quest for the Holy Grail*, trans. Burns, 171; *La Queste del Saint Graal*, ed. Pauphilet, 279–80: "Et quant Boorz ot contees les aventures del Seint Graal telles come il les avoit veues, si furent mises en escrit et gardees en l'almiere de Salebieres, dont Mestre Gautier Map les trest a

fere son livre del Seint Graal por l'amour del roi Henri son seignor, qui fist l'estoire translater de latin en François. Si se test a tant li contes, que plus n'en dist des Aventures del Seint Graal."

2. Edited in *Vitae Sanctorum Britanniae et Genealogiae*, 313–15; and in *Early Welsh Genealogical Tracts*, 14–16. The gloss appears on fol. 11r.

3. Blom, "Welsh Glosses in the Vocabularium," 38 n. 65. However, in the *De situ Brecheniauc*, the glossator never indicates an abbreviation with a punctus. Instead, he only uses a punctus to signal the end of the gloss. Only three glosses end without a punctus, one of which ends with an abbreviation instead: ".i. cū dentib" (fol. 11r); ".i. trūcate barbe" (fol.11r); ".i. inagere lacus caltiõis" (fol. 11r).

4. *The Anglo-Norman Dictionary*, accessed March 6, 2016, http://www.anglo-norman.net /D/eurus.

Bibliography

EDITIONS AND TRANSLATIONS OF WALTER MAP

Boutemy, André. *Gautier Map, conteur anglais: Extraits du "De Nugis Curialium."* Brussels: Office de Publicité, 1945.

Contes pour les gens de cour. Trans. Alan Keith Bate. Turnhout: Brepols, 1993.

De nugis curialium: Courtiers' Trifles. Ed. and trans. M. R. James, rev. C. N. L. Brooke and R. A. B. Mynors. Oxford: Clarendon Press, 1983.

Early Fiction in England from Geoffrey of Monmouth to Chaucer. Ed. and introd. Laura Ashe. London: Penguin, 2015. [This work contains Richard Sowerby's translations of three of Walter's stories at 153–88.]

Gualteri Mapes "De nugis curialium": Dinstinctiones quinque. Ed. Thomas Wright. London: J. B. Nichols and Son, 1850.

Gautier Map: Contes de courtisans. Trans. Marylene Perez. Third cycle doctorate's thesis, Lille, 1982.

The Latin Poems Commonly Attributed to Walter Mapes. Ed. Thomas Wright. London: Printed for the Camden Society by J. B. Nichols and Son, 1841.

Master Walter Map's Book "De Nugis Curialium" (Courtiers' Trifles). Trans. Frederick Tupper and Marbury Bladen Ogle. London: Chatto and Windus, 1924.

Storiau Gwallter Map. Trans. R. T. Jenkins. Llandybie: Llyfrau'r Dryw, 1941.

Svaghi di corte. Trans. Fortunata Latella. 2 vols. Parma: Pratiche Editrice, 1990.

Walter Map: De Nugis Curialium. Ed. Montague Rhodes James. Oxford: Clarendon Press, 1914.

    Walter Map's "De Nugis Curialium." Trans. Montague Rhodes James; with historical notes by John Edward Lloyd; ed. E. Sidney Hartland. London: Honourable Society of Cymmrodorion, 1923.

"Walter Map's 'Dissuasio Valerii.'" In *Jankyn's Book of Wikked Wyves*, vol. 1, *The Primary Texts*, ed. Ralph Hanna III and Traugott Lawler, 121–48. Athens: University of Georgia Press, 1997.

MANUSCRIPTS

British Library Additional 34749
British Library, Cotton Vespasian A.v
British Library, Cotton Vespasian A.xiv
British Library, Egerton 2810
British Library, Royal 6 D.ix
British Library, Royal 19 C.xiii

Cambridge, Corpus Christi College 32
General Collection, Beinecke Rare Book and Manuscript Library, Yale University, 229
Oxford, Bodleian Library, Bodley 851

PRIMARY SOURCES

The Acts of Welsh Rulers, 1120–1283. Ed. Huw Pryce. Cardiff: University of Wales Press, 2005.

The Anglo-Saxon Chronicle. Ed. and trans. Michael Swanton. New York: Routledge, 1998.

The Anglo-Saxon Chronicle: A Collaborative Edition. Vol. 5, *MS C.* Ed. Katherine O'Brien O'Keeffe. Cambridge: D. S. Brewer, 2001.

Annales Cambriae. Ed. John Williams ab Ithel. London: Longman, Green, Longman, and Roberts, 1860.

Annales Cambriae, A.D. 682–954: Texts A–C in Parallel. Ed. and trans. David N. Dumville. Cambridge: University of Cambridge Press, 2002.

Annales de Margan. In *Annales Monastici,* vol. 1, ed. Henry Richards Luard, 1–40. London: Longman, Green, Longman, Roberts, and Green, 1864.

An Anonymous Short English Metrical Chronicle. Ed. Ewald Zettl. London: Oxford University Press, 1935. Reprint, 1991.

Bodel, Jehan. *La Chanson des Saisnes.* Ed. Annette Brasseur. 2 vols. Geneva: Librairie Droz, 1989.

Brut y Tywysogyon; or, The Chronicle of the Princes: Red Book of Hergest Version. Ed. and trans. Thomas Jones. Cardiff: University of Wales Press, 1955.

Calendar of Inquisitions Post Mortem and Other Analogous Documents. Vol. 5, *Edward II.* London: Printed for His Majesty's Stationery Office by Mackie, 1908.

Cartularium Prioratus S. Johannis Evangelistae de Brecon. Ed. R. W. Banks. London: Whiting, 1884. *Cyfranc Lludd a Llefelys,* ed. Brynley F. Roberts. Dublin: Dublin Institute for Advanced Studies, 1975.

Cyfreithiau Hywel Dda yn ôl Llyfr Blegywryd. Ed. Stephen J. Williams and J. Enoch. 2nd. ed. Powell. Cardiff: University of Wales Press, 1961.

The Death of Arthur. Trans. Norris J. Lacy. Vol. 7 of *Lancelot-Grail: The Old French Arthurian Vulgate and Post-Vulgate in Translation,* ed. Norris J. Lacy. Cambridge: D. S. Brewer, 2010. First published by Garland, 1992–96.

Early Welsh Genealogical Tracts. Ed. P. C. Bartrum. Cardiff: University of Wales Press, 1966.

English Benedictine Kalendars After A.D. 1000. Ed. Francis Wormwald. 2 vols. London: Harrison and Sons, 1939.

English Benedictine Libraries: The Shorter Catalogues. Ed. R. Sharpe et al. Corpus of British Medieval Library Catalogues 4. London: British Library in association with the British Academy, 1996.

Episcopal Acts and Cognate Documents Relating to Welsh Dioceses, 1066–1272. Ed. J. Conway Davies. 2 vols. Cardiff: Historical Society of the Church in Wales, 1946–48.

L'Estoire del Saint Graal. Ed. Jean-Paul Ponceau. 2 vols. Paris: H. Champion, 1997.

Geoffrey of Monmouth. *The History of the Kings of Britain: An Edition and Translation of "De gestis Britonum."* Ed. Michael D. Reeve, trans. Neil Wright. Woodbridge: Boydell Press, 2007.

Giraldi Cambrensis opera. Ed. J. S. Brewer, James F. Dimock, and George F. Warner. 8 vols. London: Longman, 1861–91.

Gwaith Meilyr Brydydd a'i Ddisgynyddion. Ed. J. E. Caerwyn Williams, Peredur I. Lynch, and R. Geraint Gruffydd. Cardiff: University of Wales Press, 1994.

Hieronymus. *Epistolae*. Ed. Johannes Andreas. Rome: Conradus Sweynheym and Arnoldus Pannartz, 1468.

Historia et cartularium monasterii Sancti Petri Gloucestriae. Ed. William Henry Hart. 3 vols. London: Longman, Green, Longman, Roberts, and Green, 1863–67.

Historia Gruffud vab Kenan. Ed. D. Simon Evans. Cardiff: University of Wales Press, 1997.

Hue de Rotelande [Hugh of Rhuddlan]. *Ipomedon: Poème de Hue de Rotelande, fin du XIIe siècle*. Ed. A. J. Holden. Paris: Klincksieck, 1979.

———. *Protheselaus*. Ed. A. J. Holden. London: Anglo-Norman Text Society, 1991.

Johannes de Hauvilla. *Architrenius*. Ed. and trans. Winthrop Wetherbee. Cambridge: Cambridge University Press, 1994.

The Kalendre of the Newe Legende of England. London, 1516.

Klaeber's Beowulf and the Fight at Finnsburg. 4th ed. Ed. R. D. Fulk, Robert E. Bjork, and John D. Niles. Toronto: University of Toronto Press, 2008.

Lai de l'Espine. In *French Arthurian Literature IV: Eleven Old French Narrative Lays*, ed. and trans. Glyn S. Burgess and Leslie C. Brook, 199–241. Cambridge: D. S. Brewer, 2007.

Lancelot: Parts V and VI. Trans. William W. Kibler and Carleton W. Carroll. Vol. 5 of *Lancelot-Grail: The Old French Arthurian Vulgate and Post-Vulgate in Translation*, ed. Norris J. Lacy. Cambridge: D. S. Brewer, 2010. First published by Garland, 1992–96.

Lancelot: Roman en prose du XIIIe siècle. Ed. Alexandre Micha. 9 vols. Geneva: Droz, 1978–83.

Lancelot-Grail: The Old French Arthurian Vulgate and Post-Vulgate in Translation. Ed. Norris J. Lacy. 10 vols. Cambridge: D. S. Brewer, 2010. First published by Garland, 1992–96.

Langland, William. *Piers Plowman: The Z Version*. Ed. A. G. Rigg and Charlotte Brewer. Texts and Studies 59. Toronto: Pontifical Institute, 1983.

Latin Arthurian Literature. Ed. and trans. Mildred Leake Day. Cambridge: D. S. Brewer, 2005.

The Latin Texts of the Welsh Laws. Ed. Hywel David Emanuel. Cardiff: University of Wales Press, 1967.

The Letters and Charters of Gilbert Foliot. Ed. Z. N. Brooke, Adrian Morey, and C. N. L. Brooke. Cambridge: Cambridge University Press, 1967.

Marie de France. *Lais*. Ed. Alfred Ewert. Oxford: Blackwell, 1944. Reprinted with a revised introduction and bibliography by Glyn S. Burgess. London: Bristol Classical Press, 1995.

La Mort le Roi Artu: Roman du XIIIe siècle. Ed. Jean Frappier. Paris: Droz, 1936.

Navigatio Sancti Brendani Abbatis: From Early Latin Manuscripts. Ed. Carl Selmer. South Bend, IN: University of Notre Dame Press, 1959.

Nigel de Longchamp's Speculum Stultorum. Ed. John H. Mozley and Robert R. Raymo. Berkeley: University of California Press, 1960.

Nova Legenda Anglie. Ed. Carl Horstman. 2 vols. Oxford: Clarendon Press, 1901.

Orderic Vitalis. *The Ecclesiastical History of Orderic Vitalis*. Ed. and trans. Marjorie Chibnall. 6 vols. Oxford: Clarendon Press, 1973.

Opera S. Bernardi. Ed. J. Leclercq and H. M. Rochais. 8 vols. Rome: Editiones Cistercienses, 1977.

The Original Acta of St. Peter's Abbey, Gloucester, c. 1122 to 1263. Ed. Robert B. Patterson. Gloucestershire Record Series. Gloucestershire: Bristol and Gloucestershire Archaeological Society, 1998.

Osbern Claudianus. *Derivazioni*. Ed. P. Busdraghi et al. 2 vols. Spoleto: Centro italiano di studi sull'Alto Medioevo, 1996.

"Petronius Rediuiuus" et Helias Tripolanensis. Ed. Marvin L. Colker. Leiden: Brill, 2007.

The Quest for the Holy Grail. Trans. E. Jane Burns. Vol. 6 of *Lancelot-Grail: The Old French*

Arthurian Vulgate and Post-Vulgate in Translation, ed. Norris J. Lacy. Cambridge: D. S. Brewer, 2010. First published by Garland, 1992–96

La Queste del Saint Graal: Roman du XIIIᵉ siècle. Ed. Albert Pauphilet. Paris: Champion, 1923.

Registrum Anglie de libris doctorum et auctorum veterum. Ed. Richard H. Rouse and Mary A. Rouse. London: British Library, 1991.

"Rhygyfarch's *Life* of St David." Ed. and trans. Richard Sharpe and John Reuben Davies. In *St David of Wales: Cult, Church and Nation*, ed. J. Wyn Evans and Jonathan M. Wooding, 107–55. Woodbridge: Boydell and Brewer, 2007.

Sir Orfeo. Ed. A. J. Bliss. Oxford: Clarendon, 1966.

Tennyson, Alfred Lord. *The Works of Alfred Lord Tennyson, Poet Laureate*. Vol. 6. Boston: Houghton, Mifflin, 1892.

The Text of the Book of Llan Dâv. Ed. J. Gwenogvryn Evans, with the cooperation of John Rhys. Oxford, 1893.

Trioedd Ynys Prydein: The Welsh Triads. Ed. and trans. Rachel Bromwich. 2nd ed. Cardiff: University of Wales Press, 1978.

Tyolet. In *"Doon" and "Tyolet": Two Old French Narrative Lays*, ed. and trans. Glyn S. Burgess and Leslie Brook. Liverpool Online Series: Critical Editions of French Texts 9. Liverpool: University of Liverpool, 2005.

"Vie de Saint Cadoc par Caradoc de Llancarfan." Ed. P. Grosjean. *Analecta Bollandiana* 60 (1942): 35–67.

Vitae Sanctorum Britanniae et Genealogiae. Ed. and trans. A. W. Wade-Evans. Cardiff: University of Wales Press, 1944. New ed., ed. Scott Lloyd. Cardiff: Welsh Academic Press, 2013.

Vita Griffini Filii Conani: The Medieval Life of Gruffudd ap Cynan. Ed. and trans. Paul Russell. Cardiff: University of Wales Press, 2005.

"'Vita Sancti Paterni': The Life of Saint Padarn and the Original 'Miniu.'" Ed. and trans. Charles Thomas and David Howlett. *Trivium* 33 (2003).

The Vulgate Version of the Arthurian Romances. Ed. H. Oskar Sommer. 8 vols. Washington, DC: Carnegie Institution of Washington, 1908–16.

Walter of Henley and Other Treatises on Estate Management and Accounting. Ed. Dorothea Oschinsky. Oxford: Clarendon Press, 1971.

Welsh Genealogies, A.D. 300–1400. Ed. Peter C. Bartrum. 8 vols. Cardiff: University of Wales Press for the Board of Celtic Studies, 1974.

William of Malmesbury. *Gesta Pontificum Anglorum*. Vol. 1, *Text and Translation*. Ed. and trans. M. Winterbottom. Oxford: Clarendon Press, 2007.

SECONDARY SOURCES

Allen, Dorena. "Orpheus and Orfeo: The Dead and the Taken." *Medium Aevum* 33 (1964): 102–11.

Arnold, Matthew. *On the Study of Celtic Literature*. London: Smith, Elder, 1867.

Aurell, Martin. "Henry II and Arthurian Legend." In *Henry II: New Interpretations*, ed. Christopher Harper-Bill and Nicholas Vincent, 362–94. Woodbridge: Boydell Press, 2007.

Barber, Richard. "Chivalry, Cistercianism and the Grail." In *A Companion to the "Lancelot-Grail Cycle,"* ed. Carol Dover, 3–12. Cambridge: D. S. Brewer, 2003.

Barlow, Frank. *William Rufus*. Berkeley: University of California Press, 1983.

Barrow, Julia. "Athelstan to Aigueblanche, 1056–1268." In *Hereford Cathedral: A History*, ed. Gerald Aylmer and John Tiller, 21–47. London: Hambledon Press, 2000.

————. "A Twelfth-Century Bishop and Literary Patron: William de Vere." *Viator* 18 (1987): 175–90.

Bartlett, Robert. *Gerald of Wales, 1146–1223.* Oxford: Oxford University Press, 1982.

Bartrum, P. C. "Rhieinwg and Reinwg." *Bulletin of the Board of Celtic Studies* 24 (1970): 23–27.

————. "Was There a British 'Book of Conquests'?" *Bulletin of the Board of Celtic Studies* 23 (1968): 1–6.

Bate, Keith. "La littérature latine d'imagination à la cour d'Henri II d'Angleterre." *Cahiers de civilisation médiévale* 34 (1991): 3–21.

Bates, David. "The Building of a Great Church: The Abbey of St Peter's, Gloucester, and Its Early Norman Benefactors." *Transactions of the Bristol and Gloucestershire Archaeological Society* 102 (1984): 129–32.

Battles, Dominique. "Chaucer's *Franklin's Tale* and Boccaccio's *Filocolo* Reconsidered." *Chaucer Review* 34, no. 1 (1999): 38–59.

Bennett, R. E. "Walter Map's *Sadius and Galo.*" *Speculum* 16 (1941): 34–56.

Bezzola, Reto Raduolf. *Les origines et la formation de la littérature courtoise en Occident (500–1200).* 3 vols. Paris: Champion, 1944–63.

Bihrer, Andreas. "Selbstvergewisserung am Hof: Eine Interpretation von Walter Maps *De nugis curialium* I, 1–12." *Jahrbuch für Internationale Germanistik* 34, no. 1 (2002): 227–58.

Birch-Hirschfeld, Adolf. *Die Sage vom Gral: Ihre Entstehung und dichterische Ausbildung in Frankreich und Deutschland im 12. und 13. Jarhundert.* Leipzig: Vogel, 1877.

Birkhan, Helmut. *Keltische Erzählungen vom Kaiser Arthur, Teil 1.* 2nd ed. Vienna: LIT Verlag, 2004.

Bliss, A. J. "Celtic Myth and Arthurian Romance." *Medium Aevum* 30 (1961): 19–25.

Blom, Alderik. "The Welsh Glosses in the Vocabularium." *Cambrian Medieval Celtic Studies* 57 (2009): 23–40.

Bolton, Julia, and Daniel T. Kline. "Literary and Cultural Contexts: Major Figures, Institutions, Topics, Events, Movements." In *The Medieval British Literature Handbook*, ed. Daniel Kline, 49–81. London, New York: Continuum, 2009.

Boureau, Alain. "Peut-on parler d'auteurs scolastiques?" In *Auctor et auctoritas: Invention et conformisme dans l'écriture médiévale*, ed. Michel Zimmerman, 267–79. Paris: École des Chartes, 2001.

Bourgain, Pascale. "The Circulation of Texts in Manuscript Culture." In *The Medieval Manuscript Book: Cultural Approaches*, ed. Michael Johnston and Michael van Dussen, 140–59. Cambridge: Cambridge University Press, 2015.

Boutémy, A. "Giraud de Barri et Pierre le Chantre: Une source de la *Gemma ecclesiastica.*" *Revue du moyen âge latin* 2 (1946): 45–62.

Boyd, Matthieu. "Melion and the Wolves of Ireland." *Neophilologus* 93 (2009): 555–70.

Bradley, Henry. "Notes on Walter Map's *De Nugis Curialium.*" *English Historical Review* 32 (1917): 393–400.

Brady, Lindy. *Writing the Welsh Borderlands in Anglo-Saxon England.* Manchester: University of Manchester Press, forthcoming 2017.

Brandsma, Frank. *The Interlace Structure of the Third Part of the Prose "Lancelot."* Cambridge: D. S. Brewer, 2010.

Breeze, Andrew. "Arthur in Early Saints' Lives." In *The Arthur of Medieval Latin Literature*, ed. Siân Echard, 26–41. Cardiff: University of Wales Press, 2011.

————. "The Name of Kayrrud in the *Franklin's Tale.*" *Chaucer Review* 37, no. 1 (2002): 95–99.

Bromwich, Rachel. "Celtic Dynastic Themes and Breton Lays." *Études Celtiques* 9 (1961): 439–74.

———. "Celtic Elements in Arthurian Romance: A General Survey." In *The Legend of Arthur in the Middle Ages: Studies Presented to Armel H. Diverres*, ed. P. B. Grout, R. A Lodge, C. E. Pickford and E. K. C. Varty, 41–55. Cambridge: D. S. Brewer, 1983.

———. "Chwedlau'r Greal." *Llên Cymru* 8 (1964–65): 48–57.

———. "First Transmission to England and France." In *The Arthur of the Welsh*, ed. Rachel Bromwich, A. O. H. Jarman, and Brynley F. Roberts, 273–98. Cardiff: University of Wales Press, 1991.

———. Review of *Professional Interpreters and the Matter of Britain*, by Constance Bullock-Davies. *Llên Cymru* 9 (1967): 249–51.

Rachel Bromwich, A. O. H. Jarman, and Brynley F. Roberts, eds. *The Arthur of the Welsh: The Arthurian Legend in Medieval Welsh Literature*. Cardiff: University of Wales Press, 1991.

Brooke, Christopher. "The Archbishops of St Davids, Llandaff, and Caerleon-on-Usk," In *Studies in the Early British Church*, ed. N. K. Chadwick et al., 201–42. Cambridge: University of Cambridge Press, 1958. Reprinted in Christopher N. L. Brooke, *The Church and the Welsh Border in the Central Middle Ages*, ed. D. N. Dumville and C. N. L. Brooke, 16–49. Studies in Celtic History, no. 8. Woodbridge: Boydell Press, 1986.

———. *The Church and the Welsh Border in the Central Middle Ages*, ed. D. N. Dumville and C. N. L. Brooke. Studies in Celtic History, no. 8. Woodbridge: Boydell Press, 1986.

———. "St Peter of Gloucester and St Cadoc of Llancarfan." In *Celt and Saxon: Studies in the Early British Border*, ed. Nora Chadwick, 258–332. Cambridge: Cambridge University Press, 1963. Reprinted in Christopher N. L. Brooke, *The Church and the Welsh Border in the Central Middle Ages*, ed. D. N. Dumville and C. N. L. Brooke, 50–94. Studies in Celtic History, no. 8. Woodbridge: Boydell Press, 1986.

Brouland, Marie-Thérèse. *Sir Orfeo: Le substrat celtique du lai breton anglais*. Paris: Didier Érudition, 1990.

Bullock-Davies, Constance. *Professional Interpreters and the Matter of Britain*. Cardiff: University of Wales Press, 1966.

———. "Welsh Minstrels at the Courts of Edward I and Edward II." Paper presented at the Transactions of the Honourable Society of Cymmrodorion, Session 1972–73, London, 1972 and 1973.

Burgess, Glyn S. *The Lais of Marie de France: Text and Context*. Athens: University of Georgia Press, 1987.

Burns, E. Jane. "Introduction." In *The History of the Holy Grail*, trans. Carol J. Chase. Vol. 1 of *Lancelot-Grail: The Old French Arthurian Vulgate and Post-Vulgate in Translation*, ed. Norris J. Lacy, xiii–xxxviii. Cambridge: D. S. Brewer, 2010.

Butrica, J. L. "Editing Propertius." *Classical Quarterly* 47, no. 1 (1997): 176–208.

Bychkov, Oleg. "The Use of the *De officiis* I in Walter Map's *De nugis curialium*." *Notes and Queries* 240 (1995): 157–59.

Caiti-Russo, Gilda. "Situation actuelle de Gautier Map, écrivain fantastique." *Revue des Langues Romanes* 101, no. 2 (1997): 125–43.

Carey, John. *Ireland and the Grail*. Aberystwyth: Celtic Studies Publications, 2007.

Carman, J. Neale. *A Study of the Pseudo-Map Cycle of Arthurian Romance*. Lawrence: University Press of Kansas.

Cartlidge, Neil. "Masters in the Art of Lying: The Literary Relationship Between Hugh of Rhuddlan and Walter Map." *Modern Language Review* 106 (2011): 1–16.

Charles, B. G. "The Welsh, Their Language and Place-Names in Archenfield and Oswestry." In *Angles and Britons: O'Donnell Lectures*, ed. Henry Lewis, 85–110. Cardiff: University of Wales Press, 1963.

Charles-Edwards, T. M. *Wales and the Britons, 350–1064*. Oxford: University of Oxford Press, 2013.

———. *The Welsh Laws*. Cardiff: University of Wales Press, 1989.

Clanchy, M. T. *From Memory to Written Record, England, 1066–1307*. Cambridge, MA: Harvard University Press, 1979.

———. "*Moderni* in Education and Government in England." *Speculum* 50 (1975): 671–88.

C. L. K. Review of *Étude sur le Lancelot en prose*, by Ferdinand Lot. *English Historical Review* 35, no. 137 (1920): 304–6.

Cohen, Jeffrey Jerome. *Hybridity, Identity, and Monstrosity in Medieval Britain: On Difficult Middles*. New York: Palgrave Macmillan, 2006.

———. "Introduction: Infinite Realms." In *Cultural Diversity in the British Middle Ages: Archipelago, Island, England*, ed. Jeffrey Jerome Cohen, 1–16. New York: Palgrave Macmillan, 2008.

———. *Of Giants: Sex, Monsters, and the Middle Ages*. Minneapolis: University of Minnesota Press, 1999.

Combes, André. *La théologie mystique de Gerson: Profil de son évolution*. 2 vols. Rome: Desclée, 1963–64.

Copeland, Rita, and Ineke Sluiter, eds. *Medieval Grammar and Rhetoric: Language Arts and Literary Theory, AD 300–1475*. Oxford: Oxford University Press, 2009.

Cormier, Raymond J. "Tradition and Sources: The Jackson-Loomis Controversy Re-examined." *Folklore* 83, no. 2 (1972): 101–21.

Cotts, John. *The Clerical Dilemma: Peter of Blois and Literate Culture in the Twelfth Century*. Washington, DC: Catholic University of America Press, 2009.

Cowley, F. G. *The Monastic Order in South Wales, 1066–1349*. Cardiff: University of Wales Press, 1977.

Cownie, Emma. "Gloucester Abbey, 1066–1135: An Illustration of Religious Patronage in Anglo-Norman England." In *England and Normandy in the Middle Ages*, ed. David Bates and Anne Curry, 143–58. London: Hambledon Press, 1994.

———. *Religious Patronage in Anglo-Norman England, 1066–1135*. Woodbridge: Boydell, 1998.

Coxon, Sebastian. "Wit, Laughter, and Authority in Walter Map's *De nugis curialium* (Courtiers' Trifles)." In *Author, Reader, Book: Medieval Authorship in Theory and Practice*, ed. Stephen Partridge and Erik Kwakkel, 38–55. Toronto: University of Toronto Press, 2012.

Davenport, Tony. "Sex, Ghosts, and Dreams: Walter Map (1135?–1210?) and Gerald of Wales (1146–1223)." In *Writers of the Reign of Henry II: Twelve Essays*, ed. Ruth Kennedy and Simon Meecham-Jones, 133–50. New York: Palgrave Macmillan, 2006.

Davies, Constance. "Classical Threads in 'Orfeo.'" *Modern Language Review* 56, no. 2 (1961): 161–66.

———. "Notes on the Sources of 'Sir Orfeo.'" *Modern Language Review* 31, no. 3 (1936): 354–57.

———. "*Sir Orfeo* and *De Nugis*." *Modern Language Notes* 51, no. 7 (1936): 492–92.

Davies, J. Conway. "Ewenny Priory: Some Recently-Found Records." *National Library of Wales Journal* 3 (1944): 107–37.

Davies, John Reuben. "The Archbishoprics of St Davids and the Bishops of *Clas Cynidr*." In *St David of Wales: Cult, Church and Nation*, ed. J. Wyn Evans and Jonathan M. Wooding, 296–304. Woodbridge: Boydell Press, 2007.

————. *The Book of Llandaf and the Norman Church in Wales*. Woodbridge: Boydell, 2003.

————. "The Cult of Saints in the Early Welsh March." In *The English Isles: Cultural Transmission and Political Conflict in Britain and Ireland, 1100–1500*, ed. Seán Duffy and Susan Foran, 37–55. Dublin: Four Courts Press, 2013.

————. "*Liber Landavensis*: Its Date and the Identity of Its Editor." *Cambrian Medieval Celtic Studies* 35 (1998): 1–11.

Davies, Michael, and Sean Davies. *The Last King of Wales: Gruffudd ap Llywelyn, c. 1013–1063*. Stroud: History Press, 2012.

Davies, R. R. *The Age of Conquest: Wales, 1063–1415*. Rev. ed. Oxford: Oxford University Press, 2000.

————. *Lordship and Society in the March of Wales, 1282–1400*. Oxford: Clarendon Press, 1978.

Davies, Wendy. "*Braint Teilo*." *Bulletin of the Board of Celtic Studies* 26 (1974–76): 123–37. Reprinted with the same pagination in *Welsh History in the Early Middle Ages*, chap. 3. Farnham: Ashgate, 2009.

————. "Property Rights and Property Claims in Welsh *Vitae* of the Eleventh Century." In *Hagiographie, cultures et sociétés, IVᵉ–XIIᵉ siècles*, ed. E. Patlagean and P. Riché, 515–53. Paris: Études Augustiniennes, 1981. Reprinted with the same pagination in *Welsh History in the Early Middle Ages*, chap. 14. Farnham: Ashgate, 2009.

————. *Welsh History in the Early Middle Ages: Texts and Societies*. Farnham: Ashgate, 2009.

Derolez, Albert. *The Paleography of Gothic Manuscript Books: From the Twelfth to the Early Sixteenth Century*. Cambridge: Cambridge University Press, 2003.

Dictionary of Medieval Latin from British Sources [*DMLBS*]. Ed. R. E. Latham et al. London: Published for the British Academy by Oxford University Press, 1975–2013.

Ditmas, E. M. R. "Geoffrey of Monmouth and the Breton Families in Cornwall." *Welsh History Review* 6 (1972): 451–61.

Divanach, Marcel. *5000 patronymes bretons francisés*. Brest: Éditions du Vieux meunier breton, 1975.

Dover, Carol, ed. *A Companion to the "Lancelot-Grail Cycle."* Cambridge: D. S. Brewer, 2003.

Duffy, Seán. "The First Ulster Plantation: John de Courcy and the Men of Cumbria." In *Colony and Frontier in Medieval Ireland: Essays Presented to J. F. Lydon*, ed. T. B. Barry, Robin Frame, and Katharine Simms, 1–28. London: Hambledon Press, 1995.

Dumville, David N. "Celtic-Latin Texts in Northern England, c. 1150–1250." *Celtica* 12 (1977): 19–49.

————. "English Square Minuscule Script: The Background and Earliest Phases." *Anglo-Saxon England* 16 (1987): 147–79.

————. "English Square Minuscule Script: The Mid-Century Phases." *Anglo-Saxon England* 23 (1994): 133–64.

————. "The Origin of the *C*-Text of the Variant Version of the *Historia Regum Britannie*." *Bulletin of the Board of Celtic Studies* 26 (1975): 315–22.

Echard, Siân. *Arthurian Narrative in the Latin Tradition*. Cambridge: Cambridge University Press, 1998.

————, ed. *The Arthur of Medieval Latin Literature: The Development and Dissemination of the Arthurian Legend in Medieval Latin*. Cardiff: University of Wales Press, 2011.

————. "Map's Metafiction: Author, Narrator and Reader in *De nugis curialum*." *Exemplaria: A Journal of Theory in Medieval and Renaissance Studies* 8, no. 2 (1996): 287–314.

Edwards, Robert R. "Walter Map: Authorship and the Space of Writing." *New Literary History: A Journal of Theory and Interpretation* 38 (2007): 273–92.

Emanuel, Hywel D. "An Analysis of the Composition of the 'Vita Cadoci.'" *National Library of Wales Journal* 7 (1951–52): 217–27.

Evans, Dylan Foster. "'Tŵr dewr gwncwerwr' ('A Brave Conqueror's Tower'): Welsh Poetic Responses to the Edwardian Castles." In *The Impact of the Edwardian Castles in Wales: The Proceedings of a Conference Held at Bangor University, 7–9 September 2007*, ed. Diane M. Williams and John R. Kenyon, 121–28. Oxford: Oxbow Books, 2010.

Faletra, Michael. "Chivalric Identity at the Frontier: Marie's Welsh Lais," *Le Cygne: Journal of the International Marie de France Society* 4 (2006): 27–41.

———. "Narrating the Matter of Britain: Geoffrey of Monmouth and the Norman Colonization of Wales." *Chaucer Review* 35, no. 1 (2000): 60–85.

———. *Wales and the Medieval Colonial Imagination: The Matters of Britain in the Twelfth Century*. New York: Palgrave Macmillan, 2014.

Falileyev, Alexander. *Llawlyfr Hen Gymraeg*. Caerfyrddin: Y Coleg Cymraeg Cenedlaethol, 2016.

Faral, Edmond. *La légende arthurienne: Études et documents*. 3 vols. Paris: H. Champion, 1929.

Farina, William. *Chrétien de Troyes and the Dawn of Arthurian Romance*. Jefferson, NC: McFarland, 2010.

Fleuriot, Léon. "Les évêques de la 'Clas Kenedyr,' évêché disparu de la région de Hereford." *Études Celtiques* 15 (1976–78): 225–26.

Fleuriot, Léon, and Auguste-Pierre Ségalen. *Héritage celtique et captation française*. Histoire littéraire et culturelle de la Bretagne, vol. 1. Paris: Champion, 1997.

Foster, Idris. "Lloring." *Bulletin of the Board of Celtic Studies* 8 (1935–37): 21–23.

Foulet, Lucien. "Marie de France et les lais bretons." *Zeitschrift für romanische Philologie* 29 (1905): 19–56.

Frappier, Jean. *Étude sur "La Mort le Roi Artu."* 2nd ed. Geneva: Droz, 1961.

Geiriadur Prifysgol Cymru. Ed. R. J. Thomas. Cardiff: University of Wales Press, 1950–2002.

Giffin, Mary E. "A Wigmore Manuscript at the University of Chicago." *National Library of Wales Journal* 7 (1951–52): 316–25.

Gillingham, John. "The Cultivation of History, Legend and Courtesy at the Court of Henry II." In *Writers of the Reign of Henry II: Twelve Essays*, ed. Ruth Kennedy and Simon Meecham-Jones, 133–50. New York: Palgrave Macmillan, 2006.

Godlove, Shannon. "'Engelond' and 'Armorik Briteyne': Reading Brittany in Chaucer's *Franklin's Tale*." *Chaucer Review* 51, no. 3 (2016): 269–94.

Golding, Brian. "Trans-Border Transactions: Patterns of Patronage in Anglo-Norman Wales." *Haskins Society Journal* 16 (2005): 27–46.

Goldschmidt, E. Ph. *Medieval Texts and Their First Appearance in Print*. Supplement to the Bibliographical Society's Transactions, no. 16. London: Printed for the Bibliographical Society at Oxford University Press, 1943.

Gordon, Stephen. "Monstrous Words, Monstrous Bodies: Irony and the Walking Dead in Walter Map's *De nugis curialium*." *English Studies* 96, no. 4 (2015): 379–402.

———. "Parody, Sarcasm, and Invective in the *Nugae* of Walter Map." *Journal of English and Germanic Studies* 116 (forthcoming 2017).

Görlach, Manfred. *The Textual Tradition of the "South English Legendary."* Leeds: University of Leeds, School of English, 1974.

Gould, S. Baring, and John Fisher. *Lives of the British Saints*. 4 vols. London: Published for the Honourable Society of Cymmrodorion by C. J. Clark, 1907–13.

Green, D. H. *The Beginnings of Medieval Romance: Fact and Fiction, 1150–1220*. Cambridge: Cambridge University Press, 2002.

Greene, Virginie. *Le sujet et la mort dans "La Mort Artu."* Saint-Genouph: Nizet, 2002.

Grimaldi, Patrizia. "Sir Orfeo as Celtic Folk-Hero, Christian Pilgrim, and Medieval King." In *Allegory, Myth, and Symbol,* ed. Morton W. Bloomfield, 147–61. Cambridge, MA: Harvard University Press, 1981.

Guy, Ben. "*De situ Brecheniauc* and Related Texts." Forthcoming.

———. "A Second Witness to the Welsh Material in Harley 3859." *Quaestio Insularis* 15 (2014): 72–91.

Hanna, Ralph. "Another Manuscript of Walter Map's '*Dissuasio Valerii.*'" *Journal of Medieval Latin* 24 (2014): 277–83.

———. "The Matter of Fulk: Romance and History in the Marches." *Journal of English and Germanic Philology* 110 (2011): 337–58.

———. "Walter Map's *Dissuasio Valerii*: Newly Identified Copies and their Clarification of the Text's Transmission." *Mittellateinisches Jahrbuch* 52 (forthcoming 2017)

Hanna, Ralph, III, and Traugott Lawler, eds. *Jankyn's Book of Wikked Wyves.* 2 vols. Athens: University of Georgia Press, 1997–2014.

Hare, Michael. "The Chronicle of Gregory of Caerwent: A Preliminary Account." *Glevensis: The Gloucester and District Archaeological Research Group Review* 27 (1993): 42–44.

Harf-Lancner, Laurence. "Des fées et des morts: La légende des fils de la morte dans le *De nugis curialium* de Gautier Map." In *"Furent les merveilles pruvees et les aventures truvees": Hommage à Francis Dubost,* ed. Francis Gingras et al., 321–31. Paris: Champion, 2005.

———. "L'Enfer de la cour: La cour d'Henri II Plantagenet et la Mesnie Hellequin (dans l'œuvre de J. de Salisbury, de Gautier Map, de Pierre de Blois et de Giraud de Barri)." In *L'État et les aristocraties: France, Angleterre, Ecosse, XIIᵉ–XVIIᵉ siècle; Actes de la table ronde,* ed. Philippe Contamine, 27–50. Paris: Presses de l'École normale supérieure, 1989.

———. "Une melusine galloise: La dame du lac de Brecknock." In *Mélanges de littérature du Moyen Âge au XXᵉ siècle offerts à Jeanne Lods par ses collègues, ses élèves et ses amis,* 323–38. Paris: École normale supérieure de jeunes filles, 1978.

Harris, Silas M. "The Kalendar of the *Vitae Sanctorum Wallensium.*" *Journal of the Historical Society of the Church in Wales* 3 (1953): 3–53.

Harward, Vernon J. "'Celtic Myth and Arthurian Romance': A Reply." *Medium Aevum* 31 (1962): 43.

———. *The Dwarfs of Arthurian Romance and Celtic Tradition.* Leiden: Brill, 1958.

Havely, N. R. *Chaucer's Boccaccio: Sources for "Troilus" and the "Knight's" and "Franklin's Tale"; Translations from the "Filostrato," "Teseida" and "Filocolo."* Woodbridge: D. S. Brewer, 1980.

Henken, Elissa R. *Traditions of the Welsh Saints.* Woodbridge: D. S. Brewer, 1987.

Henley, Georgia. "Gerald of Wales and Welsh Society." In *A Handbook on Medieval Wales,* ed. Emma Cavell and Kathryn Hurlock. Leiden: Brill, forthcoming 2018.

Hinton, James. "Notes on Walter Map's 'De Nugis Curialium." *Studies in Philology* 20 (1923): 448–68.

———. "Walter Map's *De nugis curialium*: Its Plan and Composition." *PMLA* 32 (1917): 81–132.

Hobbins, Daniel. *Authorship and Publicity Before Print: Jean Gerson and the Transformation of Late Medieval Learning.* Philadelphia: University of Pennsylvania Press, 2010.

Holden, Brock. *Lords of the Central Marches: English Aristocracy and Frontier Society, 1087–1265.* Oxford: Oxford University Press, 2008.

Hughes, Kathleen. "British Library MS. Cotton Vespasian A. xiv (*Vitae Sanctorum Wallensium*): Its Purpose and Provenance." In *Celtic Britain in the Early Middle Ages: Studies in Scottish and Welsh Sources*, ed. David. N. Dumville, 53–66. Woodbridge: Boydell, 1980. An earlier version appears in *Studies in the Early British Church*, ed. Nora K. Chadwick, 183–200. New York: Cambridge University Press, 1958.

Hume, Kathryn. "The Composition of a Medieval Romance: Walter Map's *Sadius and Galo*." *Neuphilologische Mitteilungen* 76 (1975): 415–23.

Hutson, A. E. *British Personal Names in the "Historia regum Britanniae."* Berkeley: University of California Press, 1940.

Huws, Daniel. "The Medieval Manuscript in Wales." In *Medieval Welsh Manuscripts*, ed. Daniel Huws, 1–23. Aberystwyth: University of Wales Press and the National Library of Wales.

Jackson, Kenneth. *Language and History in Early Britain: A Chronological Survey of the Brittonic Languages, First to Twelfth Century A.D.* Edinburgh: Edinburgh University Press, 1953.

———. "Les sources celtiques du roman du Graal." In *Les romans du Graal aux XIIᵉ et XIIIᵉ siècles, Strasbourg, 29 mars–3 avril 1954*, 213–31. Paris: Centre national de la recherche scientifique, 1956.

Jaeger, C. Stephen. *Ennobling Love: In Search of a Lost Sensibility*. Philadelphia: University of Pennsylvania Press, 1999.

———. "Patrons and the Beginnings of Courtly Romance." In *The Medieval Opus: Imitation, Rewriting and Transmission in the French Tradition: Proceedings of the Symposium Held at the Institute for Research in the Humanities, October 5–7, 1995, at the University of Wisconsin–Madison*, ed. Douglas Kelly, 45–58. Amsterdam: Rodopi, 1996.

———. "Pessimism in the Twelfth-Century 'Renaissance.'" *Speculum* 78 (2003): 1151–83.

Jankulak, Karen. *Geoffrey of Monmouth*. Cardiff: University of Wales Press, 2010.

Jewers, Caroline. "Myth and the *matière de Bretagne*." In *The Cambridge History of French Literature*, ed. William Burgwinkle, Nicholas Hammond, and Emma Wilson, 47–56. Cambridge: Cambridge University Press, 2011.

Jones, John Morris. *A Welsh Grammar: Historical and Comparative*. Oxford: Clarendon Press, 1913.

Jones, Nerys Ann, and Morfydd E. Owen. "Twelfth-Century Welsh Hagiography: The Gogynfeirdd Poems to the Saints." In *Celtic Hagiography*, ed. Jane Cartwright, 45–67. Cardiff: University of Wales Press, 2003.

Jones, Thomas. "Lloring." *Bulletin of the Board of Celtic Studies* 13 (1948–50): 75.

Kauntze, Mark. *Authority and Imitation: A Study of the "Cosmographia" of Bernard Silvestris*. Leiden: Brill, 2014.

Kennedy, Elspeth. "The Making of the *Lancelot-Grail Cycle*." In *A Companion to the "Lancelot-Grail Cycle,"* ed. Carol Dover, 13–22. Cambridge: D. S. Brewer, 2003.

———. "Variations in the Patterns of Interlace in the Lancelot-Grail." In *The Lancelot-Grail Cycle: Text and Transformations*, ed. William W. Kibler, 31–50. Austin: University of Texas Press, 1994.

Kennedy, Ruth, and Simon Meecham-Jones, eds. *Authority and Subjugation in Writing of Medieval Wales*. New York: Palgrave Macmillan, 2008.

———, eds. *Writers of the Reign of Henry II: Twelve Essays*. New York: Palgrave Macmillan, 2006

Keynes, Simon. "Diocese and Cathedral Before 1056." In *Hereford Cathedral: A History*, ed. Gerald Aylmer and John Tiller, 4–20. London: Hambledon Press, 2000.

Kibler, William W., ed. *The Lancelot-Grail Cycle: Text and Transformations*. Austin: University of Texas Press, 1994.

Kittredge, George Lyman. "Sir Orfeo." *American Journal of Philology* 7, no. 2 (1886): 176–202.

Knight, Jeremy K. "St. Tatheus of Caerwent: An Analysis of the Vespasian Life." *Monmouthshire Antiquary* 3 (1970–71): 29–36.

Knowles, David. *The Monastic Order in England, 940–1216*. 2nd ed. Cambridge: Cambridge University Press, 1963.

Koch, John. *Cunedda, Cynan, Cadwallon, Cynddylan: Four Welsh Poems and Britain, 383–655*. Aberystwyth: University of Wales Centre for Advanced Welsh and Celtic Studies, 2013.

Lapidge, Michael. "The Medieval Hagiography of St. Ecgwine." *Research Papers: The Vale of Evesham Historical Society* 6 (1977): 77–93.

———. "The Welsh-Latin Poetry of Sulien's Family." *Studia Celtica* 8–9 (1973–74): 68–106.

Laradjii, Aline. *La légende de Roland: De la genèse française à l'épuisement de la figure du héros en Italie*. Paris: Harmattan, 2008.

Legge, Dominica. *Anglo-Norman Literature and Its Background*. Oxford: Clarendon Press, 1963.

Lehmann, Paul. *Mittellateinische Verse in "Distinctiones monasticae et morales" vom Anfang des 13. Jahrhunderts*. Sitzungsberichte der Bayerischen Akademie der Wissenschaften, Philosophische-Philologische und Historische Klasse, Jhrg. 1922, Abh. 2. Munich: Bayerischen Akademie der Wissenschaften, 1922.

Levine, Robert. "How to Read Walter Map." *Mittellateinisches Jahrbuch* 23 (1988): 91–105.

Livingston, Charles H. "Old French Herluin." *Modern Language Notes* 60, no. 3 (1945): 178–80.

Lloyd, John Edward. *A History of Wales from the Earliest Times to the Edwardian Conquest*. 3rd ed. London: Longmans, 1939.

Lloyd, John Edward, and R. T. Jenkins, eds. *Y Bywgraffiadur Cymreig hyd 1940*. London: Honourable Society of Cymmrodorion, 1953. English version published as *The Dictionary of Welsh Biography down to 1940*. London: Honourable Society of Cymmrodorion, 1959.

Lloyd-Morgan, Ceridwen. "Crossing the Borders: Literary Borrowing in Medieval Wales and England." In *Authority and Subjugation in Writing of Medieval Wales*, ed. Ruth Kennedy and Simon Meecham-Jones, 159–73. New York: Palgrave Macmillan, 2008.

———. "Nodiadau Ychwanegol ar Achau Arthuriaidd a'u Ffynonellau Ffrangeg." *National Library of Wales Journal* 21 (1980): 329–39.

Loomis, Roger Sherman. *Arthurian Tradition and Chrétien de Troyes*. New York: Columbia University Press, 1949. Reprint, 1961.

———. *The Grail: From Celtic Myth to Christian Symbol*. Cardiff: University of Wales, 1963.

———. "King Arthur and the Antipodes." *Modern Philology* 38 (1941): 298–304.

———. "Objections to the Celtic Origin of the 'Matière de Bretagne.'" *Romania* 78 (1958): 47–77.

———. "The Oral Diffusion of the Arthurian Legend." In *Arthurian Literature in the Middle Ages: A Collaborative History*, ed. Roger Sherman Loomis, 52–63. Oxford: Oxford University Press, 1959.

———. "*Sir Orfeo* and Walter Map's *De Nugis*." *Modern Language Notes* 51, no. 1 (1936): 28–30.

———. "The Spoils of Annwn: An Early Arthurian Poem." *PMLA* 56 (1941): 887–936.

Lot, Ferdinand. *Étude sur le Lancelot en prose*. Paris: É. Champion, 1918.

———. "Études sur la provenance du cycle arthurien." *Romania* 24 (1895): 497–528.

———. "Nouvelles études sur la provenance du cycle arthurien." *Romania* 28 (1899): 321–47; and 30 (1901): 1–21.

———. "Provenance du cycle arthurien." *Romania* 28 (1899): 1–48.

———. "Sur la date du *Lancelot* en prose." *Romania* 57 (1931): 137–46.

Loth, Joseph. *Contributions à l'étude des romans de la Table Ronde*. Paris: H. Champion, 1912.

———. "Des nouvelles theories sur l'origine des romans arthuriens." *Revue Celtique* 13 (1892): 475–503.

Lucas, Peter. "Chaucer's Franklin's Dorigen: Her Name." *Notes and Queries* 37 (1990): 398–400.

Mackley, J. S. *The Legend of St. Brendan: A Comparative Study of the Latin and Anglo-Norman Versions*. Brill: Leiden, 2008.

Manitius, Max. *Geschichte der Lateinischen Literatur des Mittelalters*. 3 vols. Munich: C. H. Beck, 1911–31.

Mann, Jill. *Feminizing Chaucer*. 2nd ed. Woodbridge: D. S. Brewer, 2002.

Manuscripts of the West Midlands: A Catalogue of Vernacular Manuscript Books of the English West Midlands, c. 1300–c. 1475. www.hrionline.ac.uk/mwm/.

Matarasso, Pauline. *The Redemption of Chivalry: A Study of the "Queste del Saint Graal."* Geneva: Droz, 1979.

Mawer, A., and F. M. Stenton. *The Place-Names of Worcestershire*. Cambridge: Cambridge University Press, 1927.

McCash, June Hall. "Chrétien's Patrons." In *A Companion to Chrétien de Troyes*, ed. Norris J. Lacy and Joan Tasker Grimbert, 26–42. Cambridge: D. S. Brewer, 2005.

McDonough, Christopher. Review of *De nugis curialium: Courtiers' Trifles*, by Walter Map, ed. and trans. M. R. James, rev. C. N. L. Brooke and R. A. B. Mynors. *Mittellateinisches Jahrbuch* 20 (1985): 294–302.

McIntosh, Angus, M. L. Samuels, and Michael Benskin. *A Linguistic Atlas of Late Mediaeval English*. 4 vols. Aberdeen: Aberdeen University Press, 1986.

McKee, Helen. *The Cambridge Juvencus Manuscript Glossed in Latin, Old Welsh and Old Irish: Text and Commentary*. Aberystwyth: CMCS Publications, 2000.

———. "The Circulation of Books Between England and the Celtic Realms." In *The Cambridge History of the Book in Britain*, vol. 1, *C. 400–1100*, ed. Richard Gameson, 338–43. Cambridge: Cambridge University Press, 2012.

———. "St Augustine's, Canterbury: Book Production in the Tenth and Eleventh Centuries." Ph.D. thesis, University of Cambridge, 1997.

Meecham-Jones, Simon. "Where Was Wales? The Erasure of Wales in Medieval English Culture." In *Authority and Subjugation in Writing of Medieval Wales*, ed. Ruth Kennedy and Simon Meecham-Jones, 27–57. New York: Palgrave Macmillan, 2008.

Meuwese, Martine. "Crossing Borders: Text and Image in Arthurian Manuscripts." *Arthurian Literature* 24 (2007): 157–77.

Minkova, Donka. *The History of Final Vowels in English: The Sound of Muting*. Berlin: Mouton de Gruyter, 1991.

Mombello, Gianni. "Les avatars d'une facétie de Cicéron." In *Grant risee? The Medieval Comic Presence*, ed. Adrian P. Tudor and Alan Hindley, 225–46. Turnhout: Brepols, 2006.

Morey, Adrian, and C. N. L. Brooke. *Gilbert Foliot and His Letters*. Cambridge: Cambridge University Press, 1965.

Morgan, Gerald. "Welsh Arthurian Literature." In *A History of Arthurian Scholarship*, ed. Norris J. Lacy, 77–94. Cambridge: D. S. Brewer, 2006.

Morgan, Richard, and R. F. Peter Powell. *A Study of Breconshire Place-Names*. Llanrwst: Gwasg Carreg Gwalch, 1999.

Morgan, T. J. *Y Treigladau a'u Cystrawen*. Cardiff: University of Wales Press, 1952.

Morgan, T. J., and Prys Morgan. *Welsh Surnames*. Cardiff: University of Wales Press, 1985.

Morrison, Elizabeth, and Anne D. Hedeman, eds. *Imagining the Past in France: History in Manuscript Painting, 1250–1500*. Los Angeles: J. Paul Getty Museum, 2010.

Murray, K. Sarah-Jane. *From Plato to Lancelot: A Preface to Chrétien de Troyes*. Syracuse, NY: Syracuse University Press, 2008.

Needham, Paul. *The Bradshaw Method: Henry Bradshaw's Contribution to Bibliography*. Seventh

Hanes Lecture Presented by the Hanes Foundation for the Study of the Origin and Development of the Book. Chapel Hill: Hanes Foundation, Rare Book Collection, University Library, University of North Carolina at Chapel Hill, 1988.

Newstead, Helaine. "Some Observations on King Herla and the Herlething." In *Medieval Literature and Folklore Studies: Essays in Honor of Francis Lee Utley*, ed. Jerome Mandel and Bruce A. Rosenberg, 105–10. New Brunswick, NJ: Rutgers University Press, 1971.

Ogle, Marbury B. "Bible Text or Liturgy." *Harvard Theological Review* 33 (1940): 194–224.

Orlandi, Giovani. "Considerazioni sulla tradizione manoscritta della *Navigatio Sancti Brendani*." *Filogia mediolatina* 9 (2002): 51–75.

Otter, Monika. *Inventiones: Fiction and Referentiality in Twelfth-Century English Historical Writing*. Chapel Hill: University of North Carolina Press, 1996.

Oxford Latin Dictionary. Ed. P. G. W. Glare. Oxford: Clarendon Press, 1996.

Padel, Oliver. "Geoffrey of Monmouth and Cornwall." *Cambridge Medieval Celtic Studies* 8 (1984): 1–28.

———. "The Nature and Date of the Old Cornish Vocabulary." *Zeitschrift für celtische Philologie* 61 (2014): 173–99.

Pepin, Ronald E. *Literature of Satire in the Twelfth Century: A Neglected Mediaeval Genre*. Lewiston, NY: Edwin Mellen Press, 1988.

———. "Walter Map and Yale MS 229." In *Essays on the 'Lancelot' of Yale 229*, ed. Elizabeth M. Willingham, 15–17. Turnhout: Brepols, 2007.

Pickens, Rupert T. "Autobiography and History in the Vulgate *Estoire* and in the *Prose Merlin*." In *The Lancelot-Grail Cycle: Text and Transformations*, ed. William W. Kibler, 98–116. Austin: University of Texas Press, 1994.

Piette, J. R. F. "Yr Agwedd Lydewig ar y Chwedlau Arthuraidd." *Llên Cymru* 8 (1965): 183–90.

Piggott, Stuart. "The Sources of Geoffrey of Monmouth I: The 'Pre-Roman' King-List." *Antiquity* 15 (1941): 269–86.

Polak, Lucie. *Chrétien de Troyes: Cligés*. Critical Guides to French Texts 23. London: Grant and Cutler, 1982.

Pope, Mildred K. *From Latin to Modern French with Especial Consideration of Anglo-Norman: Phonology and Morphology*. Manchester: Manchester University Press, 1934.

Powell, R. F. Peter. "Llyn Llan-gors." *Brycheiniog* 22 (1986–87): 39–41.

Pryce, Huw. "British or Welsh? National Identity in Twelfth-Century Wales." *English Historical Review* 116, no. 468 (2001): 775–801.

———. "Gerald's Journey Through Wales." *Journal of Welsh Ecclesiastical History* 6 (1989): 17–34.

Pughe, William Owen. *The Cambrian Biography; or, Historical Notices of Celebrated Men Among the Ancient Britons*. London: E. Williams, 1803.

Rhys, John. *Celtic Folklore: Welsh and Manx*. Oxford: Clarendon Press, 1901.

Rickard, P. *Britain in Medieval French Literature, 1100–1500*. Cambridge: Cambridge University Press, 1956.

Rigg, A. G. "Golias and Other Pseudonyms." *Studi Medievali* 18 (1977): 65–109.

———. *A History of Anglo-Latin Literature, 1066–1422*. Cambridge: Cambridge University Press, 1992.

———. "Medieval Latin Poetic Anthologies (II)." *Mediaeval Studies* 40 (1978): 387–407.

———. Review of *De nugis curialium: Courtiers' Trifles*, by Walter Map, ed. and trans. M. R. James, rev. C. N. L. Brooke and R. A. B. Mynors. *Speculum* 60, no. 1 (1985): 177–82.

———. "Walter Map, the Shaggy Dog Story, and the *Quaesitio Disputata*." In *Roma, Magistra Mundi: Itineraria Culturae Medievalis; Mélanges offerts au Père L. E. Boyle à l'occasion de son*

75e anniversaire, ed. Jacqueline Hamesse, 723–35. Louvain-la-Neuve: Fédération des Instituts d'Études Médiévales, 1998.

Roberts, Brynley F. "Geoffrey of Monmouth and Welsh Historical Tradition." *Nottingham Medieval Studies* 20 (1976): 29–40.

———. "Melusina: Medieval Welsh and English Analogues." In *Mélusines continentales et insulaires: Actes du colloque international tenu les 27 et 28 mars 1997 à l'Université Paris XII et au Collège des Irlandais*, ed. Jeanne-Marie Boivin and Proinsias MacCana, 281–96. Paris: Champion, 1999.

———. "The Treatment of Personal Names in the Early Welsh Versions of *Historia Regum Britanniae*." *Bulletin of the Board of Celtic Studies* 25 (1973): 274–90.

Roberts, Sara Elin. "Legal Practice in Fifteenth-Century Brycheiniog." *Studia Celtica* 35 (2001): 307–23.

Rolands, I. W. "William de Braose and the Lordship of Brecon." *Bulletin of the Board of Celtic Studies* 30 (1982–83): 123–33.

Rubellin, Michel. "Au temps où Valdès n'était pas hérétique: Hypothèses sur le rôle de Valdès à Lyon (1170–1183)." In *Inventer l'hérésie? Discours polémiques et pouvoirs avant l'Inquisition*, ed. Monique Zerner, 193–217. Nice: Centre d'Études Médiévales, 1998.

Russell, Paul. *Celtic Word-Formation: The Velar Suffixes*. Dublin: School of Celtic Studies, Dublin Institute of Advanced Studies, 1990.

———. "Old Welsh *Dinacat, Cunedag, Tutagual*: Fossilised Phonology in Brittonic Personal Names." In *Indo-European Perspectives in Honour of Anna Morpurgo Davies*, ed. J. H. W. Penney, 447–60. Oxford: Oxford University Press, 2004.

———. *Read It in a Glossary: Glossaries and Learned Discourse in Medieval Ireland*. Cambridge: Hughes Hall and Department of Anglo-Saxon, Norse and Celtic, University of Cambridge, 2008.

———. "Some Neglected Sources for Middle Welsh Phonology." *Études Celtiques* 29 (1992): 383–90.

Sanford, E. M. "Giraldus Cambrensis' Debt to Petrus Cantor." *Medievalia et humanistica* 3 (1945): 16–32.

Sargent, Amelia Borrego. "Gerald of Wales's *Topographia Hibernica*: Dates, Versions, Readers." *Viator* 43 (2012): 241–61.

———. "Visions and Revisions: Gerald of Wales, Authorship, and the Construction of Political, Religious, and Legal Geographies in Twelfth and Thirteenth Century Britain." Ph.D. diss., University of California, Berkeley, 2011.

Schofield, William Henry. "Chaucer's *Franklin's Tale*." *PMLA* 16 (1901): 405–49.

Schwieterman, Patrick Joseph. "Fairies, Kingship, and the British Past in Walter Map's *De Nugis Curialium* and *Sir Orfeo*." Ph.D. diss., University of California, Berkeley, 2010.

Scott, John. *The Early History of Glastonbury: An Edition, Translation and Study of William of Malmesbury's "De antiquitate Glastonie Ecclesie."* Woodbridge: Boydell Press, 1981.

Seibt, Ferdinand. "Über den Plan der Schrift 'De nugis curialium' des Magisters Walter Map." *Archiv für Kulturgeschichte* 37 (1955): 183–203.

Severs, J. Burke. "The Antecedents of Sir Orfeo." In *Studies in Medieval Literature: In Honor of Professor Albert Croll Baugh*, ed. MacEdward Leach, 187–207. Philadelphia: University of Pennsylvania Press, 1961.

Short, Ian. "Literary Culture at the Court of Henry II." In *Henry II: New Interpretations*, ed. Christopher Harper-Bill and Nicholas Vincent, 335–61. Woodbridge: Boydell Press, 2007.

———. *A Manual of Anglo-Norman*. 2nd ed. Oxford: Anglo-Norman Text Society, 2013.

Sims-Williams, Patrick. "Celtic Civilization: Continuity or Coincidence?" *Cambrian Medieval Celtic Studies* 64 (2012): 1–45.

———. "Celtomania and Celtoscepticism." *Cambrian Medieval Celtic Studies* 36 (1998): 1–35.

———. "Did Itinerant Breton *Conteurs* Transmit the *Matière de Bretagne?*" *Romania* 116 (1998): 72–111.

———. "The Emergence of Old Welsh, Cornish and Breton Orthography, 600–800: The Evidence of Archaic Old Welsh." *Bulletin of the Board of Celtic Studies* 38 (1991): 20–86.

———. "The Invention of Celtic Nature Poetry." In *Celticism*, ed. Terrence Brown, 97–124. Amsterdam: Rodopi, 1996.

———. *Irish Influence on Medieval Welsh Literature*. Oxford: Oxford University Press, 2011.

———. "The Provenance of the Llywarch Hen Poems: A Case for Llan-gors, Brycheiniog." *Cambrian Medieval Celtic Studies* 26 (1993): 27–63.

———. "A Turkish-Celtic Problem in Chrétien de Troyes: The Name *Cligés*." In *Ildánach Ildírech: A Festschrift for Proinsias Mac Cana*, ed. John Carey, John T. Koch, and Pierre-Yves Lambert, 215–30. Andover, MA: Celtic Studies Publications, 1999.

———. "The Visionary Celt: The Construction of an 'Ethnic Preconception.'" *Cambrian Medieval Celtic Studies* 11 (1986): 71–96.

Sinex, Margaret. "Echoic Irony in Walter Map's Satire Against the Cistercians." *Comparative Literature* 54, no. 4 (2002): 275–90.

Smith, Joshua Byron. "An Edition, Translation, and Introduction to Benedict of Gloucester's *Vita Dubricii*." *Arthurian Literature* 29 (2012): 53–100.

———. "'The First Writer in the Welsh Language': Walter Map's Reception in Nineteenth-Century Wales." *National Library of Wales Journal* 36, no. 2 (2015): 183–97. https://www.llgc.org.uk/collections/activities/research/nlw-journal/

———. "Gerald of Wales, Walter Map, and the Anglo-Saxon Past of Lydbury North." In *New Perspectives on Gerald of Wales: Texts and Contexts*, ed. Georgia Henley and Joseph McMullen. Cardiff: University of Wales Press, forthcoming.

Smith, Llinos Beverley. "The Welsh and English Languages in Late-Medieval Wales." In *Multilingualism in Later Medieval Britain*, ed. David Trotter, 7–21. Cambridge: D. S. Brewer, 2000.

Spitzer, Leo. "Anglo-French Etymologies." *Studies in Philology* 41 (1944): 521–43.

Stacey, Robin Chapman. "King, Queen, and *Edling* in the Laws of Court." In *The Welsh King and His Court*, ed. T. M. Charles-Edwards, Morfydd E. Owen, and Paul Russell, 29–62. Cardiff: University of Wales Press, 2000.

Stephens, Thomas. *The Literature of the Kymry*. 2nd ed. London: Longman, Green, 1876.

Stock, Brian. "Antiqui and Moderni as 'Giants' and 'Dwarfs': A Reflection of Popular Culture?" *Modern Philology* 76 (1979): 370–74.

———. *Listen for the Text: On the Uses of the Past*. Baltimore: Johns Hopkins University Press, 1990.

Stollberg, Gunnar. *Die soziale Stellung der intellektuellen Oberschicht im England des 12. Jahrhunderts*. Lübeck: Matthiesen, 1973.

Stotz, Peter. *Handbuch zur lateinische Sprache des Mittelalters*. 5 vols. Munich: Beck, 1996–2004.

Suppe, Frederick C. "Interpreter Families and Anglo-Welsh Relations in the Shropshire-Powys Marches in the Twelfth Century." *Anglo-Norman Studies* 30 (2007): 196–212.

———. *Military Institutions on the Welsh Marches: Shropshire, A.D. 1066–1300*. Woodbridge: Boydell Press, 1994.

Tatlock, John S. P. *The Legendary History of Britain: Geoffrey of Monmouth's "Historia Regum*

Britanniae" and Its Early Vernacular Versions. Berkeley: University of California Press, 1950. Reprint, New York: Gordian, 1974.

———. *The Scene of the Franklin's Tale Visited*. London: Published for the Chaucer Society by Kegan Paul, Trench, Trübner, 1914.

Tengvik, Gösta. *Old English Bynames*. Uppsala: Almqvist & Wiksells Boktryckeri-A.-B., 1938.

Thomas, Charles. *And Shall These Mute Stones Speak? Post-Roman Inscriptions in Western Britain*. Cardiff: University of Wales Press, 1994.

Thomson, Rodney. "Books and Learning at Gloucester Abbey in the Twelfth and Thirteenth Centuries." In *Books and Collectors, 1200–1700*, ed. James P. Carley and Colin G. C. Tite, 3–26. London: British Library, 1997.

Thornton, David E. "Hey, Mac! The Name *Maccus*, Tenth to Fifteenth Centuries." *Nomina* 20 (1997): 67–94.

Thorpe, Lewis. "Walter Map and Gerald of Wales." *Medium Aevum* 47 (1978): 6–21.

Trachsler, Richard. "Gautier Map, une vieille connaissance." In *Façonner son personnage au Moyen Âge*, ed. Chantal Connochie-Bourgne, 319–28. Aix-en-Provence: Presses universitaires de Provence, 2007.

Türk, Egbert. *Nugae curialium: La règne d'Henri II Plantegenêt (1145–1189) et l'éthique politique*. Genève: Librairie Droz, 1977.

Várvaro, Alberto. *Apparizioni fantastiche: Tradizioni folcoriche e letteratura nel medioevo—Walter Map*. Bologna: Il Mulino, 1994.

Vincent, Nicholas. "The Court of Henry II." In *Henry II: New Interpretations*, ed. Christopher Harper-Bill and Nicholas Vincent, 278–334. Woodbridge: Boydell Press, 2007.

Voth, Christine. "Irish Pilgrims, Welsh Manuscripts and Anglo-Saxon Monasteries: Was Script Change in Tenth-Century England a Legacy of the Celtic World?" *Select Proceedings from the International Society of Anglo-Saxonists, Dublin 2013*, forthcoming.

Wade, James. *Fairies in Medieval Romance*. New York: Palgrave Macmillan, 2011.

Wahlgren, Lena. *The Letter Collections of Peter of Blois*. Göteborg, Sweden: Acta Universitas Gothoburgensis, 1993.

Ward, H. L. D., and J. A. Herbert. *Catalogue of Romances in the Department of Manuscripts in the British Museum*. 3 vols, London: Trustees of the British Museum, 1883–1910.

Warren, W. L. *Henry II*. Berkeley: University of California Press, 1973.

Waugh, Scott. "Histoire, hagiographie et le souverain idéal à la cour des Plantagenêt." In *Plantagenêts et Capétiens: Confrontations et héritages*, ed. Martin Aurell and Noël-Yves Tonnerre, 429–46. Turnhout: Brepols, 2006.

Webster, K. G. T. "Walter Map's French Things." *Speculum* (1940): 272–79.

Whetter, K. S. *Understanding Genre and Medieval Romance*. Burlington, VT: Ashgate, 2008.

Whitaker, Muriel A. "Otherworld Castles in Middle English Romance." In *Late Medieval Castles*, ed. Robert Liddiard, 393–408. Woodbridge: Boydell Press, 2016.

Williams, Albert Hughes. *An Introduction to the History of Wales*. 2 vols. Cardiff: University of Wales, 1941–48.

Williams, Griffith John. *Traddodiad Llendyddol Morgannwg*. Cardiff: University of Wales Press, 1948.

Williams, J. E. Caerwyn. "Brittany and the Arthurian Legend." In *The Arthur of the Welsh*, ed. Rachel Bromwich, A. O. H. Jarman, and Brynley F. Roberts, 249–72. Cardiff: University of Wales Press, 1991.

Wood, Juliette. "Walter Map: The Contents and Context of *De Nugis Curialium*." *Transactions of the Honourable Society of Cymmrodorion* (1985): 91–103.

Index

Acknowledgments

Many of the ideas of this book owe their initial development to a fellowship from the Institute of Historical Research, funded by the Andrew W. Mellon Foundation. I am also grateful to Northwestern University, the Medieval Academy of America, the English-Speaking Union, and the University of Arkansas, all of whom generously supported my research. I would also like to thank the Department of Anglo-Saxon, Norse, and Celtic at the University of Cambridge, where I spent an invigorating year as a Visiting Scholar. I am also grateful to the Rare Book School, whose Andrew W. Mellon Fellowship in Critical Bibliography has provided a remarkable community of scholars; their imprint is felt throughout this book. The excellent staff at the University of Arkansas's Interlibrary Loan Department quite literally make it possible for me to do my job. Without their constant aid, I would be forced to study American literature.

I am delighted to have worked with Jerome Singerman and the University of Pennsylvania Press, who have been professional and prompt at every turn. Northwestern University provided me with an ideal mix of teachers and friends, all of whom shaped my thinking and this book in profound ways. Particularly deserving of my thanks are Katelyn Mesler, Richard Kieckhefer, Susan Philips, and William Paden. I also am grateful to the community of scholars at the University of Arkansas for their support and friendship, especially to Brian Hurley, Mary Beth Long, Lynda Coon, Casey Kayser, Joy Reeber, James Gigantino, Vivian Davis, David Jolliffe, Gwynne Gertz, and Benjamin Fagan. The Department of English, and in particular my chair, Dorothy Stephens, supported the researching and writing of this book. My learned colleague Daniel Levine politely asked me to thank him, so I do. I have also valued the weekly discussion groups led by Casey Jones and Rob Billingsley. Above all, William Quinn has been a wonderful mentor and friend, supporting me as I wrote, rewrote, and wrote again.

Ben Guy, Georgia Henley, David Callander, and Barry Lewis all read chapter drafts and provided excellent suggestions and critique. Mark Kauntze's eye for detail greatly improved my chapters on textual criticism. Lindsey Panxhi read an early draft of the entire manuscript, catching many errors and offering innumerable improvements. Daler Mehndi's infectious encouragement helped me as I worked through the final stages of this book. Siân Echard and an anonymous reader provided superb and timely feedback on the manuscript; among many other improvements, the book's current shape results from their excellent advice. Lindy Brady deserves no small amount of thanks. Our writing group forced me to compete with her frightening work ethic, spurring me to finish this project in a timely manner.

Walter Map himself knew that we do not create our own knowledge, so much as take from those who have come before: "Non est a nobis nostra peritia," he laments. Similarly, if I have displayed any *peritia* in this book, it is merely borrowed from Paul Russell and Barbara Newman. I owe many things to Paul, but foremost is an appreciation for and love of detail. Barbara's kindness, erudition, and constant felicity in all things medieval have been a true gift.

To my parents I owe an inestimable debt of gratitude. They have always supported me and have never once questioned the utility of pursuing dead languages (at least not in my presence). My children, who have hindered the completion of this book in many ingenious ways, have nonetheless given me the motivation to forge ahead when I needed it most. And while I have spent the better part of my career studying a man who wrote a wildly popular treatise against marriage, Lora Walsh, whose love, intelligence, and companionship I enjoy daily, has provided a better rebuttal to Walter Map than any scholastic ever could. Her attention to detail, however, is nothing short of scholastic: she read and greatly improved this book with her suggestions and critique.

Finally, if anything is to blame for my becoming a medievalist, it is the encouragement, guidance, and teaching of Charlie Wright. Thus, any faults in this book, though they are certainly mine, are ultimately his.